MEDIEVAL TOWNS

A READER

edited by

MARYANNE KOWALESKI

UTP

Library and Archives Canada Cataloguing in Publication

Originally published by Broadview Press 2006

Medieval towns : a reader / edited by Maryanne Kowaleski.
(Readings in medieval civilizations and cultures ; XI)
Includes bibliographical references and index.
ISBN 1-44260-091-1
(Previous ISBN 1-55111-449-6)

1. Cities and towns, Medieval. I. Kowaleski, Maryanne, 1952–   II. Series.

HT115.M43 2006   307.76094'0902   C2006-902015-9

We welcome comments and suggestions regarding any aspect of our publications—please feel free to contact us at the addresses below or at news@utphighereducation.com.

North America:

5201 Dufferin Street, North York,
Ontario, Canada M3H 5T8

2250 Military Road,
Tonawanda, NY, USA 14150

Tel: (416) 978-2239;
Fax: (416) 978-4738
E-mail: customerservice@
utphighereducation.com

UK, Ireland, and continental Europe:

NBN International
Estover Road
Plymouth PL6 7PY UK

Tel: 44 (0) 1752 202300
Fax: 44 (0) 1752 2023310
E-mail: enquiries@nbninternational.com

www.utphighereducation.com

Higher Education University of Toronto Press gratefully acknowledges the financial support of the Government of Canada through the Book Publishing Industry Development Program for our publishing activities.

Typesetting by Aldo Fierro

PRINTED IN CANADA

CONTENTS

CHRONOLOGICAL TABLE OF CONTENTS

(Numbers in brackets refer to selections in the Reader)

CONTENTS

CONTENTS

LIST OF TABLES

LIST OF FIGURES

CONTENTS

LIST OF MAPS

INTRODUCTION

Scholars have spent a lot of time trying to offer a precise definition of the medieval town. I adopt a simple explanation that most scholars would accept: a medieval town was a relatively large settlement in which the majority of inhabitants made their living from non-agricultural pursuits. These pursuits included trade (primarily retail), industry (handicrafts), and service (from carters and barbers to innkeepers and domestic servants), although a small number of medieval town residents were always engaged in some sort of agricultural labor (farming and raising livestock). The point is that towns were distinguished by their occupational diversity and multiple economic functions.

The next question is how large were they? Medieval towns were small by modern standards, with populations of barely 2,000 in some cases, but usually in the range of 3,000 to 15,000. Not many towns were larger than 15,000, even in the early fourteenth century when medieval town populations reached their zenith. There were only a few towns with populations over 100,000. Paris was probably the largest, with some 200,000 inhabitants in 1300, followed by Venice, Genoa, and Milan in northern Italy and Granada in southern Spain, with populations of 100,000 to 150,000. London c. 1300 may have had a population as large as that of Paris, but perhaps closer to 120,000. Ghent in Flanders, Florence in Italy, and Seville in Spain had about 80,000 residents, followed by a second tier of towns with populations of about 50,000, including Bruges in Flanders, Cologne in Germany, Barcelona in Spain, and Siena in northern Italy. These towns were usually called "cities" because of their large size and their administrative functions as regional or national capitals. Towns that had cathedrals and served as diocesan centers were also called cities in the Middle Ages. Most of the documents in this collection concern these larger towns or cities; indeed, they tend to dominate the study of medieval urban history because of their size, the variety and complexity of their institutions, their importance on the national and even international stage, and the fortunate survival of a wide range of their records. I have tried, however, to include material on small and medium-sized towns in this collection as well, such as a range of archival evidence from the small town of Exeter in southwestern England, which had a population of about 5,000 in 1300 and perhaps only 3,200 in the late fourteenth century.

While there is a chapter of documents in this volume that covers the early Middle Ages, the majority focus on the central Middle Ages when urbanization quickened in western Europe from 1100 to 1300, and on the late Middle Ages when documentation for towns became more abundant. Towns were considerably smaller in the later Middle Ages, however, after the demographic crises of the Black Death in 1348–49 and subsequent outbreaks of plague and epidemics. The population of Paris, for example, had shrunk to only 30,000 by the early fifteenth century, affected not only by disease, but also by the occupation of the city by the English during the

Hundred Years War between France and England. And although the city increased in size once the French regained it from the English in 1437, Paris and most other European cities did not attain the size they had reached in the early fourteenth century until sometime in the sixteenth or even seventeenth century.

I assembled the documents for this collection with two aims in mind. The first is to provide an array of different types of source material—prescriptive charters, guild regulations, and town ordinances; narrative chronicles and literary works; administrative documents of practice such as contracts, tax rolls, inventories, wills, court rolls, and account rolls; and pictorial and archaeological evidence—to promote an understanding of the rich and varied history of medieval towns. In so doing, I hope to encourage readers to realize how much we can profit from examining towns through different disciplinary lenses, including archaeology, architecture, demography, feminist studies, material culture, and literature, as well as cultural, economic, environmental, legal, political, and social history. To encourage students to think about how such sources can be exploited, the Reader often groups disparate documents together under one heading or issue, furnishes cross-references to documents that consider similar issues, provides supplementary illustrations drawn from medieval manuscripts and other art forms, and includes tables that summarize data drawn from documentary sources.

The second aim of the collection is to focus attention on different aspects of urban history, which too often tends to be studied via a constitutional approach that emphasizes the emergence of urban political autonomy, or an economic approach that focuses on the distinctive commercial and industrial functions of towns. Both these approaches receive their due in the documents included here, particularly in Chapters 1 through 4. But the focus here is on what might be termed "everyday town life": on the experiences of urban residents from childhood through marriage and old age, on the roles of and attitudes toward medieval townswomen, on the piety and charitable impulses of townspeople of all classes, and on their education, sports, and entertainment. Special attention is given to what made town life different from life in the village, castle, or monastery. Urban life, for example, as today, entailed particular dangers because of the population density of towns, their openness to (and, indeed, need for) migrants from all walks of life to maintain their populations in the face of high urban mortality, and the extreme variations in wealth and status among urban residents. Social revolt, fire, famine, disease, war, and crime all had especially devastating effects on medieval towns. Many features of the urban setting also distinguished towns from rural villages, including the built environment of houses, public buildings, and commercial venues, as well as the distinctive smells, sounds, and even the "fast food" associated with cities.

Although the variety of documents included in this collection is wide, readers should be aware that the majority come from political or administrative authorities, or are filtered through a clerical voice. Most surviving medieval documents were produced by a small, elite, literate class of clerks, clerics, and notaries whose interests were not always the same as the townspeople who are the subject of this volume. Nor were these documents usually written to illuminate exactly what we want to know. Instead, like all historians, readers must exercise both caution and imagination in ferreting out information about specific aspects of medieval towns and town life. In assessing what individual documents tell us, readers should always consider the aims, beliefs, and agendas of those responsible for writing the selected documents. Information given in the brief introductions to each passage provides some guidance here, as do some of the study questions appended to each entry.

Students reading these documents should consider how factors such as gender and "class," as measured in variations in wealth and status, might have shaped the experience of medieval town dwellers. They should also keep in mind how the history of towns changed both over time (for example, towns became more powerful politically in the national arena during the late Middle Ages although, paradoxically, they were smaller in size than they had been in the pre-plague period) and according to the region where the town was located. Some of the specific differences between northern and southern European towns that scholars have remarked upon include the faster pace of commercialization and urbanization in northern Italy than elsewhere, the formation of "city-states" throughout Italy, the tendency for women to marry at an earlier age in southern European towns (which in turn could have reflected different attitudes toward women), the importance of urban militias in the frontier towns of Spain, and the prevalence of the family-owned towers that dotted the urban landscape in Italy. These differences, however, should not be too greatly emphasized since the commonalities of urban life across medieval Europe are striking, as many of the documents in this Reader will attest. The geographical distribution of the readings focuses on the more urbanized regions of Europe, especially northern Italy and Flanders, and also England, France, and Germany. The peripheral regions of Europe are, admittedly, less well covered, although an attempt has been made to include some documents from Spain, Scandinavia, and eastern Europe.

The choices about which documents to include have been dictated not only by an interest in offering a full, balanced, interdisciplinary, and methodologically diverse view of medieval urban history, but also by a concern to keep the cost and size of the Reader reasonable. Alongside the new translations made for this volume are many standard—but seminal—documents upon which scholars have long relied to interpret the history of medieval towns. Some of these appear in older translations that have been modernized or revised so that the English reads more fluidly; revisions that involve more than the modernization of archaic phrasing have been made with reference to the work in the original language. Technical or foreign terms are explained by editorial insertions within square brackets. When knowing the value of medieval money is necessary to understand the context of particular passages, I have added such guidance in the brief introductions before each passage; these indications of the relative value of different medieval currencies may also be found in the index under "money."

I am happy to acknowledge the many debts I have accumulated in producing this volume, which is the fruit of considerable collaboration. Although this Reader is based on a collection of primary sources I gathered many years ago for my undergraduate course on medieval towns, it has been enhanced greatly because of suggestions for additional readings from Paul Dutton, Richard Gyug, Joseph Huffman, Nils Hybel, Dan Smail, and an anonymous reader for Broadview Press. For advice on specific translations, I turned to experts, including Bill Caferro, Martha Carlin, Remie Constable, Paul Dutton, Mary Erler, Elizabeth Ewan, Stephanie Hovland, Nils Hybel, and Dan Smail, but I owe special thanks to Richard Gyug, who generously checked my translation of especially difficult passages from Latin, and Thelma Fenster, who provided invaluable guidance on translating difficult passages from Old French and Anglo-Norman. Jeremy Goldberg, Vanessa Harding, and Margery Rowe kindly granted me permission to reprint their translations of key sources. Paul Clark was especially helpful in turning the texts of my original collection into computer-readable texts, while Kris Christian guided the text through the initial copy-editing process with an expert's eye. Grad assistants and student workers at the Center for Medieval Studies, including Heather Burns, Liz Michael, Dawn Ritchotte, and Kristin Uscinski, also lent a hand at crucial junctures, particularly Kristin Canzano, who helped me find and label many of the figures. Thanks also go to Morgan Franck for her help in preparing the final manuscript and part of the index. I am also grateful for the encouragement and editorial guidance of Paul Dutton. My biggest debt, however, is to those who did new translations for this reader, including Martin Chase, Allison Clark, Caroline Dunn, Thelma Fenster, Anne Lester, Laura Morreale, Dan Smail, and Jennifer Speed; fuller notice of their translations is given in a list at the end of this book.

Thanks also go to the students in my undergraduate course on medieval urban history, who served as guinea pigs for the Reader, and especially to Sarah Alexander and Anna Moscatiello for their suggestions on study questions. Finally, I want to express my gratitude to the librarians of Fordham University whose willingness to secure new, out-of-print, and interlibrary loan books and articles was crucial to the success of this project and others I have completed while at Fordham. Particular thanks go to Jim McCabe, the Director of Fordham Libraries, and to Betty Garity, Jan Kelsey, Charlotte Labbe and her staff, and Michael Wares; it is to them and all the librarians and library staff at Fordham University that I dedicate this book.

CHAPTER ONE

THE EARLY MIDDLE AGES

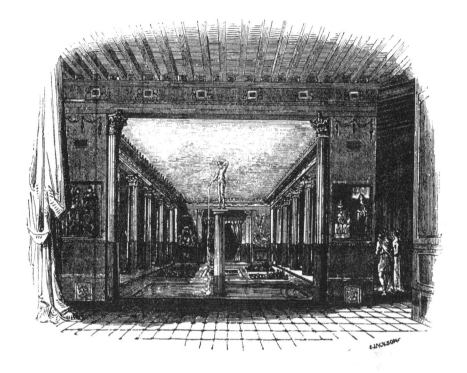

Figure 1.1

A Roman Villa

Reproduced from Charles Knight, *Old England: A Pictorial Museum of Regal, Ecclesiastical, Municipal, Baronial, and Popular Antiquities*, 2 vols. (London: James Sangster and Co., 1850), fig. 180.

1. THE GRANDEUR OF ROME

These two descriptions of ancient Rome illustrate the impressive size of the city, the magnificence of its many public buildings and spaces, and the organization of services into administrative districts. The first extract was written around the middle of the first century by Strabo, a Greek-speaking geographer who lived in Rome for a while and wrote Geography, a 17–book systematic study of the "inhabited world." The second document is from the Curiosum Urbis Romae or Notitia, which was composed around the middle of the fourth century by an anonymous author interested in cataloguing buildings, roads, bridges, and other public spaces in Rome. Extracts from the descriptions of four of Rome's fourteen districts are included here. The unit loca is a measure of seating capacity that if halved roughly equaled the number of spectators that could be accommodated.

Source: (A) trans. H.L. Jones, *The Geography of Strabo*, 8 vols. (New York: G.P. Putnam's Sons, 1923) II, pp. 405, 407; (B) trans. N. Lewis and M. Reinhold, *Roman Civilisation Sourcebook II: The Empire* (New York: Columbia University Press, 1955; reprinted New York: Harper and Row Torchbooks, 1966), pp. 488–89.

(A) Strabo's Description of the City of Rome in the First Century

Book 5, iii, 8. So much, then, for the blessings with which nature supplies the city; but the Romans have added still others, which are the result of their foresight. For if the Greeks had the reputation of being most felicitous in the founding of cities, in that they aimed at beauty, strength of position, harbors, and productive soil, the Romans had the best foresight in those matters which the Greeks took but little account of, such as the construction of roads and aqueducts, and of sewers that could wash out the filth of the city into the Tiber.... The sewers, vaulted with close-fitting stones, have in some places left room enough for wagons loaded with hay to pass through them. And water is brought into the city through the aqueducts in such quantities that veritable rivers flow through the city and the sewers; and almost every house has cisterns and service pipes and copious fountains—with which Marcus Agrippa concerned himself most, though he also adorned the city with many other structures. In a word, the early Romans took but little account of the beauty of Rome, because they were occupied with other—greater and more necessary—matters; whereas the later Romans, and particularly those of today and in my time, have not fallen short in this respect either but have filled the city with many beautiful structures. Pompey, the deified Caesar, Augustus, his sons and friends, and wife and sister, have outdone all others in their zeal for buildings and in the expense incurred. The Campus Martius contains most of these, and thus, in addition to its natural beauty, it has received still further adornment as the result of foresight. The size of the Campus is awe-inspiring, since it affords space at the same time for chariot races and every other equestrian exercise unhindered by the great multitude of people exercising themselves by playing ball, trundling hoops, and wrestling; and the works of art situated around the Campus Martius, and the ground covered with grass throughout the year, and the crowns of the hills that rise above the river and extend as far as its bed, presenting the appearance of a stage painting—all this affords a spectacle from which it is hard to tear one's self away. And near this Campus is still another, and colonnades around it in very great numbers, and sacred precincts, and three theaters, and an amphitheater, and very costly temples in close succession to one another.... Believing this place most sacred, they also erected in it the tombs of their most illustrious men and women. The most noteworthy is the one called the Mausoleum, a great mound near the river on a lofty foundation of white marble, thickly covered with evergreen trees to the very summit. On top is a bronze image of Augustus Caesar; beneath the mound are the tombs of himself and his kinsmen and intimates; behind the mound is a large sacred precinct with wonderful promenades; and in the center of the Campus around his crematorium is a wall, this too of white marble, surrounded by a circular iron fence and planted with black poplars inside. And again if, on passing to the Old Forum, one should see forum after forum ranged alongside it, and basilicas, and temples, and should see also the Capitol and the works of art there and those on the Palatine and in Livia's Promenade, one would easily forget the things outside. Such is Rome.

(B) Catalogue of Notable Features in Four Districts of Rome in the Mid-Fourth Century

District II, Caelimonitum contains:
Temple of Claudius; great meat market; ... Grotto of the Cyclops; Cohort V of the night patrol; ... sacred tree; Peregrine Barracks; house of Philip; ... training school for gladiators in the Morning Games.... Wards—7; crossroads shrines—7; block captains—48; commissioners—2; blocks of tenements—4,600; private houses—127; storehouses—27; baths—85; fountains—65; bakeries [or mills]—15; area—12,200 feet [in circumference].

District III, Isis and Serapis, contains:
Mint; amphitheater [the Colosseum], which has 87,000 *loca*; great training school for gladiators; house of Bruttius Praesens; central theatrical storehouse; Shepherds' Fountain; ... Baths of Titus and Trajan; Portico of Livia; camp of the sailors of the Misenum fleet. Wards—12; crossroads shrines—12; block captains—48; commissioners—2; blocks of tenements—2,757; private houses—60; storehouses—18; baths—80; fountains—65; bakeries—16; area—12,350 feet.

District VIII, Great Roman Forum, contains:
Three rostra [platforms for speakers]; [shrine of the] Genius of the People;
Senate House; Atrium of Minerva; Forums of Caesar, of Augustus, of Nerva, of
Trajan; Temple of Trajan, and the spiral column 128½ feet high, with 185 steps
and 45 windows inside; Cohort VI of the night patrol; bank basilica; Temples of
Concord, of Saturn, or Vespasian and Titus; Capitolium; Golden Milestone
[where all great roads to the city converged]; … Julian Basilica; Temple of
Castor and Pollux; [Temple of] Vesta; storehouses of Agrippa; … Attrium of Cacus;
Portico of the Pearl Dealers; [statue of the] elephant eating grass [?]. Wards—34;
crossroads shrines—34; block captains—48; commissioners—2; blocks of tenements—3,480; private houses—130; storehouses—18; baths—86; fountains—120;
bakeries—20; area—14,067 feet.

District IX, Circus Flaminius, contains:
Six stables of the four circus factions; Portico of Philip; the Minucian porticoes
—the old one and the one for the grain dole; Grotto of Balbus; three theaters:
Balbus's which has 11,510 *loca*, Pompey's, with 17,580 *loca*, Marcellus's, with 20,000
loca; Odeum [for musical performances] with 10,600 *loca*; Stadium, with 30,088
loca; Campus Martius; Trigarium [an open space for exercising horses]; Kneeling
Storks [a statue]; Pantheon; Basilicas of Neptune, of Matidia, of Marcianus; Temple
of Antonius and the spiral column 175½ feet high, with 203 steps and 56 windows
inside; Baths of Alexander and of Agrippa; Portico of the Argonauts and Melegar;
[Temple of] Isis and Serapis; … [Temple of the] Deified Emperors; Pelicles tenement. Wards—35; crossroads shrines—35; block captains—48; commissioners—2;
blocks of tenements—2,777; private houses—140; storehouses—25; baths—63;
fountains—120; bakeries—20; area—32,500 feet.

[Summary]
Libraries—28; obelisks—6: two in the Circus Maximus (the smaller 87½ feet
high, the taller 122½), one on the Vatican (75 feet high), one in the Campus
Martius (72½ feet high), two at the Mausoleum of Augustus (each 42½ feet high);
bridges—8 …; hills—7 …; fields—8 …; forums—11 …; basilicas—10 …; [great
public] baths—11 …; aqueducts—19 …; roads—29 ….

*Questions: What kind of picture do these two descriptions give us of the physical appearance
of Rome? Of the types of public, commercial, and private buildings there? What features
do the two writers find especially worthy of mention? Do these descriptions reveal anything
about the religion, literacy, entertainment, or living conditions of Roman inhabitants? Can
you detect any significant change in the physical appearance of the city between the first and
fourth centuries?*

2. THE ROMAN BATHS

Every city in the Roman Empire, even those on the frontiers, had public baths where men (and women if separate facilities were provided) gathered for personal grooming, recreation, and socializing. The first extract is attributed to a Greek-speaking rhetorician, Lucian, who describes one of the great public baths of a Roman city in the second century. The second extract focuses on the activities of a bath's clientele and was written by Seneca, a Roman citizen and writer who lived in the first century.

Sources: (A) trans. A.M. Harmon, Lucian, *Hippias, or The Bath*, by Lucian (Cambridge, MA: Harvard University Press, 1913), pp. 39, 41, 43, abridged; (B) trans. R.M. Gummere, *Ad Lucilium Epistulae Morales*, by Seneca (New York: G.P. Putnam's Sons, 1918), pp. 373, 375, revised.

(A) Description of a Great Public Bath in the Second Century

... The building suits the magnitude of the site, accords well with the accepted idea of such an establishment, and shows regard for the principles of lighting. The entrance is high, with a flight of broad steps of which the tread is greater than the pitch, to make them easy to ascend. On entering, one is received into a public hall of good size, with ample accommodation for servants and attendants. On the left are the lounging rooms, also of just the right sort for a bath, attractive, brightly lighted retreats. Then, beside them, a hall, larger than need be for the purposes of a bath, but necessary for the reception of richer persons. Next ... locker rooms to undress in, on each side, with a very high and brilliantly lighted hall between them, in which are three swimming pools of cold water; it is finished in Laconian marble, and has two statues of white marble in the ancient style ....

On leaving this hall, you come into another which is slightly warmed instead of meeting you at once with fierce heat; it is oblong, and has an apse on each side. Next to it, on the right, is a very bright hall, nicely fitted up for massage, which has on each side an entrance decorated with Phrygian marble, and receives those who come in from the exercising floor. Then near this is another hall, the most beautiful in the world, in which one can stand or sit with comfort, linger without danger, and stroll about with profit. It also is resplendent with Phrygian marble clear to the roof. Next comes the hot corridor, faced with Numidian marble. The hall before [it] is very beautiful, full of abundant light and aglow with color like that of purple hangings. It contains three hot tubs.

When you have bathed, you need not go back through the same rooms, but can go directly to the cold room through a slightly warmed chamber. Everywhere there is copious illumination and full indoor daylight ... Why should I go on to tell you of the exercising floor and the cloak rooms? ... Moreover, it is beautified

with all other marks of thoughtfulness—with two toilets, many exits, and two devices for telling time, a water clock that makes a bellowing sound and a sundial.

(B) Seneca's Description of a Roman Bath House in the First Century

I live over a bathing establishment. Picture to yourself now the assortment of
voices, the sound of which is enough to sicken one. When the stronger fellows
are exercising and swinging heavy leaden weights in their hands, when they are
working hard or pretending to be working hard, I hear their groans; and whenever
they release their pent-up breath, I hear their hissing and jarring breathing. When I
have to do with a lazy fellow who is content with a cheap rubdown, I hear the slap
of the hand pummeling his shoulders, changing its sound according as the hand
is laid on flat or curved. If now a professional ball player comes along and begins
to keep score, I am done for. Add to this the arrest of a brawler or a thief, and the
fellow who always likes to hear his own voice in the bath, and those who jump into
the pool with a mighty splash as they strike the water. In addition to those whose
voices are, if nothing else, natural, imagine the hair plucker keeping up a constant
chatter in his thin and strident voice, to attract more attention, and never silent
except when he is plucking armpits and making the customer yell instead of yell-
ing himself. It disgusts me to enumerate the varied cries of the sausage dealer and
confectioner and of all the peddlers of the cook shops, hawking their wares, each
with his own peculiar intonation.

*Questions: How does the Roman bath described by Lucian fit in with the Roman buildings
described in doc. 1? What types of people visited the baths and why did they go there?*

3. THE HUMBLE TOWNSPEOPLE: GRAFFITI AND ELECTION NOTICES ON THE WALLS OF POMPEII

*These inscriptions were found scratched or painted on the walls of houses and other buildings
in the city of Pompeii, which was largely destroyed by a volcano in 79 C.E. They reflect all
different aspects of life in a busy Roman town of some 25,000 inhabitants. An as was a small
copper coin of low value; sesterces were worth about 4 asses, and a denarius was a silver
coin worth about 16 asses.*

Source: trans. N. Lewis and M. Reinhold, *Roman Civilisation Sourcebook II: The Empire* (New York:
Columbia University Press, 1955; reprinted New York: Harper and Row Torchbooks, 1966), pp.
326-27, 358-60, selections.

1. Twenty pairs of gladiators of Decimus Lucretius Satrius Valens, lifetime *flamen* [priest for the cult] of Nero son of Caesar Augustus, and ten pairs of gladiators of Decimus Lucretius Valens, his son, will fight at Pompeii on April 8, 9, 10, 11, 12. There will be a full card of wild beast combats, and awnings [for the spectators]. Aemilius Celer [painted this sign], all alone in the moonlight.

2. Market days: Saturday in Pompeii, Sunday in Nuceria, Monday in Atella, Tuesday in Nola, Wednesday in Cumae, Thursday in Puteoli, Friday in Rome.

3. 6th [day of the month]: cheese 1 [as], bread 8 [asses], oil 3 [asses], wine 3 [asses]
   7th: bread 8, oil 5, onions 5, bowl 1, bread for the slave [?] 2, wine 2
   8th: bread 8, bread for the slave [?] 4, grits 3
   9th: wine for the winner 1 *denarius*, bread 8, wine 2, cheese 2
   10th: … 1 *denarius*, bread 2, for women 8, wheat 1 *denarius*, cucumber 1, dates 1, incense 1, cheese 2, sausage 1, soft cheese 4, oil 7.

4. Pleasure says: "You can get a drink here for an *as*, a better drink for two, Falernian [a good wine] for four."

5. A copper pot is missing from this shop. 65 *sesterces* reward if anybody brings it back, 20 *sesterces* if he reveals the thief so we can get our property back.

6. The weaver Successus loves the innkeeper's slave girl, Iris by name. She doesn't care for him, but he begs her to take pity on him. Written by his rival. So long.
   [Answer by the rival:] Just because you're bursting with envy, don't pick on a handsomer man, a lady-killer and a gallant.
   [Answer by the first writer:] There's nothing more to say or write. You love Iris, who doesn't care for you.

7. Take your lewd looks and flirting eyes off another man's wife, and show some decency on your face!

8. Anybody in love, come here. I want to break Venus's ribs with a club and cripple the goddess's loins. If she can pierce my tender breast, why can't I break her head with a club?

9. [A prostitute's sign:] I am yours for 2 *asses* cash.

10. His neighbors urge you to elect Lucius Statius Receptus as *duovir* with judicial power; he is worthy. Aemilius Celer, a neighbor, wrote this. May you take sick if you maliciously erase this!

11. The petty thieves support the election of Vatia as *aedile*.

12. I ask you to elect Marcus Cerrinius Vatia to the *aedileship*. All the late drinkers support him.

13. I ask you to elect Aulus Vettius Firmus *aedile*. He is worthy of the city. I ask you to elect him, ballplayers. Elect him!

14. I wonder, O wall, that you may not have fallen in ruins from supporting the stupidities of so many scribblers!

4. THE IMPACT OF THE "BARBARIAN INVASIONS" ON FIFTH-CENTURY TOWNS

Although Jerome, one of the early Church Fathers, lived in Bethlehem in the still relatively peaceful eastern Empire, he was obviously distraught at the news of the troubles in the western empire.

Source: trans. P. Schaff and H. Wace, *A Select Library of Nicene and Post-Nicene Fathers of the Christian Church*, Series II, vol. VI, *St Jerome* (New York: The Christian Literature Co., 1893), pp. 236–37, revised.

Savage tribes in countless numbers have overrun all parts of Gaul. The whole country between the Alps and the Pyrenees, between the Rhine and the ocean, has been laid waste by the Quadi, Vandals, Sarmaratians, Alans, Gepids, Herules, Saxons, Burgundians, Allemanni—alas! For the commonweal!—even for the Pannonians.... The once noble city of Mainz has been captured and destroyed. In its church many thousands have been massacred. The people of Worms after standing a long siege have succumbed. The powerful city of Rheims, the people of Amiens, the people of Artois ... Tournai, Nîmes, and Strasbourg have fallen to the Germans, while the provinces of Aquitaine and of the Nine Nations, of Lyons and Narbonne are with the exception of a few cities one universal scene of desolation. And those which the sword spares without, famine ravages within. I cannot speak without tears of Toulouse which has thus far been kept from falling by the merits of its reverend bishop Exuperus. Even the Spaniards are on the brink of ruin and tremble daily as they recall the invasion of the Cimbri. And while others suffer misfortune once in actual fact, they suffer them continually in anticipation.

I say nothing of other places that I may not seem to despair of God's mercy. All that is ours now from the Pontic Sea to the Julian Alps in days gone by once ceased to be ours. For thirty years the barbarians burst the barrier of the Danube [River] and fought in the heart of the Roman Empire.... The poet Lucan describing the power of the city [of Rome] in a glowing passage says: "If Rome be weak, where shall we look for strength?" We may vary his words and say: "If Rome be lost, where shall we look for help?"...

Questions: What were the problems facing towns in the fifth century and how widespread were they? Why was Jerome, who lived some distance away in the eastern Roman empire, so worried about what was happening to these western European cities?

5. GREGORY OF TOURS'S ODE TO DIJON IN THE SIXTH CENTURY

Gregory of Tours was a Gallo-Roman bishop of Tours who chronicled the history of the early Frankish kings of the Merovingian dynasty. The sixth century, when he wrote, was a period of considerable political disorder and social tumult, which made life difficult for the inhabitants of the old Roman towns, many of which had been severely damaged during the first wave of Germanic invasions in the fourth and fifth centuries. Yet the northern French town of Dijon described by Gregory seems far removed from these problems and reminds us that urban life continued in some of the northern European towns.

Source: trans E. Brehaut, *History of the Franks, by Gregory, Bishop of Tours* (New York: Columbia University Press, 1916), p. 65.

I think it not unpleasing to insert in this place an account of the site of Dijon, where he [Gregory, a local bishop] was especially active. It is a stronghold with very solid walls, built in the midst of a plain, a very pleasant place, the lands rich and fruitful, so that when the fields are ploughed and once the seed is sown, a great wealth of produce comes in due season. On the south it has the Ouche, a river very rich in fish, and from the north comes another little stream, which runs in at the gate and flows under a bridge and again passes out by another gate, flowing around the whole fortified place with its quiet waters, and turning with wonderful speed the mills before the gate. The four gates face the four regions of the universe, and thirty-three towers adorn the whole structure, and the wall is thirty feet high and fifteen feet thick, built of squared stones up to twenty feet, and above of small stone. And why it is not called a city I do not know. It has all around it abundant springs, and on the west are hills, very fertile and full of vineyards, which produce for the inhabitants such a noble Falernian [wine] that they disdain wine of Ascalon. The ancients say this place was built by the emperor Aurelian.

Question: Why does Gregory think that Dijon deserves to be called a city?

6. TOLL EXEMPTIONS IN FRENCH TOWNS

This grant of exemption from tolls was written in the second half of the seventh century, a period after the first wave of Germanic migrations, but before the relative stability that came with the establishment of the Carolingian empire. This was a period of transition when remnants of the old Roman empire were still evident. Indeed, most of the towns mentioned in the document were Roman foundations. The exemption is part of a formulary, which is a collection of documents covering common petitions, grants, and other administrative matters that scribes could use as models when preparing documents to order. The scribe basically copied the wording of the document in the formulary, but substituted the appropriate names for "this bishop" or "this town." The mere presence in a formulary of a document treating tolls as a common occurrence suggests that the level of local and regional trade during this period was more regular than many scholars used to believe was possible.

Source: trans. M. Kowaleski, from *Textes et documents d'histoire au moyen âge, I: Ve - milieu VIIIe siècle*, ed. P. Riché and G. Tate (Paris: Société d'Édition d'Enseignement Supérieur, 1972), pp. 220–21.

Exemption. The king of France to his nobles, patricians, counts, toll collectors, and all those public interest. We have full confidence that our ceaseless efforts to accord suitable benefits to the places of the saints [and their] churches or priests will repay us in eternal blessing. Therefore, knowing your grandeur and your fidelity, we, at the request of "this bishop," prelate of "this town," have granted this favor, in the name of our Lord, in consideration of the merits of this [prelate]. Know that each year the blessed one [the bishop] or his representatives, who make purchases in Marseille or in the other trading towns of our kingdom in the measure of so many cartloads, may trade in any place or travel for any other necessity without paying there any toll or other tax to our treasury. Therefore, by this present order, which we order to be kept perpetually, we decree that neither you, nor your agents, nor your successors should require or exact any toll from the sizeable cartloads of goods belonging to this prelate, neither in Marseille itself, nor in Toulon, nor in Fos, Arles, Avignon, Soyons, Valence, Vienne, Lyons, Chalon-sur-Saône, or in other cities or villages or wherever toll is exacted in our kingdom, whether transported by water or land, nor [should you collect] any tax assessed on the roads, bridges, travelers, gates, grazing lands or any tax that our treasury could hope [to collect]. Whatever the source, all these tolls are granted in the name of our Lord, to the said prelate, his successors and his church, in order to profit the blessed ones of this saintly place. This concession takes effect right away by our authority. We have decided to corroborate it below with our own signature.

Questions: What were the different types of tolls that people buying goods in these towns normally had to pay? What does this text tell us about the role of towns in trading activity during the second half of the seventh century?

7. THE RAIDS OF THE NORTHMEN

A second wave of invasion by the Moslems from the south, the Northmen from Scandinavia, and the Magyars or Hungarians to the east hit Europe in the ninth and tenth centuries. Particularly devastating to the towns of England, France, and the Low Countries were the raids by the Northmen (also called the Vikings or Danes). The first extracts come from the Annals of St. Bertin, a monastic chronicle, while the second description of an attack on the city of Paris comes from a poem written by a monk, Abbo of St. Germain-des-Prés in Paris.

Source: trans. F.A. Ogg, *A Source Book of Medieval History* (New York: American Book Company, 1907), pp. 165–68; and pp. 168–71, which are revised by P. Dutton, *Carolingian Civilization: A Reader* (Peterborough, Ontario: Broadview Press, 1993), pp. 483–85.

(A) The Early Raids of the Northmen, 843–59

843. Pirates of the Northmen's race came to Nantes, killed the bishop and many of the clergy and laymen, both men and women, and pillaged the city....

844. The Northmen ascended the Garonne as far as Toulouse and pillaged the lands along both banks with impunity....

845. The Northmen with 100 ships entered the Seine on 20 March and, after ravaging first one bank and then the other, came without meeting any resistance to Paris. Charles [the Bald] resolved to hold out against them, but seeing the impossibility of gaining a victory, he made with them a certain agreement and by a gift of 7,000 pounds he bought them off from advancing farther and persuaded them to return.... The Northmen returned [from Paris] down the Seine and coming to the ocean pillaged, destroyed, and burned all the regions along the coast....

853–54. The Danish pirates, making their way into the country eastward from the city of Nantes, arrived without opposition, on 8 November, before Tours. This they burned, together with the church of St. Martin and the neighboring places. But that incursion had been foreseen with certainty and the body of St. Martin had been removed to Cormery, a monastery of that church, and from there to the city of Orleans. The pirates went to the chateau of Blois and burned it, proposing then to proceed to Orleans and destroy that city in the same fashion. But Agius, bishop of Orleans, and Burchard, bishop of Chartres, had gathered soldiers and ships to meet them, so they abandoned their design and returned to the lower Loire, though the following year [855] they ascended it anew to the city of Angers.

855. They left their ships behind and undertook to go overland to the city of Poitiers, but the Aquitanians came to meet them and defeated them, so that not more than 300 escaped.

856. On 18 April, the Danish pirates came to the city of Orleans, pillaged it, and went away without meeting opposition....

859. The Danish pirates having made a long sea-voyage (for they had sailed between Spain and Africa) entered the Rhone where they pillaged many cities and monasteries and established themselves on the island called Camargue.... They devastated everything as far as the city of Valence. Then after ravaging all these regions they returned to the island where they had fixed their habitation. Thence they went on toward Italy, capturing and plundering Pisa and other cities.

(B) The Siege of Paris, 885

[The Northmen] came to Paris with 700 sailing ships, not counting those of smaller size which are commonly called barques. At one stretch the Seine [River] was lined with the vessels for more than two leagues, so that one might ask in astonishment in what cavern the river had been swallowed up, for nothing was visible there, since ships covered that [river] as if with oak trees, elms, and alders. On the second day after the fleet of the Northmen arrived under the walls of the city, Siegfred, who was then king in name only but who was in command of the expedition, came to the dwelling of the illustrious bishop. He bowed his head and said: "Gauzelin, have compassion on yourself and on your flock. We beseech you to listen to us, in order that you may escape death. Allow us only the freedom of the city. We will do no harm and we will see to it that whatever belongs either to you or to Odo shall be strictly respected." Count Odo, who later became king, was then the defender of the city. The bishop replied to Siegfred, "Paris has been entrusted to us by the Emperor Charles, who, after God, king and lord of the powerful, rules over almost all the world. He has put it in our care, not at all that the kingdom may be ruined by our misconduct, but that he may keep it and be assured of its peace. If, like us, you had been given the duty of defending these walls, and if you should have done that which you ask us to do, what treatment do you think you would deserve?" Siegfred replied: "I should deserve that my head be cut off and thrown to the dogs. Nevertheless, if you do not listen to my demand, on the morrow our war machines will destroy you with poisoned arrows. You will be prey to famine and pestilence and these evils will renew themselves perpetually every year." So saying, he departed and gathered together his comrades.

In the morning the Northmen, boarding their ships, approached the tower and attacked it. They shook it with their engines and stormed it with arrows. The city resounded with clamor, the people were aroused, the bridges trembled. All came together to defend the tower. There Odo, his brother Robert, and the Count Ragenar distinguished themselves for bravery; likewise the courageous Abbot Ebolus, the nephew of the bishop. A keen arrow wounded the prelate, while at his side the young warrior Frederick was struck by a sword. Frederick died, but the old man, thanks to God, survived. For many this was their last moment of life, but they inflicted bitter blows on many of the enemy. At the last the enemy withdrew, carrying off a vast number of Danish dead....

No longer did the tower appear as fine as it once did, but its foundations were still solid and it delighted a little in the windows that had been opened up to the sun. The people spent the night repairing the holes with boards. By the next day, on the old citadel had been erected a new tower of wood, a half higher than the former one. In the morning, the sun and the Danes fell on the tower together. They engaged the Christians in violent combat. On every side arrows sped and blood flowed. With the arrows mingled the stones hurled by catapults and war-machines; the air was filled with them. The tower which had been built during the night groaned under the strokes of the darts, the city shook with the struggle, the people ran hither and thither, the bells jangled. The warriors rushed together to defend the tottering tower and to repel the fierce assault.

Among these warriors two, a count and an abbot [Ebolus], surpassed all the rest in courage. The former was the redoubtable Odo who never experienced defeat and who continually revived the spirits of the worn-out defenders. He ran along the ramparts and hurled back the enemy. On those who were secreting themselves so as to undermine the tower he poured oil, wax, and pitch, which, being mixed and heated, burned the Danes and tore off their scalps. Some of them died; others threw themselves into the river to escape the awful substance....

Meanwhile Paris was suffering not only from the sword outside but also from a pestilence which brought death to many noble men. Within the walls there was not enough ground in which to bury the dead ... Odo, the future king, was sent to Charles, emperor of the Franks, to implore help for the stricken city.

One day Odo, powerful with his arms, suddenly appeared on Montmartre in splendor in the midst of three bands of warriors. The sun made his armor glisten and greeted him before it illuminated the country around. The Parisians saw their beloved chief at a distance, but the enemy, hoping to prevent his gaining entrance to the tower, crossed the Seine and took up their position on the bank. Nevertheless Odo, his horse at a gallop, got past the Northmen and reached the tower, whose gates Ebolus opened to him. The enemy pursued the comrades of the count who were trying to keep up with him and get refuge in the tower.... [The Danes were defeated in the attack.]

Now came the Emperor Charles [the Fat], surrounded by soldiers from many lands, even as the sky is adorned with resplendent stars. A great throng, speaking many languages, accompanied him. He established his camp at the foot of the heights of Montmartre, near the tower. He allowed the Northmen to have the country of Sens to plunder; and in the spring he gave them 700 pounds of silver on condition that by the month of March they leave France for their own kingdom. Then Charles returned [home]; he was not to live long.

Questions: Did the cities meet the Viking raids with any type of resistance? Who led the resistance in Paris? What role did ordinary townspeople play in the defense of Paris? How did Emperor Charles [the Fat] choose to deal with the attackers?

8. THE MAGYAR RAIDS

The last wave of "barbarian invasions" of Europe was conducted by the Magyars, or Hungarians, a nomadic group from the Asian steppes who had little experience with towns. They penetrated much of eastern Europe, reaching as far west as France and as far south as Italy, but they focused in particular on German lands. These reports of the Magyar raids were written by Flodoard, a canon of the town of Reims in northern France, who recorded them in his Annals, *a year-by-year account of events during his own time.*

Source: trans. S. Fanning and B.S. Bachrach, *The* Annals *of Flodoard of Reims 919–966* (Peterborough, ON: Broadview Press, 2004), pp. 11–12, 15, 23, 26, 29, 56, 61, selections.

[In the year 924] ... King Berengar [of Italy], rejected by the Lombards, led the Magyars as they devastated Italy. They set fire to the rich and populous town of Pavia, destroying vast resources there. Forty-four churches were set afire and the bishop of that city [John], along with the bishop of Vercelli [Ragamfridus], who had been with him, was killed by the fire and the smoke. From the almost innumerable multitude of inhabitants of Pavia, only 200 are said to have survived. They gave the Magyars eight measures of silver gathered from the ashes of the remains of the city, thus ransoming the life and walls of the empty city. When this was completed, the Magyars crossed the steep ridges of the Alps and came into Gaul. Rudolf [II], the king of Cisalpine Gaul [Upper Burgundy] and Hugh of Vienne, closed them up in the passes of the Alps but the Magyars escaped from this inhospitable place through narrow mountain passes and entered Gothia....

It was reported that the Magyars who were ravaging Gothia suffered a plague, which caused dysentery and swelling of their heads, and very few survived....

[In the year 926] ... the Magyars crossed the Rhine and raged as far as the Voncq region, taking booty and setting fires. There was an eclipse of the moon, in its fourteenth day, on 1 April, the Saturday of Easter, and it became pale, with just a little light remaining, just like a two-day old moon. As dawn broke, the entire moon became the color of blood. For fear of the Magyars the body of St-Rémi and the relics of other saints were taken from the monasteries and brought to Reims, to be placed among the relics of Saint Walburgis, and many miracles were performed there....

[In the year 933] ... The Magyars divided their forces into three units. One of them went to Italy and another invaded the lands of Henry [king of Germany] across the Rhine. Henry set out against them, along with the Bavarians and Saxons and other peoples who were subject to him. He cut down all of them, almost exterminating them. It is said that 36,000 were killed, not including those who drowned in the river or those taken alive....

[In the year 935] ... The Magyars attacked throughout Burgundy, raging with plunderings, fires, and murder. However, this raiding lasted for only a short time, for when the Magyars learned of King Raoul's coming, they moved on into Italy....

[In the year 937] ... A part of the sky seemed to be burning and afterwards there was an invasion of Francia by the Magyars from that direction, with villas and fields laid waste, houses and basilicas burned, and large number of captives led away....

[In the year 951] ... The Magyars left Italy, crossed the Alps and invaded Aquitaine, staying there almost the entire summer. They exhausted that region with their plunderings and killings and then returned through Italy into their own land....

In the year 955, King Otto [of Germany] set out from his own lands and went out to meet the Magyars, who were plundering while they advanced. He fought and defeated them, preventing them from entering his realms....

A very large force of Magyars attacked Bavaria, seeking to invade Francia. King Otto [of Germany], along with Boleslav [duke of Bohemia], the prince of the Sarmatians, and Conrad of [Lotharingia], who was now reconciled to the king, fought against them [at the battle of the Lechfeld]. He cut down the Magyars, almost annihilating them....

Questions: How far-ranging were the Hungarian incursions and what impact did they have on towns? Why did towns act as magnets for the invaders? Did towns or townspeople have anything to do with their defeat?

9. THE CREATION OF BRUGES

This account from a monastic chronicle of how Bruges became a town focuses on the consumer needs of those dwelling in a castle built by the count of Flanders in the ninth century.

Source: trans. M. Kowaleski, from "Création d'une ville," *Documents relatifs à l'histoire de l'industrie et du commerce en France*, ed. G. Fagniez, vol. 1 (Paris: Alphonse Picard et Fils, 1898), pp. 54–55.

After this, for the labor or needs of those in the castle [built by the count of Flanders], traders began to stream in—that is, merchants of precious goods—who set themselves up in front of the gate, at the castle's bridge. Then there followed tavern-keepers, then inn-keepers to provide food and lodging for those who came to do business before the prince, who was often there. Houses began to be built and inns prepared, where those who could not be put up inside the castle were received. And they used to say these words: "Let's go to the bridge." Many dwellings grew up there so that very soon it became a large town which to this day bears the name "Brugghe," which, in their tongue, means "bridge."

Questions: What factors helped make Bruges a town? Who were the earliest settlers and why did they come to Bruges?

10. OTTO I GRANTS A MARKET IN BREMEN TO THE ARCHBISHOP OF HAMBURG, 965

The right to grant the privilege of holding a market or fair was usually reserved to kings and emperors who made such grants to reward loyal followers or, in this case, to gain salvation by agreeing to the request of important clergymen, such as the archbishop of Hamburg, who was also lord of a town called Bremen in northern Germany.

Source: trans. O.J. Thatcher and E.H. McNeal, *A Source Book for Mediaeval History* (New York: Charles Scribner's Sons, 1905), p. 580, revised.

In the name of the undivided Trinity. Otto, by the favor of God Emperor, Augustus. If we grant the requests of clergymen and liberally endow the places which are dedicated to the worship of God, we believe that it will undoubtedly assist in securing for us the eternal reward. Therefore, let all know that for the love of God we have granted the petition of Adaldgus, the reverend archbishop of Hamburg, and have given him permission to establish a market in the place called Bremen. In connection with the market we grant him jurisdiction, tolls, a mint, and all other related things to which our royal treasury would have a right. We also take under our special protection all the merchants who live in that place, and grant them the same protection and rights as those merchants have who live in other royal cities. And no one shall have any jurisdiction there except the aforesaid archbishop and those to whom he may delegate. Signed with our hand and sealed with our ring.

Questions: What privileges does the German emperor award to the archbishop on behalf of Bremen? Why was the archbishop seeking these particular privileges for the town? Why would these privileges be valuable for an early medieval town?

11. THE ORIGINS OF THE SAXON TOWNS

Henry I (919–36), the first German king of the Saxon house, focused his attention not on reviving imperial claims to Italy but on strengthening his own authority in Saxony and defending the frontiers of his kingdom from the Magyar (Hungarian) invasions. This selection is from a history of the Saxons written by Widukind, a monk who wrote in the latter part of the tenth century. The passage illustrates the relations between the Germans and the Slavs to the east and the military origin of many Saxon cities. The Slavs had moved as far west as the Elbe river, occupying the lands left vacant by the Germanic tribes after the migrations. From the time of Henry, however, much of this territory was gradually recovered by the Germans who systematically colonized these lands after conquering them. Here we see the capture of the city of Brandenburg and the reduction of Bohemia.

Source: O.J. Thatcher and E.H. McNeal, *A Source Book for Mediaeval History* (New York: Charles Scribner's Sons, 1905), pp. 71–72.

It lies beyond my power to relate in detail how King Henry, after he had made a nine years' truce with the Hungarians, undertook to develop the defenses of his own land [Saxony] and to subdue the barbarians; and yet this must not be passed over in silence. From the free peasants subject to military service he chose one out of every nine, and ordered these selected persons to move into the fortified places and build dwellings for the others. One third of all the produce was to be stored up in these fortified places, and the other peasants were to sow and reap and gather the crops and take them there. The king also commanded all courts and meetings and celebrations to be held in these places, that during a time of peace the inhabitants might accustom themselves to meeting together in them, as he wished them to do in case of an invasion. The work on these strongholds was pushed night and day. Outside of these fortified places there were no walled towns. While the inhabitants of his new cities were being trained in this way, the king suddenly fell upon the Heveldi [the Slavs who dwell on the Havel], defeated them in several engagements, and finally captured the city of Brandenburg. This was in the dead of winter, the besieging army encamping on the ice and storming the city after the garrison had been exhausted by hunger and cold. Having thus won with the capture of Brandenburg the whole territory of the Heveldi, he proceeded against Dalamantia which his father had attacked on a former occasion, and then besieged Jahna and took it after twenty days.... Then he made an attack in force upon Prague, the fortress of the Bohemians, and reduced the king of Bohemia to subjection.

Questions: Which places did King Henry choose to make into cities, and what steps did he take to accomplish this end? How do the origins of these Saxon towns compare to the town origins related in docs. 9 and 10?

12. THE CUSTOMS AND RENTS OF HEREFORD ACCORDING TO DOMESDAY BOOK, 1086

After Duke William of Normandy conquered England in 1066, he wanted to know the extent and value of his newly won lands, so he initiated a survey of all lands and manors held by his tenants-in-chief, including many (but not all) towns in England since they were, like manors, controlled by individual lords who had the right to collect taxes and administer the local courts. Known as Domesday Book, this survey sometimes recorded the customs and laws of individual towns and manors. The following document gives the entry for the English town of Hereford, which was located near the Welsh border and had the king himself as its lord. A burgage was a plot of land in a town that contained a building (usually a house and/or a shop) and a large yard.

Source: trans. J.H. Round, "Domesday Book," in *The Victoria History of the County of Hereford*, vol. I, ed. W. Page (London: Archibald Constable and Co., Ltd., 1908), pp. 309–10, revised.

In the city of Hereford in the time of King Edward there were 103 men dwelling together within and without the wall, and they had the following customs.

If any one of them wished to withdraw from the city he could with the consent of the reeve sell his house to another man who was willing to do the service due for it, and the reeve [a supervisory officer usually chosen from among the tenants] had the third penny of this sale. But if anyone through his poverty could not perform his service, he surrendered his house without payment to the reeve, who saw that the house did not remain empty and that the king did not lose [his] service.

Within the wall of the city each whole burgage [plot of land with a house] rendered 7½ pence, and 4 pence for the hire of horses, and on three days in August reaped at Marden, and [its tenant] was [present] on one day for gathering the hay where the sheriff pleased. He who had a horse proceeded three times a year with the sheriff to the pleas and to the hundred [courts] at Wormelow. When the king was hunting, from each house according to custom went one man to the beating in the wood.

Other men who had not whole burgages provided guards for the hall when the king was in the city.

When a burgess serving with a horse died, the king had his horse and weapons. If someone died who did not have a horse, the king had either 10 shillings or his land with the houses [thereon]. If anyone, when he died, had not bequeathed his possessions, the king had his goods. These customs were for those who lived in the city, and others likewise who dwelt without the wall, except only that a whole burgage outside the wall only gave 3½ pence. The other customs were common [to both]. Those whose wives brewed within or without the city gave 10 pence according to custom.

There were six smiths in the city; each of them rendered one penny from his forge, and each of them made 120 shoes of the king's iron, and to each one of them was given 3 pence on that account according to custom, and those smiths were freed from every other service.

There were seven moneyers there. One of these was the bishop's moneyer. When the coinage was renewed each of them gave 18 shillings for receiving the dies, and from the day on which they returned, for one month, each of them gave the king 20 shillings, and likewise the bishop had from his moneyer 20 shillings.

When the king came into the city the moneyers coined money as much as he willed for him, that is, of the king's silver.

And these seven had their own sac and soc [rights and profits of jurisdiction].

Upon the death of any of the king's moneyers the king had 20 shillings for relief.

But if he should die intestate, the king had all his income.

If the sheriff went into Wales with the army these men went with him. So that if anyone commanded to go did not go, he was fined 40 shillings for the king.

In the same city Earl Harold had 27 burgesses who had the same customs as the other burgesses.

From the same city the reeve rendered 12 pounds to the king and 6 pounds to the Earl Harold, and he had in his farm [lease] all the aforesaid customs.

The king, however, had in his demesne the three forfeitures, namely [for] breaking his peace, for house-breaking, and for assault.

Whosoever committed one of these [crimes], was fined 100 shillings paid to the king no matter whose man he might be.

The king now has the city of Hereford in demesne, and the English burgesses dwelling there have their former customs, but the French burgesses are quit for 12 pounds from all their forfeitures, except the three aforesaid.

The city renders to the king 60 pounds by tale of blanched money [money purified by being melted down and assayed].

Questions: How "urban" was Hereford in this period? What rights did the lord of the town possess? Are there any signs of the impact of the recent conquest of England on the town?

13. GRANT OF PRIVILEGES TO THE CASTILIANS, MOZARABS, AND FRANKS OF TOLEDO, 1086–1118

This document is a confirmation given in 1118 of a charter (now lost) granted by King Alfonso VII in 1086 to the citizens of Toledo, which had been recently seized from the Moslems. The charter highlights some of the differences between towns in Spain and elsewhere in western Europe, particularly the focus on the duties and rights of citizen-knights and the interest in military security, a reflection of the ongoing "Reconquista," which is what the Christian campaign to conquer southern Spain from its Moslem rulers (called Moors) was called. Also noteworthy are the distinctions made between five different citizen groups in Toledo. The Castilians were the new Christian conquerors from northern Spain; the Mozarabs were local Christians who had lived under the rule of the Moslems and spoke Arabic; and the Franks were immigrants from France who had come as merchants, pilgrims (to the great shrine of Santiago de Compostela in the north), or warriors in the Reconquista. The Galicians were from the northwestern part of the Iberian peninsula, the area around the shrine of Compostela. The charter also recognizes the separate status of Jews in Toledo, and refers back to the law code of the Visigoths, a Germanic group that migrated and settled in Iberia in the fifth century.

Source: trans. M. Kowaleski, from *Coleccion de fueros municipales y cartas pueblos*, vol. 1, ed. Tomás Muñoz y Romero (Madrid: Jose Maria Alonso, 1847; repr. Madrid: Lope de Vega, 1972), pp. 363–69, abridged.

Under the rule of the protective and indivisible Trinity, that is to say, both the Son and the Holy Spirit of the one, all-powerful God, the venerable King Alfonso, son of Raymond, has ordered again the renewal and confirmation of this pact and this most firm agreement for all the citizens of Toledo, namely the Castilians, Mozarabs, and Franks, on account of their fidelity and their equality. And he has augmented and confirmed for the love of God and for the remission of all of their sins, these privileges that had been given to them by his grandfather, King Alfonso, to whom God should give the best repose....

Likewise, all the clergy, who pray night and day to God all-powerful for themselves and every Christian, should have all their hereditary goods exempt from tithes.

He has also exempted all knights from toll at the gates on horses and mules in the city of Toledo.

And any Christian prisoner who escapes from Moorish captivity will not owe toll at the gates. And all that the king may give to the knights of Toledo, as gifts or in money, should be divided among them, namely Castilians, and Galicians [*Gallecos*], and Mozarabs, according to their numbers in relation to each other. And that knights as well as other citizens of Toledo should not be held for debt in his entire kingdom. If anyone should attempt to distrain one of them for debt in any of his territories, he should [pay] double the pledge, and pay 60 shillings to the king.

And this also: and those knights who do not do *abnudba* [service of guarding animal herds on the frontier from enemy attack] but [are expected to do] one *fossatum* [service on a military expedition into Muslim territory between May and September] and who have not participated in that *fossatum* without a good excuse, should pay the king 10 shillings.

And if one among them should die who holds a horse or a hauberk [a type of armor] or any arms from the king, their sons or nearest kin will inherit all, and those so honored shall remain with their mother, and shall be without obligations in their father's honor, until they are capable of riding a horse....

Likewise all charges arising from disputes and quarrels occurring among those who reside within the town or outside in the countryside on their own lands belong to them [the citizens]....

If any of them wishes to go to France or to Castile or to Galicia or some other land, he should leave a horseman at home, who will serve on his behalf during this time, and he [the knight] may go with the grace of God.

Whoever wants to go away with his wife to his lands beyond the mountains [perhaps the Guadarrama range separating Toledo from Castile] should leave a horseman at home and depart in October and return in May. If he does not return by this date and does not have a valid excuse, he should pay the king 60 shillings. If, however, he does not take his wife, nor leave a horseman with her, he must then appear before the court. Similarly, cultivators of the soil and of vines should pay the king tithes on wheat, and barley, and the fruits of vines, but not more, and faithful God-fearing men, accepting the pay of the king, should be chosen to record this tithe. And the tithe crops should be brought at the time of threshing the harvest to the granaries of the king, and at the time of the grape harvest to the king's wine press, and it should be accepted from them under the supervision of two or three faithful men of the city with true and equal measures. And those who pay this tithe to the king do not owe any service for their beasts, nor labor service, nor *fossatoria* [a tax paid to avoid military service between 1 May and the end of September], nor guard-duty in the city, nor in the castle, but they should be honored, and free, and governed without any vexation. And whoever of them wishes to ride on horseback may ride on horseback now and adopt the status of knight.

Whoever possesses an inheritance or villa next to a tributary of the rivers of Toledo, if he wishes to construct a mill on the tributary itself, or a waterwheel or a fishery, can do so without fear. And not only may they, their sons, and their heirs possess all these goods in fixity and stability for perpetuity, but they can also sell them and buy from each other, and give them to whomever they wish, and each one may do whatever he wishes with his inheritance…. And also whoever has inheritances in any lands of this empire, it is commanded that the bailiffs may not enter these lands, nor their agents; they are given these orders for love of the people of Toledo. For also, with the assistance of God, concerning the properties of the Moors of the city, those, who were from those cities, should have assurance [that] they will [be able to] return to recover their inherited properties and may try to sell those same inherited properties in Toledo to those who reside in Toledo….

If anyone kills any man within Toledo or within five miles of its circuit, he should die a most shameful death by stoning. If, however, he will have been accused of the murder of a Christian, or Moor, or Jew, and there is no trustworthy or faithful testimony concerning him, they will judge him according to the *librum judicum* [the book of the judges, which refers to the Visigothic code of law].

He also confirms the honor of the Christians, so that if a Moor or a Jew should have a legal case with a Christian, they must go to the trial before a Christian judge, and that no arms or any saddle horse may leave Toledo for Moorish lands.

And it pleases him that the city of Toledo should not be *prestamo* [a temporary fief to pay for military service], and that it should have no other master than him, neither man nor woman, and that in the time of siege, he will hasten to defend Toledo from all who wish to oppress it whether they are Christians or Moors….

… [The charter ends with a list, divided according to districts, of 48 named men, presumably residents of Toledo who served as witnesses in swearing to uphold the charter; eleven of the names are written in Arabic.]

Questions: Who were the "knights" of Toledo and what privileges did they receive? What were they expected to do in exchange for these privileges? Did the different religious and ethnic groups in Toledo enjoy the same privileges and responsibilities? To what extent does this charter illustrate harmony or tension between the different ethnic and religious groups of Toledo?

14. GERMAN COLONIZATION IN THE EAST

Towns developed later in eastern Europe, which was far less populated than western Europe and had not experienced the influence of Roman settlement and civilization. To attract more settlers to these relatively empty lands, the local counts sent brokers or agents to more heavily urbanized regions (such as the Low Countries) to extol the advantages of moving east, where they promised that opportunities for advancement were plentiful. This extract from a chronicle describes this process as well as the foundation of the great northern German town of Lübeck.

Source: trans. F.J. Tschan, *The Chronicle of the Slavs, by Helmold, priest of Bosau* (New York: Columbia University Press, 1935), pp. 168–69, abridged.

... Adolf [the count of Holstein] began to rebuild the fortress at Segeberg and girded it with a wall. But because the land was without inhabitants, he sent messengers into all regions, namely to Flanders and Holland, to Utrecht, Westphalia, and Frisia, proclaiming that those who were in difficult straits because of a shortage of fields should come with their families and receive very good land—a spacious land, rich in crops, abounding in fish and meat, and exceedingly good pastures....

An innumerable multitude of different peoples rose up at this invitation and they came with their families and possessions into the land of Wagria to Count Adolph that they might possess the country which he had promised them. First of all the Holzations [people from Holstein] received abodes in the safest places to the west in the region of Segeberg along the River Trave ... The Westphalians settled in the region of Dargune, the Hollanders around Eutin, and the Frisians around Süssel. The country around Plön, however, was still uninhabited. Oldenburg and Lütjenburg and the rest of the lands bordering on the sea he gave to the Slavs to live in, and they became his tributaries.

Count Adolf came later to a place known as Bucu and found there the wall of an abandoned fortress which Cruto, the tyrant of God, had built, and a very large island, encircled by two rivers. The Trave flows on one side, the Wakenitz on the other. Each of these streams has swampy and impassable banks. On the side, however, on which the land road runs there is a little hill surmounted by the wall of the fort. When, therefore, the circumspect man saw the advantages of the site and beheld the noble harbor, he began to build there a city. He called it Lübeck because it was not far from the old port and city which Prince Henry had at one time constructed. He sent messengers to Niclot, prince of the Abodrites, to make friends with him, and by means of gifts drew to himself all men of consequence, to the end that they would all strive to accommodate themselves to him and bring peace upon his land. Thus the deserted places of the land of Wagria began to be occupied and the number of its inhabitants was multiplied. Vicelin, the priest too, on the invitation as well as with the assistance of the count, got back the properties near the castle of Segeberg which Emperor Lothar had in times past given him for the construction of a monastery and for the support of the servants of God.

Questions: Why did Count Adolf decide to build a city at Lübeck? What factors helped to make Lübeck a town?

15. ARCHAEOLOGICAL EXCAVATIONS IN TENTH-CENTURY YORK

York was founded as a military base by the Romans and was a royal capital and seat of an important bishopric for the Anglo-Saxon kingdom of Northumbria from the seventh to ninth centuries. But the Northmen captured the city in 866 (during the second wave of "barbarian invasions") and controlled it—as part of a larger kingdom ruled by Danish and Norwegian kings—until 954. There always remained a strong Scandinavian element in York (called Jorvik in the tenth century) which was particularly evident in the place names and personal names of its residents. Our understanding of life in Viking-age York has been considerably enhanced by a series of archaeological excavations at Coppergate (coppr means "cup" and gata means "street" in Old Norse) in the middle of the city of York. The heavily water-logged site helped to preserve many objects that normally decompose over the centuries.

Source: Richard Hall, *The Viking Dig: The Excavations at York* (London: The Bodley Head, 1984), summary of pp. 67–116 in Nos. 1–10, below, and Figures 65, 93, 108, 137, 138.

These are some of the tenth-century structures and objects found in the archaeological excavations of York:

1. Buildings with wattle walls [made of wooden posts with strong, flexible branches of wood woven around them], a central hearth, and wall-benches along two interior walls.

2. Pathways made of wattle that connected buildings.

3. The workshop of a woodturner, with broken or partially finished wooden bowls and cups. The wood types found included ash, yew, and maple.

4. Disc brooches made of silver, silver-plated lead alloy, copper alloy, or lead alloy, about 2–5 cm wide, and decorated with animal motifs, runic inscriptions, foliage designs, or curving lines. Most were made of a cheap lead alloy.

5. Beads made of amber and jet.

6. Red-painted pottery made on the continent.

7. Contemporary forgery of a tenth-century Islamic silver coin, made of lead and tin on a copper alloy base.

8. Fragments of woolen textiles including one complete woolen sock made from single-needle knitting [a technique known in Scandinavia].

9. Combs and a comb case made from antler and bone.

10. Hundreds of leather shoes and boots with a single-piece flat sole sewn on to the upper, but without a heel. Worn soles were the most common find, suggesting that soles were thrown away and replaced when sufficiently worn.

11. Three gravestone markers carved by masons; one had a cross carved on one side and a chevron on the other; another had Scandinavian-style interlaced animal designs.

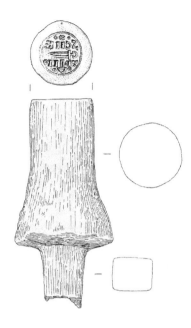

Figure 1.2

Iron Coin Die for an Early Tenth-Century Penny

Minters used these dies to make coins by putting the die-head (pictured at the top) onto softened metal and hammering on the tang (which here is broken off) so that the die-head made an impression of the coin on the metal. The die-head is engraved with a Latin inscription meaning "the money of St. Peter," which probably refers to the cathedral church of York, dedicated to St. Peter. But the engraving also includes a sword and hammer, both of which can be interpreted as pagan Viking symbols. Note also that the die-head reads backwards, so that the inscription and symbols come out the right way when the coin is stamped out. A coin struck from this die has been found in Denmark. Reproduced with permission from Richard Hall, *The Viking Dig: The Excavations at York* (London: The Bodley Head, 1984), fig. 65, p. 62.

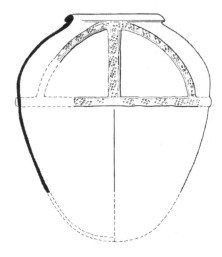

Figure 1.3

Reconstruction of a Wine Pitcher from the Rhineland

Enough fragments of this large (36 cm. high) pottery pitcher were discovered to reconstruct what it looked like. We know the pitcher held wine, and the shape and style are distinctive of pottery produced in the German Rhineland (called Badorf ware), which indicates that large quantities of wine were being brought from Germany to York in the tenth century. Reproduced with permission from Richard Hall, *The Viking Dig: The Excavations at York* (London: The Bodley Head, 1984), fig. 93, p. 88.

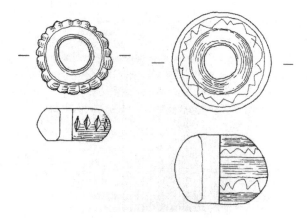

Figure 1.4

Viking Age Stone Spindle-Whorls

Spindle-whorls are common finds in archaeological excavations. These weights made from animal bone, pottery shards, or stone were used to weigh down the hand-held spindles used in spinning thread. Spinning was clearly a daily activity. Reproduced with permission from Richard Hall, *The Viking Dig: The Excavations at York* (London: The Bodley Head, 1984), fig.108, p. 98.

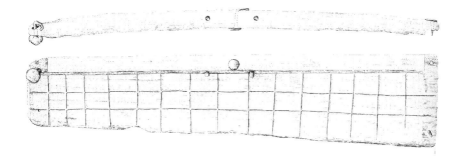

Figure 1.5

Fragment of a Wooden Gaming Board

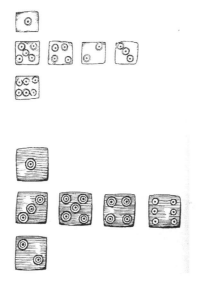

and Figure 1.6

Bone and Jet Dice

Finds such as this game board fragment and sets of dice give us some insight into how the Anglo-Scandinavian population of York spent their leisure time. The board was probably used for *hnefatafl*, a game of skill for two players, similar to chess or draughts. The dice indicate that games of chance were played. Reproduced with permission from Richard Hall, *The Viking Dig: The Excavations at York* (London: The Bodley Head, 1984), fig.137, 138, p. 114.

Questions: What do these structures and objects tell us about everyday life in Viking-age York? What insights do they offer into the trade and industry of tenth-century York? About the influence of the Scandinavian conquerors on this northern English town? How can archaeological evidence add to (or even challenge) documentary evidence?

CHAPTER TWO

COMMUNES, GOVERNMENT, AND EXTERNAL RELATIONS

Figure 2.1

The Burghers of Ghent at the Court of the Count of Flanders

Representatives from the civic rulers or burghers of Ghent beg the pardon of Louis II, Count of Flanders, after their 1397 revolt against him. While communes such as Ghent were self-governing, they were still responsible to the king (or in this case, the count) who had granted their civic charter. Miniature from a manuscript of Froissart. Reproduced from Paul LaCroix, *Manners, Customs, and Dress During the Middle Ages and During the Renaissance Period* (London: Bickers and Son, 1870), fig. 38.

16. THE PEOPLE OF COLOGNE REBEL
AGAINST THEIR ARCHBISHOP, 1074

This extract from the Annals of Lambert of Hersfeld *shows how the arbitrary exactions of the lord of Cologne—the city's archbishop—provoked a violent rebellion led by the son of a wealthy merchant. The Cologne mob was also inspired by news of a similar revolt the year before by the people of Worms, who had driven their lord—also a bishop—out of town because of his rigid rule. Revolts of this period, which were often led by the wealthier citizens, reflected the expanding wealth and confidence of urban inhabitants and their interest in ruling themselves rather than being ruled by a lord.*

Source: trans. O.J. Thatcher and E.H. McNeal, *A Source Book for Mediaeval History* (New York: Charles Scribner's Sons, 1905), pp. 585–86.

The archbishop spent Easter in Cologne with his friend, the bishop of Münster, whom he had invited to celebrate this festival with him. When the bishop was ready to go home, the archbishop ordered his servants to get a suitable boat ready for him. They looked all about, and finally found a good boat which belonged to a rich merchant of the city, and demanded it for the archbishop's use. They ordered it to be got ready at once and threw out all the merchandise with which it was loaded. The merchant's servants, who had charge of the boat, resisted, but the archbishop's men threatened them with violence unless they immediately obeyed. The merchant's servants hastily ran to their lord and told him what had happened to the boat, and asked him what they should do. The merchant had a son who was both bold and strong. He was related to the great families of the city, and, because of his character, very popular. He hastily collected his servants and as many of the young men of the city as he could, rushed to the boat, ordered the servants of the archbishop to get out of it, and violently ejected them from it. The advocate of the city [an official appointed to protect ecclesiastical property and rights] was called in, but his arrival only increased the tumult, and the merchant's son drove him off and put him to flight. The friends of both parties seized their arms and came to their aid, and it looked as if there were going to be a great battle fought in the city. The news of the struggle was carried to the archbishop, who immediately sent men to quell the riot, and being very angry, he threatened the rebellious young men with dire punishment in the next session of court. Now the archbishop was endowed with all virtues, and his uprightness in all matters, both of the state and of the church, had often been proved. But he had one vice. When he became angry, he could not control his tongue, but overwhelmed everybody, without distinction, with bitter upbraidings and violent vituperation. When his anger had passed, he regretted his fault and reproached himself for it. The riot in the city was finally quieted a little, but the young man, who was very angry as well as elated over his first success, kept on making all the disturbance he could. He went about the city making speeches to the people about the harsh government of the archbishop, and accused him of laying unjust burdens on the people, of depriving innocent persons of their property, and of insulting honorable citizens with his violent and offensive words.... It was not difficult for him to raise a mob.... Besides, they all regarded it as a great and glorious deed on the part of the people of Worms that they had driven out their bishop because he was governing them too rigidly. And since they were more numerous and wealthy than the people of Worms, and had arms, they disliked to have it thought that they were not equal to the people of Worms in courage, and it seemed to them a disgrace to submit like women to the rule of the archbishop who was governing them in a tyrannical manner....

Questions: What provoked the revolt? Is there any indication of the reasons why the revolt drew such support from the townspeople? Who were the leaders of the revolt?

17. THE FORMATION OF A COMMUNE AT LAON, 1116

This passage about the formation of a sworn commune by townsmen fed up with the burdensome rule of their lord, the local bishop, was written by a contemporary abbot, Guibert of Nogent. The first commune at Laon was formed among the local clergy, nobles, and townspeople, but three years later, after the bishop reneged on his agreement to recognize this commune, a second commune emerged that was composed primarily of townspeople, who turned their anger against the bishop.

Source: trans. C.C. Swinton-Bland, revised by J.F. Benton, *Self and Society in Medieval France: The Memoirs of Abbot Guibert of Nogent (1064-c.1125)*, ed. J.F. Benton (Toronto: Medieval Academy reprints for teaching, no. 15, 1984), pp.165–68, 171–76, selections.

Some time after the bishop [of Laon] had set out for England to extract money from the English king, whom he had served and who had been his friend, the archdeacons Gautier and Guy and the nobles of the city devised the following plan. Since ancient times it had been the misfortune of the city that neither God nor any lord was feared there, but, according to each man's power and desire, the public authority was involved in rapine and murder. To begin with the source of the plague, whenever the king, who ought to have exacted respect for himself with royal severity, happened to visit the city, he was himself first shamefully fined on his own property. When his horses were led to the water morning or evening, his grooms were beaten and the horses seized. It was known that the clergy themselves were held in such contempt, that neither their persons nor their goods were spared, but the situation then followed the text, "As it is with the people, so with the priest." But what shall I say about the lower classes? None of the peasants came into the city (no one who did not have the best guaranteed safe-conduct even approached it) who was not thrown into prison and held to ransom, or, if the opportunity occurred, was not drawn into some lawless lawsuit.... No one was safe going out at night, for he would surely be either robbed or captured or killed.

The clergy and the archdeacons and the nobles, taking account of these conditions and looking out for ways of exacting money from the people, offered them through their agents the opportunity to have authorization to create a commune, if they would offer an appropriate sum of money. Now "commune" is a new and evil name for an arrangement for them all to pay the customary head tax, which they owe to their lords as a servile due, in a lump sum once a year, and if anyone commits a crime, he shall pay a fine set by law, and all other financial exactions which are customarily imposed on serfs are completely abolished. Seizing on this opportunity for commuting their dues, the people gathered huge sums of money to fill the gaping purses of so many greedy men. Pleased with the shower of income poured upon them, those men established their good faith by proferring oaths that they would keep their word in this matter.

After this sworn association of mutual aid among the clergy, nobles, and people had been established, the bishop returned with much wealth from England. Angered by those responsible for this innovation, for a long time kept away from the city....

Although he said that he was moved by relentless wrath against those who had sworn an oath to the association and those who were the principals in the transaction, in the end his high-sounding words were suddenly quieted by the offer of a great heap of silver and gold. Then he swore that he would maintain the rights of the commune, following the terms of the charters of the city of Noyon and the town of Saint-Quentin. The king too was induced to confirm the same thing by oath with a bribe from the people.

O my God, who can describe the controversy that broke out when, after accepting so many gifts from the people, they then took oaths to overturn what they had sworn; that is, when they tried to return the serfs to their former condition after once freeing them from the yoke of their exactions? The hatred of the bishop and nobles for the burghers was indeed implacable ... Whenever one of the people was brought into a court of law, he was judged not on his condition in the eyes of God, but, if I may put it this way, on his bargaining power, and he was drained of his substance to the last penny....

Calling together the nobles and certain of the clergy in the last days of Lent in the most holy Passiontide of Our Lord, the bishop determined to attack the commune, to which he had sworn, and had with presents induced the king to swear.

He had summoned the king to that pious duty and, on the day before Good Friday—that is, on Maundy Thursday—he instructed the king and all his people to break their oaths....

After the bonds of the association were broken, such rage, such amazement seized the burghers that all the craftsmen abandoned their jobs and the stalls of the tanners and cobblers were closed and nothing was exposed for sale by the inn-keepers and chapmen, who expected to have nothing left when the lords began plundering. For at once the property of such individuals was calculated by the bishop and nobles, and the amount any man was known to have given to establish the commune was demanded of him to pay for its annulment....

To be brief, all the efforts of the bishop and the nobles in these days were reserved for fleecing their inferiors. But those inferiors were no longer merely angry, but were goaded into an animal rage. Binding themselves by mutual oaths, they conspired for the death, or rather the murder, of the bishop and his accomplices. They say that forty took the oath. Their great undertaking could not be kept completely secret, and when it came to the attention of Master Anselm toward evening of Holy Saturday, he sent word to the bishop, who was retiring to rest, not to go out to the service of matins, knowing that if he did he would be killed. With excessive pride, the bishop stupidly said, "Nonsense, I'm not likely to die at the hands of such people." But although he scorned them orally, he did not dare to go out for matins or to enter the church.

The next day, as he followed the clergy in procession, he ordered the people of his household and all the knights to come behind him carrying short swords under their garments. During this procession, when a little disorder began to arise, as often happens in a crowd, one of the burghers came out of the church and thought the time had come for the murder to which they were sworn. He then began to cry out in a loud voice, as if he were signaling, "Commune, Commune!" over and over again. Because it was a feast day, this was easily stopped, yet it brought suspicion on the opposition....

On Wednesday I went to him because through his disorders he had robbed me of my grain supply and of some legs of pork, called *bacons* in French. When I requested him to relieve the city of these great disturbances, he replied, "What do you think they can do by their riots? If John, my moor, were to take by the nose the most powerful man amongst them, he would not even dare to grunt. For just now I have compelled them to renounce what they call their commune for so long as I live." I said something, and then seeing the man was overcome with arrogance, I stopped. But before I left the city, because of his instability we quarreled with mutual recriminations. But although he was warned by many of the imminent peril, he took no notice of anyone.

The next day, that is, on the Thursday—when the bishop and Archdeacon Gautier were engaged after the noon offices in collecting money, suddenly there arose throughout the city the tumult of men shouting "Commune" then through the nave of the cathedral of Notre-Dame, and through the very door by which Gerard's killers had come and gone, a great crowd of burghers attacked the bishop's palace armed with rapiers, double-edged swords, bows and axes, and carrying clubs and lances. As soon as this sudden attack was discovered, the nobles rallied from all sides to the bishop, having sworn to give him aid against such an assault if it should occur. In this rally Guimar the castellan, an older nobleman of handsome presence and guiltless character, armed only with shield and spear, ran out through the church. Just as he entered the bishop's hall, he was the first to fall, struck on the back of the head with a sword by a man named Rainbert, who had been his close friend.... Adon, the *vidame* [one of the bishop's officials], sharp in small matters and even keener in important ones, separated from the rest and able to do little by himself among so many, encountered the full force of the attack as he was striving to reach the bishop's palace. With his spear and sword, he made such a stand that in a moment he struck down three of those who rushed at him. Then he mounted the dining-table in the hall, where he was wounded in the knees and other parts of the body. At last, falling on his knees and striking at his assailants all around him, he kept them off for a long time, until someone pierced his exhausted body with a javelin. After a little he was burned to ashes by the fire in that house.

While the insolent mob was attacking the bishop, and howling before the walls of his palace, the bishop and the people who were aiding him fought them off as best they could by hurling stones and shooting arrows. Now, as at all times, he showed great spirit as a fighter; but because he had wrongly and in vain taken up that other sword, he perished by the sword. Unable to stand against the reckless assaults of the people, he put on the clothes of one of his servants and fled into the warehouse of the church, where he hid himself in a container. When the cover had been fastened on by a faithful follower, he thought himself safely hidden. As those looking for him ran hither and thither, they did not call out for the bishop but for a felon. They seized one of his pages, but he remained faithful and they could get nothing out of him. Laying hands on another, they learned from the traitor's nod where to look for him. Entering the warehouse and searching everywhere, at last they found him....

And as he implored them piteously, ready to swear that he would give them unlimited riches, that he would leave the country, with hardened hearts they jeered at him. Then a man named Bernard of Bruyères raised his sword and brutally dashed out that sinner's brains from his holy head. Slipping between the hands of those who held him, before he died he was struck by someone else with a blow running under his eye-sockets and across the middle of his nose. Brought to his end there, his legs were hacked off and many other wounds inflicted....

Questions: How does Guibert of Nogent define a "commune"? Did the interest groups involved in the formation of the commune fit with Guibert's definition? What role did oaths play in the formation of the commune and the revolt against Laon's lord, the bishop? What tactics did the townspeople employ to secure their commune after the bishop revokes it? What did the bishop fear about the formation of the commune? How does this revolt compare with that in Cologne (doc. 16) in terms of motivation, leadership, and aims?

18. THE CUSTOMS OF LORRIS, 1155

Many towns started down the path toward self-government by seeking written ratification of their customs and additional privileges from their lords in a charter. The charter of Lorris, granted by the king of France, served as a model for many town charters in northern France in laying out the customary laws governing the town. These charters, however, normally reflect only a step in the movement toward self-government since the lords were reluctant to part with all of their privileges in the town at once.

Source: trans. F.A. Ogg, *A Source Book of Medieval History* (New York: American Book Co., 1907), pp. 328–30, revised.

1. Every one who has a house in the parish of Lorris shall pay as rent only 6 pence for his house, and for each acre of land that he possesses in the parish.

2. No inhabitant of the parish of Lorris shall be required to pay a toll or any other tax on his provisions; and let him not be made to pay any measurage fee on the grain which he has raised by his own labor.

3. No burgher shall go on an expedition, on foot or on horseback, from which he cannot return the same day to his home if he desires.

4. No burgher shall pay toll on the road to Étampes, to Orleans, to Milly (which is in the Gâtinais), or to Melun.

5. No one who has property in the parish of Lorris shall forfeit it for any offense whatsoever, unless the offense shall have been committed against us or any of our *hôtes* [those receiving land from the king and under his direct protection].

6. No person while on his way to the fairs and markets of Lorris, or returning, shall be arrested or disturbed, unless he shall have committed an offense on the same day....

9. No one, neither we nor any other, shall exact from the burghers of Lorris any tallage, tax, or subsidy....

12. If a man shall have had a quarrel with another, but without breaking into a fortified house, and if the parties shall have reached an agreement without bringing a suit before the provost, no fine shall be due to us or our provost on account of the affair....

15. No inhabitant of Lorris is to render us the obligation of *corvée* [labor services], except twice a year, when our wine is to be carried to Orleans, and not elsewhere.

16. No one shall be detained in prison if he can furnish surety that he will present himself for judgment.

17. Any burgher who wishes to sell his property shall have the privilege of doing so; and, having received the price of the sale, he shall have the right to go from the town freely and without molestation, if he so desires, unless he has committed some offense in it.

18. Any one who shall dwell a year and a day in the parish of Lorris, without any claim having pursued him there, and without having refused to lay his case before us or our provost, shall abide there freely and without molestation....

35. We ordain that every time there shall be a change of provosts in the town the new provost shall take an oath faithfully to observe these regulations; and the same thing shall be done by new sergeants every time that they are installed.

Questions: What types of privileges were the townspeople of Lorris especially anxious to make into law? What do these laws tell us about the chief concerns of the townspeople? To what extent does the charter reflect the concerns of a specifically "urban" populace? What governing powers does the charter give to the townspeople?

19. THE LOMBARD COMMUNES AS VIEWED
BY A GERMAN BISHOP

Otto of Freising, a German bishop who accompanied Emperor Frederick Barbarossa (his nephew) during his invasion of Italy in 1154, wrote this account of the governing structure of towns in Lombardy, in northern Italy. Since the Lombard towns were part of the Holy Roman Empire, they were theoretically subject to the emperor (here referred to as their "prince"), but in fact their growing wealth and independence made it difficult for the emperor to exercise true control over these towns, most of which had become communes and enjoyed some measure of self-government. Indeed, Barbarossa's "invasion" was an attempt to re-establish at least the emperor's fiscal rights in these towns, particularly in Milan, the region's largest city, which had openly flouted the emperor's wishes.

Source: trans. U. Balzani, *Early Chroniclers of Europe: Italy* (London: Society for Promoting Christian Knowledge; New York: E. & J.B. Young and Co., 1883), pp. 253–56.

They [the Lombards] also imitate the activity of the ancient Romans in the management of the cities and in the preservation of the state.... they are so attached to their liberty that, to avoid the insolence of rulers, they prefer to be reigned over by consuls than by princes. And since, as it is known, there are three orders among them, of captains, vassals, and the commons [*plebs*], in order to keep down arrogance, these consuls are chosen, not from one order, but from each, and, lest they should be seized with a greed for power, they are changed nearly every year. From which it happens that that territory is all divided into cities, which have each reduced those of their own province to live with them, so that there is hardly to be found any noble or great man with so great an influence, as not to owe obedience to the rule of his own city. And they are all accustomed to call these various territories their own *comitatus* [county], from this privilege of living together. And in order that the means of restraining their neighbors may not fail, they do not disdain to raise to the badge of knighthood, and to all grades of authority, young men of low condition, and even workmen of contemptible mechanical arts, such as other people drive away like the plague from the more honorable and liberal pursuits. From which it happens that they are preeminent among the other countries of the world for riches and power. And to this they are helped also, as has been said, by their own industrious habits, and by the absence of their princes, accustomed to reside north of the Alps.

In this, however, they retain a trace of their barbarous dregs, forgetful of ancient nobility, that while they boast of living by law they do not obey the laws. For they seldom or never receive the prince reverently, to whom it would be their duty to show a willing reverence of submission, nor do they obediently accept those things which he, according to the justice of the laws, ordains, unless they are made to feel his authority, constrained by the gathering of many soldiers. On this account it frequently happens that, whereas a citizen has only to be restrained by the law, and an adversary must be coerced with arms according to the law; they find him, from whom as their proper prince they should receive clemency, more often having recourse to hostilities for his own rights. From which results a double evil for the state, both that the prince has his thoughts distracted by the collecting of an army for the subjection of the citizen, while the citizen has to be compelled to obedience to his prince, not without a great expenditure of his own substance. Whence, for the same reason that the people are in such an instance guilty of rashness, the prince is to be excused, by the necessity of the case, before God and man.

Among the other cities of that nation, Milan, situated between the Po [River] and the Alps, now possesses supremacy.... And it is considered more famous than other cities, not only on account of its greater size and its large number of armed men, but also because it has added to its jurisdiction two other cities placed in the same region, namely Como and Lodi. Then, as happens in human affairs, through the blandishments of a smiling fortune, it swelled out into such daring of pride, being elated with success, that it not only did not refrain from attacking all its neighbors, but ventured even without alarm to incur the recently offended majesty of the prince.

Questions: What does the writer find unique about the Lombard cities? How were these cities governed? What was their relationship to their overlord, the prince (the emperor of Germany)? What are Otto's views about the proper relationship between the Lombard cities and the emperor, and what does his explanation of the current situation tell us about his political views?

20. ROYAL CHARTERS GRANTED TO DUBLIN, 1192–1229

Established in 841 by the Northmen, Dublin had become Ireland's most important city by the mid-eleventh century when it was ruled directly by the Irish kings. In 1171, King Henry II of England invaded Ireland and took over most of the country, including Dublin. The English kings were thus lords of Dublin for much of the Middle Ages, although in 1192, the date of the first charter printed here, its lord was the king's son, John, Earl of Mortain (later King John of England). The charters below show the escalation of rights granted to Dublin from its royal lords over a thirty-year period. The "Hundred" refers to the Hundred Court, which represented the larger regional jurisdiction to which the city belonged. All those who did not enjoy Dublin citizenship were called "foreigners," even citizens from neighboring towns.

Source: trans. J.T. Gilbert, *Calendar of Ancient Records of Dublin in the Possession of the Municipal Corporation of that City* (Dublin: Joseph Dollard, Wellington-Quay; London: Bernard Quaritch, 1889), pp. 2–8, revised.

May 15, 1192.... John, Lord of Ireland, Earl of Mortain, grants to his citizens of Dublin, both within and without the walls there, to have their boundaries as perambulated on oath by good men of the city under precept from his father, King Henry [the boundaries of the city are then recited]. The liberties and free customs granted are as follows:

1.   No citizen of Dublin shall plead beyond the walls of the city in any plea, except pleas of external tenements not pertaining to the Hundred of the city.

2.   Citizens are exempted from [collective] fines for murder within the boundaries of the city.

3.   No citizen can wage battle in the city on any appeal brought against him, but should clear himself by the oath of forty lawful men of the city.

4.   No man can take lodging within the walls, by order or billeting by the marshals, against the will of the citizens.

5.   The citizens are exempted from toll, lastage, passage, pontage, and all other customs throughout the entire land and dominion of John.

6.   No citizen should be amerced [fined] in money unless according to the law of the Hundred, that is to say, by forfeiture of 40 shillings, so that he who is amerced should be quit of half of it, and should pay the other half as

amercement [fine], except for three fines, namely, those of bread, ale, and watch, which are amercements of 2 shillings and 6 pence, one-half of which shall be condonable, and the other to be paid as amercements.

7.   The Hundred Court shall be held only once in the week.

8.   No citizen shall be aggrieved by meskenning [a fine for a mistake in oral pleadings] in any plea.

9.   The citizens should legally have their lands, tenures, mortgages, and debts throughout John's entire land and dominion, whoever may be indebted to them.

10.   They may distrain [arrest to insure appearance in court] their debtors by their chattels in Dublin.

11.   In relation to the citizens' lands and tenures within the city, right should be done according to the customs of the city.

12.   Pleas on debts contracted in the city, and mortgages made there, shall be held in the city, according to the customs of the city.

13.   If anyone within John's land or dominion should exact toll from men of Dublin, and refuse to refund it on demand, the Provost of that city may distrain his chattels at Dublin and enforce repayment.

14.   No foreign merchant can buy, within the city, grain, hides, or wool, from a foreigner, but only from citizens.

15.   No foreign merchant can have a wine tavern, unless on ship-board, liberty being reserved to John that, out of every ship arriving with wines in Dublin, his bailiff in his place may select two butts of wine, one before and one behind the mast, for John's use [paying the merchant owner] 40 shillings, each being at the price of 20 shillings. Nothing more should be taken by him unless with the consent of the merchant.

16.   No foreigner can sell cloth in the city by retail.

17.   No foreign merchant can stay in the city, with his wares for sale, beyond forty days.

18. No citizen of Dublin can be distrained for debt anywhere within John's land or dominion, unless he be the debtor or surety.

19. The citizens may contract marriages for themselves, their sons, daughters, and widows, without license from their lords.

20. None of their lords should, on account of their external lands, have custody [guardianship] or donation of the sons, daughters, or widows of citizens, but only the custody of their tenements which are of the lord's fee until they come of age.

21. No [assize of] recognition shall be held in the city.

22. The citizens may have all their reasonable guilds, as the burgesses of Bristol have or had, and in the most advantageous manner.

23. No citizen may, against his will, be compelled to replevy [to pay bail for] any man, although he dwell on his land.

The following rights are also granted by John to the citizens.

24. All tenures within and without the walls, within the above-named boundaries, should be disposed of according to their pleasure by the common consent of the citizens, in messuages and in plantings, in buildings over the water, and elsewhere in the city, to be held in free burgage, namely, by service of landgable [to pay ground rent] rendered by the citizens within the walls.

25. Every citizen may, for his own advantage, build wherever he wishes on the bank [of the river], but without damage to the city or citizens.

26. The citizens may have and possess all lands and vacant places within the above-named boundaries for building upon, as they may desire.

27. Neither Templars nor Hospitallers [monastic military orders] should, within the city boundaries, have more than one man or one messuage exempt from the common customs of the city.

28. The grants here made are not to interfere with the tenures and lands of any who, by John's charters, have lands and tenures outside the walls within the aforesaid boundaries. The city of Dublin is not empowered to dispose of these

lands and tenures as of others, but the holders of them are to be liable with the citizens to all the customs of the city. This applies to those holding John's charters for lands within the boundaries outside the walls, before he granted to the city of Dublin the above-named liberties and this charter. The citizens shall have all the liberties and free customs granted to them by John in the best and most advantageous mode, without impediment or molestations.

July 3, 1215 ... King John grants in perpetuity to his citizens of Dublin his city of Dublin, with the provostship and all other appurtenances, to be held by them in fee-farm, with the citizens' part of the water of the Liffey [river], together with his part of the same water. He reserves the boat-fishings which he had previously given in free alms, and boat-fishings which others have, of ancient tenure, and retains for his own use the sites of mills on the same water. For the present grant the citizens are to pay annually to the king and his heirs, at his exchequer in Dublin, 200 marks, at two periods of the year, namely 100 marks on the feast of St. Michael [29 September], and 100 at the following Easter. John also grants to the citizens permission to make a bridge beyond the Liffey, wherever they consider may be most advantageous for them and for his city. He grants and confirms to the citizens all the liberties and free customs previously conferred upon them by his father, King Henry, and by himself, according to the tenor of their charters, reserving to the king pleas of the crown, prisage of wines, and other matters set forth in his charters. John likewise grants to the citizen all the lands which belonged to the city of Dublin within the limits specified in his charter, subject to the terms of their agreement with the monks of St. Mary's Abbey, outside Dublin. He further grants and confirms to the citizens permission to hold one fair every year at Dublin within their boundaries, commencing on the vigil of the festival of the Finding of the Holy Cross [3 May], and to continue during the fifteen following days, with all the liberties and free customs pertaining to such a fair, reserving to the archbishop of Dublin the fair during two days, namely, the vigil of the above-named festival and the day of the festival itself.

July 18, 1221 ... Henry III [grants] permission to his good men of Dublin, in aid of enclosing that city, and for the security and protection of it, as well as of the adjacent parts, to levy tolls as follow on articles brought to Dublin for sale: 3 pence on every sack of wool; 6 pence on every last of hides [a last has 200 hides]; and 2 pence on every butt of wine. This permission to continue only until the king reaches his majority, and no longer.

June 15, 1229 ... Henry III [grants] permission to the citizens of Dublin, and their heirs, to elect from among themselves annually a loyal and discreet mayor, proper for the government of that city, and who, on his election, shall swear fealty to the king, or to his justiciary in his absence. The mayor is to hold office during one year, at the expiration of which the citizens may retain him or elect another.

Questions: What types of privileges were the citizens of Dublin most interested in securing from their lord? How do their interests compare to those of the citizens of Lorris (doc. 18)? What new privileges were added as the years went by?

21. LÜBECK IS MADE AN IMPERIAL CITY, 1226

Lübeck was once a city subject to the count of Holstein (doc. 14), then the king of Denmark, and finally, in 1226, it was declared the first imperial city east of the Elbe river in recognition of its exceptional commercial growth. The designation of "imperial city" was widely coveted (some towns even rebelled against their own lords in order to secure the recognition of the emperor) because of the special protection, relative independence, and status it brought. The emperors, for their part, were happy to designate the larger towns as "imperial cities" because it ensured their loyalty (and often, their financial contributions) in the midst of the unstable territorial rivalries of the German Empire.

Source: trans. M. Kowaleski, "Lübeck, ville impériale: 1226," in *L'Europe au moyen âge: Documents expliqués. Tome III: fin IXe siècle – fin XIIIe siècle*, eds. Ch.-M. de la Roncière, P. Contamine, R. Delort, and M. Rouche (Paris: Librairie Armand Colin, 1969), p. 243.

In the name of the holy and indivisible Trinity, Frederick II, by divine favor and clemency emperor of the Romans, always august, king of Jerusalem and of Sicily.... We have conceded and firmly prescribed that the city of Lübeck should be free in perpetuity, that is, it is immediately a city and imperial place and dependent immediately on the imperial sovereignty and can never be separated from this immediate sovereignty. We have also decided that if the emperor ever decides to appoint a rector to direct the city, only someone originally from the vicinity and the area from around the town itself may be designated for this office, and also that the castle, which is called Travemunde, should be governed in the same manner by this rector.

Wishing besides that the territory of the town, in our happy epoch, should be enlarged and grown, we concede and add to this its territory; that henceforth this city should run from the Padelügge river to the Trave river and, going along the Padelügge river, the length of the territorial limits that can be distinguished, to the river of Krempelsdorf and from this river of Krempelsdorf to Sec Alleu and from there to the Trave. And we grant to these burgesses that the toll of Oldesloe [a town through which goods passed on their way to Lübeck] can not be demanded from any of them. And we grant to them besides the right of making and minting money in their town in our name, this during our life and that of Henry, king of the Romans, our illustrious and dear son, and for this act they should pay 60 marks of silver to our court each year....

Moreover, all the faithful merchants who come into this city by land or by water for their business should enjoy a perpetual security when coming as well as going, as long as they pay duty to those who are owed it. And also when the burgesses of Lübeck go to England, we release them entirely from the abuses and exactions which the people of Cologne, Tiel [two other German towns which regularly traded in London], and their members wish, it is said, to charge wrongfully. We completely annul this abuse and [order that] they should enjoy the right and conditions that the people of Cologne, Tiel, and their members enjoy. And we grant them the island, situated in front of the castle of Travemunde, that is called Priwalc. We strictly forbid an outside lawyer from practicing or rendering justice in the city's territory.... Moreover, no prince, lord, or noble of the bordering provinces should dare to prevent from arriving at the city of Lübeck anything necessary to it wherever it may come from, including Hamburg, Ratzebourg, Wittenburg, Schwerin and all the territory of Buruwin and of his son.... And we confirm for them in perpetuity all the rights, the good usages, and the good customs that they have enjoyed since the time of Emperor Frederick, our grandfather of happy memory....

Questions: What new privileges did the status of imperial city bring to Lübeck? How did these privileges differ from the usual rights granted by rulers to towns, as evident in Lorris (doc. 18) or Dublin (doc. 20)?

22. THE GERMAN EMPEROR ANNULS ALL CITY CHARTERS, 1231–32

As towns became more wealthy and powerful, the lords of towns turned to the king for help in subduing the aspirations of their citizen-subjects. Here the German emperor, Frederick II, responds to the complaints of the lords by insisting on their right to rule their cities and by revoking the rights previously given to the communes. In the long run, however, these decisions had little influence on towns, which continued to grow more independent of their lords.

Source: trans. O.J. Thatcher and E.H. McNeal, *A Source Book for Mediaeval History* (New York: Charles Scribner's Sons, 1905), pp. 590–91.

In the name of the holy and undivided Trinity. Frederick, etc.... (2) In the various parts of Germany, through the failure to enforce the law and through neglect, certain detestable customs have become established which hide their bad character under a good appearance. By them the rights and honor of the princes of the empire are diminished and the imperial authority is weakened. It is our duty to see that these bad customs, or rather these corrupt practices, shall no longer be in force. (3) Wishing, therefore, that all the grants and concessions of liberties and privileges which we have made to the princes of the empire shall have the broadest interpretation and that the said princes may have full and undisturbed possession of them, we hereby remove and depose in every town and city of Germany all the city councils, burgomasters, mayors, aldermen, and all other officials, by whatever name they may be called, who have been established by the people of the said cities without the permission of their archbishop or bishop. (4) We also dissolve all fraternities or societies, by whatever name they may be called. (5) We also decree that, in every city or town where there is a mint, no kind of money except that which is coined in that place shall be used in the sale and purchase of all kinds of goods and provisions. (6) In times past the archbishops and bishops governed the cities and all the lands which were given them by the emperor, and we wish them to continue to do so forever, either in person or through the officials whom they may appoint for this purpose, in spite of the fact that certain abuses have crept in, and in some cities there are those who resist them. But this resistance to their lord is illegal. (7) In order that these wicked abuses may be stopped and may not have even a pretence of authority, we revoke and declare invalid and worthless all the privileges, open letters, and sealed letters, which we or our predecessors or the archbishops or bishops have given to any person, either public or private, or to any city, in favor of these societies, communes, or councils, to the disadvantage of the princes and of the empire. This document has the form of a judicial decision, being published by a decree of the princes with our full knowledge....

Questions: What are the "bad customs" to which the emperor is referring? How would the decrees of the emperor here help the lords? How would the decrees affect the German communes?

23. ELECTION OF THE PODESTÀ, CONSULS, AND OFFICIALS OF VOLTERRA, 1224

This extract from the Statutes of the Tuscan commune of Volterra spells out how the podestà, consuls, and other civic officials were selected, as well as the obligations of these officials. The statutes also try to address some of the problems that Volterra's political leaders faced in governing the city.

Source: trans. P. Riesenberg, "The Statutes of Volterra, 1224," in *The Medieval Town*, ed. J.H. Mundy and P. Riesenberg (New York: Van Nostrand Co., 1958; repr. Huntington, NY: Robert E. Krieger, 1979), pp. 154–57.

A. On the Election of the Consuls and How They are to be Summoned
If the person elected consul is not in the city of Volterra, the consuls or the podestà should send for him, and they may take whatever steps are necessary to do this. This holds true for the podestà elect also. And whosoever may be named consul will be asked by the consuls or the podestà whether he will accept the office, and if he rejects it or refuses to swear to the consuls or the podestà that he will accept the consulship, the consuls or the podestà will then summon another to be consul instead. And they shall do this within three days of the refusal. But he who accepts the consulship, or promises that he will accept it, that man shall be consul. And he who serves as consul for a term will not be eligible again for the office for three years. Likewise, he who is podestà for a term shall not serve again as podestà until three years have passed.

B. On the Election of Officials for the Commune of Volterra
The new consuls or the podestà are bound to choose one good man who will choose two better and more suitable men whom he may know; and these will swear to choose for the commune, in good faith, six councilors, a treasurer, a notary, overseers, a treasurer of the customs house, and messengers, all good and true men.

C. On Not Changing the Constitution for a Year
No chapter of this constitution shall be changed for a whole year unless by certain constitutional experts who shall be chosen for this purpose, and these alone may change the constitution for the coming year. And we say that no emendation may be placed in the laws of the commune of Volterra save by these designated experts. These men shall be called before the full assembly of citizens or before the council where the advisors of the commune sit together with the consuls of the merchants and the lords of the district, or the majority of these, and where also there are 100 men of the town. And, when the experts are questioned, they should be questioned by the person who swore in good faith to choose them. And if any one of the consuls, or the podestà or any other person of this city or its territory should do other-

wise, or cause the contrary to be done, he shall be fined 100 pounds; and the person who writes any illegal constitution will be fined 25 pounds and will lose his office for ten years. Moreover, when the consuls or the podestà believe that the constitution should be emended or changed for the following year, they should summon the constitutional experts three months before the expiration of their office.

D. With Regard to Anyone Making a Conspiracy Against the Commune

Should anyone order or make any organization or conspiracy or sworn association against the well-being of the commune of Volterra, he shall pay a fine of 50 pounds; and whoever writes this agreement will pay a fine of 10 pounds; and whoever joins this conspiracy or association will pay a fine of 100 shillings unless this should be done by the word of the consuls or the podestà with the consent of all or of the majority of them and of the consuls of the merchants.

E. Oath of the Citizens of Volterra

In the name of the Lord, amen. I, N [citizen's name inserted here], swear on the holy gospels of God to observe and fulfill and never violate by fraud each and every order which the consuls or podestà of Volterra should have me obey, during the term of their office, for the honor of the commune. Likewise, the advice which the consuls or the podestà may ask of me I shall give to the best of my ability, and in all honesty. Likewise, the confidence or secrets which may be made to me by the consuls or the podestà or by some other person in the name of the commune of Volterra, these trusts I shall hold and not violate save with the consent of the consuls or the podestà, lest he who trusted me be injured. Likewise, if I should hear the great bell sound once the call to assembly I shall come to the public meeting without arms, and I shall remain in good faith until the end of the meeting, should there be one, and I shall not leave except by permission of the consuls or the podestà or their designated representative. Likewise, if I should hear the two great bells sounding the call to assembly I shall appear at the designated place armed, and shall not leave save by the express wish of the consuls or the podestà or their delegates. Likewise, if the said consuls or podestà should ask me, or if one of them should ask me for my tower or any other fortified place, I shall give it to them for their purposes, and I shall not take it back or attempt to take it back against their will. Likewise, I swear to help maintain the salt monopoly. And all this I swear to do and observe in good faith without deceit throughout the tenure of the consuls and the podestà. And let this document stand unaltered, and let nothing be added to it.

Questions: How were the chief officials of Volterra selected? What were the responsibilities of the consuls, the podestà, and the citizens themselves in the governing of Volterra? What potential abuses were the citizens of Volterra trying to prevent in these ordinances?

24. THE MAGNATES AND THE RISE OF THE *POPOLO* AND GUILDS IN FLORENCE, 1207–1328

Giovanni Villani was a loyal citizen who began in 1300 to survey the history of Florence from its early days to his own time in his New Chronicle. *In these extracts, Villani summarizes the early struggles between the aristocracy or magnates on the one hand, and the mercantile ele-ment on the other, for control of the city. The outlaw behavior of the magnates (who generally sympathized with the Ghibelline [the pro-imperial party]) led the Florentine people, called the* popolo *or* popolani *(who mostly championed the cause of the Guelf or pro-papal, anti-impe-rial party), to take extreme measures to exclude them from government and harness their ex-cesseses, a movement that culminated in 1292 with the passage of the Ordinances of Justice. The last passage makes clearer the role of the merchant guilds in the constitutional reform, as well as the steps taken to introduce a fairer electoral process. The Ancients (later called "priors") were the elected leaders of the popolo, some chosen by the guilds, others by neighborhood disticts.*

Source: trans. R.E. Selfe, *Villani's Chronicle: Being Selections from the First Nine Books of the* Croniche Fiorentine *of Giovanni Villani*, ed. P.H. Wicksteed, 2nd ed. (Westminster: Archibald Constable & Co., 1906), pp. 117–18, 149–50, 269–71, 301–03, 313–14, revised; (B) Book X, §108: trans. T. Dean, *The Towns of Italy in the Later Middle Ages* (Manchester: Manchester University Press; New York: St Martin's Press, 2000), pp. 222–24.

Book V. 32. How the Florentines elected their first podestà
In the year of Christ 1207, the Florentines chose for the first time a foreign mag-istrate, for until that time the city had been ruled by the government of citizen consuls, of the greatest and best of the city, with the council of the senate, to wit of 100 good men. And these consuls, after the manner of Rome, entirely guided and governed the city, and administered law and executed justice, and they remained in office for one year. And there were four consuls so long as the city was divided into quarters, one to each gate; and afterwards there were six, when the city was divided into *sesti*.... But afterwards when the city was increased in inhabitants and in vices, and there came to be more ill-deeds, it was agreed for the good of the common-wealth, to the end the citizens might not have so great a burden of government, and that justice might not miscarry by reason of prayers, or fear, or private malice, or any other cause, that they should invite a gentleman from some other city, who might be their podestà for a year, and administer civil justice with his assessors and judges, and carry into execution sentences and penalties on the person. And the first podestà in Florence was Gualfredotto of Milan, in this year, and he dwelt in the Bishop's Palace, forasmuch as there was as yet no palace of the commonwealth in Florence. Yet the government of the consuls did not therefore cease, but they reserved to themselves the administration of all other things in the commonwealth. And by the said government the city was ruled until the time of the *Primo Popolo* in Florence, as hereafter we shall make mention, and then was created the office of the Ancients.

Book VI. 39. How the Primo Popolo was formed in Florence

[1250] When the said host came back to Florence there was great contention amongst the citizens, inasmuch as the Ghibellines, who ruled the land, crushed the people with insupportable burdens, taxes, and imposts, and with little to show for it because the Guelfs were already established up and down in the territory of Florence, holding many fortresses and making war upon the city. And besides this, they of the house of Uberti and all the other Ghibelline nobles tyrannized over the people with ruthless extortion and violence and outrage. Wherefore the good citizens of Florence, tumultuously gathering together, assembled themselves at the church of San Firenze, but not daring to remain there because of the power of the Uberti, they went and took their stand at the church of the Minor Friars at Santa Croce, and remaining there under arms they dared not to return to their homes, lest when they laid down their arms they should be broken by the Uberti and the other nobles and condemned by the magistrates. So they went under arms to the houses of the Anchioni of San Lorenzo, which were very strong, and there, still under arms, they forcibly elected 36 corporals of the people, and took away the rule from the podestà, which was then in Florence, and removed all the officials. And this done with no further conflict they ordained and created a popular government with certain new ordinances and statutes. They elected captain of the people M. Uberto da Lucca, and he was the first captain of Florence, and they elected twelve Ancients of the people, two for each *sesto*, to guide the people and counsel the captain, and they were to meet in the homes of the Badia over the gate which goes to Santa Margherita, and to return to their own homes to eat and sleep, and this was done on 20 October, 1250. And on this day the captain distributed twenty standards amongst the people, giving them to certain corporals divided according to companies of arms and districts, including sundry parishes, in order that when need arose, every man should arm himself and draw to the standard of his company, and then with the standards draw to the said captain of the people. And they had a bell made which the captain kept in the Lion's Tower. And the chief standard of the people, which was the captain's, was dimidiated in white and red.

Book VI. 79: How the office of Priors was first created in Florence

In the year of Christ 1282 the city of Florence was governed by the regime of the Fourteen good men as Cardinal Latino had left it, to wit eight Guelfs and six Ghibellines.... It seemed to the citizens that this government of the Fourteen was too numerous and confused, and thus so many divided hearts might be at one, and, above all, because it was not pleasing to the Guelfs to have the Ghibellines as partners in government by reason of the events which were to come to pass (such as the loss which King Charles [of Anjou] had already sustained in the island of Sicily, and the arrival in Tuscany of an imperial vicar, and the wars begun in Romagna by

the ... Ghibellines). So, for the safety and welfare of the city of Florence, they annulled the office of the Fourteen and created and made a new office to govern the
city, to wit, the Priors of the Arts [guilds]. The name meant the first elected above
others, and derived from the gospels, where Christ said to his disciples *"Vos estis
prior."* The pressure for this change and innovation began with the consuls and the
council of the Calimala guild, of which the wisest and most powerful citizens were
members, with the greatest following of magnates and *popolani*. They attended especially to the pursuit of trade, and most adhered to the Guelf Party and the Holy
Church. And the first priors of the guilds were three in number, their names being
Bartolo de' Bardi, from the *sesto* of Oltrarno and for the Calimala guild, Rosso
Bacherelli, from the *sesto* of San Piero Schieraggio and the Bankers' Guild, and
Salvi Girolami for the *sesto* of San Brancazio and the Wool Guild. And their term
of office began in mid-June and lasted two months ... and so, every two months,
there were to follow three priors for the three major guilds. They ate, slept, and
gave audience in secure lodgings in the Badia, at the commune's expense, where
the *anziani* [Ancients] of the old *popolo* used to meet, and after them the Fourteen....
And these priors, with the captain of the *popolo*, had the task of governing the great
and weighty affairs of the commune, of convening councils and issuing ordinances.
During the first two months, the citizens liked this office, so for the next two
months six priors were appointed, one per *sesto*, and to the three major guilds were
added those of physicians and spicers, of Por Santa Maria, and of furriers. Then
successively other guilds were added, up to the number of the twelve major guilds,
and they included magnates as well as *popolani*, men of good reputation and deeds,
who were artisans or merchants. And so it continued, until the second government
of the *popolo* was instituted in Florence ... from which time no more magnates were
included and a Standard-bearer of Justice was added.... Election to the office of
prior was made by the outgoing priors with the leaders of the twelve major guilds
and with certain additional members elected by the priors from each *sesto*; they
elected by secret ballot, such that whoever got most votes was made prior; and this
election was held in the church of San Piero Scheraggio.

Book VIII. 1. How the Second Popolo *arose in the city of Florence*
In the year of Christ 1292, on the first day of February, the city of Florence being
in great and powerful state, and prosperous in all things, and the citizens thereof
waxing fat and rich, and by reason of excessive tranquility, which naturally en-
genders pride and novelties, being envious and arrogant among themselves, many
murders, and wounds, and outrages were done by citizens upon each other. And
above all the nobles known as magnates and potentates in the country and city
alike wrought upon the people who might not resist them, force and violence
both against person and goods, taking possession thereof. For the whole thing
certain good men, artificers and merchants of Florence, who desired a good life,

considered how to set a remedy and defence against the said plague, and one of their leaders, among others, was a man of worth, an ancient and noble citizen from among the *popolani*, rich and powerful, whose name was Giano della Bella, of the people of St. Martin, with the following and counsel of other wise and powerful *popolani*. And instituting in Florence an order of judges to correct the statutes and our laws, as by our ordinances the custom of old to do, they ordained certain laws and statutes, very strong and weighty, against such magnates and men of power as should do wrong or violence against the people. [They] increased the common penalties in diverse ways, and enacting that one member of a family of magnates should be held answerable for the others, and two bearing witness to public fame and report should be held to prove such crimes, and the public accounts should be revised. And these laws they called the Ordinances of Justice. And to the intent they might be maintained and put into execution, it was decreed that beyond the number of six priors which governed the city, there should be a gonfalonier of justice appointed by the several *sesti* in succession, changing every two months, as do the priors. And when the hammer-bells were sounded, the people were to rally to the church of San Piero Scheraggio and give out the banner of justice, which before was not the custom. And they decreed that not one of the priors should be of the noble houses called magnates, for before this good and true merchants had often been made priors, albeit they chanced to be of some great and noble house. And the ensign and standards of the said *popolo* was decreed to be a white field with a red cross, and there were chosen 1,000 citizens, divided according to the *sesti*, with certain standard-bearers for each region, with 50 footmen to each standard, who were to be armed, each one with hauberk and shield marked with the cross. And they were to assemble at every tumult or summons of the gonfalonier, at his house or at the palace of the priors, to do execution against the magnates, and afterwards the number of the chosen footmen increased to 2,000 and then to 4,000.

... And in this new thing and the beginning of the *popolo*, the *popolani* would have been hindered by the power of the magnates had it not been that in those times the said magnates of Florence were in broils and discords among themselves, since that the Guelfs were returned to Florence, and there was great war between the Adimari and the Tosinghi, and between the Rossi and the Tornaquinci, and between the Bardi and the Mozzi [eight other family disputes are then listed]....

Book VIII. 12. How the magnates of Florence raised a tumult in the city to break up the popolo
On 6 July 1295, the magnates and great men of the city of Florence seeing themselves mightily oppressed by the new Ordinances of Justice made by the people—and especially by that ordinance which declares that one kinsman is to be held responsible to account for another, and that two witnessses establish public report—having their own friends in the priorate, gave themselves to breaking down the ordinances of the people. And first they made up their great quarrels amongst themselves.... And this

done, on an appointed day, they made a great gathering of folk, and petitioned the priors to have the said articles amended. Whereupon, all the people of Florence rose in tumult and rushed to arms. The magnates [were] on armored horses themselves, and with retainers from the country and other troops on foot in great numbers, and one set of them drew up in the piazza of San Giovanni, over whom M. Forese degli Adimari held the royal ensign; another set assembled at the Piazza a Ponte ... and a third set in the Mercato Nuovo ... with intent to overrun the city. The *popolani* were all in arms, in their ranks, with ensigns and banners, in great numbers, and they barricaded the streets of the city at sundry points to hinder the horsemen from overrunning the place, and they gathered at the palace of the podestà, and at the house of the priors, who at that time dwelled at the house of the Cerchi behind San Brocolo. And the people found themselves in great power and well ordered, with force of arms and folk, and they associated with the priors, whom they did not trust, a number of the greatest and most powerful and discreet of the *popolani* of Florence, one for each *sesto*. Wherefore the magnates had no strength nor power against them, and the people might have overthrown them, but consulting for the best and to avoid civil battle, by the mediation of certain friars between the better sort of each side, each party disarmed and the city returned to peace and quiet without any change.... But for all that this disturbance was the root and beginning of the dismal and ill estate of the city of Florence which thereafter followed, for thenceforth the magnates never ceased to search for means to beat down the people, to their utmost power, and the leaders of the people sought every way of strengthening the people and abasing the magnates by reinforcing the Ordinances of Justice....

Book X. 108. Electoral reform
[1328] After Florence had heard the news of the death of the duke [of Calabria, son of the king of Naples] they held various councils and discussions on how they should reform the city's government along communal lines, so as to eliminate factions among citizens. And, as it pleased God, those who were then priors, with the advice of one good man from each *sesto*, agreed on the following method of electing the priors and standard-bearers: that the priors, with two additional *popolani* from each *sesto*, should make a choice and list of all the citizens—Guelfs, *popolani*, and men aged over thirty—who were worthy of the office of the priorate; and likewise, the gonfaloniers [standard-bearers], with two additional *popolani* from each *gonfalone* [policing precincts or neighborhoods within the city], should do the same, as should the captains of the Guelf Party and their council, the five officials of the Mercatanzia with the advice of the seven leaders of the major guilds, and two consuls per guild. Once these lists were done, the priors and standard-bearers should convene in the priors' council-chamber at the beginning of December, along with the Twelve Goodmen (the priors' advisors in serious business), the nineteen gonfaloniers, two consuls from each of the twelve major guilds,

and six additional members from each *sesto* appointed by the priors and the Twelve Goodmen: the total of all these was ninety-eight. Each man listed should be put to a secret ballot of black and white beans, gathered by wise, discreet foreign friars (two Franciscans, two Dominicans, and two hermit-friars), some of whom should be in the chamber by turns to collect the beans and count them. And whoever had sixty-eight votes [or more], that is sixty-eight black beans, was approved for the office of prior, and his name was written both into a secret register that remained with the Dominican friars, and on to a small ticket placed into a bag according to his *sesto*. These bags were then placed in a strongbox locked with three keys and kept in the Franciscans' sacristy. The *conversi* friars of Settimo kept one key ... the captain of the *popolo* another, and the minister of the friars the third. And when, every two months, the office of priors finished—or rather three days before they left office—the outgoing priors, with the captain, convened the council, had the strongbox brought in and opened, and, *sesto* by *sesto*, the bags were opened, the name-tickets mixed up, and tickets then drawn at random. Those who were drawn became priors, though observing the following prohibitions: of two years, during which the same person could not again be prior; of one year, during which his son, father, or brother could not be prior; of six months, during which anyone of his wider family could not be prior. And this arrangement was decided first by the requisite councils, then in a full public assembly on the piazza, on 11 December 1328, when many people gathered, and when many speeches were made praising and confirming it.... And [it was decided] that every two years in January the whole process should be started again, but that whoever's name was still in the register as not having been drawn [from the bags] should stay there, and those names approved in the new process should have their tickets mixed with those that had not yet been drawn.... In this way, the city's government and officials were reformed ... and from this ensued for a while a very tranquil and peaceful state ... but, as wanting to make frequent changes is a Florentine habit, these good arrangements were very soon corrupted and vitiated by the factions of wicked citizens, who wanted to rule over everyone else.

Questions: What did the popolo *see as the chief problems with magnate rule of the city? How did the people eventually oust the magnates from power? What steps did they take to dampen the power of the magnates? What role did the merchant guilds play in reforming the electoral process, and what was the balance of power like after the reforms of 1328?*

25. THE GREATER VERSUS THE LESSER
CITIZENS IN BRISTOL, 1316

The democratic trend evident in Florence and the Flemish towns also occurred elsewhere, although with less success. This extract from a chronicle of the early fourteenth century, attributed to a monk of Malmesbury, describes a riot that broke out in the Gloucestershire town of Bristol—at that time the third-largest city in Britain—over the monopolistic commercial and taxation practices of a clique of fourteen civic officials. Although the oligarchic government of the fourteen was temporarily overthrown, they were eventually reinstated. Indeed, the Bristol form of government, in which power was vested in the hands of a relatively small group of merchants who often acted out of self-interest, was typical of most late medieval English towns.

Source: trans. C.W. Colby, *Selections from the Sources of English History* (New York: Longmans, Green, and Co., 1899), pp. 94–95, revised.

Some time ago trouble arose in the town of Bristol over the customs in the seaport and market, privileges, and other things, in which fourteen of the greater persons of this town seemed to have a special right. The community resisted, stating that the burgesses were all of one condition and therefore equal as to liberties and privileges. Frequent domestic quarrels over matters of this sort arose, until in the king's court they asked for and received judges to examine the case and bring it to just conclusion. Forthwith the said fourteen procured that outsiders should be associated in the inquiry. These, moreover, were believed to have been bribed and wholly brought over to the side of the fourteen. The community alleged that it would be contrary to the liberties of the town to try a local matter by the judgment of outsiders, but the judges held that such allegations were idle; so that in this respect they [the judges] did not regard the liberties and privileges of the citizens. The leader of the community, seeing that their exceptions were not admitted and their right was being taken from them by favor rather than by reason, left the hall, where according to custom the trial was going on, in a great state of agitation, and thus spoke to the commonalty: "Judges have come who favor our adversaries and admit outsiders to our prejudice, whereby we shall forever lose our rights." On these words the foolish crowd started a riot and all the people were smitten with fear of a tumult. Forthwith returning with a large company they entered the hall where they proceeded to turn their right into outrage. With fists and sticks they began to assail the opposing party, and that day about twenty lives were suddenly and stupidly lost. Since a natural fear so attacked both gentle and simple, many jumped out of the windows from the top of the balcony, and in falling to the ground broke their legs or shins very badly. As for the judges, they feared for their lives and humbly sought leave to depart in peace. The mayor of the town, after he had with the greatest difficulty calmed the fury of the mob, sent them away unharmed.

On account of this disturbance about eighty men were indicted, and after a careful inquiry held before the royal judges at Gloucester, were condemned. They were then ordered to surrender themselves, but they did not come or obey and so were declared to be exiles. But they remained well-fortified within their town, nor would they obey the royal mandate unless it was carried out by force.

The said fourteen who were striving against the community gave up their homes and revenues and left the town because they deemed it useless to remain among their opponents at such a time. This rebellion of the community lasted two years or more, and yet for the king's part he often tried to make peace, for he preferred to qualify the sentence of the rioters if they were willing, rather than to destroy a good town by taking full vengeance. But they still persisted in the rebellion, always despising the royal order and precept. They did not come when called; they did not obey when threatened, but said that all suits against them were unjust, because wholly contrary to their privileges and liberties.

The king, therefore, unwilling any further to satisfy their malice, summoned the knights and chief persons of Gloucestershire to London, and enjoined upon them by virtue of the oath they took there to make clearly known the case of Bristol, and who was at fault. They all said that the community of Bristol had the wrong side, and that the eighty were responsible for the violence. Therefore he sent Adolmar, Earl of Pembroke, to Bristol, who having convened the chief persons of the community spoke to them thus on the king's behalf: "Our lord the king," he said, "having taken action in your case has found you guilty, and enjoins you to obey the law. Give up these murderers and culprits, and you and your town will remain in peace. I promise that if you do so you will find the king placable and merciful enough." The community replied, "We were not responsible for the outrage; we have not transgressed against our lord the king. Certain persons strove to take away our rights, and we on the other hand strove as was fit, to defend them. Therefore if the king will remit those things with which we have been burdened, if he will give us life and limb, revenues and estates, we will obey him as lord and do whatever he wishes; otherwise we will keep on as we have begun and will defend our liberties and privileges even to death."

Questions: Can we discern what were the "liberties and privileges" of the urban commonalty from this document (or from docs. 18, 20, 26, or 27)? What exactly were the "fourteen" doing to provoke the ire of the rest of the urban community? Which side did the king support and why? How did the king use his power to enforce his will?

26. "MOTHER" TOWNS: BRESLAU ADOPTS
THE CHARTER OF MAGDEBURG, 1261

As new towns were established, or smaller settlements became cities, they often looked to older cities for examples of how to rule themselves. In many cases the newer towns copied all or most of the charter of the older or "mother" city. One such "mother" city was Magdeburg, located on the frontier between the Germans and the Slavs (which included the Wends and Poles) of the interior. It was thus an important commercial center for trade between the Germans and Slavs, and it became the seat of an archbishop as well, whose work included Christianizing the Slavs. Magdeburg's importance was also evident in the organization of new Slavic cities, which were generally established by German colonists who insisted that their new towns have the charter of Magdeburg. This passage records part of the response of the schoeffen, *the civic magistrates of Magdeburg, to the request of the citizens of Breslau for a copy of its charter. The burgrave was the representative of the local lord; the schultheiss was the chief official of the citizenry, equivalent to a type of mayor. The charter is long and unorganized but covers a wide range of laws about elections, the powers of different civic officials, market jurisdiction, legal procedures, inheritance, and a host of other urban problems. The extracts printed below are those focusing on the powers of the municipal officials; for the clauses on inheritance, see doc. 78.*

Source: trans. O.J. Thatcher and E.H. McNeal, *A Source Book for Mediaeval History* (New York: Charles Scribner's Sons, 1905), pp. 592–602, selections.

1. When Magdeburg was founded the inhabitants were given a charter such as they wished. They determined that they would choose aldermen every year, who, on their election, should swear that they would guard the law, honor, and interests of the city to the best of their ability and with the advice of the wisest people of the city.

2. The aldermen have under their jurisdiction false measures, false scales, false weights, offences in the sale of all sorts of provisions, and all kinds of deception in buying and selling. If they find anyone guilty of such things, he shall pay a fine of 3 Wendish marks, that is, 36 shillings.

3. The aldermen shall take counsel with the wisest people and then appoint their courts at whatever time they wish. Their decisions rendered in court are binding and must be obeyed. If anyone resists their decisions, they shall punish him....

6. If anyone is convicted of using false weights or measures, the aldermen shall punish him according to the custom of the city, or fine him 36 shillings.

7. The burgrave is the highest judge. He must hold three courts every year: the first one at St. Agatha's day [February 5], the second one at St. John's day [June 24], and the third one a week after St. Martin's day [November 11]. If these days fall on holy days or on "bound times" [holidays when no courts could be held], the court must be put off. If plaintiffs do not appear, the case must be put off. If the *schultheiss* does not come, the case must be put off. But the *schultheiss* who fails to come must pay the burgrave 10 pounds, unless it was impossible for him to come.

8. All crimes committed fourteen days before the burgrave's court meets belong solely to the jurisdiction of the burgrave. But if the burgrave is not there, the citizens shall choose someone else to judge in his place, if anyone has been taken in the very act of committing a crime. The fee of the burgrave is 3 pounds. When the burgrave rises from the judge's chair, his court is dissolved, and he then appoints the court of the *schultheiss* to be held fourteen days from the next day.

9. The *schultheiss* holds three regular courts every year: the first one, twelve days after Christmas, the second, on the first Tuesday after Easter week, and the third, at the end of the week of Pentecost. At the close of each of these courts he shall appoint another court [if necessary], to be held fourteen days later. If these courts fall on a holy day, he may put off his court for a day or two.

10. The fee of the *schultheiss* is 8 shillings. No one shall be summoned to his court except by the *schultheiss* himself or by his beadle. His servant shall not summon anyone. If the *schultheiss* is not at home when a crime is committed, the people shall choose someone to judge in his place, in case they have taken some offender in the act. The *schultheiss* shall receive his authority as a fief from the lord of the land, and he shall have a fief [besides], and he must be of legitimate birth, and born a citizen of the town....

12. Neither the burgrave nor the *schultheiss* shall compel citizens to render decisions [that is, assist in holding court] at any other time than the regular sessions of the court, except when a criminal has been taken in the act. But the burgrave and the *schultheiss* must, every day, try the cases which are brought before them....

23. If a man transfers a piece of property to another in the presence of the judge and of the *schoeffen,* the *schoeffen* shall receive a fee of 1 shilling....

32. If anyone reviles a *schoeffen* while he is on the bench [that is, while he is performing the duties of his office], he shall pay the *schoeffen* the regular fine [for an offence against a *schoeffen*], that is, 30 shillings, and he shall also pay the judge his fee.

33. If a man reviles the *schoeffen* after they have given a decision, he shall pay each of them the regular fine, that is, 30 shillings, and also pay the judge his regular fine. He shall pay the judge's fine as many times as there are *schoeffen* whom he reviled....

40. The burgrave and not the *schultheiss* shall have jurisdiction over the three crimes of attacking from an ambush, violating women, and attacking with intent to kill. If the one attacked has wounds and shows them to the judge and has witnesses who heard him cry for help, the accused shall answer in court to the charges.

The honorable *schoeffen* and the aldermen of Magdeburg drew up this law of Magdeburg for the noble duke, Henry, and his citizens of Breslau, and, if necessary, will aid them in keeping it. They gave it at the request of Henry the duke and of his citizens of Breslau. In the year 1261....

Questions: How were aldermen selected? What were their obligations and duties? What types of power and obligations did the burgrave, the schultheiss, *and the* schoeffen *have? What are the similarities and differences between the ruling powers of the town government in Magdeburg and Breslau compared to the government of the Italian cities of Volterra (doc. 23) and Florence (doc. 24)?*

27. "DAUGHTER" TOWNS: THE CITIZENS OF CULM SEEK ADVICE FROM THE CITY RULERS OF MAGDEBURG, 1338

When a "daughter" town such as Culm (in Germany) was confronted with problems that could not be solved by recourse to its charter, it sent a deputation to the mother town—in this case, Magdeburg—to seek advice on specific points. This passage represents the questions posed by the citizens of Culm, along with the answers of the schoeffen *of Magdeburg (doc. 26).*

Source: trans. O.J. Thatcher and E.H. McNeal, *A Source Book for Mediaeval History* (New York: Charles Scribner's Sons, 1905), pp. 602–04.

1. May aldermen be deposed?

To the honorable aldermen of Culm, we the *schoeffen* of Magdeburg, your obedient servants [send greeting]. You have asked us in your letter whether aldermen may choose other aldermen, and whether they may choose from among themselves burgomasters and *schoeffen* without the consent of the burgrave. And also whether the burgrave may depose some of the aldermen and appoint others in their place. We answer, that the aldermen may choose other aldermen for a year, and one or two burgomasters from their own number also for a year. But the burgrave has no right to depose aldermen and put others in their place.

2. Who shall choose other *schoeffen*?

The *schoeffen* shall elect other *schoeffen,* and those elected shall remain *schoeffen* as long as they live. The aldermen have no right to elect *schoeffen*. The burgrave shall confirm the *schoeffen* who are elected.

3. May the aldermen make laws?

You have also asked us whether the aldermen with the consent of their citizens may make laws among themselves and fix the penalties for offences against them, without the consent of the burgrave, and whether the aldermen have the right to collect such penal ties and retain them, or shall the burgrave and the *schultheiss* have a share in them. And you have also asked if a man breaks the laws and refuses to pay the fine, how it is to be collected from him. We answer, that the aldermen may make laws and fix their penalties provided these laws do not conflict with the laws of the city. And they may do this without the consent of the burgrave. And they have the right to demand the payment of fines, and they may keep them for the benefit of the city; the burgrave and the *schultheiss* shall have no part in them.

4. What if a man refuses to pay a fine?

If a man refuses to pay a fine but admits that he owes it, the aldermen may seize and imprison him until he pays it. If he says he does not owe the fine, he shall prove it by taking an oath by the saints.

5. About false measures.
You have further asked whether the aldermen have jurisdiction over weights and measures, false measures, and the sale of provisions, and if a man refuses to pay a fine how it shall be collected. We answer, that aldermen have jurisdiction over the said things, and that if a man refuses to pay his fine, they may seize and imprison him until he pays it, as is written above.

6. About damage done to a forest.
You asked us if a man cuts wood in a forest, how he shall pay the damage. We answer, if a man cuts down trees in another's forest, or cuts his grass, or fishes in his streams, he shall pay for the damage and a fine besides.

7. How far shall a guest live from the city?
You also asked us how far a man must live from the court if he wishes to have the right of a guest. We answer, if a guest is accused before the court, if he swears by the saints that he lives more than twelve miles from the court, he shall have his trial at once. If a guest enters suit against a citizen in the same court, the citizen shall answer in court that same day if the guest demands it.

8. About attaching the property of a guest.
You further asked us how you should proceed, if a man attaches the property of a guest from a far country, so that justice may be done to both. We answer, if a man attaches the property of a guest who lives so far away that you cannot get hold of him, the attachment is not to be put into execution until the guest is informed of it. If the guest does not then appear to defend his property, the attached property may be taken.

9. About taxes.
You further asked us, if the citizens have property outside of the territory of the city which they hold from some lord and from which they receive an income, are they bound to pay the tax which may be assessed on property outside the city, just the same as they do on their ordinary property? We answer that, according to the law and practice of our city, every man must pay taxes on his property outside as well as inside the city, no matter where it is, and he must take an oath to its value and pay a tax accordingly.

Questions: What further details do these answers give us about the responsibilities and limits on the power of aldermen, the burgrave, shultheiss, and schoeffen? What were the other concerns of the citizens of Culm that they needed the "mother" town to address for them?

28. BRUNSWICK EXTENDS CIVIC RULE TO
ITS SUBURBS, 1269

After a town achieved a measure of freedom, new settlements—often in the suburbs of the old town—frequently sprang up as the city grew and prospered. These new settlements at first usually had no share in the government of the town, but over time they were normally incorporated into the older town. In this passage, the aldermen from the old town and two previously unincorporated quarters of the town get together to establish common civic rule, which entails some financial arrangements, as well as agreements about electing the town leaders.

Source: trans. O.J. Thatcher and E.H. McNeal, *A Source Book for Mediaeval History* (New York: Charles Scribner's Sons, 1905), pp. 588–89.

[From] all the aldermen of the city of Brunswick, etc.... We wish it to be made known that after having taken counsel with the older and wiser men for the best interests of the city, we have, under oath, issued the following decree which shall be observed forever, to the effect that hereafter we [the aldermen from the three different parts of the city which up to this time have had a separate organization] shall meet in one house to take counsel together about the affairs of the whole city. All the income of the city, from whatever source, shall be kept in a common fund and spent for the common good of the whole city. In the old town wine may be sold all the time. In that quarter of the city called Indago [that is, the Park], however, when one vat of wine has been sold no more shall be sold there until a vat has been sold in the new town, and vice versa. New aldermen shall be elected every year as follows. Seven new aldermen shall be elected in the old town, and three of the former aldermen from the same quarter shall be chosen to remain in office another year. In Indago [the quarter called the Park] four new aldermen shall be elected and two of the former aldermen shall remain in office. In the new town three shall be elected and one of the former shall remain in office. Thus there shall always be twenty aldermen. They shall take a special oath, among other things, to preserve this union [of the three towns in one]. And that no doubt may arise about this, we have caused this document to be written and the seal of the city to be attached to it. Witnesses ...

Questions: How were the new quarters integrated into the "old town" in terms of officials, elections, and other rules? Did any distinctions remain between the "old" and "new" sections of the town after consolidation?

29. FLORENCE EXPANDS ITS *CONTADO*, 1202–89

These extracts from the chronicle of Giovanni Villani (doc. 24) show the expansion of the city of Florence's control into its surrounding countryside, called the "contado." Such territorial expansion was typical of the larger northern Italian communes, which by the thirteenth century were in the process of becoming true "city-states." As such, they had their own armies, foreign policy, tax system, and coinage, while also imposing their rule (and taxes) on the towns and villages they conquered in their contado. *In this passage, the "commonwealth" refers to Florence.*

Source: trans. R.E. Selfe, *Villani's Chronicle: Being Selections from the First Nine Books of the* Croniche Fiorentine *of Giovanni Villani*, ed. P.H. Wicksteed, 2nd ed. (Westminster: Archibald Constable & Co., 1906), pp. 116–17, 125–26, 291–92, revised.

Book V. 30 . How the Florentines destroyed the strongholds of Simifonti and of Combiata
In the year of Christ 1202, when Aldobrandino, of the Barucci of Santa Maria Maggiore (a very ancient family), and his colleagues were consuls in Florence, the Florentines took the stronghold of Simifonti, and destroyed it, and took the hill into possession of the commonwealth, since it had been at war with the Florentines for a long time. And the Florentines gained it by the treachery of a certain man of Sandonato in Poci, which surrendered a tower, and claimed for this cause that he and his descendants should be free in Florence from all taxes; and this was granted, although this traitor was first slain in this tower by the inhabitants as it was being attacked. And in that year the Florentines went with their army against the fortress of Combiata, which was very strong, at the head of the river Marina, towards Mugello, which pertained to Cattani of the country which would not obey the commonwealth and made war against it. And when these strongholds were destroyed, they made a decree that they should never be rebuilt.

Book V. 31. Destruction of Montelupo, and how the Florentines gained Montemurlo
In the year of Christ 1203, when Brunellino Brunelli de' Razzanti was consul in Florence with his colleagues, the Florentines destroyed the fortress of Montelupo because it would not obey the commonwealth. And in this same year the Pistoians took the castle of Montenurlo from the Counts Guidi; but a little while after, in September, the Florentines went there with an army to help the Counts Guidi, and re-took it, and gave it back to the Counts Guidi. And afterwards, in 1207, the Florentines made peace between the Pistoians and the Counts Guidi, but afterwards the counts not being well able to defend Montemurlo from the Pistoians, because it was too near to them, and they had built over against it the fortress of Montale, the Counts Guidi sold it to the commonwealth of Florence for 5,000 lbs. of small florins, which would now be worth 5,000 golden florins; and this was in

the year of Christ 1209, but the Counts of Porciano never would give their word for their share in the sale....

Book V. 41. How the Florentines caused the dwellers in the country around to swear fealty to the city, and how the new Carraia Bridge was begun
In the year of Christ 1218, when Otto da Mandella of Milan was podestà of Florence, the Florentines caused all the dwellers in the country around to swear fealty to the commonwealth, seeing that before that time the greater part had obeyed the rule of the Counts Guidi, and of them of Mangone, and of them of Capraia, and of Certaldo, and of many Cattani which had taken possession of the lands by privileges and some by force of the emperors....

Book VII. 132. How the Florentines besieged the city of Arezzo, and laid waste the region round about
[1289] After the victory of the commonwealth over the Aretines, the trumpet was sounded for the return from pursuing the fugitives, and the Florentine host was marshaled upon the field; and this done, they departed to Bibbiena, and took it without any resistance; and having plundered and despoiled it of all its wealth and much booty, they caused the walls and the fortified houses to be destroyed to the foundations, and many other villages round about and they stayed there eight days. Whereas, if on the day following, the Florentine host had ridden upon Arezzo, without doubt they would have taken the city; but during that sojourn they that had escaped from the battle returned there, and the peasants round about took refuge there, and order was taken for the defense and guard of the city. The host of the Florentines came there after some days, and laid siege to the city, continually laying waste the region round about, and taking their fortresses, so that they gained them nearly all, some by force, and some on conditions; and the Florentines caused many of them to be destroyed, but they kept possession of Castiglione of Arezzo, and Montecchio, and Rondine, and Civitella, and Laterina, and Montesansavino....

Questions: Whom did Florence fight against to gain more control over its "contado" or surrounding countryside, and why were large Italian cities such as Florence so anxious to do this? What methods or tactics did they use to consolidate their territorial control? What is Villani's attitude toward this consolidation and extension of Florentine influence?

30. THE STRUGGLE BETWEEN THE GUELFS
AND GHIBELLINES

One remnant of factional strife in the Tuscan cities (doc. 38) was the Parte Guelfa or "Guelf party," which sought to combat the Ghibellines, a political party that retained more loyalty to imperial policies. The Parte Guelfa was by far the stronger faction in Florence, where civic policies regularly privileged Guelf affiliation and penalized those with Ghibelline sympathies. The Guelfs tended to align with the pope against the German emperor, and also allied with the French Angevins, who under Count Charles of Anjou (later King Charles) conquered Sicily and much of southern and central Italy. The popolo *or* popolani *were both wealthy merchants and artisans as well as middling citizens who together opposed the power of the rich magnates, from whom they had wrested control of Florence in 1250 (doc. 24).*

Source: trans. R.E. Selfe, *Villani's Chronicle: Being Selections from the First Nine Books of the* Croniche Fiorentine *of Giovanni Villani*, ed. P.H. Wicksteed, 2nd ed. (Westminster: Archibald Constable & Co., 1906), pp. 224–28, revised.

Book VII. 15. How the popolo *restored the Guelfs to Florence, and how they afterwards threw out the Ghibellines*

… And by a treaty of peace, the following January [1267] the *popolo* restored to Florence both Guelfs and Ghibellines, and caused many marriages and alliances to be made between them, among which these were the chief: that M. Bonaccorso Bellincioni degli Adimari gave for wife to M. Forese, his son, the daughter of Count Guido Novello, and M. Bindo, his brother, took one of the Ubaldini; and M. Cavalcante, of the Cavalcanti, gave for wife to his son Guido the daughter of M. Farinata degli Uberti; and M. Simone Donati gave his daughter to M. Azzolino, son of M. Farinata degli Uberti. Because of these alliances, the other Guelfs of Florence distrusted their loyalty to the party, so the peace endured but for a little while. For, when these Guelfs had returned to Florence, feeling themselves stronger and emboldened by the victory which they had gained over Manfred [the son of Emperor Frederick II], with King Charles, they sent secretly into Apulia to King Charles for soldiers, and for a captain, and he sent Count Guy de Montfort, with 800 French horsemen, and he came to Florence on Easter Day of the Resurrection in the year of Christ 1267. And when the Ghibellines heard of his coming, the night before they departed from Florence without stroke of sword, and some went to Siena, and some to Pisa, and to other places. The Florentine Guelfs gave the lordship over the city to King Charles for ten years, and when they sent him their free and full election by solemn embassy, with authority over life and death and in lesser judgments, the king answered that he desired from the Florentines their love and good will and no other jurisdiction. Nevertheless, at the prayer of the commonwealth he accepted it simply, and every year sent there his vicars [his own official]; and he appointed twelve good citizens to rule the city with the vicar. And it may be noted concerning this banishment of the Ghibellines, that it was on the same day, Easter Day of the Resurrection, whereon they had committed the murder of M. Bondelmonte de' Bondelmonti, whence the factions in Florence broke out, and the city was laid waste; and it seemed like a judgment from God, for never afterwards did they return to their estate.

Book VII. 16. How, after the Ghibellines had been driven from Florence, the ordinances and councils of the city were reorganized
When the Guelf party had returned to Florence, and the vicar or podestà was come from King Charles (the first of them being M....), and after twelve good men had been appointed, as of old the Ancients, to rule the republic, the council of 100 good men of the people was restored, without whose deliberation no great thing or cost could be carried out; and after any measure had been passed in this council, it was put to the vote in the council of the colleges of consuls of the greater Arts [guilds], and the council of the *credenza* [privy council of the captain of the people] of eighty. These councillors, which, when united with the general council, numbered 300, were all *popolani* and Guelfs. After measures had been passed in the said councils, the following day the same proposals were brought before the councils of the podestà, first before the council of ninety, including both magnates and *popolani* (and with them associated yet again the colleges of consuls of the Arts), and then before the general council, which was of 300 men of every condition; and these were called the occasional councils; and they had in their gift governorships of fortresses, and dignities, and small and great offices. And this ordered, they appointed revisors, and corrected all statutes and ordinances, and ordered that they should be issued next year. In this manner was ordered the state and course of the commonwealth and of the people of Florence at the return of the Guelfs; and the chancellors of finance were the monks of Settimo and of Ognissanti on alternate half-years.

Book VII. 17. How the Guelfs of Florence instituted the Ordinances of the Party
In these times, when the Ghibellines had been driven out from Florence, the Guelfs who had returned there were fighting over the goods of the Ghibelline rebels, so they sent ambassadors to the court, to Pope Urban and to King Charles, to order their affairs, which Pope Urban and King Charles for their estate and peace ordered them in this manner, that the goods should be divided into three parts—one part to be given to the commonwealth, the second to be awarded in compensation to the Guelfs who had been ruined and exiled, the third to be awarded for a certain time to the "Guelf Party." But afterwards all these goods fell to the Party, whence they formed a fund, and increased it every day, as a re-

serve against the day of need of the Party. When the Cardinal Ottaviano degli Ubaldini heard of this fund, he said, "Since the Guelfs of Florence have funded a reserve, the Ghibellines will never return there." And by the command of the pope and the king, the Guelfs made three knights heads of the Party, and called them at first consuls of the knights, and afterwards they called them Captains of the Party, and they held office for two months, the *sesti* electing them alternately, three and three; and they gathered to their councils in the new church of Santa Maria Sopra Porta, being the most central place in the city, and where there are many Guelf houses around. Their privy council consisted of fourteen, and their larger council of seventy magnates and *popolani*, by whose vote were elected the Captains of the Party and other officers. And they called three magnates and three *popolani* Priors of the Party, to whom were committed the order and care of the money of the Party; and also one to hold the seal, and a syndic to prosecute the Ghibellines. And all their secret documents they deposited in the church of the Servi Sancte Marie. After like manner the Ghibelline refugees made ordinances and captains....

Questions: What methods did the popolo government of Florence first employ to reconcile the Guelf and Ghibelline factions? Why did these efforts fail? What actions did the Guelfs take once they consolidated power in Florence?

31. THE ESTABLISHMENT OF THE RHINE LEAGUE AND OF ITS PEACE, 1254

The political situation in thirteenth-century Germany was chaotic as the emperors were either diverted to problems in other parts of the empire, or were simply too weak to impose peace. Left to their own devices to combat the private warfare that raged in many areas of Germany, the cities of the Rhine valley joined together to combat the problems. This extract recites the first legislation of the League, which formed in the same year.

Source: trans. O.J. Thatcher and E.H. McNeal, *A Source Book for Mediaeval History* (New York: Charles Scribner's Sons, 1905), pp. 606–07.

In the name of the holy and undivided Trinity. The judges, consuls [aldermen], and all the citizens of Mainz, Cologne, Worms, Speyer, Strassburg, Basel, and other cities which are bound together in the league of holy peace, to all the faithful of Christ, greeting in him who is the author of peace and the ground of salvation.

1. Since now for a long time many of our citizens have been completely ruined by the violence and wrongs which have been inflicted on them in the country

and along the roads, and through their ruin others have also been ruined, so that innocent people, through no fault of their own, have suffered great loss, it is high time that some way be found for preventing such violence, and for restoring peace in all our lands in an equitable manner.

2. Therefore we wish to inform all that, with the aid of our Lord Jesus Christ, the author and lover of peace, and for the purpose of fostering peace and rendering justice, we have all unanimously agreed on the following terms of peace: We have mutually bound ourselves by oath to observe a general peace for ten years from St. Margaret's day [July 13, 1254]. The venerable archbishops, Gerhard of Mainz, Conrad of Cologne, Arnold of Trier, and the bishops, Richard of Worms, Henry of Strassburg, Jacob of Metz, Bertold of Basel, and many counts and nobles of the land have joined us in this oath, and they as well as we have all surrendered the unjust tolls which we have been collecting both by land and water, and we will collect them no longer.

3. This promise shall be kept in such a way that not only the greater ones among us shall have the advantage of this common protection, but all, the small with the great, the secular clergy, monks of every order, laymen, and Jews, shall enjoy this protection and live in the tranquility of holy peace. If anyone breaks this peace, we will all go against him with all our forces, and compel him to make proper satisfaction.

4. In regard to the quarrels or differences which now exist between members of this peace, or which may hereafter arise, they shall be settled in the following way: Each city and each lord, who are members of this league, shall choose four reliable men and give them full authority to settle all quarrels in an amicable way, or in some legal manner....

Questions: What do the clauses in this agreement tell us about the common interests of the Rhineland cities? What steps did the League take to ensure that the agreement would be kept? What does the establishment of this League suggest about the expanding influence of cities in the larger political sphere?

32. DECREES OF THE HANSEATIC LEAGUE, 1260–64

The Hanseatic League (from Old German hansa, *a confederacy) seems to have begun in the eleventh century with an alliance of Lübeck and Hamburg to safeguard traffic on the Elbe River against robbers and feudal lords. It grew rapidly, and at the period of its greatest power there were some eighty Hanseatic cities along the Baltic Sea and in the inland districts of northern Germany. These decrees shed light on the early development of the League.*

Source: trans. O.J. Thatcher and E.H. McNeal, *A Source Book for Mediaeval History* (New York: Charles Scribner's Sons, 1905), pp. 611–12.

We wish to inform you of the action taken in support of all merchants who are governed by the law of Lübeck.

1. Each city shall, to the best of its ability, keep the sea clear of pirates, so that merchants may freely carry on their business by sea.

2. Whoever is expelled from one city because of a crime shall not be received in another.

3. If a citizen is seized [by pirates or bandits] he shall not be ransomed, but his sword-belt and knife shall be sent to him [as a threat to his captors].

4. Any merchant ransoming him shall lose all his possessions in all the cities which have the law of Lübeck.

5. Whoever is proscribed in one city for robbery or theft shall be proscribed in all.

6. If a lord besieges a city, no one shall aid him in any way to the detriment of the besieged city, unless the besieger is his lord.

7. If there is a war in the country, no city shall on that account injure a citizen from the other cities, either in his person or goods, but shall give him protection.

8. If any man marries a woman in one city, and another woman from some other city comes and proves that he is her lawful husband, he shall be beheaded.

9. If a citizen gives his daughter or niece in marriage to a man [from another city] and another man comes and says that she is his lawful wife, but cannot prove it, he shall be beheaded.

This law shall be binding for a year, and after that the cities shall inform each other by letter of what decisions they make.

Questions: What were the chief concerns of the early Hanseatic League? What are we to make of the concerns expressed over bigamy in nos. 8 and 9? Whose interests were most served by the League's laws?

33. THE CINQUE PORTS CONFEDERATION

The Cinque Ports (supposedly named for the original five members) were a group of over thirty ports on the English Channel that received considerable tax exemptions and legal privileges in exchange for supplying to the king of England 57 fully manned ships for a two-week period every year. The Ports' common economic interests, however, were probably responsible for bringing them together in the first place, particularly to defend their interests at the large port of Yarmouth during the autumn herring season, when thousands of traders and fishers flocked to its six-week herring fair to ply their trade. The "barons" of the Cinque Ports were the towns' ruling elites, most of whom were merchants and shipowners. Yarmouth was not a member of the Cinque Ports.

Source: *Calendar of Patent Rolls, 1272–1281* (London: H.M.S.O., 1901), pp. 203–04, revised.

Award between the barons of the ports and the men of Great Yarmouth [in 1277]. The barons are to have their easement in strand and den [access to the beach and dunes] which they claim at Yarmouth, without any appropriation of the soil and in the time of the fair without giving any manner of custom [toll]. The men of the town of Yarmouth are to clear the strand and den of old ships and timber where people are to put in and dry their nets, except of such ships as are being made, and of the masts upon which the said drying is carried on. And they are not to raise more than five windmills upon the den more than they have formerly raised, and those mills to be raised to the least damage and nuisance of the den and of those who are to dry their nets there. The barons are to have and enjoy peaceably their rents [on properties] which they hold in the town of Yarmouth, and if anyone denies them [rent], the provost and bailiffs of Yarmouth are to help them levy this rent according to law and right. And if the barons believe themselves to have rights to other rents, which they are denied by the people of Yarmouth, they are to recover [the rents] by writ or by the law and by custom used in the said town. With regard to the claim of the barons to have at Yarmouth royal justice and the keeping of the king's peace in time of the fair lasting for 40 days, they are to have the keeping of the king's peace and to do royal justice together with the provost of Yarmouth, as follows; that is, during the fair they are to have four sergeants, of whom one shall carry the king's banner, and another sound a horn to assemble the people and to be better heard, and two shall carry wands for keeping the king's peace, and this office they shall do on horseback if they wish it. The bailiffs of the Ports, together with the provost of Yarmouth, are to make attachments [arrests] and plead pleas and determine complaints during the fair, according to law-merchant, and the amercements and profits of the people of the Ports are to remain to the barons of the Ports at the time of the fair, and the profits and amercements of all others who are not of the Ports are to remain to the king by the bailiffs of Yarmouth. The bailiffs of the barons of the Ports, together with the provost of Yarmouth, is to have the keeping of the prison of Yarmouth during the fair, and if any prisoner be taken for so grave a trespass that it cannot be determined by them during the time of the fair by merchant law, nor the prisons delivered, such person is to remain in the prison of Yarmouth until the coming of the justices. The bailiffs of the barons of the Ports are to receive the customary 2 pence from each ship [docking], called "fire pence," to keep up fires [as beacons] in the usual places for the safety of the shore by night as long as they are willing to keep up the fires, and if they fail to keep up these fires the provost of Yarmouth may receive the said pence and keep up the fires. In discharge of the custom of 4 pence from each ship claimed by the barons, they shall receive £6 sterling from year to year from the provost of Yarmouth at their departure from the fair. With regard to the claim of the barons to distrain [take sureties] for their debts by land and sea, their bailiffs are not to make any distraint without the provost of Yarmouth, except upon the people of the Ports, and it is to be reasonable according to the law-merchant so that the fair does not suffer thereby. No guard is to be put henceforth on ships, merchants, and merchandise by the men of Yarmouth, whereby merchants are prevented from selling their goods freely. Neither the barons or the men of Yarmouth are to take anything from minstrels and wayward women (*femmes de vie*). The barons are not to take anything for window tax or stallage [the toll for setting up a sale stall].

Questions: What economic rights did the men of the Cinque Ports enjoy in the town of Yarmouth during the autumn herring fair? Why would the towns of the Cinque Ports confederation seek these specific rights? What did these rights mean to them? What effect could the upholding of Cinque Ports' rights have on the finances and autonomy of the port of Yarmouth?

Figure 2.2

The Seal of Dover

Figure 2.3

The Seal of Yarmouth

Communes proudly announced their independence by making their own seals, which they used to seal all official town documents. Since the choice of what to put on the seal lay with the civic authorities, seals can tell us much about civic identity. These two seals come from Dover and Yarmouth, important port towns in England. Both proclaim their maritime commercial focus by depicting ships on their seals, but note too the herring at the bottom of the Yarmouth seal, an indication of Yarmouth's economic reliance on the autumn herring fishery. Reproduced from Paul LaCroix, *Military and Religious Life in the Middle Ages and the Renaissance* (New York: Frederick Ungar Publishing, 1964), figs. 79, 80.

34. PARLIAMENTARY SUMMONS TO ENGLISH BOROUGHS, 1295

English kings generally convened a Parliament when they needed to raise funds for special efforts, such as fighting wars. Towns were first called to send representatives to Parliament in 1265, during a power struggle between the king and a group of powerful nobles. It was only in 1295, however, that the principle of calling urban representatives was embraced by the reigning king, Edward I. In England, about 166 towns were of sufficient stature to warrant a summons to send two representatives to Parliament. Not all towns had the means to finance the expense of sending representatives, however, so the number of towns responding to these summons averaged about 86 in the 1290s and dropped further in the fourteenth century before rising once again in the late fifteenth century.

Source: trans. C.W. Colby, *Selections from the Sources of English History* (London: Longmans, Green and Co., 1899), pp. 88–90, revised.

The king to the sheriff of Northamptonshire. Desiring to hold counsel and treat with the earls, barons, and other nobles of our realm, as to provision against the perils which now threaten it, we have ordered them to meet us at Westminster, on the Sunday next following the feast of St. Martin's in the coming winter [13 November], to discuss, ordain, and do whatever may be necessary to guard against this danger. We therefore firmly enjoin you to have chosen without delay and sent to us at the said day and place two knights from the said county and two citizens from each city of the said county, and two burgesses from each borough, of those more discreet and powerful to achieve in such a way that the said knights, citizens, and burgesses may each have full and sufficient power, on behalf of themselves and the community of the county, cities, and boroughs to do what may then be ordained by the common counsel in the premises; so that the present business may not in any way rest undone through lack of this power. And bring with you the names of the knights, citizens, and burgesses, and this writ. Witnessed by the king at Canterbury, 3 October.

Questions: What does this summons tell us about the political power achieved by English towns in the governance of the country? Why would the king want to have urban representatives at Parliament?

35. THE POPE AND CITY POLITICS IN SIENA, FIFTEENTH CENTURY

The balance of power between the magnates and nobles on one hand, and the popolo *of wealthy merchants and artisans in Tuscan towns on the other, was always changing (docs. 24 and 30). This extract focuses in particular on how this balance of power could be shifted when an outside power—in this case, the pope himself—interfered with local civic relations.*

Source: trans. F.A. Gragg, *The Commentaries of Pius II, Books II and III* (Northampton, MA: Smith College Studies in History, vol. 25, nos. 1–4, Oct. 1939–July 1940), pp. 135–37, 153.

... We can assert that in this city there were many nobles and very powerful men who erected lofty palaces, high towers, and very splendid churches while they administered the state. When, however, the nobler families began to quarrel about the government and sometimes appealed even to armed force, the nobility decided to resign the management of affairs to the people, reserving for themselves only a few offices; for they thought that the popular party, though they might be administering the government, would do nothing without the permission of the nobles, of whose power they would continue to stand in awe. This turned out to be the case for a time, but when the people became accustomed to rule and had once tasted the sweets of office and the fruits of power, in their increased wealth and splendor they disdained the nobility, banished certain noble families, and sent the rest under the yoke like slaves, although they shared with them a few minor offices.

There were five parties in the city (not counting the populace) as follows: the Nine, so named because when they alone were in power, they appointed nine chief magistrates; the Twelve, named on the same principle; the Reformers, so called because it was thought they had made certain reforms in the state; the Nobles who retained the title originally conferred because of their antiquity and influence; the rest were called the Populari [the *popolo*]. The Twelve had long since been deposed and no longer had any part in the government; the Nobles were entrusted with a fourth part of certain offices, but they were not permitted to command citadels or to live as priors in the palace or to keep the keys of the gates. The entire strength of the government remained in the hands of the Nine, the Reformers, and the Populari. In the course of time during the pontificate of Calixtus III bitter feuds grew up among these three parties and a considerable number of those in power were accused of having conspired to betray the city to Piccinino. On this charge some were beheaded, some driven into exile, some banished and fined; and the whole city was so torn with civil discord that it was the universal opinion that it would soon lose its liberty.

But the great God looked with loving eyes on a state dedicated to his Mother, the Virgin Mary; for when Pope Pius succeeded to the papacy on the death of

Calixtus, he at once took thought for his dearly loved country. He disrupted the schemes set on foot against it and frightened off its enemies by his authority. Moreover he thought it greatly concerned the city's welfare that the places of citizens who had been removed from the government should be filled from the Nobles and that it did not befit its dignity that the Nobles, to whom he himself belonged by birth, should be regarded as slaves in his native city. The Sienese, suspecting this would happen, in order to forestall any complaint, elected to office Pius's own family, the Piccolomini, thinking that he would demand nothing further. But Pius, who was concerned not for his own house but for the whole state, thought that nothing had been accomplished unless all the nobles were returned to power, and he sent ambassadors to demand that all the rest of that order should be made equal to the Piccolomini. The people were violently excited by this demand; they declared that the pope's request was outrageous and that the state would never consent, even if they were compelled to stand a siege and starved into eating their own children. Pius on the other hand insisted and swore that, if they did not obey, he would withdraw his favor from a city which refused to comply with just demands....

The council was recalled repeatedly; a vote was taken again and again, but still it was impossible to get two-thirds of the senators to accept the pope's terms. When, however, he grew more insistent and demanded a reply before he left, and it appeared that he would be furious if he did not prevail, the senate finally voted to admit the Nobles to all offices and to grant them a fourth of some privileges and an eighth of the others. The announcement of this vote soon filled the whole city with rejoicing. The entire senate and all the magistrates went to acquaint the pope with what had been done. Pius, though he realized that his wishes had not been fully met, still, in order not to cast gloom on the city, appeared pleased and thanked the senate, praising what they had done and saying that he hoped for something more when he returned from Mantua.

Questions: How does the factionalism in Siena compare to that in Florence (docs. 37 and 38)? Why did Pope Pius interfere in Sienese politics? Whose side was he on and why? In the end, what impact did his interference have on the way Siena was ruled?

CHAPTER THREE

URBAN SOCIETY AND SOCIAL CONFLICT

Figure 3.1

Thirteenth-Century Burgesses

The rise of towns made possible the development of a "middle class," to which these burgesses would have belonged. These men were perhaps merchants or high-ranking members of craft guilds. Reproduced from Paul LaCroix, *Manners, Customs, and Dress During the Middle Ages and During the Renaissance Period* (London: Bickers and Son, 1870), fig. 20.

Figure 3.2

A Rich Citizen

This is from a brass engraving made on the top of the tomb slab of Robert Atte Lache, a rich merchant of the town of King's Lynn in England, who died c. 1376. Only the very wealthy could afford this type of sepulchral monument. Given the detailed carving of his hair, beard, and clothing, this depiction is probably close to what Atte Lache really looked like. Reproduced from G.G. Coulton, *Social Life in Britain From the Conquest to the Reformation* (Cambridge: Cambridge University Press, 1919), fig. 21, facing p. 322.

Figure 3.3

Craftsmen

The title, "*Gens de mestier*" means "craftspeople." Each of these fourteenth-century craftsmen carries the tools of his trade. The man in the center wears a heavy leather apron to protect his clothing. Facsimile of a miniature from a Belgian manuscript. Reproduced from Paul LaCroix, *Manners, Customs, and Dress During the Middle Ages and During the Renaissance Period* (London: Bickers and Son, 1870), fig. 202.

36. CHARTER TO THE NON-NOBLE
KNIGHTS OF BURGOS, 1256

The charters of privileges granted by the Castilian kings to the towns within their territories often singled out a class of non-noble knights to receive special financial and legal rights so that the kings could win the support of this group in their struggles against the troublesome and powerful nobility. In Burgos, as in most other Castilian cities, these "knights" were landowners, merchants, and even wealthy artisans, but they were distinguished from other town residents by their wealth. These royal charters bolstered the privileges accorded to the non-noble knights and helped them become the most powerful political and social group in Castilian towns. The laws or statutes that were promulgated by the kings were called fueros. *This extract is from the Fuero Royal, a Roman-based code of law that the Castilian kings granted to most of the Spanish towns in order to create a standardized legal system.*

Source: trans. T. Ruiz, "Charter to the Non-Noble Knights of Burgos (1256)," *Medieval Iberia: Readings*, ed. O.R. Constable (Philadelphia: University of Pennsylvania Press, 1997), pp. 225–27.

Christus, Alpha and Omega. Let it be known to all the men who would read this letter, how I, Don Alfonso, by the grace of God, king of Castile, of Toledo, of León, of Galicia, of Seville, of Córdoba, of Murcia, and of Jaen, found that the noble city of Burgos, which is the head of Castile, did not have a complete statute [*fuero*], so that they [the citizens of Burgos] would have judgments as they should, and for this reason [that Burgos did not have a *fuero*] there were many doubts, many disputes, and many enmities, and justice was not exercised as it should have been. I, the aforementioned king Don Alfonso, wishing to put an end to these problems, together with the queen Doña Yolant[e], my wife, and with my son, the infante Don Fernando, give and grant to the city council of Burgos, to those of the town as well as of the hamlets, the *fuero* [*Fuero real*] that I drew with the counsel of my court, written into a book and sealed with my lead seal, so that they [the citizens of Burgos] be judged by it [the *Fuero real*] in all things for ever more, they and those who come from them. And [I] also [grant this law] to do them good and mercy, and to reward them for the many services that they did to the most noble, and most high, and most honored king Don Alfonso [VIII], my great-grandfather, and to the most noble, and most high, and most honored king Don Fernando [III], my father and to me before and after the beginning of my rule. I give and grant these privileges that are written in the charter.

And I order that the knights who have the great houses in the town with their wives and children, and those [knights] who do not have wives with the company they have, and who inhabit [these houses] from eight days before Christmas until eight days after Quinquagesima Sunday [the Sunday before Ash Wednesday], and who have horses and weapons: the horse of a value of over thirty *maravedíes* (*mrs.*), shield, lance, an iron helmet, sword, coat of mail, armor, and quilted under waist-coat, that they be excused from taxes. And for other properties which they may own in other towns of my realm, let them [also] be exempted. Their servants, plow-men, millers, gardeners, sheepherders—who keep their mares and cattle—and their nannies, [let them be also] exempted from taxes. These exempted servants and retainers are to be excused from taxes if their properties and goods are valued under 100 *mrs.*, but if over 100 *mrs.*, let them pay taxes to the king.

And when the knight dies, and his wife remains alive, I order that she retain this privilege while she is a widow. If she marries a knight with horse and weapon let her have the privilege of a knight as knights do. And if she marries a taxpayer [*pechero*] let her pay. If the widow had children under age, let them be excused from taxes until the age of sixteen. When they come of age, if they have horses and weapons and do their obligations as other knights [do], let them have this honor and exemption from taxes and if not, let them pay the taxes.... [The charter continues granting the council of Burgos rights of pasture and other exemptions] Moreover, I grant that the knights can fence pasture lands for their cattle in their properties, and that these pasture lands be fenced in a manner that will not dam-age [the well-being] of nearby villages. In addition, I grant them [the knights] that the year that the [militia] of the city of Burgos joins the army by order of the king, that those serving will be exempted from *marzadga* [a national tax paid in March]. And I order that no one should dare to go against, break, or lessen this privilege under a penalty of 10,000 *mrs.* and double that amount to [be paid] to the council of Burgos.

Questions: What qualifications did a Burgos resident need to be classified as a knight? What privileges did knightly status bring? What did the king expect in return for granting this special status? Why do you think the status of non-noble knight developed in Castilian towns, but not elsewhere?

37. TOWER FELLOWSHIPS AND FACTIONALISM
IN FLORENCE

Most of the northern Italian towns witnessed severe strife or factionalism among different groups of the ruling elite who were vying with each other for influence within the town government. This strife took several different forms, including the formation of alliances between families who supported the construction of a fortified tower in which they could seek refuge, the institutionalization of feuds and vendettas, and even all-out warfare between different factions, which were often based on family loyalties. To suppress this factionalism, towns appointed outsiders (called a podestà) as town managers, passed laws controlling vendettas, and eventually, in Florence, restricted the rights of the elite magnate class which was most involved in this factionalism. (See also docs. 23, 24, 31, and 145.)

Source: trans. R.E. Selfe, *Villani's Chronicle: Being Selections from the First Nine Books of the* Croniche Fiorentine *of Giovanni Villani*, ed. P.H. Wicksteed, 2nd ed. (Westminster: Archibald Constable & Co., 1906), pp. 109–10, revised.

Book V. 9. How civil war began in Florence between the Uberti and the government of the Consul

Then in the same year [1177] there began in Florence dissension and great war among the citizens, the worst that had ever been in Florence; and this was by reason of too great prosperity and repose, together with pride and ingratitude. Thus the house of the Uberti, which were the most powerful and the greatest citizens of Florence, with their allies, both magnates and *popolo*, began war against the Consuls (who were the lords and rulers of the commonwealth for a certain time and under certain ordinances), from envy of the government, which was to their mind not run well. And the war was so fierce and unnatural that just about every day, or every other day, the citizens fought against one another in different parts of the city, from district to district, according to their factions. And they had fortified their towers, which were very numerous in the city, in height 100 or 120 cubits [about 150–180 feet]. And in those times, by reason of this war, many towers were newly fortified by the communities of the districts, from the common funds of the neighborhood, which were called Towers of the Fellowships, and upon them were set engines to shoot forth one at another, and the city was barricaded in many places. This trouble endured more than two years, and many died by reason thereof, and much peril and hurt was brought upon the city; but this war among the citizens became so habitual that one day they would be fighting, and the next day they would be eating and drinking together, and telling tales of one another's valor and prowess in these battles. At last they ceased fighting because they grew weary from it, and they made peace, and the Consuls remained in their government; although they were responsible for begetting and bringing out the accursed factions, which were afterwards in Florence, as hereafter in due time we will make mention.

Questions: Why was factional strife so much more virulent and long-lasting in Italian towns than elsewhere? Why did the factions form fellowships to build towers? What were the different purposes—practical and symbolic—that the towers might have served?

38. FACTIONALISM AND THE CONCERNS OF AN EXILE, 1312

Neri degli Strinati was a member of one of Florence's oldest and most well-established families, the Strinati, whose status was fixed as early as the thirteenth century with their inclusion in the list of grandi *(the "great" or magnate families) as opposed to the* popolo *(the common people) in the Ordinances of Justice of 1292. In 1312, Neri degli Strinati began writing a chronicle about his family's experiences in the years before they were exiled to Padua, following the Black Guelfs' rise to power in Florence in the first decade of the fourteenth century. The Black Guelfs' prominence came at the expense of their rivals, the White Guelfs, who backed an opposing faction in Guelf-dominated Florence, and the Ghibellines, who supported the imperial presence in northern Italy (doc. 31). The following excerpts illustrate the experiences of Neri and his family in Florence before their departure, and the concerns they had while away from all the riches they possessed in their home town.*

Source: trans. L. Morreale, from "Chronichetta di Neri degli Strinati," in *Storia della Guerra di Semifonte scritta da Mess Pace da Certaldo e Cronichetta di Neri Degli Strinati*, ed. Domenico Maria Manni (Florence: Stampa Imperiale, 1753), pp. 97–127.

In the name of Lord Jesus Christ and his blessed and glorious Mother, and all the saints in heaven.

I, Neri Alfieri dello Strinato Raminghi, in order to memorialize those things which have happened, will write about the facts of my family as they have really and personally transpired, and will begin in the year 1312.... I, Neri, am in the city of Padua with all my family, as a man banished from Florence for what is now ten years, because of that treacherous tyrant [Charles of Valois, brother of the king of France]. And due to his arrival in Florence and because of the deceitful Black Guelfs, many other Ghibellines and White Guelfs, both magnates and *popolo*, were banished along with me. Among my family there are four of us who were banished, including Baldo, and Cambino, and Alfieri, who is the son of Marbottino. Alfieri and I came to Padua, and Baldo went to Orvieto, and Cambino went to Rome. [He then traces his family history from the first ancestor until he reaches his father.] From Alfieri my father, there remains Belfradello, Albertiono, and I, Neri. Belfradello and Albertino had no issue, and I, Neri, have Giovanni and Mattio. Mattio died in 1312. [He goes on to describe the other branches of the family.] …

And from Villanuzzo descended the side of the sons of Alfieri, and the side of the sons of Davanzato, so that half of the inheritance comes to our side, that is the sons of Sir Belfredello, and the sons of Marabottino, and the sons of Alfieri, who was my father, and in this way we should share a third among ourselves…. [He then documents the accumulation of properties, especially shops, by his father between 1252 and 1282.]

In 1282, the sons of Sir Belfradello made a new contract with the Marabottini sons and with me, Neri, as the third part, because all the houses on the market-place side belonged to us, and we pledged these houses in the contract. We had these contracts made up and there were agreements about these houses, but they were burned in a trunk, when I had to flee for safety to the inn of the sons of Tieri Dietisalvi in Calimala with all my papers and my clothes, and that was when the faithless Guelfs drowned Florence because they were fearful of losing land.

Here I will document all of the possessions on our side, and all of the houses that come from our half of the inheritance, and the agreements that we have made for the seven shops that came to us, excluding the Palazzo that was included in the inheritance. [Several passages then describe how the estates were divided among family members and business associates.]

At the request of Arriguccio, Boniface, and the sons of St. Leo, peace was demanded after that time, so that the Ghibellines could return to Florence to make peace with the help of the church of Rome, at the time of Pope Nicholas of the Roman Orisini [family], who sent his cardinal, Brother Latino, who was a Dominican friar, in order to first obtain peace among the Guelfs, and then between the Guelfs and Ghibellines, and then have the Ghibellines return to Florence, except for the Uberti family. And this cardinal pressured every person and demanded peace from everyone he could, and this was done in 1290 or around this time, and so peace was pledged to the cardinal despite the difficult times…. [He then recounts several land transfers during the period between 1290 and 1301.]

Sir Charles [Valois], brother of the king of France, came to Florence on 27 October 1301. On 2 November, the citizens of Florence, that is the Ghibellines and the White Guelfs, were robbed, and the suburbs were robbed and burned, as I said, by these people. The men and the supporters of the sons of the della Tosa house, with a group of armed solders, came to our house where the three sons of Marabottini and I, Neri, lived, and in our house they stole all they found there; fortunately the night before we had hidden all of the most expensive things; and that group sent for Sir Odaldo and Sir Rosilino della Tosa, and that night, thank goodness, Pinuccio di Nanni came to the house in his nightclothes, like a man who was in bed, and he ordered these brigands to leave, and we would have been lost had it not been for his goodness. When we had been robbed, Sir Oldaldo had told our women that we were no longer men, and that we had ceased to be men the night before; in this way, the sons of the della Tosa broke the peace.

Also during the very same night, those from the Medici family entered our house, sending Bernardino di Uombono dei Medici, who stole all that remained. And when everything in this house was stolen, they sent Averardo di Medici to swear at our women. And this I would not like to remain on my pen; in that night they left all the children, both male and female, naked in their bed-sheets, and took all their clothes and rags away; a deed so terrible that it was not even done by the Saracens in Acre.

When Sir Rosso della Tosa was an officer over the Ghibellines he was charged with ensuring obedience to the commune, and he caused the destruction of three houses of the sons of Marabottini behind the Vecchetti house, and tore down the house of the Villa da Scandiccio di Baldo, and cut the vines and the fruit trees and removed the vats and other household goods and sent them home; and the first was Sir Brunetto de'Brunelleschi, and Sir Arrigo, brother of Sir Rosso, and they made no apologies for this. [Neri describes many other transactions that took place under the Guelf regime, including a case involving members of the *popolo*.] ...

Maffeo and I, since we were *grandi*, could not take action against the Gone family, or revenue from Ghigo di Ghoso, because they were from the *popolo*.... And in another case, we could not [reconcile this debt] because of the Ordinances of the *popolo* against the *grandi*, and I could not believe that this affair was so drawn out, but we believe that Mr. Lamberto and his sons will pay the debt.... [The chronicle ends abruptly with the description of another business transaction complicated by the rules of the Ordinances of Justice.]

Questions: What were the effects of Florentine factionalism for city inhabitants, as described by Neri degli Strinati? How did factional discord affect different members of his family? What tools (e.g., petty thievery, insults, religious pressure) were used to exert power, and what does the manipulation of these mechanisms of power tell us about the scope of factionalism in northern Italian cities?

39. COMMERCIAL STATUS, WEALTH, AND POLITICAL OFFICE IN MEDIEVAL EXETER

In most larger English towns, full citizenship rights, which included the right to vote and run for city office, exemption from market tolls, and legal privileges, only came with membership in the "freedom" of the city (which was usually the same as the "guild merchant"). The first extract (A) lists the names of new members in two years and illustrates the different ways that men gained entry to the freedom of Exeter. While the percentage of householders enjoying access to this privileged group varied from town to town, they usually represented considerably less than one half of all householders, even though they held all of the most important civic offices. In Exeter, the wealth of the freedom members can be measured in the percentage who engaged in the lucrative trade overseas, or by the number of servants in their household, or, most directly, from the returns of a 1377 tax assessed on the value of the property and goods of 420 of the 525 householders; taxes ranged from 2 pence to 15 shillings, but 54 per cent paid 6 pence or less. Selections from this tax record (called a "murage" tax because its revenues went toward the repair of the town walls), which was organized by the four city districts or quarters, are in the second extract (B). The political rank achieved by these householders can be seen in the many election returns that survive (the third extract, in C), including that for the same year as the 1377 tax. The fourth extract (D) summarizes in tabular form the data collected from longer series of the first three records, as well as additional data on the sea-trading activities and servants of the householders in 1377. The "A" rank of the merchant oligarchy of Exeter were those who held the office of mayor, steward, or councillor; "B" rank officeholders served as elector or bridge-wardens; "C" rank officials were elected to policing positions such as gatekeeper and alderman; and "D" rank men never held any civic office at all.

Source: (A) trans. M.M. Rowe and A.M. Jackson, *Exeter Freemen 1266–1967* (Devon and Cornwall Record Society, extra series 1, 1973), pp. 32–33; (B) trans. M. Kowaleski, from Devon Record Office, Exeter Miscellaneous Roll 72; (C) trans. M. Kowaleski, from Devon Record Office, Exeter Mayor's Court Roll, 1–2 Richard II, mm. 1d, 2d; (D) M. Kowaleski, *Local Markets and Regional Trade in Medieval Exeter* (Cambridge: Cambridge University Press, 1995), p. 102.

(A) Extracts from the Entries to the Freedom of Exeter for 1364 and 1380

[1364, Mayor's Court Roll of Exeter]
 April 1: Richard Frensshe, brazier, fine of £1 6s 8d
 Sept. 16: John Bridlegh', fine of £1, granted to Martin [de Battishull], clerk, in aid of his fee
 Sept. 16: William Comere, fine of £1
 Sept. 16: Robert Comere, fine of £1
 Sept. 23: Richard Bealde, fine of £1 6s 8d
 Nov. 4: Walter Fouke, fine of £1
 Nov. 4: Andrew Bonevill, fine of £1

Nov. 18: Walter Chedlyngton, fine of £1
Nov. 18: John Trywell, fine of £1 6s 8d

[1380, Mayor's Court Roll of Exeter]
　　Jan. 16: Stephen Hul, son of John Hul, by succession
　　Jan. 16: Henry Archer, apprentice of Robert Wilford for nine years
　　Jan. 16: Robert, servant and apprentice of Thomas Glasiere for ten years
　　Jan. 23: John Leghe, skinner, fine of £1
　　Feb. 13: Walter Wylde, fine of £1
　　Feb. 13: John Crystowe, fine of £1
　　Feb. 20: William Malpe, fine of £1
　　July 23: Robert Nevyle, fine of £1 6s 8d
　　Sept. 24: Henry Holl, apprentice of Robert Wylford
　　Sept. 24: Thomas Smalecombe, fine of £1
　　Oct. 29: Henry Veisy, fine of £1
　　Nov. 5: William Jul, fine of £1
　　Nov. 5: Roger Truel, fine of £1
　　Nov. 5: Nicholas Goldyng, fine of £1
　　Nov. 5: William Mannyng, fine of £1
　　Nov. 5: Simon Hony, fine of £1
　　Nov. 5: William Wymark, fine of £1
　　Nov. 5: John Baigge, fine of £1
　　Nov. 12: John Kyng, weaver, fine of £1
　　Nov. 12: John Tyrel, fine of £1 2s
　　Nov. 12: Stephen Cotelere, fine of £1
　　Nov. 12: John Waddon, fine of £1
　　Nov. 12: Henry Spycer, skinner, fine of £1
　　Nov. 12: Andrew Poleworthy, fine of £1 6s 8d
　　Nov. 12: Roger Hore, fine of £1 4s
　　Nov. 12: William Hodel, son of Walter Hodel, by succession
　　Nov. 12: Thomas Criditon, by succession to his father
　　Nov. 12: Richard Carseyes, smith, fine of £1

(B) The Murage Tax Roll of Exeter, 1377

Exeter. Tax first levied for the repair of the gates, walls, and ditches.

East Quarter: The names of the collectors of this quarter: Richard Stayre, John Barber.
[There follows a list of 137 householders and the tax each paid, including:]
　　William Wygham, 2 shillings

Hugh Thornyng, 12 pence
William Baillesford, 12 pence
Thomas Smythesheghes, 2 shillings

...Sum of that quarter, £3 17s 7d....

South Quarter: The collectors of this quarter: Nicholas Bynnecote, William Criditon.
[List of 139 householders and the tax each paid, including:]
William Criditon, 12 pence
John Domet, 2 shillings
Adam Scut, 7 shillings
John Bridleghe, 5 shillings
Matthew Ekesbonere, 2 shillings
John Grey, 5 shillings
...

Sum of that quarter: £7 12 shillings ... And 6 pence that was assessed on Jocelin Smabbe is waived. Also 6 pence on John Somerforde [waived] because he is poor ... And 6 pence assessed on John Graas [waived] because it cannot be raised....

West Quarter: The collectors of this quarter: William Coscombe, Walter Lyndeseye.
[List of 59 householders and the tax each paid, including:]
John Russel, 4 shillings
William Coscombe, 4 shillings
John Westcote, 2 shillings
...
Sum of this quarter: 78 shillings, 2 pence....

North Quarter: The collectors of this quarter: John Talbot, Thomas Webber.
[List of 85 householders and the tax each paid, including:]
John Talbot, 1 mark [13 shillings, 4 pence]
Robert Wylford, 15 shillings
John Rede, 10 shillings
John Gist, 8 shillings
John Aisshe, 12 pence
Raymond Goos, 4 shillings
John Webbere, 5 shillings
...

Sum from this quarter: £6 2 shillings ... And 4 pence from Richard Beuman is waived because he has nothing ...

(C) Election Returns for the City of Exeter, 1377

Exeter. Election of the mayor and stewards of the city done on the date noted above [5 October 1377] by the oath of: [these are the Electors]

Martin Battishull	Henry Westcote	John Belchiere
William Gerveys	Nicholas Pees	John Veisy
Robert Wilford	John Bole	Robert Scot
John Gyst	Walter Fouke	Baldwin Whitesleghe
John Talbot	Richard Frensshe	Walter Lyndeseye
Raymond Goos	William Doune	Walter Thomas
John Webber	Walter Donsterre	Robert Dene
John Russel	Thomas Smythesheghes	Thomas Glasiere
Henry Forbour	Richard Bealde	Richard Digoun
William Rok	John Aisshe	William Wygham
John Bridleghe	John Piers	Ralph Uppexe
William Coscombe	Richard Bradecroft	Peter Hadleghe

Who by their oath elect Robert Wilford as mayor. And he is sworn in. Adam Scut as steward and receiver. And he is sworn in. William Gerveys, John Russel, Raymond Goos as stewards, sworn in.

The names of those being on the Common Council:

John Gyst	John Talbot	John Webber
Martin Batteshull	John Nymet	William Rok
John Grey	Adam Golde	Henry Forbour
John Rede	Walter atte Wode	John Bridlegh

Election of the wardens of the Exe Bridge, the [Leper] House of St. Mary Magdalene, and other offices of the city done on the same day by the oath of:

John Talbot	Nicholas Bynnecote	William Louche
Henry Forbour	Walter Fouke	Thomas Smythesheghes
Adam Golde	William Doune	Henry Westcote
William Rok	Robert Dene	William Wygham

Who by their oath elect William Doune and Robert Dene as bridge-wardens for the next year, Richard Bealde as warden of the House of St. Mary Magdalene. And they are sworn in.

Gate-Keepers:

For the East Gate: John Webber. And the said John is replaced by Gregory Bony (sworn in) in his place. Pledge Richard Dygoun.

At the South Gate: Walter Donsterre, and he is sworn in.

At the West Gate: Richard Wyndovere, and he is sworn in.

At the North Gate: Roger Morhay, and he is sworn in.

Aldermen:

Outside the East Gate: Robert Plomere, Robert Mareschal, and they are sworn in.

Outside the South Gate: Thomas Canon, Lawrence Spealte, and they are sworn in.

Outside the North Gate: John Tadyford smith, Thomas Sampson, and they are sworn in.

Sergeants:

Henry Swan, pledged by Adam Golde, John Aisshe, Richard Digoun, Thomas Smythesheghes

William atte Wille, pledged by John Gist, Henry Westcote, Richard Digoun, Robert Dene

William Focergay, pledged by William Bremelham, Hugh Thornyng, John Ponton, Thomas Smythesheghes

William Spycer, pledged by William Bremelham, Hugh Thornyng, Matthew Ekesbonere, Ralph Uppexe

(D) The Commercial Status and Wealth of Exeter Householders in 1377 According to Political Rank

Table 3.1: The Commercial Status and Wealth of Exeter Householders in 1377 According to Political Rank

Political rank	(No.) % of total householders		(No.) % in freedom		Aver. tax (in pence)	(No.) % active in sea trade		Aver. no. of servants
A (Highest Offices)	(32)	6%	(32)	100%	53.8	(24)	75%	1.53
B (Electors)	(34)	6%	(34)	100%	24.7	(11)	2%	1.24
C (Lower offices)	(31)	6%	(8)	26%	12.4	(1)	6%	.97
D (No offices)	(428)	82%	(38)	9%	8.4	(21)	5%	.61
Total	(525)	100%	(112)			(58)		
Average		21%			13.0		11%	.73

Questions: What were the most common ways for men to enter the freedom of the city in Exeter? What different sorts of information do the freedom register (A), murage tax (B) and election returns (C) of Exeter offer us? Which type of men, in terms of occupation, status, and wealth, were most likely to rise to high political office in the town?

40. THE POLITICAL FORTUNES OF A FLORENTINE MERCHANT

In the fourteenth to sixteenth centuries, many Florentine businessmen kept ricordi *or private diaries where they recorded not only their commercial dealings and business investments (sometimes deliberately referred to as their "secret" account books), but also much information on their family affairs and political actitivies. One such diary was written by Gregorio Dati, who started off rather humbly by working as a shop assistant, but rose to become a silk merchant and partner in trading companies doing business in Aragon and Catalonia. His diary reveals the many ups and downs of his business dealing, as well as the political positions that came with increased wealth. In 1429, for example, he served as Standard-Bearer of Justice, one of the the highest offices in the Florentine republic.*

Source: trans. J. Martines, "The Diary of Gregorio Dati," in *Two Memoirs of Renaissance Florence*, ed. G. Brucker (Prospect Heights, IL: Waveland Press, 1991; first printed 1967), pp. 107–08, 125–26, 136–37, 139–40, selections.

In the name of God, his Mother, and all the saints of Paradise, I shall begin this book wherein I shall set forth an account of our activities so as to have a record of them, and wherein having once more and always invoked the name of God, I shall record the secret affairs of our company and their progress from year to year. This ledger belongs to Gregorio, son of Stagio Dati, and I shall call it the secret ledger. In the name of God, Father, Son, and Holy Ghost, I shall here record some particular things known to myself....

I was born on 15 April 1362.... Our father left this world for a better one on 11 September 1374, when he was a consul of the Wool Guild and treasurer of the Commission on the Salt Tax and Forced Loans.... On 15 April 1375, when I had learned enough arithmetic, I went to work in a silk merchant's shop belonging to Giovanni di Giano and his partners. I was thirteen years old and I won their esteem.... I left Giovanni di Giano on 2 October 1380, spent fifteen months with the wool guild, and returned to him on 1 January 1382....

[In 1405, Dati served on the Ten of Liberty, a magistracy that settled disputes between citizens, and as guild consul for the third time. He also held this office in 1408.] ... On 28 April [1412], my name was drawn as standard-bearer of the Militia Company [a member of one of the Signoria's advisory Colleges]. Up until then I had not been sure whether my name was in the purses for that office, although I was eager that it should be both for my own honor and that of my heirs. I recalled that my father Stagio had held a number of appointments in the course of his life, being frequently a consul of the Guild of Por Santa Maria, a member of the Merchants' Court and one of the officials in charge of gabelles [salt taxes] and the treasurers. Yet he was never drawn for any of the Colleges during his lifetime, though shortly before his death he was drawn as a prior. I recalled that I had aroused a great deal of animosity eight years ago because of my business in Catalonia, and that last year I had only just escaped being arrested for debt by the commune. On the very day my name was drawn for this office, only fifteen minutes before it was drawn, I had taken advantage of the reprieve granted by the new laws and finished paying off my debt to the commune. That was a veritable inspiration from God, may his name be praised and blessed! Now that I can obtain other offices, it seems to me that, having had a great benefit, I should be content to know that I have sat once in the Colleges and should aspire no further. So, lest I should ungratefully give way to the insatiable appetites of those in whom success breeds renewed ambition, I have resolved and sworn to myself that I shall not henceforth invoke the aid of any or attempt to get myself elected to public offices or to have my name included in new purses. Rather, I should let things take their course without interfering. I shall abide by God's will, accepting those offices of the guilds or commune for which my name shall be drawn, and not refusing the labor but serving and doing what good I may. In this way I shall restrain my own presumption and tendency towards ambition and shall live in freedom and without demeaning myself by begging favors from any. And if I should depart from this resolve, I condemn myself each time to distribute two gold florins in alms within a month. I have taken this resolve in my fiftieth year.

Knowing my weakness in the face of sin, I made another resolve on the same day. In order to ensure the peace and good of my own conscience, I vowed that I would never accept any office, if my name should be drawn, wherein I would have the power to wield the death penalty. If I should depart from this resolution, I condemn myself to give 25 gold florins in alms to the poor within three months for each such office that I have agreed to accept....

I was guild consul for the eighth time from the beginning of May 1423. With me served [he lists 5 men]. Angolo died during his term in office, and his place was taken by Lorenzo di Piero di Lenzo.

I agreed to serve as podestà of Montale and Agliana in order to avoid the plague. My term of office was from 12 April to 12 October 1424. A great number of people accompanied me there and, by God's grace, none of us got sick. I was the first to stay in the residence at Montale and I saw to it that it was properly furnished and arranged. I acquired little wealth there but was highly esteemed by the inhabitants. Thanks be to God.

... My name was drawn to serve among the Lord Priors of the city of Florence for a term of two months, starting on 1 July and finishing on the last day of August 1425. Serving with me were [he lists 8 men]. The war [with the Visconti ruler of Milan] made our task extremely onerous but, by the grace of God, we left matters in a better way than we found them.

By the grace of God, I was Standard-Bearer of Justice for two months from 1 March 1429. The priors serving with me were: Zanobi di Tommaso Bartoli, a feather-bed maker; Bianco d'Agnoli, a maker of wine glasses, as artisans of the quarter of St. Spirito; ... [he lists six others, two for each of the other three quarters] and Ser Iacopo Salvestri, our notary. By God's grace we worked harmoniously together and accomplished a number of good things. I had a column placed in Piazza S. Felice; it was brought from the Mercato Vecchio, and the decision was taken by the Priorate.

... The same year 1412, my name was drawn to be standard-bearer of justice, and I served in that office. This was the beginning of my recovery [in 1414, from debt] ... our brother Lionardo was made Father General of his Order [the Dominicans]. So our trust in God aided and comforted us.

After reaching the settlement with Piero Lana's heirs in 1412, I found myself in debt for about 3,000 florins. God came to my aid then with the promotion of my brother who, as Father General, was in a position to help me pay off the debt. The assistance he gave me from time to time and according to his means is recorded in ledger B, page 94. The sums he paid out to me and in my name up to the year 1420 amounted to 2,330 florins, and he made me a gift of them....

Questions: What information does this selection offer on how men rose to political office in Florence? What types of office did Gregorio Dati hold? What did holding political office mean to him? What advantages and disadvantages do historians face in mining the ricordi for information on the past?

41. THE DISTRIBUTION OF WEALTH IN TWO TOWNS

We can get some idea of the distribution of wealth in medieval towns from urban tax returns, although few survive that include all of a city's households. The basis of urban taxes also varied from town to town or even from year to year within one town. The 1377 tax roll of the small English town of Exeter, for example, taxed heads of households according to their wealth in landed property, rents, and moveables (such as shop inventory, household furnishings, or grain surpluses), with the proceeds going toward the repair of the town wall (doc. 39B). The 1427 catasto for the large city of Florence (doc. 66) is probably the most comprehensive extant medieval tax return since it enumerated all the members of each household, as well as the household's wealth in terms of real property, moveables, and investments in the Monte, *the town's debt fund (citizens who loaned money to the city purchased "shares" in the fund, which theoretically gained in value through interest on the "bonds" or shares).*

Source: (A) data drawn from: M. Kowaleski, "Taxpayers in Late 14th Century Exeter: The 1377 Murage Roll," *Devon and Cornwall Notes and Queries* 34 (1980): 220; (B) data drawn from: D. Herlihy, "Family and Property in Renaissance Florence," in *The Medieval City*, ed. H.A. Miskimin, D. Herlihy, and A.L. Udovitch (New Haven, CT: Yale University Press, 1977), pp. 6, 8.

(A) Table 3.2: The Distribution of Taxable Wealth of 416 Households in Exeter, 1377

Tax Group	(No.)	% of Households	% of Wealth
Paid 2–6 pence	(227)	54.6%	20.6%
Paid 7–18 pence	(122)	29.3%	28.5%
Paid 24–180 pence	(67)	16.1%	50.9%
Total tax = 5440 pence	(416)	100.0%	100.0

(B) Table 3.3: The Distribution of Taxable Wealth of 9,946 Households in Florence, 1427

% of Households in Tax Group		% of Real Property Owned	% of Moveable Property Owned	% of Bonds in Public Debt Owned	Total % of Wealth Owned
Richest	10%	53%	71%	86%	68%
Middle	30%	39%	23%	13%	27%
Poorest	60%	8%	6%	1%	5%
Total Taxes:		4,128,024 florins	3,467,707 florins	2,573,378 florins	100%

Questions: How evenly distributed was wealth in these two towns? Are there any significant differences in the distribution of wealth? What differences can be seen in the nature of the wealth held by different income groups in Florence?

42. A BONDMAN SEEKS REFUGE IN AN ENGLISH TOWN, 1237–38

Since towns relied on immigration to maintain and bolster their population, they tended to look the other way when bondmen (semi-free peasants also called serfs or villeins) seeking a better life left their rural manors to live in the town. Indeed, one of the most common clauses in town charters gave freedom to those serfs who lived in the town for a year and a day without being detected by their lord. The serf in this court case, however, was tracked down by his lord, although it appears the lord transferred his rights over the serf and his family to the king, who was lord of the town of Andover.

Source: trans. A.E. Bland, P.A. Brown and R.H. Tawney, *English Economic History: Select Documents* (London: G. Bell and Sons, 1914), p. 125, revised.

Order was made to the bailiffs of Andover that, at the first coming of the lord king to Clarendon, they should show the lord king, why they have detained from Everard le Tyeis William of Amesbury, his bondman and fugitive, inasmuch as he claims him at the time and hours, as he says, etc.

And Adam de Marisco and other bailiffs of Andover come and say that this William was at one time dwelling at Wilton and was a traveling merchant and married a woman in the town of Andover, and within the year in which he married her, the same Everard came and sought him as his bondman and fugitive, but they refused to deliver him to him and dared not without the lord king's command.

Afterwards the same Everard comes, and remits and quitclaims to the lord king and his heirs the aforesaid William with his whole brood, etc.

Questions: How was William of Amesbury, the former bondman from a country village, integrated into the town of Andover?

43. GRIEVANCES OF THE COMMON FOLK OF DUBLIN, 1316–18

In many towns like Dublin, a "middling" group of prosperous shopkeepers and artisans sometimes became sufficiently upset at their exclusion from the higher reaches of urban government, which tended to be run by a relatively small merchant oligarchy (doc. 39 D), to voice their complaints in an organized fashion. Resentments about an unfair distribution of financial burdens, such as paying an unequal share of taxes while the ruling elite manipulated the tax system and city revenues in their favor, or about favoritism in handing out city contracts or escaping particularly burdensome civic duties, were the biggest causes of complaint. At times their resentment of the ruling elite could boil over into violence (docs. 25, 47–49), but in other towns organized but peaceful presentations of grievances to the city's lord could also lead to changes. In this period, Dublin was under extra stress because of a Scottish invasion in 1315 that came close to capturing Dublin itself.

Source: trans. J.T. Gilbert, *Calendar of Ancient Records of Dublin in the Possession of the Municipal Corporation of that City* (Dublin: Joseph Dollard, Wellington-Quay; London: Bernard Quaritch, 1889), pp. 132–35, revised.

Statement of grievances under which the common folk of Dublin suffered in consequence of the inefficient government of city rulers, as well as non-observance of the city usages, and for which remedies were sought and granted as follow:

For the honor of the King, and the safety and maintenance of the city, the common folk pray the mayor, bailiffs, and commonalty to accept and carry out the following recommendations, and to quash such of the proposals as may be deemed inexpedient:

Under penalty of grievous amercement, at least one man should come to muster from every house at the tolling of the public bell by day or night, while the land is troubled by the Scotch enemies, and by the hostile Irish, who daily threaten to burn the suburb and to do all possible damage to the city.

Guards to be assigned to every gate; no sally to be made unless by order of the Mayor and under command of the captains.

The city rent and the revenues of the provostship are to be punctually collected, and, any surplus of tallages and fees to be applied to the public works and other necessary expenses of the city. Hitherto the common folk have been heavily pressed by the city rent, commonly in arrears, and by unreasonable taxes which interfered with their trade and obliged them to close their warehouses.

Tallages are to be levied according to the returns made by the citizens on their own oaths or those of their neighbors.

Tenants of the archbishop resident within the city franchise are to be taxed like other citizens.

Tallages and imposts are to be collected under the supervision of four or six good men duly sworn, and accounts to be rendered of receipts and payments before the commonalty or their auditors.

None are to be admitted to the franchise of the city except with the assent of all the commonalty, or at least of the twenty-four jurats [the chief elected officials], and in consideration of liberal payment.

Inquests of offices in the four quarters of the city are to be taken before the mayor and bailiffs at least twice annually, and in relation to the city rents and dues concealed or embezzled.

Heavy amercements are to be levied on citizens within the franchise who contrary to the charter carry on elsewhere actions which should be tried before the mayor and bailiffs in the city court. Such amercements are to be expended on the city works.

A fine of 2 shillings is to be levied on every man who when summoned by the sergeant does not come to the Assembly or elsewhere to the mayor on business for the commonalty, and who cannot allege a reasonable excuse. The amounts to be accounted for by the bailiffs and to be charged to them.

The expenses of the watch are to be contributed to both by rich and poor, and forfeitures to be levied without respect to any, especially in time of war.

The purchase of any ship's cargo is not to be monopolized by the combination of two or three persons, but left open to all merchants within the franchise.

Merchandise is not to be bought by citizens, unless in the markets, nor until after it has been warehoused.

The assize of bread and ale [which tested for quality and fair price) is to be more strictly kept and to be made more frequently than heretofore, and transgressors are to be speedily punished as in former times.

Severe amercements and forfeitures of goods are to be imposed on those of the franchise who privately make purchases for the use of foreigners [non-residents of Dublin].

The goods of those who privately traffic with merchandise of foreigners who are not of the franchise and do not pay taxes are to be forfeited.

More severe punishments than hitherto are to be inflicted on regraters [those who bought early and sold late when the goods were scarce], who purchase fish and other victuals coming to the city and sell them in small parcels privately, thus greatly raising prices on the people.

Proceedings by exchequer process to be taken for the recovery of the numerous debts are due to the city from lands and rents of living and deceased persons.

At the election of the mayor, on Michaelmas-day [29 September], every citizen then resident is to attend, under penalty of 100 shillings, unless he can prove reasonable cause for absence. Those who on election refuse to serve as mayor or bailiffs are to be expelled from the commonalty and their houses to be prostrated. No mayor nor bailiff is to be elected except by the commonalty on Michaelmas-day.

In the four quarters of the city on Wednesdays and Thursdays weekly, after dinner, one man at least shall come from each house to do public works. Meanwhile all the shops to be closed, and those who during that time sell goods contrary to this order to be fined, and the amount applied to the public works of the city.

Application is to be made to the king's court and his officials, to ordain that victuals or other goods be not taken by force in the city except for the use of his Majesty and his chief justiciary, and only by the marshals or persons who are known, and under supervision of a sergeant of the city appointed by the mayor. To the damage of the citizens, the common people of the poor class, apprehensive of seizures, fear at present to bring their goods to the city for sale.

Questions: What were the chief grievances of the commoners of Dublin? Is it possible to see in the complaints that the common folk made how richer citizens were abusing their position? What solutions did the common folk propose to address these problems? Are there any points of comparision between the complaints of the Dubliners and the problems in Bristol (doc. 25)?

44. A DAY IN THE LIFE OF A CARPENTER

Written in the voice of an urban carpenter by the anonymous author of Li Roman de Renart le Contrefait, *an Old French poem of the thirteenth century, this extract offers a somewhat optimistic view of the simple pleasures experienced by an artisan at work.*

Source: trans. T. Fenster and M. Kowaleski, from "Un charpentier décrit plaisamment sa journée de travail," in *Le Moyen Age*, ed. M. Mollat and R. van Santbergen (Liege: H. Dessain, 1961), pp. 114–15.

I'll say, "Put the building site in order and plane the side of this beam. Get rid of this mess and take away that rubbish."

My apprentice will say: "Gladly."

"I need some hay right away to make ash, and I need a fire—there isn't any. I also need wood and dry logs."

And my apprentice will set off to work and I'll go and sharpen my axe, and after my axe, my saw. And everything gets done by other people!

At that point, I'll dawdle for awhile, then I'll put a piece of wood out in the yard. I'll do it slowly, and then I'll smack it a bit and remove the bark.

Well, then it'll be time for lunch, which invites drinking. I go off to the tavern and truly take my ease. I come back with the intention of making a mortise [one part of a wooden joint]. I take my auger to be sharpened and make a hole in the dead center of the wood. Then I come back to wet my whistle with a friend who's waiting for me.

When I see my master upon returning, I seem tough and busy enough to bring down a great castle or a tower ... As soon as my master leaves, I no longer want to bring anything down or disturb anything, but now it's time to have the afternoon drink....

Questions: What does this literary work tell us about the tools, materials, and tasks of a medieval artisan? About what the poet thinks about the artisan's attitude toward work?

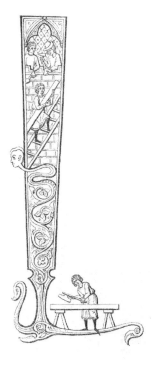

Figure 3.4
Carpenters at Work
The workman at the bottom of this image is hewing timber into beams, another man is hauling finished beams up a ladder, and the two at the top are finishing a stone battlement. From a manuscript of a bible of King Edward III. Reproduced from Thomas Wright, *The Archaeological Album* (London: Chapman and Hall, 1845), p. 70.

45. A LONDONER'S HOUSEHOLD GOODS, 1337

We can get some idea of the standard of living enjoyed by those lower down the social lad-
der from inventories of their goods, which were occasionally recorded to probate a will, or, in
this case, because the owner was forced to forfeit his goods when convicted of a felony. This
inventory was compiled for Hugh le Bevere of London, who was accused of killing his wife,
Alice, and condemned to die in prison for his crime. Hugh's surname and the occupation of
the chief appraiser of his goods suggest he was a furrier, while the variety and value of his
goods suggest he was of a prosperous "middling" status typical of urban artisans. Note that
a "robe" referred to a complete outfit—what we might today think of as a "suit" but in the
form of a gown rather than a jacket and trousers. To get some idea of the value of Hugh's
goods, remember that in this period, the average daily wage of a laborer was about 3 pence,
while a large loaf of bread cost about ¼ penny. There were 12 pence in one shilling; 1 mark
was worth 13 shillings 4 pence.

Source: trans. H.T. Riley, *Memorials of London and London Life* (London: Longmans, Green, and Co., 1868), pp. 199–200, revised.

Be it remembered, that on Saturday next before the Feast of the Apostles Simon and Jude [28 October], in [1337] ... came John Fot, citizen and vintner of London, before [the Recorder and Chamberlain of the Guildhall of London] ... and acknowledged that he had received from Walter de Mordone and Ralph de Uptone, recently sheriffs of London, the goods and chattels written below, in the presence of ... [the coroner and sheriffs of London] as appraised on the oath of Edward Mohaut, furrier, and others. Which goods belonged to Hugh le Bevere, who was indicted before the same coroner and sheriffs for the death of Alice, his wife, for which Hugh, being questioned about this death before the justiciars of our lord the king who were assigned to deliver Newgate jail, refused the law of England [he refused to submit himself to a jury]. Whereupon, by award of the justiciars, Hugh was committed to prison, there in penance to remain until he should be dead. The same being:
> One mattress, value 4 shillings
> Six blankets and one serge [woolen bed-cover], 13 shillings 4 pence
> One green carpet, 2 shillings
> One torn coverlet, with shields of cendale [silk], 4 shillings
> One coat, and one surcoat of worsted [a woolen fabric], 40 pence
> One robe of perset [a blue color], 7 shillings
> One surcoat, with a hood of ray [a striped cloth], 2 shillings 6 pence
> One coat, with a hood of perset, 18 pence
> One surcoat, and one coat of ray, 6 shillings 1 pence
> One green hood of cendale with edging, 6 pence

Seven linen sheets, 5 shillings
One tablecloth, 2 shillings
Three tablecloths, 18 pence
One camise [a long under-tunic] and one *savenape* [a cloth runner to protect tablecloth], 4 pence
One canvas, 8 pence
Three feather-beds, 8 shillings
Five cushions, 6 pence
One haketone [padded jacket worn under armor], 12 pence
Three brass pots, 12 shillings
One brass pot, 6 shillings
Two pairs of brass pots, 2 shillings 6 pence
One broken brass pot, 2 shillings 6 pence
One candlestick of latten [a copper/tin alloy], and one plate, with one small brass plate, 2 shillings
Two pieces of lead, 6 pence
One grate, 3 pence
Two andirons [to support logs in fireplace], 18 pence
Two basins, with one washing-vessel, 5 shillings
One iron herce [a large frame for candles], 12 pence
One tripod, 2 pence
One iron headpiece, 12 pence
One iron spit, 3 pence
One frying pan, 1 pence
One funnel, 1 pence
One small canvas bag, 1 pence
Seven *savenapes* [cloth runners to protect tablecloth], 5 pence
One old linen sheet, 1 pence
Two pillows, 3 pence
One cap, 1 pence
One counter [a table for counting money], 4 shillings
Two coffers [small chests], 8 pence
Two curtains, 8 pence
Two remnants of cloth, 1 pence
Six chests, 10 shillings
One folding table, 12 pence
Two chairs, 8 pence
One portable cupboard, 6 pence
Two large tubs, 2 shillings
Also firewood, sold for 3 shillings
One mazer [made of maple wood] cup, 6 shillings

Six casks of wine, 6 marks, the value of each cask being one mark [which equaled 13 shillings 4 pence]

Total, £12, 18 shillings 4 pence

The same John also received, of the goods of Hugh, from Richard de Pulham:

One cup called "*note*," [made out of a nut-wood] with a foot and cover of silver, value 30 shillings

Six silver spoons, 6 shillings

Also, from John Whytsand, one surcoat, and one woman's coat, value 8 shillings, which was pledged [probably for a loan] to Hugh by Paul le Botiller, for one mark.

Total, 44 shillings.

Questions: Can you categorize and detail the clothing, furniture, household goods, and kitchen equipment of Hugh's house? How do his clothing and household goods compare to those in the home of a craftsman today? How comfortable was his standard of living?

46. DOMESTIC SLAVES

Slave-owning became more common in Iberian and Italian towns, particularly in the seaports, during the late Middle Ages, perhaps in part as a response to the labor shortages following the Black Death. Florence legalized owning non-Christian slaves in 1364, although slaves who converted to Christianity were not automatically freed. Most of the slaves in Italy came from the area around the Black Sea; those in Iberia were also Muslims and Africans. Most slaves were women, and most worked as domestic slaves in their master's household, where they often lived out their days, although some might be freed by their master. Only wealthy people could afford the high price of a slave (doc. 55).

Source: trans. M. Kowaleski, from "Esclaves domestiques," in *Archives de l'Occident. Tome Premier. Le Moyen Age (Ve-XVe siècle)*, ed. O. Guyotjeannin (Paris: Fayard, 1992), pp. 708–10.

Searching for a Runaway Slave in Florence, 1388

Lodovico Marini has written to you this morning how last night a slave ran away, aged about 20 years, with brown hair and brown eyes, a well-formed bust, that is, neither fat or thin. She is quite petite and she hardly looks Tartar, but more the opposite. She is not skilled in our language. She is called Margherita, and I purchased her several months ago from Marco di Bellaccio, who told me he had her from a friend in Naples. Here is the description I can give you. She escaped from Marignolla this evening, as I have told you, with her clothes—that is, a skirt of mixed fabrics which is a bluish color and new, a sleeveless vest, a head-veil and other trifles, and also an old skirt in lambskin with a black sash on top of it, and she wears a hood most of the time. If I remember other details, I will write about them to you, but one could be fooled with all of these details. We have had no news, except that I have sent information with several travelers on the way to Pisa; and they say they encountered knights who told them of finding in Empoli a slave who matched the description I gave you, though she was only wearing a sleeveless dress, though she could have changed something in her get-up so she would not be recognized. It seems she was with a shoemaker from here; and behind them there was a box with a bundle of belongings, which perhaps included her clothes. At the moment, I don't know any more. I pray you, for the love of Lodovico and me, continue to look for her; if she came or should come to you, have her arrested and give proof of her flight. Besides, I pray you to dispatch a message to Livourne to stop her, if she goes there to embark, and another to the Arno [River] ferrymen to prevent her from going to Genoa; or do what seems best to you and go along with Bartolomeo, who is staying with Francesco di Bonaccorso and who has been informed by Lodovico. And both of you do me this service, so that I will be able to say, if I get news, that it is due to your kindness. I am much obliged to you. God keep you.

Farewell, Franco Sanchetti, of Florence.

P.S. Sometimes, one finds them in a brothel; you could also look into this. Send a letter to Michele Guinigi in Lucques; he will include it with what we have written to him on this matter.

Contract for the Purchase of a Slave in Ferrara

In the name of Christ, amen. 19 May 1441.... Ser Domenico, once of the household of Moricon, guardian of the *fondaco* [an entrepôt of foreign merchants within the city], inhabitant of Venice in the quarter of St. Antoinino, has spontaneously, freely, and in full consciousness given, sold and remitted, under the bond of perpetual servitude, to Nicolo Filippi of Marano de Ferrara, present, buying for himself and his heirs, stipulating and receiving as his own slave, a Circassian [from the area northwest of the Caucasus Mountains, near the Black Sea], aged around 17 years old, called in her language Comora and called Franceschina in sacred baptism and in Latin, healthy and without defect of spirit or body and with all her limbs, hidden and visible, [not suffering] from any illness; according to the usage of Venice, for the price of 45 gold ducats, with which the seller is content, he [Ser Domenico] has recognized to have had and entirely received from the said buyer ..., giving and conferring to the said buyer and his heirs the entire and absolute ownership of the said slave with full authority and power to do and dispose of this slave as he wishes....

Questions: What do these texts tell us about what slave owners were looking for in a slave? What do these selections tell us about the slaves themselves? What do these selections (and the end of the letter sent by the Genoese agents of the merchant, Francesco Datini of Prato, in doc. 55) tell us about the "market" for slaves in medieval Italian towns?

47. THE REVOLT OF THE COMMONS IN LONDON, 1194

The divisions between rich and poor had become the source of considerable anxiety by the late twelfth century in the larger cities, where these divisions were most severe. Circumstances that highlighted these divisions, such as fiscal mismanagement in the collection of a tallage or tax owed to the king, could make such resentment boil over (docs. 25, 43). Although the common folk were rarely strong or united enough to counteract the power of the urban elite in this period, they could make their voices heard, particularly if they found an articulate and well-respected champion from the ruling elite who sympathized with their plight. In this incident, the champion suffered greatly for his sympathies.

Source: trans. J.A. Giles, *Roger of Wendover's Flowers of History* (London: Bohn, 1849), v. 2, pp. 146–47, revised.

About this time there arose a dispute in the city of London between the poor and the rich on account of the tallage, which was exacted by the king's agents for the benefit of the Exchequer [the royal treasury]. For the principal men of the city, whom we call mayors and aldermen, having held a deliberation at their hustings [court], wished to preserve themselves free from the burden, and to oppress the poorer classes. Wherefore William Fitz-Robert, surnamed "with the beard," because his ancestors in anger against the Normans never shaved, opposed this, and called the mayors of the city traitors to our lord the king for the above-mentioned cause, and the disturbances were so great in the city that recourse was had to arms. William stirred up a large number of the middle and lower classes against the mayors and aldermen, but by their pusillanimity and cowardice the plans of William's confederates in resisting the injury done them were dissipated and defeated. The middle and lower classes were repressed, and the king, his ministers, and the chief men of the city charged the whole crime on William. As the king's party were about to arrest him, he, being a distinguished character in the city, tall of stature and of great personal strength, escaped, notwithstanding their exertions, defending himself with nothing but a knife, and flying into the church of St. Mary of the Arches, demanded the protection of our Lord, St. Mary, and her church, saying that he had resisted an unjust decree for no other purpose than that all might bear an equal share of the public burden, and contribute according to their means. His expostulations, however, were not listened to, the majority prevailed, and the archbishop, to the surprise of many, ordered that he should be dragged from the church to take his trial, because he had created a sedition and made such a disturbance among the people of the city. When this was told to William, he took refuge in the tower of the church, for he knew that the mayors, whom he had contradicted, sought to take away his life. In their obstinacy they applied fire, and sacrilegiously burnt down a great part of the church. Thus William was forced to leave the tower, almost suffocated with the heat and smoke. He was then seized, dragged out of the church, stripped, and, with his hands tied behind his back, conveyed away to the Tower of London. Soon after, at the instigation of the archbishop, the principal citizens, and the king's ministers, he was taken from the Tower, and dragged, tied to a horse's tail, through the middle of London to Ulmet, a pitiable sight to the citizens and to his own respectable relations in the city: after which he was hung in chains on a gallows. Thus William of the Beard was shamefully put to death by his fellow citizens for asserting the truth and defending the cause of the poor: and if the justice of one's cause constitutes a martyr, we may surely set him down as one. With him also were hanged nine of his neighbors or of his family, who espoused his cause.

Questions: Why did William rebel against the mayor and aldermen of London? How did he manage to gain the support of other Londoners? Why was he so cruelly punished? Where did the sympathies of the monastic chronicler of this passage lie?

48. THE RISINGS IN GHENT AND BRUGES AGAINST
THE PATRICIANS, 1301–02

Corruption and inequality in the management of urban finances also provided the trigger for rebellion in many Flemish cities, which relied almost exclusively on (regressive) indirect sales taxes for revenues rather than direct taxation which assessed people according to their means. Although these Flemish cities were highly industrialized and famous for their cloth manufactures, the refusal of their ruling patriciate of merchant-landowners to allow any political voice to the artisans' guilds provoked considerable unrest from the late 1270s on. This situation was made more complicated when King Philip IV of France, in an effort to lessen the influence of the count of Flanders, allied with the patricians. This selection from a local Ghent chronicle describes risings in Ghent and Bruges that succeeded in giving more political power to artisans, particularly those in the cloth industry. These risings, moreover, led to the famous victory of the Flemish foot-soldiers over the flower of French knighthood at the Battle of Courtrai in 1302.

Source: trans. H. Johnstone, *Annals of Ghent* (New York: Oxford University Press, 1951), pp. 12–19, abridged.

In the year of our Lord 1301, about the end of May, King Philip [of France] came into Flanders with the Queen of Navarre, his wife, as new prince and direct lord.... He came first to Douai, next to Lille, afterwards to Ghent.... Now when the king entered Ghent, the commonalty hastening to meet him, cried out loudly and begged earnestly to be freed from a certain heavy tax which there was at Ghent and Bruges upon articles for sale, especially beer and mead. The men of Ghent called it "the evil money," those of Bruges, the "assize." And the king, in cheerful mood and freshly arrived, acceded to the requests of those who clamored thus. This greatly displeased the patricians of the town, who were used to making profit from the said exaction, as at Bruges also. From Ghent the king went ... to Bruges. The men of Bruges came to meet him with extravagant adornments of their garments, and with diverse joustings sent him presents of great value. Now the *échevins* [the chief civic officials] and patricians of Bruges had forbidden the commonalty on pain of death, to clamor to the king for the abolition of the assize, or make supplication to him, as had been done at Ghent. The commonalty, offended by this, stood on the king's arrival as though they were dumb, at which, it is said, the king was very much surprised. When the king had gone on to Wynendaele, a very beautiful residence of the former court, the *échevins* and patricians of Bruges, being desirous that the presents made to the king and the ornaments of the garments which they had prepared to wear when meeting him should be paid for out of the assize, and that the tunics and raiment of the commonalty should be paid for out of the commonalty's own resources, still further excited the commonalty to anger. Great disturbance and dissension therefore arose in the town. Its originator is said to have been a certain weaver called Peter, surnamed Coninck, and some of his adherents. So the bailiff, on the advice of the patricians and *échevins* of Bruges, seized him, together with about twenty-five leaders of the commonalty, and shut him up in the king's prison, formerly the court's, that is called the Steen. When the commonalty heard of this, stirred and provoked, they gathered together, forced those in charge of the prison to open it and brought out all their friends unharmed, both Peter and his followers. So their agitation calmed down for a while, though they were still suspicious of the ill-will of the patricians....

James of St. Pol, still left by the king as ruler and governor of Flanders, proud and spirited as he was, much resented the contumacy of the city of Bruges in having broken the king's prison, that is to say, having caused it to be opened by force. So he assembled a force of about 500 mounted men and stationed it near Bruges, and by the advice of Sir John of Ghistelles, who had always borne that city ill-will, and of the patricians of Bruges, tried by various subtleties and deceptions to take vengeance for the action of the commonalty and grind it under foot. After consultation, therefore, on the ringing of a certain bell, arranged by them for this purpose, all the patricians armed themselves (the commonalty suspecting no evil), intending with the help of the aforesaid James, who was ready outside the gate of the town, and whom they meant to admit by one of the gates as soon as the fighting had begun, swiftly to destroy and weaken the power of the commonalty. When the commonalty discovered this, they most manfully resisted the patricians, who began to advance against them at the signal. They forced the patricians to flee to a safe place called the Bourg, near [the church of] St. Donatian. Finally they attacked that place also and obtained it by assault, slew some of the patricians, wounded many, and took the rest prisoner.... James [called in] ... a great army of Flemish nobles and patricians of other Flemish towns.... By the efforts of certain mediators, peace was made ... on the following terms. Those of the commonalty who admitted themselves responsible for the disturbance and fighting were to leave the town of Bruges and the land of Flanders within a fixed period, as though banished, never to return. Peter Coninck and his followers did this. The rest of the townsfolk were to submit to the decision and judgment of the count and his brothers ... [who] caused certain stone towers and gates to be destroyed, the wooden towers and all fortifications to be thrown into the ditch, ... and the rampart encircling the town to be at various points thoroughly dug up and destroyed. They said and decreed that through the aforesaid fight the town had forfeited all the liberties and noble customs and privileges granted to it by the kings of France or counts of Flanders....

The following winter, John, count of Namur and Guy his brother, the count's sons, with William of Jülich, son of their sister, their hearts touched by the cruel and unjust imprisonment of their father and brothers, began like men of spirit to conspire and hold secret counsel with some of their Flemish friends and to send private messangers and letters to some of the commonalities of Flanders who were unsettled and disturbed, [desirous of] recovering the rich land of their ancestors. So about mid-winter Peter Coninck, with some of his followers, returned by their advice to Bruges, and obtained such a hold over the weavers, fullers, and some others of the commonalty (for he was genial, and won them with smooth and sweet words) that the king's bailiff and the *échevins* and patricians of Bruges dared not touch him or his associates.... And Peter Coninck gained such a hold upon the commonalty of Bruges that he publicly forbade those who were destroying the rampart of Bruges and filling up the ditch, by order of James of St. Pol, to continue to obey his command, and threatened them from the rampart. When this became known, the king's bailiff and his judge and the *échevins* of Bruges, and many of the patricians, fearing for their lives, fled from the town, and Peter and his friends remained as it were lords of it.

... [The *échevins* and patricians of Ghent tried to reimpose the tax to pay for the debts they had contracted in making presents to the king, and threatened to banish or behead all who opposed it.] Assembling in consultation about dusk, the men of the commonalty came to an agreement that the next day they would do no work at their crafts, but would remain idle and discuss among themselves how they could get rid of the exaction. When the king's bailiff and the *échevins* and the patricians heard of this, they ... designed to capture or massacre those of the commonalty who were unwilling to work. When the commonalty saw the patricians in arms, and heard the haughty words of some, they remained quiet for the time being, and many of them went to work. But about terce on the second day ... some of the commonalty secretly armed themselves ... and went forth openly. By beating upon [metal] bowls (as they dared not approach the town bell), they roused all the commonalty, who left their work en masse and took up arms, and meeting the patricians in conflict began a fight. They forced ... about 600 to flee to the castle.... The commonalty, therefore, possessed with rage and massing together, attacked the said castle with crossbowmen on every side, and before noon took it, on the surrender of the patricians. Of the latter they slew two *échevins* and eleven others, and sorely wounded about a hundred. They compelled the rest, with the bailiff, to swear fidelity to them....

In the year of our Lord 1302, there began a painful and deadly war, long in incubation and incapable of appeasement, which came to birth at last with horrible and copious shedding of the blood of innumerable men....

Questions: What were the main complaints of the common folk and how did they compare to the complaints of townspeople in Bristol (doc. 25), Dublin (doc. 43), and London (doc. 47)? What actions did the townspeople of Ghent take to bring about change? Who were their leaders? What opposition did they face?

49. THE DEMANDS OF THE CIOMPI IN FLORENCE, 1378

The largest and, some might argue, most dramatic urban social revolt was the uprising of the Ciompi in Florence in 1378. The Ciompi were the mass of cloth workers who did not belong to guilds—indeed, they were even forbidden to organize into religious fraternities since these organizations might form the basis of labor agitation. As part of the popolo minuto, *their poverty, low status, and lack of political power distinguished them from the* popolo grasso, *the more well-off merchants, shopkeepers, and guild artisans. The initial impact of their revolt was bolstered when discontented artisans from the lesser guilds, who also had little say in civic government, joined ranks with the Ciompi. The powerful Lana guild of cloth manufacturers was especially resented by the cloth laborers of the* popolo minuto *who were subject to its discipline, but were not allowed to enjoy the benefits of membership.*

Source: trans. G. Brucker, *The Society of Renaissance Florence: A Documentary Study* (New York: Harper and Row Torchbooks, 1971), pp. 236–39.

[July 21, 1378] When the *popolo* and the guildsmen had seized the palace [of the podestà], they sent a message to the Signoria [which included nine priors, chosen from a select group of wealthy guildsmen] ... that they wished to make certain demands by means of petitions, which were just and reasonable.... They said that, for the peace and repose of the city, they wanted certain things which they had decided among themselves ... and they begged the priors to have them read, and then to deliberate on them, and to present them to their colleges....

The first chapter [of the petition] stated that the Lana guild would no longer have a [police] official of the guild. Another was that the combers, carders, trimmers, washers, and other cloth workers would have their own [guild] consuls, and would no longer be subject to the Lana guild. Another chapter [stated that] the commune's funded debt would no longer pay interest, but the capital would be restored [to the shareholders] within twelve years.... Another chapter was that all outlaws and those who had been condemned by the commune ... except rebels and traitors would be pardoned. Moreover, all penalties involving a loss of a limb would be canceled, and those who were condemned would pay a money fine.... Furthermore, for two years none of the poor people could be prosecuted for debts of 50 florins or less. For a period of six months, no forced loans were to be levied.... And within that six months' period, a schedule for levying direct taxes [*estimo*] was to be compiled....

The *popolo* entered the palace and [the podestà] departed, without any harm being done to him. They ascended the bell tower and placed there the emblem of the blacksmiths' guild, that is, the tongs. Then the banners of the other guilds, both great and small, were unfurled from the windows of the [palace of] the podestà, and also the standard of justice, but there was no flag of the Lana guild. Those inside the palace threw out and burned ... every document which they found. And they remained there, all that day and night, in honor of God. Both rich and poor were there, each one to protect the standard of his guild.

The next morning the *popolo* brought the standard of justice from the palace and they marched, all armed, to the Piazza della Signoria, shouting: "Long live the *popolo minuto!*" ... Then they began to cry that "the Signoria should leave, and if they didn't wish to depart, they would be taken to their homes." Into the piazza came a certain Michele di Lando, a wool-comber, who was the son of Monna Simona, who sold provisions to the prisoners in the Stinche ... and he was seized and the standard of justice placed in his hands.... Then the *popolo* ordered the priors to abandon the palace. It was well furnished with supplies necessary [for defense] but they were frightened men and they left [the palace], which was the best course. Then the *popolo* entered, taking with them the standard of justice ... and they entered all the rooms and they found many ropes which [the authorities] had bought to hang the poor people.... Several young men climbed the bell tower and rang the bells to signal the victory which they had won in seizing the palace, in God's honor. Then they decided to do everything necessary to fortify themselves and to liberate the *popolo minuto*. Then they acclaimed the woolcomber, Michele di Lando, as *signore* and standard-bearer of justice, and he was *signore* for two days.... Then [the *popolo*] decided to call other priors who would be good comrades and who would fill up the office of those priors who had been expelled. And so by acclamation, they named eight priors and the Twelve and the [Sixteen] standard-bearers....

When they wished to convene a council, these priors called together the colleges and the consuls of the guilds.... This council enacted a decree that everyone who had been proscribed as a Ghibelline since 1357 was to be restored to Guelf status. And this was done to give a part to more people, and so that each would be content, and each would have a share of the offices and so that all of the citizens would be united. Thus, poor men would have their due, for they had always borne the expenses [of government], and only the rich have profited.

... And they deliberated to expand the lower guilds, and where there had been fourteen, there would now be seventeen, and thus they would be stronger, and this was done. The first new guild comprised those who worked in the woolen industry: factors, brokers in wool and in thread, workers who were employed in the dye shops and the stretching sheds, menders, sorters, shearers, beaters, combers, and weavers. These were all banded together, some nine thousand men.... The second new guild was made up of dyers, washers, carders, and makers of combs.... In the third guild were menders, trimmers, stretchers, washers, shirtmakers, tailors, stocking-makers, and makers of flags.... So all together the lower guilds increased by some thirteen thousand men.

The lord priors and the colleges decided to burn the old communal scrutiny lists, and this was done. Then a new scrutiny was held. The offices were divided as follows: the [seven] greater guilds had three priors; the fourteen [lower] guilds had another three, and the three new guilds had three priors. And so a new scrutiny was completed, which satisfied many who had never before had any share of the offices, and had always borne the expenses.

Questions: Who presented the petition and what were their demands? What political and economic changes did they envision? How revolutionary were the changes they wanted to make? How did the Ciompi revolt compare to that of London (doc. 47) and Ghent (doc. 48) in terms of the main complaints and demands being made, participants in the revolt, and outcome?

CHAPTER FOUR

THE URBAN ECONOMY

Figure 4.1
Urban Shops
This street scene depicts typical urban shops, which were usually open to the street in order to display the wares being sold. Workshops were often at the back of the shop, with living quarters above the shop. From a fifteenth-century manuscript of the "Régime des Princes". Reproduced from Paul LaCroix, *Science and Literature in the Middle Ages and at the Period of the Renaissance* (New York: D. Appleton and Co., 1878), fig. 111.

50. MARKET REGULATIONS IN MUSLIM SEVILLE

In the late eleventh and early twelfth centuries, the Muslim cities in Andalusia, in southern Spain, were bigger and more commercially active than the cities of Christian Spain in the north. Some idea of the vitality and diversity of Seville's markets can be gleaned from this extract from a hisba, *a manual that guided a market inspector (*muhtasib*) about his duties, which included regulating business dealings in the market and ensuring quality and price controls, as well as a range of other responsibilities concerning proper moral conduct and religious observance.*

Source: trans. B. Lewis, *Islam from the Prophet Muhammad to the Capture of Constantinople* (New York: Harper and Row, 1974; reprint Oxford: Oxford University Press, 1987), II, pp. 157–61.

Shopkeepers must be forbidden to reserve regular places for themselves in the forecourt of the great mosque or elsewhere, for this amounts to a usurpation of property rights and always gives rise to quarrels and trouble among them. Instead, whoever comes first should take his place.

The *muhtasib* must arrange the crafts in order, putting like with like in fixed places. This is the best and most orderly way.

There must be no sellers of olive oil around the mosque, nor of dirty products, nor of anything from which an irremoveable stain can be feared.

Rabbits and poultry should not be allowed around the mosque, but should have a fixed place. Partridges and slaughtered barnyard birds should only be sold with the crop plucked, so that the bad and rotten can be distinguished from the good ones. Rabbits should only be sold skinned, so that the bad ones may be seen. If they are left lying in their skins, they go bad.

Egg sellers must have bowls of water in front of them, so that bad eggs may be recognized.

Truffles should not be sold around the mosque, for this is a delicacy of the dissolute.

Bread should only be sold by weight. Both the baking and the crumbs must be supervised, as it is often "dressed up." By this I mean that they take a small quantity of good dough and use it to "dress up" the front of the bread which is made with bad flour. A large loaf should not be made up out of the *poya* rolls [a roll given to the baker as payment for the use of his oven]. These should be baked separately and as they are.

The glaziers must be forbidden to make fine goblets for wine; likewise the potters.

The *ratl* weights for meat and fish and *harisa* [dish made of meat, cracked wheat, and sour milk] and fritters and bread should be made of iron only, with a visible seal on them. The *ratl* weights of the shopkeepers should always be inspected, for they are bad people.

The cheese which comes from al-Madā'in [a region south of Seville] should not be sold, for it is the foul residue of the curds, of no value. If people saw how it is made, no one would ever eat it. Cheese should only be sold in small leather bottles, which can be washed and cleaned every day. That which is in bowls cannot be secured from worms and mold.

Mixed meats should not be sold on one stall, nor should fat and lean meat be sold on one stall. Tripe should only be sold dry on boards, for water both spoils it and increases its weight. The entrails of sheep must be taken out, so that they should not be sold with the meat and at the same price, which would be a fraud. The heads of sheep should not be skinned, except for the young. The guts must always be removed from the bodies of animals, except lambs, and should not be left there, for this too would be an occasion for fraud.

No slaughtering should take place in the market, except in the closed slaughterhouses, and the blood and refuse should be taken outside the market. Animals should be slaughtered only with a long knife. All slaughtering knives should be of this kind. No animal which is good for field work may be slaughtered, and a trustworthy and incorruptible commissioner should go to the slaughterhouse every day to make sure of this; the only exception is an animal with a defect. Nor should a female still capable of producing young be slaughtered. No animal should be sold in the market which has been brought already slaughtered, until its owner establishes that it is not stolen. The entrails should not be sold together with the meat and at the same price. A lamb weighing six *ratls* with its offal shall not be sold at the same price as a lamb the meat of which alone is of that weight.

Fish, whether salt or fresh, shall not be washed in water for this makes it go bad. Nor should salted fish be soaked in water, for this also spoils and rots it.

[Word missing in text] should only be sold cut into small pieces and with the bones removed. Jerked meat should not be sold, for it is prepared with bad and rotten meat. There is no goodness in it, and it is a deadly poison.

Left-over and rotten fish should not be sold.

Sausages and grilled rissoles should only be made with fresh meat and not with meat coming from a sick animal and bought for its cheapness.

Flour should not be mixed with the cheese used for fritters. This is fraud, and the *muhtasib* must watch out for it.

The cream must always be pure and not mixed with cheese. The leftovers of the cooks and fryers should not be sold....

Women should not sit by the river bank in the summer if men appear there.

No barber may remain alone with a woman in his booth. He should work in the open market in a place where he can be seen and observed.

The cupper. He should only let blood into a special jar with graduation marks, so that he can see how much blood he has let. He should not let blood at his discretion, for this can lead to sickness and death....

No one may be allowed to claim knowledge of a matter in which he is not competent, especially in the craft of medicine, for this can lead to loss of life. The error of a physician is hidden by the earth. Likewise a joiner. Each should keep to his own trade and not claim any skill of which he is not an acknowledged master—especially with women, since ignorance and error are greater among them.

Only a skilled physician should sell potions and electuaries and mix drugs. These things should not be bought from the grocer or the apothecary whose only concern is to take money without knowledge; they spoil the prescriptions and kill the sick, for they mix medicines which are unknown and of contrary effect.

The sale of tame pigeons must be prohibited, for they are used only by thieves and people of no religion. The sale of cats should also be banned. Any broker who is known to be treacherous and dishonest should be excluded from the market, for he is a thief. He must be watched and not employed.

The lime stores and [other] empty places must be forbidden, because men go there to be alone with women.

Only good and trustworthy men, known as such among people, may be allowed to have dealings with women in buying and in selling. The tradespeople must watch over this carefully. The women who weave brocades must be banned from the market, for they are nothing but harlots.

On festival days men and women shall not walk on the same path when they go to cross the river....

Questions: What do the regulations that shopkeepers were required to follow tell us about their commercial activities? What types of control were placed on other occupations? What commodities were most regulated, and what limits were put on their sale? What seem to have been the biggest concerns or anxieties behind these regulations? Were the regulations consumer-oriented or shaped by religious concerns?

51. THE CHAMPAGNE FAIR TOWNS

The county of Champagne, which lay to the east of the kingdom of France, was ruled by powerful counts and countesses until it was incorporated into the French royal domain in 1284. During the twelfth and thirteenth centuries the Champagne fairs were the most important market centers in northern France, fostered by the protection of early counts who guaranteed safe passage and protection to visiting merchants, ensured standard weights and measures, and guaranteed a strong currency, the pound provinois. The annual cycle of fairs that emerged effectively created a continuous market in local and international goods frequented by merchants from all over Europe: the winter fair in Lagny, the early spring fair in Bar-sur-Aube, and the summer and autumn fairs alternating between the comital capitals of Provins and Troyes. The first selections are from a detailed assessment of the extent and value of the count's properties and privileges in Troyes and Provins, and the obligations and privileges of the towns' residents. The second selection shows how the number of people attracted to the annual fairs displaced some of the permanent residents of these towns, as described in a rental agreement that indicates how permanent residents in Bar-sur-Aube, who rented a house from the nuns of Foissy, were required by their nun-landlords to make accommodations for the annual fair.

Source: (A) trans. A.E. Lester, from "Extenta Terre Comitatus Campanie et Brie (1276–1278)," in Auguste Longnon, ed. *Documents Relatifs au Comté de Champagne et de Brie 1172–1361*, 3 vols. (Paris: Imprimerie nationale, 1901–14), vol. 2, pp. 9–11, 68–70; (B) trans. A.E. Lester, from *Les villes de foires de Champagne*, by E. Chapin (Paris: Honoré Champion, 1937), pièces justificatives, no. 17, pp. 313–14.

(A) Extent of the Lands of the Count of Champagne and Brie, 1276–78

In Troyes:

The count has lordship there over the fair of St. Jean, which begins on the first Tuesday fifteen days after the Feast of John the Baptist [24 June], and will end on or around the Nativity of the Blessed Virgin [8 September]. The value of the fair is currently estimated at 1000 pounds, in addition to what is paid in fief which is valued at 13 pounds, and he holds a similar fief in another fair, called "the warm [summer] fair" [probably the May fair at Provins].

Likewise the count has lordship over the other fair which is called that of St. Remy or the "cold fair," which begins on the day after the Feast of All Saints [1 November] and ends the week before the Nativity of the Lord [25 December]. The value of the fair is currently estimated at 700 pounds.

Likewise he has a market in Troyes and by right of lordship he holds the tolls on looms and weights which are called *Urmellum*, which he takes in front of the house of Urmello, and it takes place here twice in the week, namely on Tuesdays and Saturdays. This is currently estimated at 100 pounds.

He likewise holds the house of the German merchants, in which their goods are sold, situated in the neighborhood of the street of Pons. This house is rented in the fair of St. Jean and in the fair of St. Remy. In the previous year of fairs it was valued at 300 pounds, minus the costs of room and board.

He also holds the butcher's stall between the street of the Temple and the "Middle" street, which the count rents for an annual rent, half of which is paid on the Feast of St. Remy [1 October] and half on the day of the Purification of the Virgin [2 February].

In Provins:

The count has lordship rights over the fair which is called St. Ayoul, which begins on the day of the exaltation of the Holy Cross [14 September] and ends on the feast of All Saints [1 November]. The fair has a value of 1000 pounds annually, and is held at St. Ayoul, in the lower town.

The count likewise holds lordship there over the fair called the May fair, which begins on the Tuesday before Ascension [37 days after Easter], depending on the day of Ascension, and lasts for forty-six days. The fair is valued at 800 pounds annually and is held in the upper walled town.

The count also has rights to the market which is held each Tuesday, where he holds rights over tolls. For this reason in any place in the market he is entitled to 1 penny per measure of cloth from those who buy cloth and from those who sell it, unless they are nobles, clerics, or townsmen of Provins ... Among those who are from outside of Provins, such that it is, for all the cloth which is sold in the aforesaid market, the count takes 1 penny from the seller and 1 from the buyer. The market is held in the upper town. It is estimated at a value of 20 pounds per year and half of the profits are held by the Hospitallers [a monastic military order]. And there are halls for the sale of cloth, of which the greatest is valued at an assigned rent of 60 pounds, the total of which is divided between the count and Hospitallers.

Likewise there is another hall there which has an annual assigned rent valued at 10 pounds, shared equally by the count and the Hospitallers.

Likewise there is a certain cellar beneath the aforesaid hall, which is divided between the count and the Hospitallers and is valued at 100 shillings.

There is also another small hall which is divided between the count and the Hospitallers. It has never been rented. As it is now, it is to be rented for 100 shillings annually.

Likewise, he holds the house of Gailard in front of St. Mary's, which will be sold in the next fair. It is worth 10 pounds.

Likewise he holds a house situated in front of the *Filias Dei*, which is called the house of Colet de Naudo, which is valued at 24 shillings a year.

Likewise the house which belonged to Colet de Mayance, which now is worth nothing.

Likewise he holds a certain house in which there is a grange and below this is a house for clerics. It is currently rented for 4 pounds.

Likewise there, next to the school [probably connected to the house of canons] are two rooms, one of which is rented for 16 shillings and the other is held by Lord Robert of Normandy [perhaps a canon at the adjoining house of canons] for his lifetime.

(B) Rental contract for a house during the period of the Fair in Bar-sur-Aube, 1275

We, master Peter, dean of the church of Bar-sur-Aube in the diocese of Langres, and John de Monasterio provost [a royal official] of Bar, make it known to all those in the present and in the future that in our presence, Theobald called *de Bayel* and Adeta his wife, who were staying in Bar, recognized freely before us that they hold a certain house with all that pertains to it for the duration of their lives from the religious persons, that is, the prioress, prior, and convent of the nunnery of Foissy, in the diocese of Troyes, outside the time of the fair of Bar. This house is located in Bar-sur-Aube in front of the lodge of Bar in a place which is commonly called *Salnaria*, next to the house of the lord King of Navarre [a title held by the count of Champagne at that time] on the one side and next to the small street that leads from *Salnaria* to the house which is called the Court of the Germans on the other side. Theobald and his wife rent this house for an annual rent of 4 pounds in the good and strong currency of Provins, which the same Theobald and his wife, under penalty of all costs and expenses, promise to render and to pay each year, while they live, to the nuns or to their proxy official if designated, during the regulated payment period of the fair of Bar, to be paid at Bar. Theobald and his wife hold the house in full possession, during the time they are living, either together or each on their own (should one die), and they have promised to maintain it and all that pertains to it in a good and praiseworthy state from their own costs and expenses. Moreover, they promise to vacate the house each year on the Tuesday following the Sunday on which the psalm *Oculi Mei* is sung [the third Sunday in Lent: the Bar fair began between 24 February and 30 March] and indeed to leave it and to remove their moveable goods until the fair of Bar has been convened and completed. After the fair is finished, Theobald and his wife will be able to return immediately to the house without any interference. If it should happen that, while Theobald and his wife are living there, the house (let it not come to pass!) is burned by fire or destroyed by chance by any other cause, they will in no way be held responsible for rebuilding the house unless they wish to. What is more, Theobald and his wife willingly agreed that if they default in the payment of the 4 pounds rent or in any of the other stipulations written above, at any time the nuns of Foissy have the right to re-mortgage the house by their own authority without making an appeal to ecclesiastical or secular justice. The nuns should also receive an inventory of the mortgage, payment and full restitution of their damages and expenses and, if it pleases the nuns, they may repossess the house and do with it as they want. When Theobald and his wife die, immediately the house with all of its improvements, except the moveable goods inside, shall revert undisputed to the nuns. As proof of this agreement we have sealed the present letters with our seals at the request of Theobald and his wife. Enacted in the year of the lord 1274, in the month of May.

Questions: What do these documents tell us about how these very profitable fairs influenced the life of the residents of the Champagne fair towns, especially during fair time? Why were the markets and fairs (many of them named after the parishes where they were located) held in front of churches? Why would the nun-landlords include a clause that required their tenants to vacate the home they were leasing during the fair?

52. TOLLS AT SOUTHAMPTON, c. 1300

Every town kept a schedule of tolls or customs it charged on goods coming into the town market for sale, or exiting after being sold in the town, whether transported over land or by sea. Customs revenues were particularly large in seaports such as Southampton because of the amount of maritime trade passing through its harbor. This schedule of Southampton's tolls gives us an idea of the types and relative value of goods traded in the town and how the goods were transported in and out of town.

Source: trans. P. Studer, *The Oak Book of Southampton* (Southampton Record Society, vol. II, 1910), pp. 2–17, revised.

Here are the customs ordained by the Town for [goods] going out by sea and by land.

The custom of bread coming to town in carts:

Of a wagon-load of bread	1 pence
Of a cart-load of bread	½ pence
Of every manner of grain, per quarter [of a ton]	½ pence
Of the cart-load of grain	½ pence

The custom of wine, cider, ale, and empty [barrels]:

Of every tun [a 252–gallon barrel] of wine which arrives in the harbor	4 pence
And of the export thereof along the coast of England	4 pence
And of a tun [of wine] freighted from beyond the sea	8 pence

And of every tun of wine going out by land	8 pence
And of every empty tun carried out of town	1 pence
And of an empty pipe [a 126–gallon barrel] carried out of town	½ pence
And of a tun of cider carried by sea or by land	2 pence
And of a pipe of ale carried by sea or by land	1 pence

The custom of plaster of Paris, of a horse bought or sold, and of bacon:

Of a wagon-load of plaster of Paris carried by land	1 pence
And of a heap [of plaster of Paris] carried by sea	1 pence
And of every horse bought or sold, [both] from the buyer and seller	2 pence
Of every bacon [a whole salted hog] carried by land or by sea	½ pence

The custom of the sack of wool and of leather:

Of every sack [364 pounds] of wool from England	4 pence
Of every poke [182 pounds] of wool	2 pence
Of every poke weighing beyond 26 cloves [=182 pounds]	4 pence
Of a hundred wool-fells	3 pence
Of cheese, by the wey [c. 180 pounds]	1 pence
Of every hide, raw or salted, dried or tanned	½ pence
Of the hide of the belly or other parts of tanned hides, carried by one man	¼ pence
And of the burden of one horse	½ pence
Of one bale of flax from Spain	2 pence
Of one sack of wool from Spain	1 pence
Of a dozen [pieces] of cordwain leather sold in the town	1 pence
Of a dozen [pieces] of basan [sheep-skin] leather sold in the town	[½ pence]
Of a bale of basan leather, as it is brought ashore from out of a ship	1 pence

The custom of honey and of grease:

Of every tun of honey, of herring grease, or of oil	1 shilling 4 pence
Of [every tun of] sardine grease, or of pork lard	1 shilling 4 pence
Of a pipe of any of these	8 pence
Of a hundredweight [c. 112 pounds] of oil and of tallow	1 pence
Of every hundred of boards for ships	4 pence
Of a hundred of boards from Eastland [the Baltic]	4 pence
Of a hundred of Irish cloth	2 pence
And of old cloths, for every dozen sold	1 pence
And of every cloth coming from beyond the sea	1 pence

And of a whole piece of English cloth	1 pence
Of a hundred of sticks for bows and crossbows	2 pence
And of a dozen of sticks	¼ pence
Of every skin or fur of rabbit	½ pence
Of a hundred of hare skins	1 pence
Of a hundred of rabbit skins, by the long hundred of 120	1½ pence
Of every coverlet of rabbit skins	1 pence
Of a hundred of sable, marten, pole-cat, fox, or cat-skins	2 pence
Of a hundred of fells of squirrels or goats [?]	1½ pence
Of a timber [40 skins] of miniver [white squirrel fur]	2 pence
Of a hundred of English lamb-skins	1½ pence
Of a hundred of budge [lamb-skin] for hoods	3 pence
Of a hundred of budge for furriers [?]	1½ pence
Of every piece of Spanish wax	4 pence
And of a bale of Spanish wax	8 pence
Of a [chest?] of quicksilver	2 pence

The custom of spices, etc.:

Of a bale of pepper, ginger, zedoary, cinnamon, galingale, mace, cubeb, cloves, saffron, grain, brazil	£1 or the value
Of a bale of almonds, cumin, rice, and licorice	2 pence
Of every wagon-load of battery-ware [metal utensils] brought by water	1 shilling 4 pence
Of a horse-load of battery-ware	2 pence
Of every silk [?] cloth	4 pence
Of every hauberk and habergeon [types of body armor]	2 pence
Of every *chief* [6 pieces] of cendal [silk]	3 pence
Of every piece [of cendal]	½ pence
Of a thousandweight [c. 1120 pounds] of tin 10 pence, or of a hundredweight	1 pence
Of a thousandweight of copper 10 pence, or of a hundredweight	1 pence
Of a hundredweight of brass	1 pence
Of a fotmel [70 pounds] of lead	¼ pence
Of a fother [2100 pounds] of lead	6 pence
Of a hundredweight of iron ¼ pence, and on the export of the same	½ pence
Of every quarter [of a tun] of woad [a blue dye]	1 pence
Of every tun of woad	6 pence
Of a pointelle [c. 7 pounds] of woad	¼ pence
Of a pipe of potash [used in the dyeing process]	4 pence

Of a barrel of potash	2 pence
Of a load [c. 240 bunches] of garlic (of 120 bunches 6 pence)	12 pence
Of a hundred of ropes from Brittany	4 pence
Of a thousand of small onions	
	1 pound [of onions] or the value of 1 pound
Of a thousand of red [cured] herring	1 pence
Of a thousand of white herring	½ pence
Of a thousand of sardines	½ pence
Of a hundred of conger [a type of fish]	4 pence
Of a hundred of cod and ling [a type of fish]	2 pence
Of a hundred of stockfish and other fresh fish	2 pence
Of a hundred of fresh mackerel	1 pence
Of a hundred of salt mackerel	½ pence
Of a barrel of mulwell [type of cod]	2 pence
Of a barrel of haddock	1 pence
Of a hundred of haddock	½ pence
Of two baskets of lamprey [type of eel]	
	1 lamprey or the value of 1 lamprey
Of a barrel of sturgeon	4 pence
Of a salt salmon	¼ pence
Of a fresh salmon, going out or coming in	½ pence
Of a hundredweight of whale	2 pence
Of a fresh or salt porpoise	2 pence
Of a hundred of "Gobettes" [lump fish?]	2 pence
Of a hundred of "Coignes" [mullet fish?]	1 pence
Of every millstone	2 pence
Of a bale of alum [mordant used in dyeing or leather making]	2 pence
Of a hundredweight of alum	2 pence
Of the passage of a man beyond the sea	2 pence
Of the passage of a horse	3½ pence
Of the berth of a ship [payment for docking]	2 pence
Of a "balenge" [coarse cloth?] of Cambrai	¼ pence
Of a hundred of "argol" [tartar deposit inside wine casks] and ink	½ pence
Of an ox or a cow	1 pence
Of a calf, pig, or sheep	¼ pence
Of every hundred of linen cloth and of canvas	2 pence
Of every chalon [blanket]	¼ pence
Of the quarter of coal coming by sea	¼ pence
Of every ton of apples or pears coming by sea	2 pence

Of every quarter of small nuts	½ pence
Of the thousand of French nuts [=walnuts]	¼ pence
Of drinking cups, basins, plates, and saucers, by the dozen	¼ pence
Of every (large) barrel of tar or of pitch	2 pence
Of every which [regular barrel]	1 pence
Of the wagon-load of timber	½ pence
Of the cope [barrel?] of figs and raisins	1 pence
Of 2, 3, or 4 gallons of oil	½ pence
Of 5, 6, 7, 8 or 9 gallons of oil	1 pence
Of 10 or 11 gallons [of oil]	1½ pence
Of 12, 13, 14, 15 or 16 gallons [of oil]	2 pence
Of 17, 18, 19, 20, 21, 22 gallons [of oil]	2½ pence
And so forth for all other [quantities of oil]	
Of the quarter [of a ton] of salt	½ pence
Of every hundred of "floats"(?)	1 pence
Of the roll of sail or sail cloth	2 pence
And if there be two rolls	2 pence
Of ropes such as cables or such manner of ropes going out unpacked	
(of a hundred pounds)	2 pence
Of a new wagon	1 pence
Of the wagon-load of charcoal	½ pence
Of a thousand of slates [roofing tiles]	¼ pence
Of the thousand of laths [wooden slats]	½ pence
Of the barrel of litmus [a dye]	1 pence
Of cables and of other ropes of whatever part they be	2 pence
Of every dozen of calf hides	2 pence
Of every hundred of garlic	12 pence
Of every piece of poldavis [a coarse canvas]	2 pence
Of every piece of "oulone" [a type of canvas]	1½ pence
Of every piece of "crestcloth," "dowlas" and "lokeram" [types of linen cloth from Brittany]	3 pence

Also, if a man buys a ship or boat he shall pay for this £1 pound sterling [as a tax] …

Questions: Which goods reached Southampton by land, and how were they carried there? If the tolls paid reflect the value of the goods customed, what were the most valuable goods traded through Southampton? What do the different types of goods listed here tell us about industry in medieval Southampton?

Figure 4.2
Measuring Salt at the Town Quay
All products entering the town were weighed and measured so that they could be "customed" or taxed by town officials. These import duties (and often export duties as well) were a source of revenue for the town. Here a Parisian official supervises the measuring of salt, while porters carry sacks of salt off the ship and into the market place. Facsimile of a woodcut of the "Ordonnances de la Prevosté des Marchands de Paris" (c. 1500). Reproduced from Paul LaCroix, *France in the Middle Ages: Customs, Classes, and Conditions* (New York: Frederick Ungar Publishing Co., 1963), fig. 280.

53. REGULATIONS ON THE SALE OF MEAT AND FISH IN BEVERLEY, 1365–1409

Meat and fish were essential foodstuffs, so towns early on regulated their processing and sale to ensure a steady and good quality product at a reasonable price. These ordinances are from the Yorkshire town of Beverley, but similar regulations doubtless existed for almost all medieval towns.

Source: trans. A.F. Leach, *Beverley Town Documents* (Selden Society, vol. 14, 1900), pp. 28–30.

Orders as to the butchers' market: Also, it was ordered, in 1365, by Richard Holme ... keepers or governors of the town of Beverley, that no market should be held for selling meat anywhere in Beverley except in the ancient butchers' market and in Barleyholme, fair and market days only excepted.

Of meat kept or sold out of season: Also, it was ordered in the year last mentioned, that if a butcher sell, or put out for sale, meat maggoty or kept beyond the proper time, or dead from murrain, or carrion, for every time any of them has been duly convicted of any of the crimes or offences aforesaid, he should pay, without remedy, to the community 6 shillings 8 pence.

Of blood or any tainted matter placed in the streets: Also, it was ordered by the community that if a butcher or any of his men put offal, blood, or any tainted thing in the high streets or Walkerbeck, or any other place except where they have been appointed by the community, everyone so offending is to pay to the community 40 pence.

Of the custody of butchers' dogs: Also, because of diverse complaints made about butchers' dogs it was ordered in 1367, by the keepers of the town of Beverley, that if any butcher's dog be found in the road without a keeper, or if he bite a stranger's pig or dog, he whose dog commits the offence should pay to the community 40 pence.

Of meat for sale: Also, proclamation was made in the lord archbishop's court on Monday, St. Mary Magdalen's day [22 July] 1370, that every butcher was to sell meat killed by himself in his own shop, and not to send it to another butcher to sell, under penalty of forfeiting the same.

Of the same: Also, that every butcher must sell his meat within four days from the time of killing, or on the fourth day put it in salt, under the same penalty [of forfeiture].

Of the market of butchers and fishmongers: Also, that town butchers stand at one end of the lord's market to be chosen by them, and strange [i.e., from outside the town] butchers at the other end; so that the fish market may be between them on market day; so that the butchers do not intermeddle with each other.

On 4 May, 1409, it was ordered that no cook was to buy fish in the market, or poultry at the cross, before 8 a.m. for the future, under penalty of 3 shillings 4 pence, to be paid to the community; and on fair-days they may buy earlier, but moderately so, under the same penalty.

Questions: What specific problems were these ordinances meant to address? Why were there such strict regulations about where and when meat and fish could be sold?

54. SHOPPING IN THE LONDON MARKETS

This poem is attributed to John Lydgate, a Benedictine monk and disciple of Chaucer. It gives us some idea of the sights, sounds, and people in the London market places, as experienced by a visitor bewildered by what he saw and heard. The poem mentions several of the city's many market-places, including Cheapside, a bustling market street in central London, Eastcheap to the south, and Cornhill, a street to the west of Cheapside.

Source: trans. N.H. Nicholas, "London Lickpenny," in *A Chronicle of London* (London: Richard Taylor, 1827), pp. 265–67, abridged.

Then unto London I did me hie [go];
    Of all the land it beareth the prize.
'Hot peascods,' one began to cry;
    'Strawberries ripe', others coaxingly advise.
    One bade me come near and buy some spice;
Pepper and saffron they gan [began to] me bid [offer me].
But for lack of money I might not be sped [succeed].
Then to Cheapside I went on,
    Where much people I saw for to stand.
One offered me velvet, silk, and lawn;
    Another he taketh me by the hand,
    'Here is Paris thread, the finest in the land.'
I never was used to such things indeed,
And wanting money, I might not spend.
Then went I forth by London Stone,
    Throughout all Canwick Street;

Drapers much cloth me offered anon.
    Then met I one, cried, 'Hot sheep's feet.'
    One cried, 'Mackerel'; 'Rushes green,' another gan greet.
One bade me buy a hood to cover my head;
But for want of money I might not be sped.
Then I hied me into Eastcheap;
    One cried, 'Ribs of beef and many a pie!'
Pewter pots they clattered on a heap;
    There was harp, pipe and minstrelsy.
    'Yea, by Cock !' 'Nay, by Cock!' some began to cry;
Some sang of Jenken and Julian for their mead,
But for lack of money I might not speed.
    Then into Cornhill I took my road,
    Where was much stolen goods among;
I saw where hung my own hood,
    That I had lost among the throng;
    To buy my own hood I thought it wrong,
I knew it well as I did my creed;
But for lack of money I could not speed.

Questions: What variety of goods could be found in the different London markets, and did the different markets specialize in certain items? What picture does the poem give of the appearance and sounds of the open-air markets, and of the behavior and honesty of the sellers?

55. LETTER FROM THE GENOA BRANCH TO THE HOME OFFICE OF THE DATINI COMPANY, 1393

Towns were the centers of international trade and banking in medieval Europe, particularly the cities of northern Italy. The wealthy merchant of Prato—Francesco Datini—was the head of a trading company that had branches all over the Mediterranean region. He and his partners and employees kept in touch by letters such as this one sent to Francesco, which is one of thousands preserved in the Datini archives in Prato, a small Tuscan town near Florence. The letter was written by Piero Benintendi, the head of the branch in Genoa, a seaport in northern Italy and near Provence in southern France.

Source: trans. R.S. Lopez and I.W. Raymond, *Medieval Trade in the Mediterranean World* (New York: Columbia University Press, 1955), pp. 400–03.

Genoa, May 23, 1393

We have written you in these days all that was needed; and the last was on the 21st [of May], and in it we told you all that was needed; [we assume] you will have received it and answered it. And then, today, we have three letters of yours, written on the 12th, 15th, and 17th [of May], and we answer by this letter what is needed.

And before we tell you anything else, this morning Lorenzo, son of Ser Niccolò, arrived here safely, praise to God [he had been sent by Datini to learn the trade in Genoa]. We shall give him a good start and treat him as one of our own; and we need say nothing further about it. Neither our people at Pisa nor those at Florence had ever told us that he had left from there, and we had no notice from them except from you; and in Pisa he stayed about eight days; and of this too, they should have informed us.

You will have received the cloth from Pisa, and you and Monna Margherita [Datini's wife] ought to be very pleased with it. We are awaiting an answer from you to learn how [well] you think we have served you—which we hope we have. We are informed of the arrival of Tieri [of the Avignon branch] there, and that in a few days from now you will send him away on a journey to Provence. We have told you that the ship of Giovanni Grisolfi is here; he says he will leave on June 4, although we think it will be the middle of June before he leaves. If you think that he [Tieri], the wife of Maestro Naddino [a physician from Prato at the papal court], or Priore [a merchant from Prato] should sail on that ship, you ought to press them to leave from there as soon as possible, else they will not be able to sail on the ship or on the new *panfano* [a small galley] of Steve Miquel, which is awaited from day to day at Pisa and will return to Provence unless it undertakes the voyage to Catalonia. We shall keep you informed of everything; then you will decide whatever you want to do about it.

We were informed that you have had a test of the woad [a dyestuff] made. We supposed you had it tested by Niccolò [Datini's associate in the dyeing workshop in Prato], and you have informed us about results. We have sent to Pisa four sacks of another lot and told them to send two sacks to you; therefore you have this also tested at once and inform us.

You have been told the reason why Luca [the chief partner of Datini in Spain] has not left for Valencia. He will leave as soon as possible. It is very serious that there is no answer as yet from Catalonia about later developments. May God send us the best news, and may the news be peace between the two peoples and likewise among all Christians. Should there be anything new, you will learn it.

In the matter of the papers and other things that are in Savona to be sent to Catalonia, we shall use such means as seem the best to us. We shall send everything by the first ship that leaves. May God keep everything safe. You will learn the later developments in this matter.

Of the wool you have with you, we agree that you should do with it whatever can be done to close it out. Hold it there: it is impossible that it will not receive a better offer there.

We are glad that you have been informed of what we told you about the lambskins sold out here, ours and those of the people of Pisa. And there is nothing else to add. Everything was done for our and their good.

You received the oranges; we are glad.

We are informed about the little slave girl you say you personally need, and about her features and age, and for what you want her. *We are informed.* We shall see if there is anyone we consider suitable and we shall get her, although at present we are badly supplied here; nevertheless so far as we are able you shall have one.

We sent a letter to Nofri [a Florentine wool worker]. We heard that he left for Prato a few days ago. About that we have spoken at length in letters of Andrea and our own, and likewise you will be fully informed by him verbally, so that there is nothing further to say about it. As yet the consuls and councillors of the guild have not met to establish what they want him to pay in order to exercise the craft. When they meet, they will do it, and you will know the developments.

From [our] people of Florence you will have been informed of the news that came yesterday from Marseille, for we told them to inform you because at that time we could not write to you ourselves. As you will have heard from them, the three ships of the corsair [privateer] of Spain and likewise two Catalan ones were at Marseille, close to the chain of the harbor, armed and fully ready to defend themselves against anyone [here follows a description of sea warfare against pirates].

We have heard later that letters have now arrived from Catalonia. It is said that the Genoese who were in Catalonia have all been seized with their goods. We think that the affair will have a good ending, so that there will be no war.

But before a ship goes from here or there to here, we think it will take a long time, because the Catalans will want to see their own people released and what they claim returned, and likewise the Genoese will want their fellow Genoese released; and, as we are telling you, matters will perhaps take a longer time than we should like....

I am informed about the little slave girl you want, and about the age and everything. And it seems to me that for the time being you could not be well served because for a long time none has come from Romania, and at present anyone who has any, keeps them. Despite this I am still trying to find you one, and I have others trying so far as possible, so that you may be served. I am telling you what we are doing—but for the time being I have little hope to succeed. Whenever ships come from Romania, they should carry some [slave girls] but keep in mind that little slave girls are as expensive as the grown ones, and there will be none that does not cost 50 to 60 florins if we want one of any value. If we find one, we shall do our best.

We have nothing further to say in this letter. May God protect you....

Questions: What commercial, transport, political, and personnel problems faced these urban trading companies which did business abroad in other cities, and how did they adjust to these problems? What goods does the company deal in?

56. RESTORING PROSPERITY TO THE PORT TOWN OF BORDEAUX, c. 1465

The Hundred Years War (1337–1453) between England and France finally ended in victory for the French, who regained territory—such as the wine region around the city of Bordeaux—held for centuries by the English. The economy of France was severely injured by the war, however, since most fighting occurred largely on French soil. This memorandum addressed to King Louis XI of France was written by Regnault Giraud, who argues that the port of Bordeaux needs to be opened immediately to English trade in order to restore prosperity to the city and its region.

Source: trans. C.T. Allmand, *Society at War: The Experience of England and France During the Hundred Years War* (New York: Harper & Row Publishers, Inc, 1973), pp. 182–83.

The city of Bordeaux is one of the large and well-populated cities of this kingdom, situated on the river Gironde: the distance between the town and the place where the river enters the sea is about 26 leagues or so. The river takes sea ships with keels, and of any size, into the city, into the harbor which is called La Lune, which is an excellent thing: one should favor a river which carries sea-going ships so deep into the land.

Item, what are its uses? We may compare it to the stomach of a person which receives meat which is offered to it, and then distributes it to the various members. Thus the said town receives ships and merchandise from all parts and coming from all kingdoms; then it distributes them to many members and to many [outside] places, such as the kingdoms of Spain, Navarre, and Aragon, and elsewhere to the lands of my lords of Armagnac, Foix, Beam, and Albret, as well as into the Languedoc and elsewhere, as these members demand it. Thus you may see the situation of Bordeaux, and how the said city is useful.

Item, the second question is, how to make it as fine and rich as it can be. It can be done through the island of England, and this is how. The island of England is a large and rich kingdom which produces much merchandise, such as fine wools (out of which they make much cloth), lead, tin, metal, coals of different kinds and other goods. They also have many ships and about twice a year, namely about All Saints' Day [1 November] and in March, the said English come, 100, 120, or 200 ships at a time, carrying the aforementioned goods, and they come to cast anchor at Bordeaux.

Item, when the ships have come from the above-mentioned countries, merchants bring money to buy their goods; and the English, too, bring gold and silver ... and they convert these into the wines of Gascony; and then all go back to their own country. And in this way the said gold and silver, in the above manner, remain in the said Bordeaux, and [consequently] in this country.

Item, the English leave the goods which they cannot immediately sell with people in Bordeaux, so as to have them sold; and these people make a great profit, for the people from the above-mentioned regions often come to seek and then buy this merchandise. Thus trade is maintained in the town by the fact that people come there. For this reason, it seems that without the relationship with, and the goods of, the kingdom of England, Bordeaux cannot be Bordeaux, for there would be no meeting place nor any congregation of merchants....

Item, as the philosophers say, it is very sensible to extract money from the hands of the enemy by subtle methods; this can be done if the king allows the said English to come for the sake of having the luxury wines of Gascony; for they will bring gold in quantity as well as goods from their country, which could be valued at 100,000 nobles [a noble was a gold English coin worth 6 shillings 8 pence] and perhaps more. This would bring much profit to the king and his kingdom.

Item, the said goods will be dispersed into the kingdoms and regions aforementioned, which will bring in much gold and silver, all of which will remain within the lordship of the king. You should know that the king has great interest that his subjects be rich, so that they may help him at the time and in the manner which they are called upon.

And if you say that many merchants, other than English, can come there, Flemings and Normans, for instance, I reply that there is very little trade with these places compared with the English trade which is accustomed to come to Bordeaux. And even if they gave the wine away at Bordeaux for nothing, the above-mentioned countries have not enough ships to carry half the wine which is produced....

Questions: What do these arguments tell us about the relationship between a port town and its hinterland? And about the reliance of port towns on overseas trading partners? And about a king's attitude toward the role of port towns in the accumulation of wealth and economic vigor?

57. REGULATION OF TRADE BY
A MERCHANT GUILD, 1257–73

The merchants of Leicester were granted a guild by the lord of the town early in the twelfth century. In many towns, the right to possess a merchant guild was one of the provisions of the early charters granted to burgesses by their lords. There was usually a close connection between the merchant guild and civic leadership since the merchants were the wealthiest and most powerful men in town. To defend their commercial interests, the merchant guild developed an internal organizational structure that in Leicester included officers and a court, called the morgenspreche *or "morning-talk," to adjudicate disputes. These court cases offer insight into the commercial interests and jurisdictional claims of powerful merchant guilds.*

Source: trans. M. Bateson, *Records of the Borough of Leicester*, vol. I (London: C.J. Clay and Sons, 1899), pp. 72–73, 79–80, 114, 123–24.

6 February, 1257. William of Barkby of Newton was found buying six woolfells in Leicester: he said he was in the Guild Merchant, and this was attested by others; and the fells were attached [arrested], and shown in the morning-talks, William being present there. And it was adjudged by the community of the guild, that, though he was in the guild, he cannot practice a guild trade unless he returns to Leicester and lives there and bears the burden and answer with others of the guild. And because he bought these fells unlawfully and against guild liberties and customs, he pledged mercy and the fells remain in the custody of Richard the reeve.

1 March, 1258. Memorandum that on Friday ... in full morning-talk, it was provided and agreed by all the community of the guild that all merchants of Leicester, who at the time of the next Stamford fair come to Stamford with cloth or wool or with fells, should have this merchandise carried to the shops, where the merchandise of Leicester is usually kept, and there they should have the merchandise

unloaded and opened in the presence of neighbors and they should keep the [merchandise] there (except the fells) for at least a day and a night, and if they want to move this merchandise elsewhere, they will be allowed to carry it well and without hindrance wherever they want; and each of them shall give for each cloth 3 pence, and for each sack of wool 6 pence, and for a hundred fells 3 pence. So that if any of them should contravene this in any way he shall fully discharge one shop [i.e., pay the whole rent on the shop].

29 November, 1273. Be it known that if any of the community or liberty of Leicester go to Chester or Shrewsbury or any other market town to carry on trade and they are distrained for the debt of any neighbor and not for his own debt, he may come home and point this out to the bailiffs of the lord earl [the lord of Leicester], and the bailiffs will give warning to the debtor once, and again, and if the debtor does not make delivery of the distrained goods of his neighbor, distrained on his account, let the bailiffs close his [the debtor's] house, whoever he may be, with bolts, and forbid him entry until he delivers his neighbors' [distrained goods] and pays his debt; and this was granted and [held] for judgment by Sir Ralph of Hengham, Walter of Hopton, judges of the lord king Edward in the hall of the earl of Leicester at the castle, on Wednesday....

c. 1260, Portmanmoot Court. Whereas at one time foreign [non-Leicester] merchants went out into the county of Leicester and bought wool in places where they should not, and caused wool to be carried to Leicester, and were convicted because they greatly offended against the community, for which they were heavily amerced and punished. Therefore, all the community assented and consented, chiefly at the petition of the merchants, that these places where they were able to buy without hindrance should be written down and publicly announced, and these places are: Melton, Loughborough, Breedon, Hinckley, Bosworth, Lutterworth, Lilbourne, and afterwards they are announced. Then it was determined that if any strange [non-Leicester] merchant should henceforth ever be convicted of committing such a trespass to the prejudice of the lord earl and against the provision of the community, he should be more heavily amerced than before the determination and provision of the agreement was settled.

Questions: What types of protection and privilege did membership in the guild merchant bring? These court disputes all deal with merchants or trading outside of Leicester; what does this tell us about the urban economy?

58. CRAFT GUILD REGULATIONS: THE SHEARERS OF ARRAS, 1236

The shearers were responsible for trimming—very carefully, with large shears or a blade—the nap raised on fine woolen cloth after undergoing fulling to felt the woven threads together. The shearers were one of the textile guilds or fraternities in the highly urbanized region of Flanders and Artois in the Low Countries, which were the largest manufacturers of woolen cloth in medieval Europe. The crafts of weaving, fulling, dyeing, and shearing, however, tended to be under the control of the merchant-drapers, who provided much of the capital to fund these different manufacturing stages and sold the finished product, thus reaping the lion's share of the profits. These regulations show the internal hierarchy and organization of the guild, as well as the efforts made to control quality, wages, and other conditions of work. Other craft guild regulations are in docs. 59, 89, and 141.

Source: trans. R.C. Cave and H.H. Coulson, *A Source Book for Medieval Economic History* (Milwaukee: The Bruce Publishing Co., 1936; reprint New York: Biblio and Tannen, 1965), pp. 250–52.

This is the first ordinance of the shearers, who were founded in the name of the Fraternity of God and St. Julian, with the agreement and consent of those who were at the time mayor and aldermen.

1. Whoever would engage in the trade of a shearer shall be in the Confraternity of St. Julian, and shall pay all the dues, and observe the decrees made by the brethren.

2. That is to say: first, that whoever is a master shearer shall pay 14 shillings to the Fraternity. And there may not be more than one master shearer working in a house. And he shall be a master shearer all the year, and have arms [be militarily prepared] for the need of the town.

3. And a journeyman shall pay 4 shillings to the Fraternity.

4. And whoever wishes to learn the trade shall be the son of a burgess or he shall live in the town for a year and a day; and he shall serve three years to learn this trade.

5. And he shall give to his master 3 *muids* for his bed and board; and he ought to bring the first *muid* to his master at the beginning of his apprenticeship, and another *muid* a year from that day, and a third *muid* at the beginning of the third year.

6.   And no one may be a master of this trade of shearer if he has not lived a year and a day in the town, in order that it may be known whether or not he comes from a good place.

8.   And if masters, or journeymen, or apprentices, stay in the town to do their work they owe 40 shillings, if they have done this without the permission of the aldermen of Arras.

9.   And whoever does work on Saturday afternoon, or on the Eve of the Feast of Our Lady, or after Vespers on the Eve of the Feast of St. Julian, and completes the day by working, shall pay, if he be a master, 12 pence, and if he be a journeyman, 5 pence. And whoever works in the four days of Christmas, or in the eight days of Easter, or in the eight days of Pentecost, owes 5 shillings.

11. And an apprentice owes to the Fraternity for his apprenticeship 5 shillings.

12. And whoever puts the cloth of another in pledge shall pay 10 shillings to the Fraternity, and he shall not work at the trade for a year and a day.

13. And whoever does work in defiance of the mayor and aldermen shall pay 5 shillings.

14. And if a master flee outside the town with another's cloth and a journeyman aids him to flee, if he does not tell the mayor and aldermen, the master shall pay 20 shillings to the Fraternity and the journeyman 10 shillings: and they shall not work at the trade for a year and a day.

16. And those who are fed at the expense of the city shall be put to work first. And he who slights them for strangers owes 5 shillings: but if the stranger be put to work he cannot be removed as long as the master wishes to keep him…. And when a master does not work hard he pays 5 shillings, and a journeyman 2 shillings.

18. And after the half year the mayor and aldermen shall fix such wages as he ought to have.

19. And whatever journeyman shall carry off from his master, or from his fellow man, or from a burgess of the town, anything for which complaint is made, shall pay 5 shillings.

20. And whoever maligns the mayor and aldermen, that is while on the business of the Fraternity, shall pay 5 shillings.

22. And no one who is not a shearer may be a master, in order that the work may be done in the best way, and no draper may cut cloth in his house, if it be not his own work, except he be a shearer, because drapers cannot be masters.

23. And if a draper or a merchant has work to do in his house, he may take such workmen as he wishes into his house, so long as the work be done in his house. And he who infringes this shall give 5 shillings to the Fraternity.

25. And each master ought to have his arms when he is summoned. And if he has not he should pay 20 shillings.

26–30. [Other regulations on military duties in the civic milita.]

31. And whatever brother has finished cloth in his house and does not inform the mayor and aldermen, and it be found in his house, whatever he may say, shall forfeit 10 shillings to the Fraternity.

32. And if a master does not give a journeyman such wage as is his due, then he shall pay 5 shillings.

33. And he who overlooks the forfeits of his Fraternity, if he does not wish to pay them when the mayor and aldermen summon him either for the army or the district, then he owes 10 shillings, and he shall not work at the trade until he has paid. Every forfeit of 5 shillings, and the fines which the mayor and aldermen command, shall be written down. All the fines of the Fraternity ought to go for the purchase of arms and for the needs of the Fraternity.

34. And whatever brother of this Fraternity shall betray his confrère for others shall not work at the trade for a year and a day.

35. And whatever brother of this Fraternity perjures himself shall not work at the trade for forty days. And if he does so he shall pay 10 shillings if he be a master, but if he be a journeyman let him pay 5 shillings.

36. And should a master of this Fraternity die and leave a male heir he may learn the trade anywhere where there is no apprentice.

37. And no apprentice shall cut to the selvage [edge of the cloth, often finished so it would not unravel] for half a year, and this is to obtain good work. And no master or journeyman may cut by himself because no one can measure cloth well alone. And whoever infringes this rule shall pay 5 shillings to the Fraternity for each offense.

38. Any brother whatsoever who lays hands on, or does wrong to, the mayor and aldermen of this Fraternity, as long as they work for the city and the Fraternity, shall not work at his trade in the city for a year and a day.

39. And the brethren of this Fraternity, and the mayor and aldermen shall not forbid any brother to give law and do right and justice to all when it is demanded of them, or when some one claims from them. And he who infringes this shall not have the help of the aldermen at all.

Questions: What obligations did each shearer have to the town, to the guild, and to his fellow guildsmen? What can we learn about the guild's internal hierarchy? What qualifications did a shearer need to be a master in the guild?

59. REGULATIONS OF THE GUILD OF SKINNERS IN COPENHAGEN

These articles governed the guild of the skinners (who flayed skins from sheep and other small animals and then preserved and assembled them for use in clothing and dress accessories) and furriers (who cured and sewed together heavier furs from such animals as squirrels, beavers, and mink to make furred garments). Given to the guild by King Christopher III of Denmark in the 1440s, these articles were confirmed in 1495 by King Hans of Denmark. In specifying rules about funerals, governance, manufacturing standards, behavior at meetings, and religious activities, the articles show the wide range of functions that craft guilds often fulfilled. Particularly interesting here is the focus on conviviality and socializing, as seen in the references to drinking and fines paid in beer. The wax collected as fines was probably made into high-quality candles for the fraternity's religious services and meetings. One Danish groat was equal to 3 shillings; the mark referred to was probably the Lübeck mark, which at this time was probably worth about 27 Danish shillings.

Source: trans. M. Chase, from *Danmarks gilde-og lavsskraaer fra Middelalderen*, 2 vols., ed. C. Nyrop (Copenhagen: Selskabet for Udgivelse af Kilder til dansk Historie, Gad, 1895–1904; repr., 1977), II, pp. 239–41.

We, Hans, by the grace of God the king of Denmark, Norway, the Wends, and the Goths, designated king of Sweden, duke of Schleswig, Holstein, Storman, and Ditmarschen, count of Oldenburg and Delmenhorst, make known to all that we, by our special favor and grace, have now confirmed and ratified and with this our open letter do confirm and ratify in word and article these named freedoms and privileges, which they may hold with perpetual authority, which our forefather Christopher, king of Denmark, granted and gave previously to the guild brothers in the skinners' trade here in Copenhagen, namely, that:

1. First, that no furrier or skinner shall work here in Copenhagen unless he satisfies the requirements for membership.

2. As soon as a brother in their guild dies, two brothers shall watch over the corpse, and all the brothers and sisters shall contribute to that, and no one shall go away before it is buried. Whosoever goes against this shall give 2 groats to the guild, or else be held in arrears.

3. All those who aspire to this office, men or apprentices, shall perform two pieces of work or labor in the alderman's workshop or place of business: a woman's leather kirtle [tunic] and a swaddle [a long garment]. If they perform the work flawlessly, they shall be accepted as full guild brothers; if they do not, then they shall go their way until they can improve their skills.

4. Before their admission [they must give] 10 shillings, and a meal worth about 6 shilling groats [18 shillings], and 4 marks worth of wax, at the behest of the guild master, to acknowledge their service.

5. No one shall do poor workmanship on a woman's leather kirtle [tunic]; whoever should do this must pay a tun of beer for each offence.

6. If anyone shall hire another man's apprentice before his appointed day [when he completes his apprenticeship], he pays a tun of beer.

7. An apprentice shall give a half tun of beer and 2 marks worth of wax.

8. He, whom the alderman makes the keeper of the candles for the chandelier in the church, shall pay one mark worth of wax as often as he neglects to light the candles.

9. Those who do not come to a meeting on time when they have been summoned, shall pay a shilling.

10. When they drink in their company, if it happens that someone offends another by his speech, he shall pay a tun of beer, whether or not the wronged party complains to the bailiff or the mayor before he complains to the alderman.

11. He who drinks until he is so drunk that he vomits, shall pay a half tun of beer and one mark worth of wax.

12. No one shall invite guests unless they are worthy of the company and inform the alderman who they are.

13. He who doesn't give the alderman silence, as soon as he bangs on the table for attention, shall pay a mark worth of wax.

14. No one shall hold a meeting of guild brothers, unless there is a *rademan* [leader] present, who can advise them about the rules of order.

15. The alderman may have two guests and a *stoellsbroder* [warden's assistant] one guest.

16. He who does something against his honor shall be as closely associated with the profession as the guild members desire.

We confirm and execute in perpetuity these [services], which the guild brothers have established and now hold in the Greyfriars' convent in Copenhagen to the praise and honor of almighty God, the Virgin Mary, and his worthy saints, to the eternal benefit and beatitude of the souls of the guild brothers and all Christians.

All under our allegiance and grace whomsoever they might be, and especially our bailiffs and officials, are forbidden to hinder, to allow to hinder, or in any way wrong the guild brothers in this. Given at our castle in Copenhagen the first Tuesday after Ascension Day [2 June], the 1495th year after the birth of God under our privy seal.

Questions: Why would skinners and furriers wish to join this guild? What activities did the guild members engage in as a group or fraternity? What were the king's interests in sanctioning such codes?

60. GUILD APPRENTICESHIPS

Most apprentices were teenagers who were apprenticed to a master by their parents. The terms of the contract—the length of the apprenticeship, the fee paid by the parents, the remuneration (in wages or room and board) paid by the master, and the conditions under which the apprenticeship could be terminated—varied greatly from town to town and from craft to craft. Early apprenticeship contracts tended to be terse, but by the late fourteenth century the conditions of employment were spelled out in much greater detail, as they are in (C) below. For other references to apprentices, see docs. 59 and 89.

Source: (A) trans. R.C. Cave and H.H. Coulson, *A Source Book for Medieval Economic History* (Milwaukee: The Bruce Publishing Co., 1936; reprint New York: Biblio and Tanne, 1965), p. 145; (B) trans. M. Kowaleski, from *Receuil de documents relatifs à l'histoire de l'industrie drapière en Flandre*, eds. G. Espinas and H. Pirenne, partie 1, tome 1 (Brussels: Académie Royale de Belgique, 1906), pp. 121–22; (C) Corporation of London Record Office, Misc. MSS 1863, revised by S. Hovland and M. Kowaleski; (D) trans. A.E. Bland, P.A. Brown, and R.H. Tawney, *English Economic History: Select Documents* (London: G. Bell and Sons, 1914), p. 148, revised.

(A) Apprenticeship to a Money-Changer in Marseille, 1248

May 12 ... 1248. I, John of St. Maximin, lawyer, place with you John Cordier, money-changer, my son William Deodat, as an apprentice, so that you may teach and instruct him in the art of money-changing, for two complete and continuous years from this date. I promise by this agreement that I will take care that my son will serve his apprenticeship with you and that he will be faithful and honest in all his dealings for the whole of the said period, and that he will not depart from you nor take anything from you. And if it should happen, which God forbid, that William should cause you any loss, I promise to reimburse you by this agreement, believing in your unsupported word, etc. Also I promise to give by this agreement for the expenses of William food, that is bread and wine and meat, 14 *heminae* [about 30 gallons worth] of good grain and 50 shillings of the money now current in Marseille, at your request, and to provide the said William with clothing and necessaries, pledging all my goods, etc.; renouncing the benefit of all laws, etc.

To this I, the said John Cordier, receive the said William as a pupil and promise you, John St. Maximin, to teach your son well and faithfully the business of money-changing, etc., pledging all my goods, etc.; renouncing the benefit of all laws, etc. Witnesses, etc.

(B) Apprenticeship to a Weaver in Arras, Late Thirteenth Century

Know all current and future *échevins* [chief civic officials] that Ouede Ferconne pledges her son Michael to Matthew Haimart on security of her house and of her person and of all her goods, and the share that Michael will have in them, so that Matthew Haimart will teach him to weave for four years. And he [Matthew] should lodge him and teach him his métier there without board. And if within two years Michael should default [on this agreement], she must restore him to [Matthew], and Ouede Ferconne, his mother, guarantees this on the security of her person and her goods. And if she wishes to purchase his freedom for the last two years, she may do it by paying 33 shillings and will pledge all that has been stated. And if he does not free himself of the last two years, he should return and Ouede, his mother, pledges this with her person and with all of her goods. And Ouede pledges that if Matthew Haimart suffers either loss or damages because of Michael her son, she must restore to him all the costs and damages on the security of herself and of all her goods, if Michael should do wrong.

(C) A Female Apprentice, 1392

This indenture witnesses that John Nougle of London, haberdasher, has put Katherine Nougle, his sister, as apprentice to Avice Wodeford, silkthrowster of London, to learn her art and to dwell with her and serve her after the manner of an apprentice from the feast of Pentecost in the fifteenth year of the reign of King Richard II [2 June 1392] until the end of seven years thence next following and fully complete. During which term Katherine shall serve Avice as her lady and mistress in all things lawful and honest, well and faithfully, courteously and diligently to her power everywhere, keep her secrets, and gladly do everywhere her lawful and honest commandments. She shall not do damage to her said mistress within the said term, nor see to be done by others to the value of 12 pence or more per annum, but to her power shall impede the same or forthwith give warning thereof to her mistress. She shall not waste inordinately the goods of her mistress nor lend them to anyone without her order or special commandment. She shall not commit fornication or adultery within the house of her mistress or without during the said term nor play any unlawful or unseemly games whereby her mistress might suffer any loss. She shall not customarily frequent a tavern except to do the business of her mistress there, nor shall she contract matrimony with any man during the said term except with the assent, will, and counsel of the said John and of Thomas Nougle, citizen and tailor of London, uncle of the apprentice. She shall not withdraw unlawfully from the service of her mistress, except for reason of matrimony during the said term, nor absent herself by day or by night. She shall not buy or sell with her own money or other's during the said term without the licence and will of her mistress, nor knowingly keep any secret that may be to the loss or prejudice of her mistress. But she should well and faithfully, honestly and obediently bear and hold herself both in words and deeds towards her mistress and all hers as a good and faithful apprentice ought to bear and hold herself according to the usage and custom of the city of London, during all the said term. And Avice shall diligently teach, treat and instruct Katherine her apprentice in her art which she uses by the best and most excellent means that she knows, or cause to be instructed by others, punishing in due manner. And also she shall find the same apprentice sufficient victuals and apparel, linen and wool caps, shoes and lodging, and all other necessaries during all the said term as is fitting to be found for such an apprentice of that art according to the custom of the said city. And for the fidelity of the said apprentice and that all and singular, the aforesaid covenants on her part shall be well and faithfully kept, fulfilled, and observed in all things as is aforesaid. Adam Byell, citizen and tailor of London, shall be pledge and mainpernor [surety], binding himself, his heirs and executors for the said apprentice, by those present, and the said apprentice binds herself firmly by all her goods present and future wherever they may be found. In witness whereof the aforesaid parties together with the forenamed pledge to these indentures interchangeably have put their seals.

(D) A Runaway Apprentice, c. 1425

To the most reverend father in God and his most gracious lord, the bishop of Winchester, chancellor of England. William Beverley of London humbly petitions that whereas William Batyngham has been arrested and detained in prison in Salisbury at the petitioner's suit because he was his apprentice and departed from his service here in London, and has been the whole time since ... wandering in different towns, such as Winchester, Bristol, and elsewhere, so that the said petitioner could not find him until now of late suddenly; and because his suit on this matter cannot be determined in Salisbury, for that the retaining and departing did not take place within that town: please it your most gracious discretion to grant to the said petitioner a writ directed to the mayor, bailiffs, and keeper of the jail there and to each of them to have the body of the said William Batyngham with such a clause "by whatsoever name he be known," before you at a certain day to be limited by you, considering that he has no other remedy, and that for God and in work of charity.

Questions: What were the different terms under which apprentices agreed to serve their masters? What terms seem to be common to all apprenticeship contracts? What problems might occur during apprenticeships? What most concerned masters and mistresses about apprentices?

61. DISPUTE BETWEEN THE MASTER SADDLERS OF LONDON AND THEIR JOURNEYMEN, 1396

The efforts of guild masters to limit membership and monopolize the craft for their own profit stimulated resentment among journeymen, those who had completed apprenticeships but had not risen to the position of master for lack of capital to open their own shop. To defend their interests, journeymen tried to form their own associations, but they were often stymied in these efforts by the masters and their allies in town government, who wanted to keep the status quo.

Source: trans. H.T. Riley, *Memorials of London and London Life* (London: Longmans, Green, and Co., 1868), pp. 542–44, revised.

Whereas there had arisen no small dissension and strife between the masters of the trade of saddlers of London, and the servingmen, called *yomen*, in that trade because the servingmen, against the consent and without leave of their masters, were all accustomed to array themselves in a new and similar garb once a year, and often times held meetings at Stratford and elsewhere outside the liberty of the said city, as well as in different places within the city. Because of this, many inconveniences and perils ensued to the trade and also very many losses might happen to them in the future, unless some quick and speedy remedy could be found by the rulers of the city. Therefore, the masters of the trade on the 10th day of the month of July, in the 20th year, etc., made grievous complaint about this to the excellent men, William More, Mayor, and the aldermen of the city, urgently entreating that, for these reasons, they would deign to send for Gilbert Dustone, William Gylowe, John Clay, John Hiltone, William Berigge, and Nicholas Mason, the then governors of these servingmen to appear before them on the 12th day of July.

And on the 10th day of July, an order was given to John Parker, sergeant of the

Chamber, to give notice to the same persons to be here on the 12th day of July, etc. The governors of the servingmen appeared, and, being interrogated as to these matters said that from time out of mind the servingmen of this trade had had a certain fraternity among themselves, and had been accustomed to array themselves all in a similar garb once a year and, after meeting together at Stratford, on the Feast of the Assumption of the Blessed Virgin Mary to go to the Church of St. Vedast, in London to hear Mass on the same day, in honor of the glorious Virgin.

But the said masters of the trade asserted to the contrary of all this, and said that the fraternity, and the being so arrayed in like garb among the servingmen, dated from only thirteen years back, and even then had been lately discontinued, and that under a certain feigned color of sanctity, many of the servingmen in the trade had influenced the journeymen among them and had formed covins, with the object of raising their wages greatly in excess, to such an extent, namely, that whereas a master in the said trade could before have had a servingman or journeyman for 40 shillings or 5 marks yearly, and his board, now such a man would not agree with his master for less than 10 or 12 marks or even 10 pounds yearly to the great deterioration of the trade.

And further, that the servingmen, according to an ordinance made among themselves, would often cause the journeymen of the said masters to be summoned by a beadle, appointed by them, to attend at Vigils of the dead members of the said fraternity, and to make offerings for them on the morrow, under a certain penalty to be levied, whereby the said masters were very greatly aggrieved, and were injured by these absences of the journeymen leaving their labors and duties against their wishes.

For amending and allaying which grievances and dissensions, the mayor and aldermen commanded that six of the said servingmen should attend in the name of the whole of the alleged fraternity, and communicate with six or eight of the master saddlers, both parties to be here, before the said mayor and aldermen on the 19th day of July to report to the Court as to an agreement between them as ordered. And further, the mayor and aldermen strictly forbade the said servingmen in any manner to hold any meeting thereafter at Stratford or elsewhere outside the liberty of the said city on pain of forfeiture of all to our lord the king and to the said city.

On the 19th day of July, the masters as well as the governors of the servingmen came and presented to the mayor and aldermen a certain petition, in these words: "Gilbert Dustone, William Gylowe, John Clay, John Hiltone, William Berigge, and Nicholas Mason, do speak on behalf of all their fraternity and do beg of the Wardens of the Saddlers that they may have and use all the points which heretofore they have used."

When the petition had been read and heard, and the masters made their arguments to the mayor and aldermen, it was determined that the servingmen in the trade should in future be under the governance and rule of the masters of the trade, as the servingmen in other trades in the same city are accustomed to do and of right are bound to be; and that in future they should have no fraternity, meetings, or covins, or other unlawful things under a penalty, etc. And that the masters must properly treat and govern their serving men in the trade in such manner as the servingmen in other trades in the city have been accustomed to be properly treated and governed. And that if any servingmen should in future wish to make complaint to the mayor and aldermen, for the time being, as to any grievance unduly inflicted upon him by the masters, the mayor and aldermen would give to him his due and speedy reward of justice as to the same.

Questions: How did the journeymen show their solidarity? Why were the master saddlers so worried about this show of solidarity, and how did they go about eliminating this threat?

62. THE BAKERS OF COVENTRY STRIKE, 1484

In Coventry, the bakers so chafed at the regulations and fines imposed on them by the town government—which was anxious to ensure a steady and cheap supply of bread to the town—that they went on a strike by leaving town, thus threatening the urban food supply. They were not numerous enough, however, to go up against the power of the civic government, which fined them heavily for their temerity.

Source: modernized by M. Kowaleski, *The Coventry Leet Book*, vol. I, ed. M.D. Harris (Early English Text Society, original series, 134, 1907), pp. 518–19.

Memorandum that the mayor called before him on the 8th day of March after the feast of the Purification the craft of the bakers, that is to say John Smyth and John Bredon, then wardens of the Craft [and 9 others named], examined them about the constitutions of their Craft, which among other things the mayor found that they were allowed 2 shillings in the farthing [worth ¼ pence] coket loaf [that is, each loaf might be lighter by the weight of 24 pence, since the size of the loaf varied according to the price of grain], if they do not come into the market [to buy grain] and hurt the market [by competing with other consumers] etc., however much the price of wheat rose or decreased, which was thought uncertain. Therefore to ensure more certain prices, these bakers in the name of all the bakers agreed there and then that when the price of a quarter [8 bushels] of wheat is above 6 shillings 6 pence, they they are to have the allowance of 2 shillings in the half-penny coket loaf. And when the price of a quarter of wheat is under 6 shillings 6 pence, they they are to be allowed 2 shillings in the farthing coket loaf. And this allowance is to be had only because they should not come into the market [to buy grain].

Memorandum that in the month of December of that year, the bakers of the city in great number, riotously disposed, assembled them and unlawfully conferred, intending the reproach of the mayor, suddenly departed the city to go to Baginton, leaving the said city destitute of bread; whereupon not only strangers resorting to the said city and the inhabitants of the same were unvictualled, but also harming the said city and the said mayor and all its officers. For this riot, various bakers were indicted, as appears in a record of the city, etc. The bakers then coming to a right mind, resorted and came to the mayor and humbly submitted themselves to his correction. Whereupon they were committed to ward, and their fine assessed by the mayor and other justices of the peace within the said city at 20 pounds, of which sum 10 pounds was returned to them again etc., the other 10 pounds was received ... and they are to give surety to obey the mayor's orders and keep the assize for the future, or pay a fine of 20 shillings.

Questions: What action of the mayor upset the bakers, and what action did the bakers take to get their way? Why was the baker's strike unsuccessful? What does this incident tell us about the interests of the mayor and other members of the ruling elite?

63. GUILD RIVALRY IN FLORENCE, 1425

This extract from the deliberations of the powerful Lana guild (of woolen cloth merchants; see doc. 49) in Florence shows the competition between guilds for honor and respect and how far the Lana guild was willing to go to ensure that their contribution to a local oratory suitably reflected their status in the city. Bankers belonged to the Cambio guild and finishers of fine cloth to the Calimala guild. The Orsanmichele was a major charitable organization that distributed alms to the poor (doc. 106).

Source: trans. G. Brucker, *The Society of Renaissance Florence: A Documentary Study* (New York: Harper and Row Torchbooks, 1971), pp. 93–94.

The consuls [of the Lana guild], assembled together in the palace of the guild in sufficient numbers and in the accustomed manner for the exercise of their office ... have diligently considered the law approved by the captains of the Society of the Blessed Virgin Mary of Orsanmichele. This law decreed, in effect, that for the ornamentation of that oratory, each of the twenty-one guilds of the city of Florence ... in a place assigned to each of them by the captains of the Society, should construct ... a tabernacle, properly and carefully decorated, for the honor of the city and the beautification of the oratory. The consuls have considered that all of the guilds have finished their tabernacles, and that those constructed by the Calimala and Cambio guilds, and by other guilds, surpass in beauty and ornamentation that of the Lana guild. So it may truly be said that this does not redound to the honor of the Lana guild, particularly when one considers the magnificence of that guild which has always sought to be the master and the superior of the other guilds.

For the splendor and honor of the guild, the lord consuls desire to provide a remedy for this…. They decree … that through the month of August, the existing lord consuls and their successors in office, by authority of the present provisions, are to construct, fabricate, and remake a tabernacle and a statue of the blessed Stephen, protomartyr, protector and defender of the renowned Lana guild, in his honor and in reverence to God. They are to do this by whatever ways and means they choose, which will most honorably contribute to the splendor of the guild, so that this tabernacle will exceed, or at least equal, in beauty and decoration the more beautiful ones. In the construction of this tabernacle and statue, the lord consuls … may spend … up to 1,000 florins. And during this time, the lord consuls may commission that statue and tabernacle to the person or persons, and for that price or prices, and with whatever agreement and time or times which seem to them to be most useful for the guild….

Questions: What were the economic consequences of this guild rivalry? What does this tell us about the concerns of a rich and powerful guild like the Lana guild? How does the story of guild rivalry here compare to the plays sponsored by the guilds of York (docs. 119 and 120)?

CHAPTER FIVE

URBAN FINANCES, JURISDICTIONS, AND JUSTICE

Figure 5.1

A Forestaller and Regrator Placed in the Town Pillory

Forestallers intercepted goods (usually foodstuffs) early in the day and then marketed the goods in town at a higher price. Regrators bought goods legally available in the market early in the day, but resold them later when shortages drove the price up. Authorities forbade these retail practices because they believed they led to unreliable supplies, higher prices, and a loss of toll for the town. From an engraving in a manuscript of c. 1500, reproduced from G.G. Coulton, *Social Life in Britain From the Conquest to the Reformation* (Cambridge: Cambridge University Press, 1919), fig. 22, facing p. 323.

64. ACCOUNTS OF THE CITY OF SIENA

The public revenues of the Tuscan town of Siena were administered by a financial magistracy made up of a chancellor (at this time, usually a monk) and three or four provisores, who were all elected for terms of six months, the same term of office held by the podestà, who was usually an impartial nobleman from outside of Siena. They operated out of a building called the Biccherna, where the chancellor made payments in the presence of at least two of the provisores, whose consent was always noted by the notary who recorded the accounts. The Council of the Bell was the main representative council in the city, responsible for all important civic legislation and elected for terms of one year. This selection—which represents only a small portion of the six-month account—shows the types of expenses borne by a large Italian city during the mid-thirteenth century. The Sienese lira was not a coin, but a money of account; it was made up of 20 shillings or 240 pennies.

Source: trans. M. Kowaleski, frrom *Libri dell'entrata e dell'uscita del comune di Siena detti della Biccherna* (Rome, 1961), pp. 74–75, 116, 119–20, 121, 123–24, selections.

Expenses in the month of July [1257]

This is the book of expenses made by Ser Ugone, monk of St. Galgano [a local Cistercian monastery], chancellor of the commune of the Sienese, decreed and presented to the lord magistrates Guido Ranucci, Ugolino Filippo Paltoneri and Griffolo [di Jacomo] ... the three provisores of the commune of the Siennese ... for dealings and business of the commune, as is contained below, made during the time of Lord Uberto, once lord of the Robbacontis of Mandello, by the grace of God, podestà of the Sienese, for the last six months, in the year of the lord 1257.

First, 500 lire to Angelerio Guardadio, at the will of Tebaldo Renaldi, Forto Dietaiuti, Ugero Ancontani, Jacobo Ciamfale, Guido Saraceni and Bertoldo Ugeri, [officials] appointed to make the walls of the city, from the chancellor of the aforesaid officials, according to the practice of the Council of the Bell, decreed and presented by the lord magistrates Guido Ranuci, Ugolino Filippi, and Griffolo di Jacomo, the three provisores of the commune.

Also 800 lire to Angelerio at the will and order of the said officials, according to the practice of the Council of the Bell, decreed and presented by the [provisores].

[Then follow 8 more payments to Angelerio for 200, 100, 100, 25, 200, 100, 50, and 50 lire for the same.]

Also 2893 lire to the magistrates Scoto Dominichi, Palmerio Raionis, and Lord Filippo, their predecessors as the three provisores of the commune ... at the will of the General Council of the Bell, for furnishing the said levy by a public instrument made by the hand of Pandulfino Orlandi, notary ...

Also 200 lire to the same ... [previous magistrates], for their work of giving and paying for property located within the city and outside....

Also 1061 lire, 5 shillings and 10 pence to the same previous magistrates of the commune of Siena, for giving and paying the creditors of the commune of Siena, from whom a loan for the commune was taken....

Also 20 shillings to Arnolfo Dainelli, for an embassy of two days, which he made to Montalcino [a township Siena was trying to bring under its control] on the occasion of the *Camilliano* [perhaps a reference to a military campaign], according to the practice of the Council....

Also 50 shillings to Lord Sterpolo Comitis, also 50 shillings to Provenzano Ildibrandini, ambassadors, for completion of an embassy for five days, which they made to Sassoforte....

Also 20 shillings to Bartalomeo Ildibrandini, messenger of the Biccherna, for his fee and salary, to complete his fee for the months of July and August....

Also 24 shillings to Ricredoni, messenger of the captain [of the *popolo*], for a journey of twelve days that he made, on the order of the lord captain and the Rossi lords [who resided in the *contado*], per the commonalty of Siena, for seizing men on behalf of the captain, who were to have transported wheat into the city of Siena....

Also 40 shillings to Benardo, messenger of the Palace of the Podestà, for his fee for the whole months of July and August, according to the practice of the General Council of the Bell....

Expenses for the month of September

... Also 8 lire and 21 pence to Pepono, cloth-seller, for the price of 170½ *brachia* [a measure of c. ½ meter] of linen cloth purchased to line the sesters [a measure of about 8 bushels] in which flour is measured for the city of Siena....

Also 20 shillings to Cittadino, courier, for his salary and purchases for ten days of a journey that he made to St. Fiora and to St. Antimo with letters from the commune of Siena....

Also 14 shillings to Guiardello, courier, for his salary and purchases for a journey of seven days that he made to Perugia with letters from the commune of Siena....

Also 100 shillings to Guido Maizi, castellan of the castle of Montichiello [a fortified town] for the commune of Siena, for his fee and salary and wages for the whole month of September....

Also 40 shillings to Raffaiono Manentis and 40 shillings to Bonfiliolo Fioris, tower-keepers for the commune of Siena in the towers of the castle of Montichiello, for their wages for the whole month of September....

Also 30 shillings to Michele Pensati [and 30 shillings paid to six other men] members of the military brigade in the castle of Montichiello for the commune of Siena, for their wages for the whole month of September, according to the practice of the General Council of the Bell....

Also 40 shillings to Ranuccio Fondacci, 40 shillings to his son Venture, 40 shillings to Arnolfo Bondii, and 40 shillings to Becco Iuncte, tower-keepers for the commune of Siena in Montelatrone, for their wages for the whole month of September....

Also 6 lire to Chiavellino Gazani, castellan [an important military official] of Prato for the commune, for his wages for the whole month of September, according to the practice of the General Council of the Bell....

Also 7 lire to Lord Bonsignroi, 6 lire to Lord Orlando Prioris, 6 lire to Lord Lantelmo, judges and advocates selected to defend the law of the *popolo* and commune of Siena, according to the practice of the General Council of the Bell and the *popolo*, for their fee and salary for the last six months, in the time of Lord Uberti de Mandello, podestà of Siena....

Also 100 lire and 10 shillings to Uberto, podestà of Siena, for his fee and salary for the month of September, that Iannes, his steward, had given to him in wheat and barley....

Also 7 lire and 10 shillings to Boscolo Albertini Boscoli, appointed to supervise the *divieto* [prohibition of food exports during times of scarcity], with a horse [that is, he was a knight], commanding the foot soldiers listed below, for his fee and salary for one month....

Also 25 shillings to Baldachino Parisi of the *popolo* of St. Anthony [parish], 25 shillings to Melio Seralii of the *popolo* of St. Martin, 25 shillings to Adoto Bernardi of the *popolo* of St. Vigilio, 25 shillings to Brunecto, once [of the] Bonifatii [family] of the *popolo* of St. Andrew, 25 shillings to Alberto Nichole of the *popolo* of Mansionis [a city district], 35 shillings to Bartalomeo Nichole de Valle of the *popolo* of St. Egidius, foot soldiers appointed with the aforesaid to guard the grain for the commune of Siena, at the will and order of the podestà....

Questions: What types of items were included among the monthly expenses of the city of Siena? Which items were most expensive? What do these expenses tell us about the problems facing the commune of Siena and the commune's ambitions? Who were the officials involved in paying out or approving these expenses?

65. THE TOWN ACCOUNTS OF LEICESTER, 1377–78

Most English towns were keeping annual accounts of their revenues and expenditures by the thirteenth century. In the larger towns, a whole series of subsidiary accounts were also kept. The first selection below is an example of a subsidiary account of profits from the markets and other activities. Subsidiary accounts were also kept to record expenditures on specific building projects (such as building new market stalls or repairing the town wall) or to keep track of the revenues and expenditures of major town properties, such as the town bridge, which both brought in revenues (from tolls or rental properties on the bridge) and spent funds on maintenance. Other examples of rental income can be found in docs. 142 and 143. At the end of the year, the sums from these subsidiary accounts usually found their way into the summary annual account, an example of which is printed below in the second extract.

Source: (A) trans. M. Bateson, *Records of the Borough of Leicester*, vol. 2 (London: C.J. Clay and Sons, 1901), pp. 163–64; (B) trans. M. Bateson, *Records of the Borough of Leicester*, vol. 2 (London: C.J. Clay and Sons, 1901), pp. 169–70, revised; (C) trans. M. Bateson, *Records of the Borough of Leicester*, vol. 2 (London: C.J. Clay and Sons, 1901), pp. 164–65, revised.

(A) Leicester Subsidiary Account of Revenues, 1377–78

Note of diverse profits arising from different causes and received by Robert Horninglow and John Prentice, bailiffs of the town from Michaelmas [29 September] 1 Richard II [1377] to the following Michaelmas [1378].

From the Butchers' Stalls:
On Saturday after Michaelmas, 2 shillings 3 pence.
[A long list of such payments for one Saturday after another follows.]
Total: £4, 3 shillings ½ pence

For Fees Taken [from non-citizens for the right to trade] and Suits [at court]:
From Robert Thakker for fee taken, 4 pence....
From fee and suit taken from two men of Thurcaston, 3 shillings.
For fees taken on two occasions, 8 pence.
From four Brabançons [men from Brabant near Flanders] and a woman, for the same, 1 shilling 8 pence.
From three men from Ireland for the same, 1 shilling.
From three strangers for the same, 1 shilling 3 pence....
From the butcher, servant of John Peterborough late dyer, 1 shilling.
From the servant of the Friars Preachers for the same, 4 pence.
From William Matressmaker for the same, 4 pence.
From three men imprisoned several times, for the same, 1 shilling.
From four strangers, one of whom had a pony, for the same, 1 shilling.

From three Welshmen and a woman, for the same, 1 shilling 4 pence.

From Michael Brabançon for suit taken from aliens sworn to the King to conduct themselves with fealty to him and his heirs, 2 shillings....

[1s each from William Irish and 10 others surnamed Irish.]

Total: £3, 12 shillings 11 pence

Rent of St. Nicholas Shambles' [market stalls] at three terms: [Total:] £3, 5 shillings

Fines:

From William Butcher of Wigston for trespass done to the lord on market day, 6 shillings 8 pence....

From Richard Flesshewer of Thorp for sale of unwholesome meat, 6 pence.

From the fine of William Wynley for entrance into the Shambles (for two gables), 10 shillings

Total: £5, 11 pence

Waifs [stolen goods abandoned by thieves] and Stray Animals:

They answer for a certain linen cloth found as a waif and sold for 4 pence.

Three cows found as waif, sold for 21 shillings.

Six lambskins and 1 lining(?) sold for 1 shilling.

For a lamb found as a stray and sold, 1 shilling 1 pence.

... Total: £1, 13 shillings 8 pence

Chattels of Felons and Fugitives:

From chattels of William Fletcher fugitive etc., 8 shillings.

From chattels of William Barbour fugitive, sold £2....

From chattels of a certain baker hanged as a felon appraised at 4 shillings 6 pence.

... Total: £2, 16 shillings 2 pence

The [sums of] this roll are entered in the paper [summary account].

(B) Leicester Mayor's Account, 1377–78

Receipts:

First he answers for £6 received from Thomas Wakefield and Nicholas Glover, chamberlains of the town this year. And for £4 received from the chamberlains as appears in the account of these chamberlains. And for 13 shillings 4 pence, by John Turner given for the work of the wall of the town. And for 2 shillings 2 pence for stone sold, found in the garden of John Braybroke. [Total] £10, 15 shillings 6 pence.

He answers for 20 shillings received from Thomas Chapman of yearly rent granted by him to the community in return for exempting him from offices, and for £1, 6 shillings 8 pence. Received from T. of Beeby and his fellows, late collectors of a tax levied by them by the King's tenth in the preceding year. Total £2, 6 shillings 8 pence.

Sum total of all receipts: £13, 2 shillings 2 pence.

Allowances:
He claims allowance of £2 for his dinner fee. And 13 shillings 4 pence for salmon fee. And 6 shillings 8 pence for parchment. And £2 for the fee of his clerk. And £1 for the common sergeant's fee. And 8 shillings of the rent of John Smith at the West Gates allowed to the Mayor of the town by custom. Total: £6, 8 shillings.

Expenses:
He accounts for 4 pence given to a certain runner of the lord king on arrival. And 4 shillings for the reward of the king's messengers bringing the king's commission for a balinger [a barge the town was ordered to fund for the war effort]. And for 2 shillings 8 pence for expenses of a supper for some messengers and the chamberlains of the town. And 6 shillings 8 pence to reward of minstrels of the lord Duke of Lancaster for the honor of the town. And for the reward of the minstrels of the Earl of Warwick. And 6 shillings 8 pence given to the minstrels of the lord duke of Lancaster when Sir Thomas of Hungerford feasted with the mayor. And 1 shilling 6 pence reward to a certain jester, named Yevan, of the lady Duchess. And 8 shillings for the expenses of the mayor and Richard of Thringstone for two days at Nottingham according to common assent in the common hall. Total: 17 shillings, 8 pence.

He accounts for 30 shillings for a dinner to Thomas of Hungerford .... And 1 shilling 8 pence as a reward to the chamberlain Thomas Hungerford at the time left ill with the mayor. Total: £1, 11 shillings, 8 pence.

He accounts concerning the expenses of the wall of the town. First for 10 shillings paid for the carriage and collection of lime and soil at the wall and for cleansing this market-place. And for 5 shillings for straw bought to be mixed with soil for the wall. And for 4 shillings for carriage of water to the same. And for 40 shillings for the salary of six laborers and makers of the wall as well as coping it [sloping the upper part of the wall to throw off rain]. And for £1, 5 shillings for straw bought and for coping the wall. And for 4 shillings for carts carrying soil to the wall for two days when it was coped. For 6 shillings 8 pence paid to the man coping the wall and for finding him payment for the coping for half the time. And for 3 shillings paid to two women serving the said coper for three weeks, each taking by day 2 pence. For 2 shillings for a cartload of wood for the stakes for the coping, these payments being made beside all kinds of donations to the said wall. Total: £4, 19 shillings, 8 pence.

Sum total of the whole allowance and of expenses £13, 17 shillings. And so there is owing from the said William a surplus of 14 shillings 10 pence.

(C) Leicester Chamberlains' Account [summary account], 1377–78

Account of Thomas Wakefield and Nicholas Glover [chamberlains].
[Receipts:]
Arrears [sums owed from last year]:
   The said Thomas and Nicholas answer for £1, 19 shillings 4 pence [from the time] of William Tailleart, mayor. And for £15, 9 shillings 1½ pence arrears received from Richard Gameston and Richard Martyn, chamberlains of Leicester this year. Total: £17, 8 shillings 5½ pence.

Rents:
   And for £1, 11 shillings 5½ pence from rents of various tenements in Leicester and of £4, 1 shilling 1½ pence from rents in the town of Whetstone. Total: £5, 12 shillings 7 pence.
   And for £12 received of various persons entering the Gild Merchant.
   And for £2, 8 pence received of ... collectors of the tenth [a tax of 1/10 the value of goods] in 1377–78.
   They answer for 1 shilling for [fines on] pigs wandering in the town.
   And for 4 pence received on a certain tax in the town of Leicester, 1 shilling 4 pence.
   Total: £37, 3 shillings.

[Expenses:]
   Of which they account for £4 paid to William Ferour.
   And for £6 paid to the same William on our account.
   And 8 shillings of rent at the West Gate allowed [excused] to the Mayor.
   And £17, 7 shillings 4½ pence spent on a chamber on the West Gate [a separate account for this work is attached] and paid to Geoffrey Clerk, Richard de Knighton, and Richard Gameston ... and various others.
   And £1, 2 shillings 1 pence paid to William Ferour for keys and timber.
   Total: £28, 17 shillings 5 pence.

And so they owe clear £8, 5 shillings 7 pence. Of which they paid 2½ pence for parchment. And the chamberlains are excused of 6 shillings 8 pence for the fine of John, husband of Matilda of Northampton, who was pardoned by the community in the [city] hall by reason of poverty. And [also excused] 6 shillings 8 pence for the fine of John Burstall by reason of his inheritance.

And so there remains in the hands of the chamberlains, £7, 12 shillings ½ pence.

[Indenture attached]. Note that by this indenture Roger Spurrier and John Spurrier, chamberlains on their account delivered to Richard Gameston and Robert Anstey chamberlains a charter of yearly rent of 6 shillings 8 pence from the tenement in Great Glen. And 4 charters of tenements in Billesdon. And a charter of a tenement in Leicester. And five charters of tenements in Stretton. Also, gages [security for good behavior] taken for trespass made with pigs.... [list of items to do with care of pigs follows.]

Questions: What were the revenue sources for the city of Leicester? Which provided the largest contribution to the city coffers? How did the city spend its revenues? How did Leceister's expenses compare to those of the larger Italian city of Siena (doc. 64)? What can we discern about the accounting methods of the city of Leicester?

66. TAX DECLARATIONS IN FLORENCE FOR THE *CATASTO* OF 1427

Faced with a fiscal crisis caused by huge expenditures on war, Florence instituted a new method of direct taxation in 1427. Called the catasto, *this new tax assessed citizens of Florence and its subject territories on the value of all of their property, including real estate, cash, business investments, and holdings in the communal debt fund. The* catasto *records still survive and provide information on the property and wealth of about 60,000 households (the basic unit of assessment), as well as the gender, ages, and family status of members of each household. In the extracts below, note that the householder's home was free from tax. These two declarations are by members of the wealthy and politically powerful Alberti family, whose male members had been exiled from the city, thus leaving their sons, wives, and widows to report their resources for tax purposes. For examples of how historians have derived evidence on the distribution of wealth and demographic structure of Florence from the* catasto, *see docs. 41 and 84.*

Source: trans. S.F. Baxendale, from *Readings in Medieval History*, ed. P.J. Geary (Peterborough, ON and Lewiston, NY: Broadview Press, 1989), pp. 812–14, 815–16, abridged.

Portata *[declaration] of Tomasso di Francesco Davizzi and his Mother*
Tommaso di Francesco Davizzi and Monna Catelena his mother in the quarter of Santa Croce, *gonfalone* [city ward] of Leon Nero; they have a *prestanzone* rate of 7 florins.

To you revered citizens, elected officials to do the *catasto* of the property of every citizen of the city of Florence. I, Tommaso di Francesco Davizzi, report to you all moveable and immoveable goods, debtors, and creditors of mine and of Monna Catelana my mother here in every detail and following all our obligations. First:

A half house, indivisible where we presently live, situated in the *gonfalone* of Leon Nero in the parish of Sant'Iacopo tralle fosse in Borgo Santa Croce. [Bounds given] ... Further, household furnishings for our use in the said house and in the summer house.

Five or 6 parts, indivisible, of a house situated in the said parish in the street called of the Alberti's house. [Bounds given] ... This house is rented by Tommaso Busini; he gives me nearly 20 florins yearly; I get for my part 16 florins 13 shillings 10 pence year.

[He goes on to list 5/6 of a farm with one parcel of land and half farm.]

I find myself in the partnership which I have with Tommaso and Simone Corsi, a base capital of 1500 florins.

We have not settled the accounts; we are overextended rather than settled; I will have to report to you what I have in the shop.

I find myself next bankrupt in the new company, current account, 270 florins.

Here next I write all the debtors I find, those whom I reckon to be good for payment ultimately.

The heirs of Cipriano and Ser Luigi di Simone Guiduccini	60 florins
Nastagio di Simone Guiduccini	35 florins
Niccolo di Sanminiato de Ricci	55 florins
Antonio, priest of Sant'Angelo	65 florins
The commune of Assisi for 10 accatti	28 florins
Benedetto da Panzano 8 florins	15 shillings
Pagolo Quaratesi 9 florins	17 shillings
Rosso di Strozzo 6 florins	11 shillings
	[Total:] 267 florins 20 shillings

Here next I will write all the credits to be recovered:

Cosimo and Lorenzo de'Medici and heirs	430 florins
Monna Vaggia di Bindo Guasconi 1	50 florins
Giovanni di Bartolo Morelli	500 florins
Llarione di Lipanno de'Bardi	42 florins
Antonio di Salvestro and partners	20 florins
Monna Antonio, wife of Piero Dini	50+ florins
The old company of Tommaso and Simone Corsi	
And with the remainder I should have	450 florins
	[Total:] 1,542 florins

Here below I will record the many debtors I find which are no-account, from which I have not been able in times past to collect, nor do I expect ever to collect. These debtors are, that is:

Tommaso di Filippo di Michele	4 ½ florins
Lorenzo and Giovanni di Scholai degli Pini:	
I paid for them to their syndic	555 florins
Santi Pisiro	1 florin

The heirs and estate of Bernardo degli Alberti, for the remainder of a finding I got against them; and I paid the *gonfalone* for them.

They don't have their property, so one must let the debt ride.

Bartolo di Maschio	765 florins
Giovanni Manini	10 florins
Monna Catelana is	aged 44
Tommaso	aged 26
Checca is a girl who Monna Catelana vowed to raise for the love of God since she has neither daddy nor mama to raise her	aged 4 or 6

[He is not given credit for Checca.]

Property 3,361 florins 4 shillings 8 pence

Obligations 2,042 florins

[Total:] Remainder: 1,319 florins 4 shillings 8 pence

Portata *of Maria wife of the late Ricciardo degli Alberti*

Before you sirs, officials of the *catasto*, I, Piero Cambini of Santa Felice in Piazza, report to you as a factor of this property of Monna Maria, wife of the late Ricciardo degli Alberti, and daughter of Messer Mainardo Cavalcanti. And today she is a widow and lives in Bologna with her daughters of whom one is a widow. And she [Maria] is ill and has a lot of difficulty making ends meet, such that she is recommended to your consideration such as it can be. And this is the property that she holds between her dowry and her bequests and monies. [He lists two farms left to her by her mother.] This Monna Maria has not had *prestanze* nor do I find her taxed with *prestanze*. She is ill and somehow she must live as a woman of substance. I, Piero Cambini, attest to these things I have written at the request of Monna Maria and I have never asked anything ever for my pains. However, I am here [in Florence] or in Venice, such that it will be necessary to find another factor to serve her. And I salute you.

Questions: What are the sources of income for these wealthy families? Why is the city of Florence concerned to keep track of these different sources of income, as well as enumerating the gender, age, and status of all household residents? Is there any indication of how these taxes were viewed by taxpayers?

67. WINCHESTER PLEADS FOR TAX RELIEF BECAUSE OF URBAN DECLINE, 1452

Late medieval towns faced a host of problems stemming in large part from depopulation following the Black Death and recurring epidemics during the late fourteenth and fifteenth centuries. Depopulation meant there were fewer households to pay taxes and rents, and fewer consumers to maintain commerce, the town's lifeblood. Competition from rural industry also cut into the business of many artisans, particularly those in the cloth crafts. In this extract, Winchester's fiscal crisis has become so bad that the town rulers turn to the king for help in paying the annual fee farm [a large rent to allow the town to keep its own revenues rather than paying them to its lord, the king].

Source: modernized by M. Kowaleski, from Dr. Ducarel, "A Petition of the City of Winchester to King Henry VI," *Archaeologia* 1 (1770): 91–94.

To the king our sovereign lord, your humble true liegemen, the mayor, bailiffs, and commonalty of your poor city of Winchester beseech full humbly, that whereas they have been charged to bear the fee farm of your said city, which annually totals the sum of 112 marks, and [they] also owe 60 shillings to the master of the hospital of Mary Magdalen near Winchester; [and] also when the 15th penny or tax is granted to your highness it amounts to the sum of £51, 10 shillings 4 pence within the city, to which, when it is to be levied, some men in the city are assessed at 4 marks and some at 5 marks because your city is desolate of people; also the expense of burgesses of the city coming to your parliaments comes to 4 shillings a day. Your bailiffs [in Winchester] have little or nothing of certainty to pay this fee farm, but only casual payments, and yearly fall short of paying the fee farm by £40 or more. For these reasons, and also for the great charges and daily costs which your poor city bears for enclosing [the city walls] and murage [taxes which went to fortifications] of your city, it has become so very desolate that many persons have withdrawn out of the said city for these reasons, and 997 houses, which used to be occupied with people now [are] empty, and because of these withdrawals 17 parish churches stand without offices at this day, which parishes and houses are more plainly expressed in a schedule attached here. And whereas your highness relieved the city on 24 May in the 19th year of your reign [1441] by granting the mayor and commonalty of the city 40 marks annually, to be taken until the end of ... by even portions from the revenues and profits of the aulnage [a tax on cloth] and subsidy of woollen cloths within the city and suburbs and its soke [suburb under the jurisdiction of the bishop of Winchester] and in all the other places within your shire of Southampton ... in relief of all these charges ... this annual payment is now void and wholly resumed to you, because of an act made in your parliament [dated 1450].... And so now your suppliants stand utterly destitute of any manner of relief from these charges to the utterest undoing of your city for ever.... That it please your said highness graciously to consider these charges and, of your most abundant grace, to grant to the mayor, bailiffs, and commonalty of your city 40 marks, which they and their successors may have each year from [29 September 1449] ... from the aulnage and subsidy of woollen cloths to be sold within your city, suburbs, and soke, and in other places within your shire of Southampton....

These are the streets that are fallen down in the city of Winchester within the last 80 years [eleven streets are listed from they claim nearly all the householders have left].... The number of householders that have left is 997 and besides these another 81 households have gone since the last parliament.

These are the parish churches that have fallen down within the said city [17 churches are named].... The desolation of this poor city is so great and yearly increasing for there is such decay and ruin that without the gracious comfort of the king our sovereign lord, the mayor and the bailiffs must of necessity cease and deliver up the city and the keys into the king's hands.

Memorandum that on the first day of February, the 30th year of the reign of King Henry the Sixth after the Conquest [1452] this bill was delivered to the lord chancellor of England at Westminster to be executed.

Questions: What were the expenses that the city of Winchester has difficulty meeting? How do they compare with the expenses of the cities of Siena (doc. 64) and Leicester (doc. 65)? What problems does the city cite as evidence it cannot meet its expenses? To what extent can we assess the city's true condition in the "rhetoric of decline" meant to elicit tax relief?

68. THE JURISDICTION OF THE WARDMOTES OF LONDON

As towns grew larger, they developed institutions to help keep the peace and handle issues of public health and defence. In London, the neighborhood unit of governance called the ward had emerged as the most important local jurisdiction by the twelfth century; each ward had its own court (called the wardmote or wardmeeting) and drew on the services of several officials, chief among them aldermen. By the thirteenth century there were twenty-four wards in London. The first extract describes what happened at these wardmeetings, while the second extract, which dates from about a century earlier, is a series of questions meant to guide the twelve jurors in making their "presentments" of those who broke one of the regulations. Frankpledge was a type of personal policing system that required all adult men to be part of a group or tithing; each member of the group was responsible for the good behavior of the others (see doc. 69).

Source: (A) trans. H.T. Riley, *Liber Albus: The White Book of the City of London* (London: Richard Griffin and Company, 1861), pp. 32–35, (B) *ibid.*, 287–92, revised.

(A) Description of the London Wardmote, 1419

The wardmote is called as being a meeting together by summons of all the inhabitants of a ward, in presence of its head, the alderman, or else his deputy, for the correction of defaults, the removal of nuisances, and the promotion of the well-being of the ward…. The aldermen were also in the habit, by virtue of warrants directed to them by the mayor for the time being, to hold their wardmotes at least twice or more often in the year, on which occasions enquiry used to be made as to the condition and tranquility of the ward, and such defaults as were presented were corrected by the alderman, as will be shown.

The process of holding a wardmote in London has customarily been as follows. The alderman, after receipt of the warrant, is to command his beadle to summon all men who are householders in his ward, as well as all hired servants, to appear before him at a certain day and hour of the day after the summons, in a certain place within the ward, for the purpose of holding the wardmote. After the persons have been duly summoned, the beadle is to have entered their names in a certain roll: namely, those of the freemen of the city who dwell in that ward, by themselves, and those of the hired servants and non-freemen, by themselves. And when at the hour appointed they have duly met together, the alderman having taken his seat with the more opulent men of the ward, each in his proper place, the clerk of the alderman is to enjoin the beadle, in behalf of the alderman, to command attention. When this is done, it is the clerk's duty to read aloud the warrant, and then to read to the beadle the names that are entered in the roll, while the beadle in his turn proclaims aloud that every person who is not there to answer to his name should be in default and shall be put down and amerced in the sum of four pence at the least. After this, the beadle is to present to the alderman a panel, arrayed by the constables of the ward, of those reputable men of the ward, who should make the inquiry, although the alderman is at liberty to amend this jury panel if he deems it expedient. This done, the jurors are to have read to them all the articles touching the wardmote. After this, a certain day for making their presentment is to be given by the alderman to the jurors. On that day the jurors are to present their verdict indented [a document with two copies that are then separated by a jagged cut]: one part of it to remain in possession of the alderman and the other with the ward. It is the duty also of the alderman to present his part to the mayor, at the sitting of his next general court, to the end that, after it has been seen and enquired if any matter pertains to the correction of the mayor and city, the indenture may be redelivered to him, to be acted upon in other respects, etc.

And at the wardmote, the alderman and reputable men of the ward and also the jurors should elect the scavagers [originally toll collectors, but supervisors of street-cleaning by this time], ale-conners [ale inspectors], beadle, and other officials, who at the general court will take the oaths befitting their respective offices. The alderman also used to be specially certified by the beadle as to the names of innkeepers, brewers, bakers, cooks, victuallers, and auctioneers who resided within the ward. Bakers also were to have their stamps there, the impressions of which were to be entered upon the alderman's paper; each baker had to pay the alderman four pence for doing this, unless it so happened that he had previously paid for an impression taken of his stamp before the same alderman of the ward, no change of alderman having taken place. It was also usual for the aldermen to seal the measures and weights in their respective wards, and to condemn those that were not sealed, receiving a remuneration for this sealing which they could keep, in the same way that the city chamber now receives it. For every ward had its own measure, made of brass, and corresponding with the royal standard of the city. Also at the wardmote, those persons who are not free of the city, and who have not previously been sworn there to that effect, were supposed to be put upon frankpledge, even if they had already been received into [frankpledge] in other wards; on which occasion they are to take the oath for persons about to be admitted to frankpledge. Every person who is about to be so received is to give one penny to the clerk for his entrance, and if any such person is absent from the wardmote, he should pay four pence to the alderman, unless indeed such person be a knight, esquire, female, apprentice-at-law, or clerk, or some other individual who has not a permanent abode in this city.

The alderman should also, in his own person, supervise and correct all defaults and nuisances presented by the jurors at the wardmote, unless perchance any matters of difficulty should arise, and of a nature bearing reference to the chamber: these matters the mayor and chamberlain, aided by the sheriffs and other officials, shall take in hand. Also if the alderman should find the officers under him remiss or negligent, he should warn them to amend their conduct, which if they neglect to do, he should reasonably punish and chastise them, or else report them to the mayor, whose duty it is to provide a suitable remedy for them.

(B) Articles of the London Wardmote, Early Fourteenth Century

Of Keeping the Peace.
In the first place, the peace of God and Holy Church, and the peace of his lordship the King, should be strictly kept between clerks and laymen, rich and poor, in common.

Of Strangers.
Also, that no person may reside or be harbored within the ward if he is not of good reputation and under frankpledge charged before the alderman of the ward, even though he may be under frankpledge in another Ward.

Of the Same.
Also, that no one is to receive a stranger in his house for more than a day and a night if he is not willing to produce him to stand trial, if it happens that he commits an offense.

Of Courtesans and Procuresses.
Also, that no woman of lewd life, or a bawd, courtesan, or common scold can reside in the ward, but should straightaway be removed by the alderman and driven out of the ward, or else be brought by the constables and beadle to the Compter [prison].

Of Erecting Furnaces.
Also, that no man or woman should erect any furnace or furnaces, or place any hearth beneath where they are, or any reredos [an open fire-grate] where a fire is made for preparing bread or ale or for cooking meat, or by partitions, laths, or boards, above or in a solar [an upper room], or any place where accident by fire may easily arise. And if any of these are erected, the scavagers should cause it to be immediately removed or destroyed. For doing this, the scavagers may have four pence for every such nuisance so removed or destroyed.

Of Chimneys.
Also, that henceforth no chimney be made except from stone, tiles, or plaster, and not of timber, under pain of being pulled down.

Of Rebellious Persons.

Also, that if anyone, whether foreigner or denizen, is not willing to be amenable to the officers of the city, who have the peace of his lordship the king to keep, then all persons upholding the peace should be ready and prepared to come in aid of the officers, to arrest and bring to justice such disobedient persons, according as the law demands.

Of Scotale.

Also, that no person of the ward make scotale in the ward, or in any other place within the franchise, under pain of imprisonment. [A scotale was a compulsory ale-drinking party one had to pay to attend.]

Of Laborers.

Also, that no one should hire or pay masons, carpenters, daubers [who applied a mixture of mud and straw], tilers, or any other laborers whatsoever, otherwise than according to the assize [regulation] ordained by the common council of the city, under pain of paying to the chamber double the amount of such excess.

Of Ladders.

Also, that all persons who dwell in great houses within the ward should have a ladder, or two, ready and prepared to help their neighbors in case misadventure might happen by fire.

Of Barrels Filled with Water.

Also, that all persons who occupy such houses, should have in summer-time, and especially between the Feast of Pentecost and the Feast of St. Bartholomew [24 August], a barrel full of water before their doors for quenching such fire, if the house does not have a fountain of its own.

Of the Carpenters' Work in the Houses.

Also, that no house within the liberties [of London] should be roofed otherwise than with lead, tile, or stone, and that if any are not, they should be taken down. And if there are any like this, they should forthwith be razed by the constables and scavagers, who can take for their troubles the [sum] stated above.

Of Crooks of Iron.

Also, that the reputable men of the ward, with the alderman, should provide a strong crook of iron with a wooden handle, together with two chains and two strong cords. And the beadle should have a good horn that sounds loudly.

Of Dirt.

Also, that no person should throw straw, dust, dung, sawdust, or other refuse into the streets or lanes, but this should be taken by the rakers or others to the places ordained for receiving such dirt, under penalty of two shillings [to be paid] to the chamber.

Of Rakers.
Also, that they should have rakers sufficient for cleansing the wards of diverse refuse, and should order the constables, with the beadle, to help them to collect their salary from the folks of the ward.

Of Swine and Cows.
Also, that no persons should rear swine, oxen, or cows within their houses, under pain of forfeiture of [the animal] to the chamber.

Of Sealed Measures.
Also, that all persons who sell by measure within the ward, that is to say, by gallon, pottle, and quart, quarter, bushel, half-bushel, and peck, should show all their measures four times in the year to the alderman, at the place he thinks proper to assign, under pain of paying two shillings to the use of the alderman; and they shall there be sealed with the seal of such alderman, if it is not sealed with the seal of the chamber. And [the person] should pay two pence for the seal of a gallon, and one penny for the seal of a pottle, and one-half penny for the seal of the quart, eight pence for the quarter, two pence for the bushel, one penny for the half-bushel, and one half-penny for the peck.

And if any measures be, upon the assay of the alderman, smaller than they should be, it should be burnt straightaway in the principal street of the ward ... and the name of the [offender] presented to the chamberlain, and [the offender] should be amerced.... And if it is found that the beadle had put the mark upon a false measure, he shall be sentenced to the pillory.

Of Stalls.
Also, that no stalls should be beyond the house of a greater breadth than two feet and a half, and the same are to be moveable and flexible, at the discretion of alderman, according to whether the streets or lanes are broad or narrow.

Of Penthouses.
Also, that the penthouses should be high enough so that persons may easily go and ride beneath them, and if any of them are lower than they ought to be, let them be altered by the end of fifteen days after notice is given about it by the constables, scavagers, or beadle, or otherwise, let it be demolished by them, taking for their trouble four [pence], as above.

Inquisitions at the Wardmotes.

You should present if the peace of his lordship the king has been broken, or any affray made within the ward since the last wardmote, and by what person or persons it was done, or if any covin or assembly against [the peace of his lordship the king] has been made.

... [Most of the charges that follow repeat the articles listed above.]

Also, if there is any huckster in the ward....

Also, if there is any leper resident in the ward....

Also, if any bargain of usury has been made within the ward since the last wardmote....

Also, if any baker of tourte bread [the coarsest brown bread] bakes white bread, or the converse....

Also, if [there are] any persons in the habit of wandering within the ward after forbidden hours, and in a manner forbidden by the common council of the city....

Also, if any officer of the city has made extortion or affray within the ward under color of his office, to the wrong or detriment of any person....

Also, if the ale-stake [a pole projecting from the front of a house advertising that ale is for sale] of any tavern is longer or extends further than is ordained....

Questions: What was the jurisdictional purview of the London wardmotes? What problems or disputes did the wardmote handle? What can we discern about the personnel and legal processes of these local courts? What powers of enforcement did the wardmote have? Could large cities such as London be "micromanaged" by these neighborhood officials and courts?

69. PROCEEDINGS IN THE COURTS OF NOTTINGHAM, 1395–96

The larger towns had several different courts, each with different responsibilities. Most English towns had leet courts, similar to the London wardmotes, which exercised jurisdiction over assaults and the many petty offenses enumerated in the articles of the wardmotes. The selections included here show the types of business handled by three different courts in Nottingham. The first selections are from presentments made by decennaries, who were the heads of the frankpledge groups [in wards often named after the closest city gate] bound to report on the misbehavior of others in their particular tithing group. As long as cities remained relatively small, the frankpledge system worked fairly well because it was inexpensive to administer (indeed, the fines assessed in the courts actually generated revenue for the towns) and the obligation to report on the wrongdoings of others in one's tithing group was reinforced by fines that could be levied on those who failed to report these misdemeanors. The second group of extracts comes from the presentments of the Great Tourn or Mickletorn Jury ("Mickle" is an Anglo-Saxon word meaning "great"), which handled mainly petty market offenses to ensure price and quality control. The third group of extracts comes from the Borough Court of Nottingham, where burgesses could sue each other; these personal pleas focused in particular on debt suits, but there were also complaints for damages from assaults and broken agreements, among other cases. For examples of court proceedings in other medieval towns, see docs. 70, 135, 136.

Source: trans. W.H. Stevenson, *Records of the Borough of Nottingham, vol. 1* (London: Bernard Quaritch; and Nottingham: Thomas Forman & Sons, 1882): (A): pp. 293, 295, 315, 317; (B): pp. 317, 319; (C) pp. 325, 326, abridged and revised.

(A) Extracts from the Presentments of Affrays, 1395–96

Presentments of all affrays, before John de Plumptre, then mayor of the town of Nottingham....

Robert de Sutton and John Daniel, decennaries of Fleschewergate, present an affray made with blood by Henry Hickling upon John Pulter, the son of Anna the wife of the said Henry, because Henry drew his knife, so blood issued between them, against the peace of our lord the king, etc..., so he is attached. And Henry comes and places himself upon the favor of the mayor, and pays 6 pence.

Walter Fletcher, decennary of Mothalgate, presents an affray made with blood by Stephen Wade upon Agnes Irish, because Stephen beat her and drew blood from Agnes with his fists ... he is attached. And Stephen comes and places himself upon the favor of the mayor and pays 6 pence.

John Lorimer and John Wyrhall, decennaries of Bridilsmythgate, present an affray made with blood by Adam Cooper upon Richard Hykot, spurrier, because

Adam struck Richard on his side with his axe … he is attached. And Adam comes and places himself on the favor of the mayor, and pays 12 pence.

… John de Mar and John Koo, decennaries of Franchegate, present an affray made without blood by Agnes, servant of William de Torlaton, because Agnes came into the house of Robert Brinklow against his will, and there nearly strangled the wife of Robert … she is attached. And Agnes comes and places herself upon the favor of the mayor, and pays 6 pence.

… John de Mampton and Gilbert Walker, decennaries of Hundegate, present that Beatrice Mather is a common scold against her neighbors in the streets of Hundegate where she dwells … she is attached. And Beatrice comes and places herself upon the favor of the mayor and pays 6 pence.

… the decennaries of Midilpament present that John de Burstall sells candles without cotton, contrary to the assize, etc. Also, they present that the wife of William de Ashbourne, the wife of Randolph Pollard, and the wife of John Burstall are common regrators and forestallers of all cheeses, butter, hens, pullets, capons and poultry, pigeons, and all such victuals coming to the town, and that they stand at the ends of the streets to buy such things before the proper hour, contrary to the assize and the proclamation of the mayor….

… John de Barrowby and Richard Roper, decennaries at the Bridge End, also present that Nicholas Tailor keeps an open shop and he is not a burgess, etc.

… John de Tamworth, junior, and Edmund de Wheatley, decennaries of Greitsmythgate, also present that John Palfreyman sells ale that is new in his own house with the sign being attached, and also sells with cups and dishes not sealed, contrary to the assize, etc.

John de Horton, wright, decennary of Gosegate, presents nothing because he is unwell, etc., excepting John de Horton, who is a common brewer and sells with cups and dishes, contrary to the assize, etc.

(B) Presentments of the Mickletorn Jury in Nottingham, 1396

Presentments of the Great Tourn taken before John de Plumptre, mayor of the town of Nottingham….

By the oath of [25 jurors named], who say that all the brewers are guilty because they brew contrary to the assize, etc., and sell with cups and dishes, contrary to the assize, etc.

Also they say that all the bakers are guilty because they take too much for baking and cooking bread from the common people, to wit, 1½ pence for a bushel of grain that is 6 pence for a quarter [which contains 8 bushels], whereas they ought to take only 4 pence for a quarter according to the statute of our lord the king, etc.

Also, they say that all the butchers sell meat which has been kept too long and is corrupt.…

Also, they say that all the fishers of Northampton, both of sea and fresh-water fish, sell dead fish which have been kept too long, and that each of them is a common forestaller of fish, etc., and they sell them at an excessive price, contrary to the statute....

... Also, they say that all the shoemakers of Northampton sell shoes too dearly, and that each of them puts calf-skin among ox-leather, and sells basan [an inferior leather] for cordwain [a high quality leather]....

... Also, they say that John Albayn of Nottingham came into the market on the eve of Easter in [1396] and there forestalled and bought a cart full of tanned hides from Richard Hudson of Bredon, to the great prejudice of John de Linby, John Ball, Thomas Holland, and Edmund de Wheatley, because they had spoken with the said Richard for these hides, and were all but agreed as to price, and then John came secretly and against the statute of the lord king and bought it for a greater sum....

(C) Personal Pleas in the Nottingham Mayor's Court, 1396

Thomas Fox, draper, brings a complaint against John Fisher on a plea of trespass and rescue, because Thomas, on the Saturday after Michaelmas [30 September 1396], came to John's house at Nottingham to seek the rent on the house he owns that John rents, but John assaulted Thomas and by force and arms with a bow and arrow would have slain Thomas there, and made rescue from Thomas of his distraint for his rent [the goods Thomas took to ensure John would pay the rent], whereby Thomas is injured and has received damages to the value of 20 shillings.... And John comes and says ... he is not guilty, and places himself on the country [asks for a jury trial].... His mainpernors [pledges] are John Russell and John Sherman.

John countersues Thomas on a plea of trespass and blood; Thomas on the same Saturday came with John Parker his servant, with two drawn daggers to John's house ... by force and arms entered the house, and followed him as far as the bed of his chamber, and would have slain him there with his dagger unless by chance certain of his neighbors had rescued him, and afterwards he [Thomas] assaulted John's son, and beat him, wounded and maltreated him, so he despaired of his life, and against the peace of our lord the king, to the damage of John of 100 shillings, to which he enters suit.... And Thomas comes in person and ... says he is not guilty and places himself on the country [seeks a jury trial].

Questions: Can you discern differences in the types of cases these three courts heard? How was justice administered in Nottingham, and how did it compare with the jurisdiction of the courts in London (doc. 68)? What problems were these courts mainly interested in addressing?

70. THE COST OF RECOVERING A DEBT IN MARSEILLE, 1331

The following extract is an itemized list of the litigation expenses paid by Guilhem Imbert during the course of his 1331 lawsuit in the courts of Marseille to recover an unpaid trading debt (for a commenda contract) of 40 pounds. His list of expenses shows the range of legal experts and other court personnel he had to hire to negotiate the complex legal procedures that had become standard by this period. The robertus *and the* valodium *were coins often used to pay professional fees; each was worth about a shilling (12 pence). Since 2 shillings (24 pence) was an average laborer's wage for the time, the plaintiff's costs alone would have represented about 108 days of work.*

Source: trans. D. Smail, from *The Consumption of Justice: Emotions, Publicity, and Legal Culture in Marseille, 1264–1423* (Ithaca, NY: Cornell University Press, 2003), pp. 67–68.

Salary of the two advocates [lawyers], 1 florin each [384 pence]
Salary of the procurator, 10 silver *robertos*
Salary of the procurator who solicited the advocates, 10 silver *robertos*
The scriptor who wrote the libel [the written charge], 5 silver *robertos*
The messenger who carried the libel to the opposing party, 2 pence
The notary who wrote the libel into the cartulary of the court, 2 silver *robertos*
The scriptor who wrote out the titles, 2 silver *robertos*
The notary who extracted a public instrument of the commenda, 10 silver *robertos*
The messenger who carried it to the opposing party, 2 pence
The notary of the court who wrote the titles into the cartulary of the court, 2 silver *robertos*
The notary of the court for a transcript of the mandament [order], 6 pence
The advocate who dictated the libel for the expenses, 10 silver *robertos*
The advocate's notary or scriptor who wrote it out, 2 silver *robertos*
The messenger who carried it to the defendant, 2 pence
The notary who wrote it out into the cartulary, 1 silver *robertus*
The messenger who cited the defendant and the notary who wrote the citation, 6 pence
The procurator, Bernat Raymon, 2 *valodios* and 5 silver *robertos*
Four more citations made to the heirs of the defendant, 12 pence
The notary of the court who wrote out two precepts, 4 *valodios*
The notary who wrote out the decision of the arbitrators, 5 silver *robertos*
The messenger of the court who collected a gage [a household item taken as security for an unpaid debt] from the heirs, 4 *valodios*
The messenger of the court for restoring the gage, 1 *valodium*
The notary who wrote out the precept, 2 *valodios*
For citing the defendant, 1 *valodium*

For writing out a recommendation of his advocate, 6 *valodios*
The messenger of the court who cited the heirs, 1 *valodium*
For writing out citations, 2 *valodios*
His lawyer, 30 shillings
The notary of the court and the scriptors, 30 shillings
Total: 10 pounds 15 shillings.

Questions: What were the largest costs associated with pursuing this civil suit? What sort of trouble did the plaintiff have in recouping his money? What tasks did the various people he paid perform for him? What were the most expensive aspects of his pursuit of justice?

71. FEUD AND VENDETTA: THE PRIVATE PURSUIT OF JUSTICE IN PISTOIA

The exaggerated sense of honor among the wealthiest citizens of Italian towns encouraged vendettas as a way to avenge slights to personal or family honor. Young men were frequently the instigators, but their actions drew their extended families into the dispute, which could turn into a long-lasting and often violent feud. Although this method of settling disagreements was tolerated among the urban nobility, the effects of feud could be devastating to the political and social stability of the town. The extract also shows how civic rulers tried to stop feuds by severely punishing and even exiling the chief offenders.

Source: trans. T. Dean, *The Towns of Italy in the Later Middle Ages* (Manchester: Manchester University Press; New York: St. Martin's Press, 2000), pp. 185–87.

[1286–1288] In this city [of Pistoia] there were many noble and powerful citizens, among whom was a clan of powerful citizens and gentlemen, called the Cancellieri, and this clan had at that time among its members eighteen knights and was so mighty and of such power that it overcame and defeated all the other *grandi*, and, on account of their power and wealth, the Cancellieri became so proud that there was no one in the city or *contado* whom they did not hold down. They insulted everyone, committed many cruelties, and had many people killed or wounded. Out of fear of them no one dared complain.

It happened that some youths, all from this one family, but from two different branches, one called the Amadori and the other the Rinieri, were gathered at a shop where wine was sold, and, having drunk to excess, a dispute arose among them as they gambled. They exchanged words, then blows, and the Rinieri lad had the better of the Amadori lad. The latter was called Dore di Messer Guglielmo, one of the leading members of his branch; he who injured him was Carlino di Messer Gualfredi Rinieri, also a leading member of his branch. Dore, seeing that he was beaten, disgraced, and vituperated by his kinsman, and unable to avenge himself there and then, because Carlino's brothers were there, left, resolving to take vengeance. And the same day, late in the evening, Dore was on the look-out and there passed by on horseback one of Carlino's brothers, called Messer Vanni, who was a judge. Dore called to him. Vanni, not knowing about what his brother had done, went over to him. Dore went to strike him on the head with his sword, but Vanni raised his hand to parry the blow, such that Dore cut his face and hand, removing all of it except the thumb. Vanni left and went home. And when his father and brothers and other kinsmen saw him wounded in this way, they and all their friends and relatives were greatly aggrieved....

The father of Messer Vanni Rinieri and his brothers resolved to make vendetta and to kill Dore, his father, brothers and kinsmen. For the Rinieri were powerful and well-connected by marriage, and the Amadori feared them greatly, indeed so afraid were they that they did not leave their house. Dore's kinsmen, thinking that they could get out of this quarrel, decided to give Dore up to Vanni's father and brothers, for them to do as they pleased, believing that they would treat him like a brother. So they arranged for Dore to be seized and sent to the house of Messer Gualfredi and his sons and put into their hands. But they, as pitiless and cruel men who disregarded the good intentions of those who had sent Dore, put him in a stable, and there one of Vanni's brothers cut off his hand, the one with which he had attacked Vanni, and cut his face on the same side as Vanni had been injured. And thus wounded and mutilated, they sent him home to his father. When his father and brothers and kinsmen saw him in this state, they were plunged into grief, and this was considered by everyone to be too cruel and severe a thing, to shed their own family's blood, especially as they had put him in their mercy. And this was the beginning of the division of the city and *contado* of Pistoia, from which followed killings, the burning of houses, castles, and villages, and the emergence of the faction names Black and White ... and war multiplied such that neither in Pistoia nor in its *contado* did there remain anyone who did not belong to one party or the other, and often neighbor fought neighbor....

The parties within the city often fought together, and on one occasion a hard fight began in the Porta Guidi district, to which Messer Detto di Messer Sinibaldo of the Black Cancellieri hurried. He was one of the most wealthy and wise members of his side, and he rode a large horse, well-armed. But during the fight, one of the White party threw a block of stone out of a window and this hit Detto on the head, such a great blow that he was completely stunned and fell forward onto his horse's neck, staying there for a long time such that he was thought to be dead. But when he came to, he left and at once each of the parties went home. Back at home, Messer Detto decided to avenge himself on one of those from whose house the stone had been thrown and, with the advice of his brothers and kinsmen, he resolved to avenge himself on the leader of that house. Messer Detto had a nephew called Messer Simone, who was a knight, young, courageous, and pitiless beyond measure, and with him Detto arranged to make vendetta. Simone promised to do it, as one who attended to these things more than to anything else. Having given the order, Messer Simone provided himself with many bold and experienced troops, and one day a judge called Piero of the Pecoroni family, from whose house the stone had been thrown, went from his house to the palace of the podestà of the city, and there, at the bar, before one of the podestà's magistrates, Messer Simone, with his band of men, killed him. The podestà's officers were powerless to defend him because of the goodly band with Messer Simone. And with his company, Messer Simone then returned home, meeting no one on the way who challenged him. The death of Messer Piero was considered a great injury, for no one thought he had deserved to die. The podestà prosecuted Messer Simone and fined him. He paid the fine and went into exile, and it was five years before he could return to Pistoia.

Questions: What started the vendetta and how did it escalate? What problems did these feuds cause? Why did private vengeance survive for so long as a means of dispute resolution in Pistoia and other Italian cities?

72. URBAN PUNISHMENTS

The following selections are ordinances in the custumals or law codes of several British towns (which are named at the beginning of each selection, along with the date of the ordinance) that specify types of punishment wrongdoers were given for particular crimes. Note that as time went on, some of these punishments were replaced by monetary fines.

Source: trans. M. Bateson, *Borough Customs*, vol. 1 (Selden Society, vol. 18, 1904), pp. 64, 65, 66, 68, 70, 73, 74, 75, 77, 78, 79–80, selections, revised.

[Preston, twelfth century] If a burgess slanders another and confesses it, he shall make amends by paying 12 pence. If he denies it, he should purge himself alone [swear an oath] before witnesses. If the slander is uttered outside the court, he pays nothing.

[Preston, twelfth century] If any one is captured for robbery or other misdeeds and condemned to death, he who prosecutes should carry out the judgment.

[Bristol, c. 1240] And that a burgess, for whatever cause he may be imprisoned, should not be taken to the castle prison, but should be taken to the town prison.

[Congleton, c. 1272] If the bailiffs of the towns take a felon, they should hold him in the stocks, if they like, for three days and then give him up to our castle of Halton with the chattels found on him, keeping to themselves the stolen goods which belong to their sergeantry [office].

[Portsmouth, c. 1272] If a woman slays a man, she shall be tied to a stake at low water and let the flood overflow her at Catt Clyff.

[Waterford, c. 1300] And if a street be set on fire by anyone, his body should be seized and cast into the midst of the fire.

[London, c. 1300] And if he has incurred the penalty of death for treason, he should be bound to a stake, at the piles which stand in the Thames [River] at the Timber-hythe where the boats are fastened, for two flows and two ebbs of the tide.

[Romney, 1352] If a man accused of murder flees, his lands and tenements and all his goods are forfeit.

[Fordwich, c. 1450] If he has no pledges (in a plea of battery or trespass), he should be taken to prison but not put in irons.

[Sandwich, c. 1450] All who are condemned for homicide are to be buried alive in the place allotted for this purpose at Sandown, called the Thiefdowns [in 1315, the penalty was drowning].

[Hythe, 1483–85] If a tenant commits a felony and flees, the lord [the archbishop of Canterbury in this town] should have [use of] the lands and tenements for a year and a day, and after a year and a day the lands and tenements should be delivered to him who owns them.

[Hereford, 1486] It was decided concerning female scolds that much mischief arose in the city through them, such as quarreling, blows, defamation, disturbance of night's rest, and strike between neighbors often arising, as well as resistance to bailiffs, officers, and others, who were abused in their very presence, and often also the raising of hues and cries in breach of the lord king's peace, and to the disturbance of their city's quiet. Wherefore, whenever scolds are taken and con-victed, they shall have the judgment of the cucking-stool without making any ransoms [payments to avoid the punishment]. And there they shall stand with bare feet and their hair down, during such time as they may be seen by all passers-by upon the road, at the pleasure of the lord king's bailiff, and not at that of the bailiff of any fee whatsoever. And after this judgment is over, they shall be brought to the lord king's jail and stay there until they make payment, at the bailiff's will, whosoever tenants they may be. And if they will not submit to be punished by such judgment, they should be cast out of the city....

Questions: How were wrongdoers punished in these medieval towns? Did the punishment fit the crime?

73. THE DUBLIN PRISON, 1486

The equipment used to restrain prisoners is here enumerated when new civic officials, the nominal supervisors of the town prison, assume office. Note that one stone of iron weighed about 12–14 pounds.

Source: modernized by M. Kowaleski, *Calendar of Ancient Records of Dublin in the Possession of the Municipal Corporation of that City,* ed. John T. Gilbert (Dublin: Joseph Dollard, Wellington-Quay; London: Bernard-Quaritch, 1889), pp. 237–38.

Memorandum: These are the instruments of iron bought with the aid of the treasury and delivered to Janico Marcus, mayor, Thomas Benet, and Robert Blanchevile, bailiffs of the city of Dublin.

First: 3 shears, 2 leg shackles, 2 bolts with 3 collars, 1 bolt with 3 points for men's hands, 3 shackles for men's legs, 1 great chain which weighs 8 stone and 11½ pounds.

And they are to deliver them to their successors when they retire from office.

Also, 2 shears weighing 2¾ stone.

Also, 2 yokes with 6 collars weighing 1 stone 13 pounds.

Also, 5 pairs of manacles weighing 1 stone 2½ pounds.

Also, 3 stock-locks on the doors. Also 2 hanging locks.

Also, 6 bolts [of] iron on the doors above.

Also, 5 bolts with collars that weigh 3 stone 1½ pounds.

Also, 3 shackles weighing 1 stone.

Questions: What might prisoners in Dublin jail experience as part of their incarceration? On whom was this equipment likely to be used?

CHAPTER SIX

MARRIAGE AND FAMILY

Figure 6.1

Marriage

Medieval marriages were supposed to be blessed by a priest, as depicted in this woodcut. Note the male friends and kin attending the groom and the female friends accompanying the bride, who together signal the approval of the kin and community. Woodcut, printed by Günther Zainer, Augsburg, 1477. Reproduced from Albert Schramm, *Der Bilderschmuck der Frühdruke*. Vol II. *Die Drucke von Günther Zainer in Augsburg* (Leipzig: Deutsches Museum für Buch und Schrift, K.W. Hiersemann, 1920), fig. 710.

74. THE DEL BENE MARRIAGE NEGOTIATIONS
IN FLORENCE, 1381

These extracts from letters sent by Giovanni d'Amerigo Del Bene in Florence to his cousin, Francesco di Jacopo Del Bene, who is away from the city, reveal not only the business side of contracting a marriage for Giovanni's daughter, Caterina, but also the extent to which marriage decisions involved the whole family. Personal letters like these are especially valuable for what they reveal about the role and thoughts of the women of the family, which here includes not only the bride and her mother, but also a jealous aunt and cousin. In relating the progress of the marriage negotiations, the letters also tell us much about the different stages of marriage in Italian cities, from the hire of a marriage broker to the gift of the ring at the betrothal ceremony.

Source: trans. G. Brucker, *The Society of Renaissance Florence: A Documentary Study* (New York: Harper and Row Torchbooks, 1971), pp. 32–37.

[February 20] In the name of God, yesterday I concluded the agreement with Giovanni di Luca [Mozzi, a marriage broker] for the marriage of Caterina [Del Bene, Giovanni's daughter] with Andrea di Castello da Quarata, with a dowry of 900 florins. I could not reduce that sum, although I tried hard to persuade Giovanni to adhere to the terms of our previous discussions. But things are very much up in the air, and Giovanni insisted upon it, alleging many reasons. So, to avoid the rupture of negotiations, I surrendered on this point.

Then I requested Giovanni to maintain secrecy about this affair, as we have agreed, and he said that he would give me a reply. Last night he said that it was impossible, because they wanted to discuss the matter with their relatives, who were so numerous that they couldn't keep the affair secret. However, they are very pleased with this match, and they didn't want to displease me on this point. So, after much effort, I persuaded them to keep it secret through Sunday, and then everyone is free to publicize it as he wishes. So, on the same day, our relatives and Amerigo's friends will be informed....

The women of your household to whom I have spoken say that the girl wishes to have a satin gown, which seems too lavish to me. Write me your opinion. On Sunday, I will meet with Giovanni [di Luca] and we will settle this affair in one day, and also the church where the betrothal ceremony will take place. And I will do the same with Lemmo [Balducci] and will explain the reason to Giovanni. And that evening I will relate everything to our women, because Lapa says that Monna Giovanna di Messer Meo has said that Amerigo [Del Bene, Giovanni's son] has a bride and that she informed her son Niccolò.

The marriage chest will be furnished in the customary manner; it will cost between 70 and 75 florins. They will provide the ring, so that everything will be ready at the proper time. In your letter, remind me of anything that, in your opinion, should be done with respect to these marriages. There is no further news concerning Antonia [Francesco's daughter] except that her mother was very unhappy about that negotiation at Borgo S. Lorenzo. It is my feeling that we shouldn't push this issue and annoy her further, and that we will find some other good prospect for her. You should advise us how we should proceed with the girls; that is, when we should go to see Amerigo's bride, and when the bridegroom should come to see Caterina. I think that Andrea [da Quarata] should come to our house first, and then Caterina, accompanied by our women, should go to see Amerigo's bride. Write me whether you think that Andrea should give the ring that day [of the betrothal ceremony] or not, so that we can arrange the matter beforehand....

[February 21] I wrote you last night and sent the letter off this morning, and so I have little to tell you save that I met Giovanni [di Luca] Mozzi today. We agreed that the betrothal would take place on the first Sunday in Lent, and we may choose the church where it will take place. I don't think that Amerigo's betrothal should be kept secret any longer, so that they won't have any excuse for complaining. I think that on Saturday, Amerigo should go to them [the Balducci] and tell them that we are arranging to marry Caterina, as well as give him a bride. He should tell them everything, and then we can settle that business, and they will learn about it a few days before it becomes public knowledge. Amerigo will write about the deliberations of the women concerning Caterina's trousseau.

I have heard that Dora [Francesco's wife] is somewhat unhappy about this marriage, seeing that Antonia [her daughter] is still unwed.... I also think that Antonia may be upset when she sees Caterina's beautiful gown. I urge you to write a comforting letter to Dora, and tell her that we will find a husband for Antonia, if God wills it. Nor should Antonia be unhappy about the new gown, for I think that it will not be long before she too will have one. I shall not be pleased, if I see any discontent in a household where there should be joy.

[February 24] ... Concerning Caterina, we have concluded the marriage agreement for 900 florins.... They wanted to hold the betrothal ceremony on the first Sunday of Lent, and Giovanni [Mozzi] and I agreed on that point, and also that it will take place in [the church of] S. Apollinare. We haven't yet discussed the guest list, but I think that they will want a large assembly. It is my feeling that we should hold the betrothal ceremony before the dinner, so there will be time afterwards to accept and to deliver the contract. I don't know whom they wish to give the ring, but tomorrow I will settle these matters of the guest list and the ring. The women have decided that Caterina's dress will be made of blue silk and that the gown will form part of the dowry; this was a wise decision. Tomorrow everything will be settled.

It is true that Dora, whom I have always considered a sensible woman, has been behaving in a way that redounds neither to her nor to our dignity. She has not wished to join in any part of this affair. Her attitude is so bizarre and so melancholy that she cries all day and says that your daughter [Antonia] will never be married and that you don't care. She says the most shocking things that I have ever heard and has made your whole family miserable. I am very annoyed by her conduct, and it would please me if you wrote to comfort and correct her, so that she will be content with this affair, and not vexed.

I was with Ser Naddo [di Ser Nepo] on Saturday and told him about Caterina's marriage, and my opinions on the betrothal of the girl [Amerigo's bride] and of Caterina, and also the question of the church and the guest lists. I also informed him of the penalty [for breaking the betrothal contract] of 2,000 florins, and every other detail concerning this affair. Today Ser Naddo told me that Lemmo is content with everything, except that if Caterina's husband gives her the ring, then he wants Amerigo to give it to his daughter; otherwise not. He also says that the penalty should be no more than 1,000 florins, since the rumors of the dowry which he has provided have ruined him. Concerning the ring, he says that he wants it to be arranged in this way, to do like the others. Concerning the penalty, I told him that you had instructed me in this matter as it was agreed, and that I could not alter it without writing you....

[Letter from Naddo di Ser Nepo to Francesco di Jacopo Del Bene, February 24, 1381] After you left here, Giovanni d'Amerigo sent for me to inform me of the marriage alliance which, by the grace of God, has been arranged between you and Lemmo. We discussed certain problems, among which was the fact that in the agreement was a clause providing for a penalty of 2,000 florins. After our discussion, I spoke with Lemmo and he agreed to everything except the penalty of 2,000 florins. He argued as follows: "The rumors of this large dowry which I have given are ruining me, with respect to the taxes which I pay to the commune. And with this matter of a 2,000 florin penalty, everyone will believe that I have given a dowry of that amount, which will destroy me, and surely they [the Del Bene] should not want this to happen. However, this business has been given by Francesco and myself to Messer Bartolomeo [Panciatichi?] for arbitration, and I will abide fully by his decision." On the 24th of this month, I met Giovanni and told him what Lemmo wanted, and that he wanted a penalty of only 1,000 florins, and the reasons for this. Giovanni told me that you had so arranged matters that he could not reply without consulting you.

Speaking with all due reverence and faith, it appears to me that this issue should not disturb or impede this marriage, considering the great friendship which has always existed between you and Lemmo, and which now should be greater than ever. Moreover, you and Amerigo should desire to further his interests, and approve a penalty of 1,000 florins and no more. They entered into this marriage with a positive attitude, and so did you, and therefore I pray you as fervently as I can to be content. I am always ready to carry out your commands.

Questions: Who participated in the various stages of contracting the marriage? What issues most concerned the men? Which issues most concerned the women? What was the role of the bride? What goods or money changed hands to mark the stages of the marriage process?

75. MARRIAGE IN THE MERCHANT CLASS

The family memoirs kept by Florentine merchants like Gregorio Dati record not only their business dealings, but also their marriages and the births of their children. Dati's marriages were themselves important business decisions, since the dowries brought by his wives were immediately channeled into his business, sometimes saving him from the brink of bankruptcy. For his political career, see doc. 40.

Source: trans. J. Martines, "The Diary of Gregorio Dati," in *Two Memoirs of Renaissance Florence*, ed. G. Brucker (Prospect Heights, IL: Waveland Press, 1991; first printed 1967), pp. 113–14, 115, 123, 132, 133–34, selections.

In the name of God and the Virgin Mary, of Blessed Michael the Archangel, of SS. John the Baptist and John the Evangelist, of SS. Peter and Paul, of the holy scholars, SS. Gregory and Jerome, and of St. Mary Magdalene and St. Elisabeth and all the blessed saints in heaven—may they ever intercede for us—I shall record here how I married my second wife, Isabetta, known as Betta, the daughter of Mari di Lorenzo Vilanuzzi and of Monna Veronica, daughter of Pagolo d'Arrigo Guglielmi, and I shall also record the promises which were made to me. May God and His saints grant by their grace that they be kept.

On 31 March 1393, I was betrothed to her and on Easter Monday, 7 April, I gave her a ring. On 22 June, a Sunday, I became her husband in the name of God and good fortune. Her first cousins, Giovanni and Lionardo di Domenico Arrighi, promised that she should have a dowry of 900 gold florins and that, apart from the dowry, she should have the income from a farm in S. Fiore a Elsa which had been left her as a legacy by her mother, Monna Veronica. It was not stated at the time how much this amounted to but it was understood that she would receive the accounts. We arranged our match very simply indeed and with scarcely any discussion. God grant that nothing but good may come of it. On the 26th of that same June, I received a payment of 800 gold florins from the bank of Giacomino and Company. This was the dowry. I invested in the shop of Buonaccorso Berardi and his partners. At the same time I received the trousseau which my wife's cousins valued at 106 florins, in the light of which they deducted 6 florins from another account, leaving me the equivalent of 100 florins. But from what I heard from her, and what I saw myself, they had overestimated it by 30 florins or more. However, from politeness, I said nothing about this....

Our Lord God was pleased to call to himself the blessed soul of ... Betta, on Monday, October 2 [1402] ... and the next day, Tuesday, at three in the afternoon she was buried in our grave in S. Spirito. May God receive her soul in his glory. Amen....

I record that on 8 May, 1403, I was betrothed to Ginevra, daughter of Antonio di Piero Piuvichese Brancacci, in the church of S. Maria sopra Porta. The dowry was 1,000 florins: 700 in cash and 300 in a farm at Campi. On 20 May, we were married, but we held no festivities or wedding celebrations as we were in mourning for Manetto Dati [Gregorio's son], who had died the week before. God grant us a good life together. Ginevra had been married before for four years to Tommaso Brancacci, by whom she had an eight-month-old son. She is now in her twenty-first year.

... After that [1411] it was God's will to recall to himself the blessed soul of my wife Ginevra. She died in childbirth after lengthy suffering, which she bore with remarkable strength and patience. She was perfectly lucid at the time of her death, when she received all the sacraments: confession, communion, extreme unction, and a papal indulgence granting absolution for all her sins.... It comforted her greatly, and she returned her soul to her Creator on September 7.... On Friday the 8th she was honorably buried and on the 9th, masses were said for her soul.

Memo that on Tuesday, 28 January, 1421, I made an agreement with Niccolo d'Andrea del Benino to take his niece Caterina for my lawful wife. She is the daughter of the late Dardano di Niccolò Guicciardini and of Monna Tita, Andrea del Benino's daughter. We were betrothed on the morning of Monday, 3 February, the Eve of Carnival. I met Piero and Giovanni di Messer Luigi [Guicciardini] in the church of S. Maria sopra Porta, and Niccolo d'Andrea del Benino was our mediator. The dowry promised me was 600 florins, and the notary was Ser Niccolo di Ser Verdiano. I went to dine with her that evening in Piero's house and the Saturday after Easter ... I gave her the ring and then on Sunday evening, 30 March, she came to live in our house simply and without ceremony....

Questions: How many times did Dati marry, and what did he look for in a wife? Did the negotiations surrounding his marriages resemble those in the Del Bene family in doc. 74?

76. CONTRACTING MARRIAGE IN YORK AND PARIS

The canon law of the medieval church required that medieval couples freely agree to marry for the marriage to be valid. The two church court cases here demonstrate the two types of marital consent. Present consent marriages consisted of vows stated in the present tense: for example, "I marry you," while future consent was essentially engagement later consummated by sexual intercourse. The emphasis on consent meant that, in theory, no man or woman could be forced into marriage through intimidation or actual physical violence. In the first of these cases, a servant named John Warrington claimed that he had been forced to marry Margaret Barker with words of present consent after his master, a shoemaker named John Bown, found the two together and threatened Warrington with imprisonment. The second case demonstrates a marriage formed by future consent and consummation, with Dyonisia Esperlon winning her case against John Sarrasin, who tried to claim that he had neither contracted marriage with her nor slept with her.

Source: (A) trans. C. Dunn, from "Barkar v. Waryington (1417)," in *Marriage Litigation in Medieval England*, ed. R.H. Helmholz (Cambridge: Cambridge University Press, 1974), pp. 224–27; (B) trans. C. Dunn, from *L'officialité archidiaconale de Paris aux XVe –XVIe siècles*, ed. L. Pommeray (Paris: University of Paris, 1933), pp. 575–76.

(A) A Marriage in York, 1417

The witness John Gamesby of the parish of St. Helen in Stayngate York, aged 40 years, says that at that time and week they were at the castle of York for a certain assize and gaol delivery [courts that tried civil and criminal pleas], and that on the first Monday of Lent [1 March 1417], after the hour of eating, around 6 o'clock in the twilight of the night, in the house of John Bown, cordwainer of York, in the presence of himself, John Bown, Bown's wife, and their servant Agnes, John Warrington and Margaret Barker offered words of matrimony in this form: the said John Warrington first taking the said Margaret by her right hand and stating, "Here I take you Margaret my wife in marriage for better or for worse and for this I give to you my troth." To whom Margaret, responding at once, stated, "Here I take you John as my husband in marriage for better or for worse and to this I give to you my troth." Both offered the words to each other according to the information and prior recitation of John Bown.

Asked if John Warrington was led to contract with Margaret by force or fear, as it is said, the witness John Gamesby says that the previous Sunday John Bown, master, told this witness how John Warrington, his servant, had intercourse with one of his servants within his residence, and that he made the same John swear on the Bible that he would not commit such an offense with another servant of his, within his house again. That oath was not opposed, yet he found the same John Warrington recently with Margaret alone together in a suspicious place, namely in his residence in a high room where hay was lying, and he believed that John had intercourse with Margaret in that place.

And therefore John Bown asked the advice of John Gamesby, how to make it better for him with the said John Warrington, and if it would be good for him to lead John Warrington to the prison of York called *Kydcot*. And then this witness John Gamesby counseled the said John Bown that he should deliberate well concerning such a proposition, and that he should first discuss with John Warrington whether he was willing to have Margaret for his wife.

And thus finally on that Monday, at night, John Bown master of John Warrington asked Warrington if he had had intercourse with Margaret, and if he had promised to take and have her as his wife.

John Warrington then said that he did not have intercourse with Margaret, nor promise his master or give faith that he wished to have her as his wife, to which Margaret then asserted the opposite, namely that John promised to take her and have her as his wife.

And then John said to Margaret and his master what it was that he said to Margaret, that "John Bown his master was able to do thus to him and to be so good and benevolent to him, that he wished to make Margaret a good woman and to do honor to her as far as he was able." And so immediately after the act John Bown, wronged by John Warrington within his residence, recited to John Warrington how he was able to oppress and punish the same John in various ways according to the common law, and he said that if he then wished to have Margaret as his wife that then the major part of his transgression would be amended.

And thus in the end John Bown his master inquired of the same John Warrington if he wished to have Margaret as his wife. To which John for a short time remained not responding; at last he said to his same master, "You are able to be so good and so kind to me that you are able to make me with great benevolence affiance and have her as my wife." And then John the master said to John Warrington, "Take her by the hand and you will say as I will say to you." And then John Warrington said, "By my faith if my father and all my friends were here now present never would I become affianced nor accept her as my wife." But nevertheless afterwards, John Warrington, because he feared that his master would make him be delivered and committed to the prison for his offense committed within his master's house, and for no other cause, as the witness steadfastly believes, John Warrington against his consenting will offered words of matrimony and entered into marriage.

Margaret Bown, age 30 years or more, says that in the house belonging to her and her husband, in the parish of St. Martin in Conyngstreet York, John Warrington and Margaret Barker offered words of matrimony between themselves. Asked how the said party demeaned themselves to a contract of this sort, and whether the said John was forced or influenced by fear to marry the said Margaret, as is said, she says that at the day and hour John Bown, master of the said

John Warrington, summoned Warrington from his shop to his hall, and said to him, "On the summer day when I recited to you the wrong which you committed in my house, you said that you wished to make amends just as I wished also to place you in my goodwill, and therefore you offered yourself to do according to my will. And for that reason here is my wish, that you will take and affiance this same Margaret Barker as your wife now here in our presence."

And then that same John Warrington, standing for a short time replying nothing, finally said: "I have friends who would be here; I will not become betrothed nor marry that same Margaret as my wife at this or at any other time." And after many diverse words were spoken then between the same John and his said master, the master to him: "Tell me, are you willing to have the same Margaret as your wife?" To which John then said to his master: "You are able to make me do so because you are able with great kindness to make me have her as my wife." And thus, finally, according to the command of his master, John took Margaret by the hand and with her contracted matrimony, as it is said, against his will. And this the same witness firmly believes, because it is well known that the said John Warrington feared that if he did not then contract marriage with Margaret on the order of his said master, that his master wished to incarcerate him and in other ways to punish him according to the common law.

And all agree to the statement of John Warrington regarding a certain wrong committed by him within the house of his master, according to the assertion of his master, saying that John had intercourse with his women servants within his house, and furthermore that he found the same John with Margaret alone in a suspicious place on the Sunday immediately preceding that Monday, namely in a room where hay was lying, in a certain remote part of his house of residence.

If indeed the said John Warrington carnally knew the said Margaret after the marriage contract this witness does not know, so she says, in so much that about seven days thereafter the same John said to her that his master was wicked to him because he made him take Margaret as his wife and to contract marriage with her, and that he strongly believed marriage of this sort was not able to stand or to exist, because he was never in his mind to have her as his wife.

(B) A Marriage in Paris, 1488

Concerning Dyonisia, daughter of Roland Esperlon, plaintiff in a cause of marriage, dowry, and provision against John Sarrasin, imprisoned defendant. The plaintiff related mutual promises concerning future marriage, particularly that on the first Sunday of May [4 May 1488] John Sarrasin gave her two Parisian coins in the name of matrimony and deflowered her and afterwards had intercourse with her many times in the name of matrimony to such a degree that she became pregnant from his act. Desiring that he be judged wedded or betrothed, she entreats for her dowry the sum of 200 pounds Tournois, and provision for herself to support expenses for the duration of the process.

The defendant, for his part, persists in his confessions by denying all other things.

Therefore because of the careful oath made by the plaintiff claiming that John Sarrasin deflowered her and knew or felt that she was pregnant from his deed around the Feast of the nativity of blessed John the Baptist [24 June 1488], the lord bishop arranged that the defendant will give for six weeks before the birth, six Parisian coins each 7th day, and, lasting for four weeks after birth, a half shield of gold saving the right of recovery, and for the first week he will grant the six Parisian coins in public.

And the plaintiff surrendered for security Roland, her father, who promised restoration of provision in the event that it was decided that the defendant was not kept and was released on the security of John Cirier ... and with consideration of the principal cause which will have proceeded to the quinzaine [the next meeting of the court], with parties secured on either side who will give two or three witnesses to swear in the presence of the plaintiff's scribe that the suit should be sent back to the ordinary [another church court] with the remaining pledges; likewise the prisoner, accepting the obligation, was received by the agent of the court and the lord bishop prevented the defendant under penalty of excommunication and 60 pounds Parisian from any secular law nor power binding him in chains.

Questions: *What do these court cases tell us about the "romantic" behavior of young men and women in medieval towns and about the conditions under which marriage was contracted? What or whom were the courts most interested in protecting, and what steps did the courts order to solve particular problems? How did John Bown, master shoemaker of York, try to control the moral behavior of his servants? To what extent were his servants part of his "family"? What did Dyonisia receive as a marriage settlement? Why did the bishop stipulate that John Sarrasin give Dyonisia her settlement in public for the first week?*

77. WOMEN, FAMILY RELATIONS, AND INHERITANCE IN ARAGON

The Fueros *of Borja and Zaragoza were municipal laws for two towns in Aragon, a kingdom in north-central Spain. This collection of statutes, issued by the kings of Aragon in the mid-twelfth century, was expanded as specific needs arose. These* Fueros *touch upon all aspects of life, including commerce, crime, inheritance, property rights, and relations between different religious groups. The* fueros *included here give a glimpse of certain aspects of social and familial life and how they were regulated by the town.*

Source: trans. J. Speed, from *Fueros de Borja y Zaragoza*, ed. Juan José Morales Gómez and Manuel José Pedraza García (Zaragoza: Anubar Ediciónes, 1986), pp. 17, 20–21, 27–28, 32, 46, 49, 52, 57, selections.

7. This regards a man who demands an inheritance or something else. It is not permitted for him to be angry, nor to make his demand in a judicial proceeding, nor in a disavowal of feudal relations nor in a delay, but as much as possible he should abbreviate his case and he ought only to make his demand so that the matter might be brought to a close more quickly and his demand might have an end. But the one who holds the inheritance or something else is permitted every kind of delay so that what he holds by a created law might remain his.

20. This regards an inheritance which two brothers have mortgaged. One is not in the country and the one who is in the country wants to take it from the pledge. They [who hold the pledge or mortgage] must not return it to him if his brother is still alive. And if he says, "My brother is dead," they must not return it to him unless he shows them the tomb where his brother lies, with the testimony of that cleric who buried him and with two other noblemen who were present at the burial, and who would swear to this according to the *Fueros* of Aragon. And if he says, "I give you in faith that they are making my brother stay in this place which is in another country," they ought to do nothing unless as written above.

43. This regards a man who gives an inheritance [of land] to a daughter, and the daughter has a husband, and the land is partly from her father and partly from her mother. If the daughter and son-in-law wish to sell the land, they may not sell it unless they give assurance that the revenues which they have received from that land they will then put toward another piece of land which is just as good and in just as good a place. If, truly, the daughter and son-in-law

have no sons or daughters, and she dies without children, after the husband becomes a widower, without any doubt, he has to return the land to the daughter's parents or to her nearest relatives.

54. This regards a sale or mortgage [of land] between brothers. A brother, if he has to sell or mortgage [the land] or in any way alienate his inheritance, he must first let his brother know, and if his brother wishes, he ought to retain it. But if he lets his brother know and the second brother says that he is not able [to buy it], or excuses himself in some way, afterwards, the first brother may sell or mortgage the land to whatever man in the world he wishes. And if the second wishes to resist, let the first brother give him a promise and let him sell and do this according to his agreement.

55. This regards the disinheriting of a son or daughter by a father. A father may not disinherit a son without clear reason. If a son beats his father, or makes him swear by something which is grievous to him, or drags him by the hair, or lies about him in front of respectable men, or if the son does anything by which the father loses those things which he has … a father can indeed disinherit his son. And if a father has sons and daughters and wishes to give everything to one and disinherit the others, he may not. But he may favor one with goods, or give one a landholding or a vineyard or houses or something else. But concerning all of these situations, it is not to be held the law that the father can favor one son or daughter and disinherit the others.

94. This regards an illegitimate son who demands a portion from his brothers or parents. If it is said to him, "We don't know or we truly doubt whether you are the son or that man whom you claim to be; therefore, prove to us that you really are his son." Then, the son must prove himself by two patrons, or by two men of the law, who would swear that he is the son of that man whom he asserted. And in this way, he is a son of that man of that place unless he demands a part of the full inheritance rights or raises up a sword.

102. This regards a father or mother who has become widowed. They cannot give a complete gift of their property if the one does not have possession of the property from the other with a charter and security, or if they never divided it. But from his or her own part of the property which has been clearly recognized, the father or mother can give a gift.

110. This regards a son or daughter who has sent a herd of cattle [as a means of support] on behalf their father or mother. If they have not sent it with a formal agreement, or with a request for security or witnesses, neither the father nor

the mother nor siblings must respond, but they should render thanks to the person who sent it. And with this, there ought to be peace according to the *Fueros* of Aragon.

126. This regards the inheritance of brothers or sons of brothers or the closest relations which has not been divided. If one of them gives away, without the mandate and consent of the others, some thing of that inheritance to the saints [a monastery], or to his wife, or to another place, it cannot be allowed. But with an oath that he would swear that he was not taking part in that kind of donation, that the inheritance had not been divided, and that he has not given permission for such a donation, he may set aside this prohibition. But if the inheritance is divided and he is able to have witnesses, he can make the donation and rightly he would do what he does.

Questions: What aspects of family relations did these statutes attempt to regulate? Why would a town step in to impose these sorts of regulations? What do these statutes suggest about women's control over property? Why are there so many regulations about the inheritance of property?

78. WOMEN, FAMILY RELATIONS, AND INHERITANCE IN MAGDEBURG AND BRESLAU

Urban charters often contained clauses about inheritance procedures because property—the source of much wealth—was at stake when householders died. In aiming to cover all contingencies, these clauses tell us much about the role of women and children, and the family disputes that could arise when settling an urban estate. The inheritance clauses printed below come from the Magdeburg charter given to the citizens of Breslau in 1261 (doc. 26). The schoeffen were the chief civic magistrates.

Source: trans. O.J. Thatcher and E.H. McNeal, *A Source Book for Mediaeval History* (New York: Charles Scribner's Sons, 1905), pp. 592–602, selections.

14. If a man dies leaving a wife, she shall have no share in his property except what he has given her in court, or has appointed for her dower. She must have six witnesses, male or female, to prove her dower. If the man made no provision for her, her children must support her as long as she does not remarry. If her husband had sheep, the widow shall take them.

15. If a man and woman have children, some of whom are married and have received their marriage portion, and the man dies, the children who are still at home [that is, unmarried], should receive the inheritance. Those

who have received their marriage portion should have no part of it [that is, the inheritance]. Children who have received an inheritance should not sell it without the consent of their heirs....

17. If a judge or *schoeffen* dies, he shall be declared deposed [that is, his office shall be declared vacant] by a session of court in which at least two *schoeffen* and four free citizens are present. Then his wife shall receive her share of his property [that is, not until his office is declared vacant may his widow claim her share of his property].

18. No one, whether man or woman, shall, on his sick-bed, give away more than 3 shillings worth of his property without the consent of his heirs, and the woman must have the consent of her husband....

20. If there are no immediate heirs [that is, children] to an inheritance, the nearest of kin shall share it equally....

22. If an inheritance is left to a boy [that is, if his father dies], and he wishes to become a priest, he shall nevertheless receive the inheritance. But if he has an unmarried sister at home, the two shall divide it between them....

28. No widow shall use the capital of her dower or sell it. If she dies it shall go to the heirs of her husband.

29. If an inheritance is left to children, and one of them dies, the others share it equally....

41. If anyone dies leaving an inheritance and no heirs appear within a year and a day to claim it, it shall go to the king.

42. If a man who has three or more children is killed, and someone is accused by one of the children of having killed his father, but is not convicted, and the court gives him a certificate that he did not commit the crime, the other children shall not renew the charge against him.

43. If a man enters suit against another, he shall make a deposit with the judge [to cover expenses?]. He shall not give this deposit to the judge, but he shall receive it back [after the suit is ended]....

47. If a man is outlawed or condemned, no one but his heirs shall take his property.

48. If a man dies without having disposed of his property, it shall go to his children, if they are his equals in birth. If one of the children dies, its share goes to its mother, but she cannot dispose of it without the consent of her heirs.

49. When a child is twelve years old it may choose whom it will as guardian. The guardian must render an account to the mother and to the children of his management of the inheritance....

52. If a man is security for anything [he had been a pledge for someone else] and dies, his children are not responsible for the security. If a man is security for a debt, he must pay it and make everything good....

55. When a man dies his wife shall give his sword, his horse and saddle, and his best coat of mail. She shall also give a bed, a pillow, a sheet, a tablecloth, two dishes and a towel. Some say that she should give other things also, but that is not necessary. If she does not have these things, she shall not give them, but she shall give proof for each article that she does not have it.

56. If two or more children inherit these things [named in no. 55, above], the oldest shall take the sword and they shall share the other things equally.

57. If the children are minors, the oldest male relative on the father's side, if he is of the same rank by birth, shall receive all these things [named in no. 55, above] and preserve them for the children. When they become of age, he shall give them to them, and in addition, all their property, unless he can prove that he has used it to their profit, or that it has been stolen or destroyed by some accident without any fault of his. He shall also be the guardian of the widow until she remarries, if he is of the same rank as she is.

58. After giving the above articles the widow shall take her dower and all that belongs to her; that is, all the sheep, geese, chests, yarn, beds, pillows, cushions, table linen, bed linen, towels, cups, candlesticks, linen, woman's clothing, finger rings, bracelets, headdress, psalters, and all prayer-books, chairs, drawers, bureaus, carpets, curtains, etc., and there are many other trinkets which belong to her, such as brushes, scissors, and mirrors, but I do not mention them. But uncut cloth and unworked gold and silver do not belong to her.

59. All the possessions of the man except those named in no. 55 [above] belong to his inheritance. If he has given anything in pledge, he who has the right to shall redeem it if he wishes to do so.

60. If one of the children becomes a priest he shall share in the inheritance equally with his brothers, but not if he becomes a monk.

Questions: What limits were put on how wives, widows, and daughters controlled property? What rights did fathers, brothers, and sons have over property that women did not have? What particular family problems do these laws address? What rights did under-age orphans have? How do the concerns about women and property expressed in these laws compare to those in the cities of Aragon (doc. 77)?

79. WIVES AT THE TAVERN

We get a completely different take on the social life of wives and husbands from this late medieval English ballad. Sung by minstrels, such ballads offer an unusual view of everyday life and relationships that would have struck a chord with listeners, most of whom were probably familiar with the type of behavior and attitudes depicted in this song. In this period a "gossip" referred to a close friend, one to whom a woman could confide. Only later did the word attain its current meaning of "idle chatter."

Source: modernized M. Kowaleski, from *Songs and Carols*, ed. T. Wright (London: Percy Society, 1843), pp. 91–95.

> How, gossip mine, gossip mine,
> When will you go to the wine?
>
> I will you now tell a full good sport,
> How gossips gather them on a sort,
> Their sick bodies for to comfort
> When they meet, in a lane or street.
>
> But I dare not, for their displeasure
> Tell of these matters half the substance;
> But yet somewhat of their governance,
> As far as I dare, I will declare.
>
> Good gossip mine, where have you been?
> It is so long since I've seen you.
> Where is the best wine? Tell you me.
> If you can tell, [then say] full well.

I know a draught of merry-go-down,
The best it is in all the town;
But yet would I not, for my gown,
My husband it wist [know], you may me trust!

Call forth your gossips by and by,
Elinor, Joan and Margery,
Margaret, Alice and Cecily;
For they will come both all and some.

And each of them will somewhat bring.
Goose, pig or capon's wing,
Pastries of pigeons, or some other thing;
For a gallon of wine they will not wring.

Go before be tweyn and tweyn [two by two],
Wisely, so you'll not be seen;
For I must home, and come again,
To witt i-wys [know truly] where my husband is.

A stripe or two God might send me,
If my husband might here see me.
She who is afraid, let her flee,
Quoth Alice then, "I dread no man."

Now we be in tavern set,
A draught of the best let him fetch,
To bring our husbands out of debt
For we will spend, till God more send.

Each of them brought forth their dish;
Some brought flesh, and some brought fish.
Quoth Margaret meek: Now with a wish,
I would Anne were here, she would make us cheer.

How say you, gossips, is this wine good?
"That it is," quoth Elinor "By the rood;
It cherishes the heart, and comforts the blood;
Such junkets among shall make us live long!"

Anne, bid fill a pot of muscatel;
For of all wines I love it well,
Sweet wines keep my body in heal;
If I had of it nought, I should take great thought.

How look you, gossip, at the board's end?
Not merry gossip? God it amend.
All shall be well, else God it defend;
Be merry and glad, and sit not so sad.

Would God I had done after your counsel!
For my husband is so fell [angry],
He beats me like the devil of hell;
And the more I cry the less mercy!

Alice with a loud voice spoke then,
"I-wis," [truly] she said "little good he can [do],
Who beats or strikes any woman,
And specially his wife; God give him short life!"

Margaret meek said, "As I may thrive
I know no man that is alive,
That give me two strokes, but I shall have five;
I am not afeared, though I have no beard!"

One cast down her shot, and went her way.
"Gossip," quoth Elinor, "what did she pay?"
"Nought but a penny." Lo, therefore I say,
She shall no more be of our lore [fellowship].

Such guests we may have i-now [enough],
That will not for their shot allow.
"With whom came she? Gossip with you?"
"Nay," quoth Joan, "I came alone."

Now reckon our shot, and go we hence,
What? Cost it each of us but three pence?
Truly, this is but a small expense,
For such a sort, and all but sport.

Turn down the street where you came out,
And we will compass round about.
"Gossip," quoth Anne "why are you doubtful?
Your husband will be pleased, when you will be reised [go out?]."

Whatsoever any man think,
We come nought but for a good drink.
Now let us go home and wynk [sleep];
For it may be seen, where we have been.

This is the thought that gossips take,
Once in the week merry will they make,
And all small drink they will forsake;
But wine of the best shall have no rest.

Some be at the tavern once a week;
And so be some every day;
Or else they will groan and make them sick.
For things used will not be refused.

What say you, women, is it not so?
Yes surely, and that you well know;
And therefore let us drink all a row,
And of our singing make a good ending.

Now fill the cup, and drink to me;
And then shall we good fellows be.
And of this talking leave will we,
And speak then good of women.

Questions: Why were these wives going to the tavern and how often did they go? What does this ballad tell us about the relationship between husbands and wives in medieval English towns? How reliable are such ballads for what urban wives in late medieval England may have done and felt?

80. CHILDHOOD DEATHS IN LONDON

English law dictated that each death had to be investigated by an official called the coroner, who convened a jury drawn from the neighborhood where the death occurred to decide if the death was a result of a felony or misadventure. The coroner's inquiries that survive for the city of London provide an unusual insight into the activities of the children of London.

Source: trans. R.R. Sharpe, *Calendar of the Coroners Rolls of the City of London A.D. 1300–1378* (London: Richard Clay and Sons, Ltd., 1913), pp. 25, 30–31, 56–57, 63–54, 83, abridged and revised.

1301 [Inquisition on the death of Richard, son of John le Mazon] ... The jurors say that ... when Richard, who was eight years of age, was walking, immediately after dinner, across London Bridge to school, he hung by his hands in play from a certain beam on the side of the bridge, so that, his hands giving way, he fell into the water and was drowned. Asked who were present, they say a great multititude of passers-by, whose names they know not, but they suspect no one of the death except the said mischance. The corpse was viewed, on which there appeared no wound or hurt....

1301 [Inquisition on the death of Petronilla, daughter of William de Wytonia, aged three years] ... The jurors say that on Tuesday the Feast of Sts. Philip and James [4 May] there came a certain Hugh Picard riding a white horse ... after the hour of vespers, when Petronilla was playing in the street, and the horse being strong, quickly carried Hugh against his will over Petronilla so that it struck her on her right side with its right forefoot. Petronilla lingered until the next day, when she died, at the hour of vespers, from the blow. Being asked who were present, the jurors know only of those mentioned. The corpse viewed, the right side of which appeared blue and badly bruised, and no other hurt. The horse valued at a mark, for which Richard de Caumpes, the sheriff, will answer. Hugh fled and has no chattels; he afterwards surrendered to John de Boreford, sheriff.

1322 [Inquisition on the death of Joan, daughter of Bernard de Irlaunde] ... The jurors say that ... before the hour of vespers, Joan was lying in her cradle alone, the shop door being open, there entered a certain sow which mortally bit the right side of the head of the said Joan. At length came Margaret, the wife of Bernard and mother of Joan, and raised the cry and snatched up Joan and kept her alive until midnight when she died of the bite and no other felony. Asked who was present, they said no one except Margaret, nor do they suspect anyone thereof except the said bite....

1322 [Inquisition on the death of Robert, son of John de St. Botulph, 7 years old] ... The jurors say that on Sunday before the Feast of St. Dunstan [19 May], Robert, Richard, son of John de Chesthunt, and two other boys, names unknown, were playing upon certain pieces of timber in a lane called Kyrounelane in the Vintry Ward, when a piece fell on Robert and broke his right leg. In the course of time Joan, his mother, arrived and rolled the timber off him, and carried him to the shop where he lingered until the Friday before the Feast of St. Margaret [20 July] when he died at the hour of prime of the broken leg and of no other felony, nor do they suspect anyone of the death, but only the accident and the fracture ...

1324 [Inquisition on the death of John, son of William de Burgh, 5 years old] ... The jurors say that on the previous Monday at the hour of Vespers John was in the house of Richard le Latthere and had taken a parcel of wool and placed it in his cap. Emma, the wife of Richard, chastising him, struck John with her right hand under his left ear, nobody else being present, so that he cried. On hearing this, Isabella, his mother, raised the hue and carried him ... where he lingered until the hour of curfew of the same day, when he died of the blow and not of any felony. Asked what became of Emma, the jurors said she fled, but where she went or who received her they know not. Order to the sheriffs to attach her when found in their bailiwick. Afterwards Emma surrendered herself to the prison of Newgate.

Question: What do these passages reveal about the activities and experiences of children in medieval towns?

81. FAMILY AND HOUSEHOLD IN MANOSQUE, 1418–26

These extracts are from the livre de raison—*a combination of a personal account book and family diary, similar to the* ricordi *of Florentine merchants—of a well-off notary named Jean Durant, who lived in the southern French town of Manosque, just north of the larger city of Marseille. The informal nature of the* livre de raison *is evident in the random jotting down of events out of date order, as well as the sometimes abbreviated and cryptic references to events and business dealings. Like other notaries, Durant earned his living by drawing up official agreements and giving them legal force by entering them into his notarial register. He mentions some of these agreements in his own diary, particularly those regarding members of his family. These business matters, as well as expenses he recorded regarding his wife, children, servants, and friends, offer an unusual glimpse into the family life and households of Durant and his friends, most of whom appear to have been of middling social status. The "spiritual kinsmen" and "kinswomen" refer to people linked by baptism to Durant, either because they were his godparents, he was their godparent, or they were godparents for one of his children. One florin was worth about 32 shillings or 384 pence, and there were 12 gros in a florin.*

Source: trans. M. Kowaleski, from *Livres de raison et de comptes en Provence*, ed. M.R. Bonnet (Aix-en-Provence: Publications de l'Université de Provence, 1995), pp. 117–36, selections.

Sunday, 28 July 1426, between 8 and 9 a.m., my daughter Borgueta was born, whose godparents were Master Jaufre Andrieu, notary, and Madame Borgueta Joliana....

Jean Dodon. On Wednesday, 18 May [1417], I gave and paid to my spiritual kinsman, Jean Dodon, 5 florins for the feeding of my daughter, Lousion. I made a final accounting of everything he had from me until this day; he has received 20 florins. I still owe him 4 florins for this past year, which ends on 1 June. It will be paid.

Memorandum of my son Arnaud. On Tuesday, 24 May, around 2 o'clock in the night, my son Arnaud was born; his godfathers, Monsieur Arnaud Savornin, vicar general, Brisset, the secretary of the Countess of Vellin, and Monsieur Jean Riquier of Thor had him baptized on Thursday....

On 26 August, I gave 1 *gros* to my servant Georges when he had his beard trimmed....

My godfather, Guillaume Riquier, owes me 1 florin that my wife Peyroneta loaned him in cash when his father died....

Monsieur Guillaume Frances, vicar of Rocquefort, owes me 6 *gros* for the remainder of two charters that I gave him for the dowry of his sister Jeanne, which came to 18 *gros*.

The heirs of Etienne Berthomieu, of Marseille, owe me 25 florins for a transfer that I made to Catherine Fediera, as appears in a notarial act taken by the hand of

P. Betonin, notary, an act that I gave into the custody and safe-keeping of Monsieur Hughes Roca of Marseille. Master Jean Senescal, tailor, owes me ... 9 *gros* for his part of a charter of donation of half of his goods to his spiritual kinsman, Jean Isnart; ½ *gros* for his part of the note regarding vines that he gave to farm [lease out] to Pierre Roqua. The aforesaid Jean Isnart owes me for an agreement made about the charter of assignment....

Remember: I have given into the custody and safe-keeping of my spiritual kinsman, Isnart [Dalmas], the butcher of Marseille, a long book with a black leather cover, which is the *livre de raison* of the company of Jean Avinhon and of P. Messier.

The agreements between Jean Bonifazi and me. On 20 September 1418, I, Jean Durant, notary, leased to my spiritual kinsman, Jean Bonifazi of Civas [a nearby village], all my cultivated and uncultivated lands, my three great gardens, the house of Madame Marguerite, reserving for me the chamber in which is found the bed and my service of *poids* [perhaps a labor service owed to him] during the grape harvest for making wine in the cistern; I have given him the cowshed of [ ] for the next five years from the Feast of St. Michael [29 September]. He must give me one-third of all the produce of these lands; the wheat will be split up into sheaves. He should give me half of all the fruits of the harvest of the trees after his expenses; he must carry them to my house and split them up there. He must well and duly work and cultivate the trees each year. Each year, he must put at least 40 *hémines* [a measure of land] of these lands to fallow [that is, let it rest by not growing crops on it] and save six rows [of land] for seed for the following year.

The same day, I settled with my aunt, Moneta de la Ciotat, for the rest of the wine that I had owed her from last year and for 3 barrels of salted tuna and a barrel of eels that she had had made for me at la Ciotat; I owed her, all total, 6 florins....

On 25 September, I gave and paid 2 florins to my spiritual kinsman, Jean Dodon, towards what I owed him for the feeding of my daughter....

On Sunday, 9 October, I gave 3 *gros* to my servant Georges towards his salary.

My aunt Madame Marguerite de Montels owes me 1 florin that I loaned and gave on her order to Madame Receveta, her companion, when she left Aubagne to go to Ollioules when I married my wife Peyroneta....

I, Jean Durant, owe 2 florins to the shop of Raimond Blanquet of Marseille, for the remainder of 4 *cannes* [measure of about 80 inches in length] of freize funerary cloth that I bought for my mother-in-law and my son Peter....

I, Jean Durant, notary, owe 3 florins 3 *gros* to Master Etienne Rahols, skinner of Marseille, for the remainder of a fur of white *avortons* [probably lamb fur] for a houppelande [a loose-fitting outer coat] for my wife Peyroneta. There is a bill for my part. It was paid.

The agreements between my nephew Jean Durant and me. On 15 November

1418 he made an agreement with me. It is thus that he must stay with me for a year in order to carry on all business, inside as well as outside, accounting to me from today until then, for the salary of 18 florins....

Jean Dodon. On 13 November, I paid 2 florins to my spiritual kinsman, Jean Dodon, towards the 8 florins I owe him for the feeding of my daughter Louison....

I have rented out half of the meadow situated in the large field to my spiritual kinswoman, Beatrice, once wife of Raimond Maurel, also guardian of her son Urbain, for 25 years to come from the Feast of All Saints [1 November]....

On the same day [23 December] I concluded an agreement and accord with Antoine Rodelhac on the subject of the charter of the company of B. d'Aviayga and for the donation that his mother made to him of the profits and other rights that she had over the goods of her husband, Antoine Ayga, and another charter of purchase; they cost him 2 florins....

Bertrand Rampalm owes me for [writing] a clause in the will of his father.

Jean Geram of Roquefort owes me 1 florin for what my wife loaned to him. Plus a quarter of wheat that I loaned him.

On Saturday, 11 February, I gave 3¾ *gros* to my nephew Jean Durant towards his salary. The same day, ½ *gros*....

Jaufre Jausselme owes me 6 *gros* for an agreement done between him and me in the presence of his father-in-law, P. Revel, for the clause in the will of Françoise Oliviera.

On Monday, 20 February, I made payment of 3 florins to my spiritual kinsman, Jean Dodon, by Pierre Fabre of Aruiol, towards 6 florins I still owed him for the feeding of my daughter Louison....

My spiritual kinswoman, Madame Jauma Jordana, and her children owe me 1 florin for the remainder of 2 charters that I gave to them concerning the death certificate of my spiritual kinsman, Hughes Jordan ...

On 22 April I concluded an agreement and accord with Madame Huguette, wife of Monsieur P. Blanc of Roquefort, deceased, regarding the charter of a transaction and the bill that Pierre Blanc made for her, a charter by which she owes me 2 florins before the Feast of St. John. She also gave me 2 florins 6 *gros* in payment of certain things that she owed me towards the 5 florins that Pierre Blanc owed her for her dowry.... She gave me in payment half of the profits of the beans and split hinge of the land that Pierre Blanc gave to her....

On Sunday, 28 April 1428, around 3 o'clock, my son Guillaume Durant was born; my spiritual kinsman, Monsieur G. de Motels, and my spiritual kinswoman, Madame Amilheta de la Sarda, were his godparents....

On Saturday 21 April 1421, in the morning, a little after the first frost, my son Louis was born; Monseigneur Lous Terralh, prévôt of Marseille, Master Antoine Vincens, notary, and his mother Dousselma were the godparents....

This same year [1418] we rented the house of St. Martin of Marseille to Master Pierre the builder, for him as well as his apprentice, for one year accounting at the Feast of St. Michael for the rent of 3½ florins for all. He immediately paid 1 florin. His apprentice paid 10 *gros* for the first third of this house on the last day of November. Then 10 *gros* for the second third....

On the last day of October 1421 was concluded the agreement, the transaction, and the bill between Peyroneta and me on one part, and Antoine Bonet on the other part, because of the demands and allowances made by each party upon the goods and inheritance of Jean Avinhon and of Madame Huguette, his mother; this transaction means that Peyroneta [who was a widow when Durant married her] has and must have all rights returned to her because of the 100 florins remaining to be paid from her dowry for other reasons and causes; that is, the paternal house of the said Jean [Avinhon] in which she actually lived... all the house of St. Martin which belonged to Madame Huguette, situated in the street of St. Martin, with all the furniture, that we have received for Jaumes Avinhon, deceased son of the said Julien and of Peyroneta, as well as half of the debt of P. Barra from the outcome of a ship voyage and all the other debts that ought to be returned to this inheritance....

On 25 November 1421, day of the Feast of St. Catherine, I rented to Monsieur P. Alcais, who used to reside with me, our house at the bridge of Aubagne, with the cellar below, and [he lists gardens and other rural properties]....

Abram Samiel, Jew, [owes] 3 florins for the purchase of a cloth of one *canne* and 2 pieces of dark cloth of Perpignan that he took for his son's celebration. He must pay at Easter....

Here are the receipts that I, Jean Durant, notary, guardian of Jaumes Avinhon, my stepson, son and heir of the hearth of Jean Avinhon of Marseille, have made.

First, on 28 October 1418, I received from the hands of my spiritual kinsman, Isnart the baker of Fermin, who leases the great house of St. Martin for a year at the price of 7 florins; I have had 28 *gros* for the first third [he goes on to list other rents received and his difficulties in securing others]....

Here are the expenses that I, Jean Durant, notary, guardian of my stepson Jaumes Avinhon ... have made.

First, on 10 March in the year of the Incarnation 1417, Jaumes Avinhon entered my house; on this day I began to support him. On the same day I paid 4 shillings for a warning letter from the officer of Marseille against all persons who would have levied or made a levy on the house [that is, the inheritance] of this child....

I paid 2 shillings to have this letter executed in St. Martin, in Acoules, and in la Major.

I paid 3 *gros* to carry several things of this child to his house; they were found in the small house of his grandmother.

I paid 1 *gros* to Master Antoine Raynaut, notary, for the notice of the recognizance of the house of this child when I went to negotiate with the men of the large shop.

I paid ½ *gros* to Master Nicholas Aymar, notary, for the notice of the recognizance of the half of the small house made to Madame Catherine of St. Jaumes.... [He continues to enumerate various expenses associated with securing the child's inheritance.]

I spent 16 florins 10 *gros* for this child, the first year when he entered my house; he had during this whole year a grave illness with fever and dysentery....

On Friday, 27 September 1420, on the day of the Feast of Sts. Cosmas and Damian, Jaumes Avinhon, son of Jean Avinhon, died; he was buried at the Franciscans' house, near his father. I paid 1 *gros* for the burial. I paid 6 *gros* for his coffin. I paid for his funeral, including the cloth that we had had from the Franciscans and the rights for the parish of St. Martin. I paid for his illness, both for the doctors, physicians, and surgeons as well as for a comforting potion and other remedies and chicken.

Questions: How many different family interactions can be seen in these extracts, whether in Durant's family or those of his friends and associates? What can we learn about the relationships between parents and children? Do these selections tell us anything about the non-family members of urban households? What insights do these selections give us on the role of godparents? Did Jean view his relations with his world as measured by money, or is that an effect of the type of document printed here?

82. A COMFORTABLE RETIREMENT FOR THE WEALTHY

Donato Velluti was a merchant and judge of Florence who rose to the civic office of Standard-Bearer of Justice in Florence in 1370. This extract is from his diary, which he used to glorify members of his own family, including this lively description of an aged relative. Although Velutti's interest in promoting the achievements of his family led him to exaggerate certain characteristics (notably the advanced age of Bonaccorso), this character portrait does offer us an idea of the experience of the aged among the wealthier members of Florentine society.

Source: trans. M. Baca, *Merchant Writers of the Italian Renaissance from Boccaccio to Machiavelli*, ed. Vittore Branca (New York: Marsilio Publishers, 1999), pp. 115–16.

Bonaccorso di Pietro was a bold, strong, hearty man, and very able in the use of arms. He accomplished great feats of valor and gallantry, both in Florence and in other places. He had received so many wounds in battles and skirmishes that he had been stitched up all over his body. He was a great opponent of the Paterins [the Albigensians] and heretics, when they were openly fighting about this type of thing, as I heard, at the time of St. Peter Martyr [a Dominican friar who promoted a citizens' crusade against the Paterins, c. 1243].

Bonaccorso was tall in stature, with strong limbs, and well put together. He lived a full 120 years, but he was blind for the last 20 years of his life. He was called Corso; and I heard that when he was very old, he had become so stiff that he couldn't bend his body. He was also an experienced, honest merchant. He enjoyed such a good reputation that when a shipment of Milanese cloth arrived in Florence (for he ordered a great deal of cloth from Milan), he would sell out of it even before the bales were untied....

After he had lost his eyesight, Bonaccorso stayed at home most of the time. He had the back part of the palazzo in the Via Maggio before it was divided up between him and his grandsons. There was a balcony along the length of the palazzo, which had three bedchambers on the back side. He would walk back and forth there every morning until he figured he had walked three or four miles. After his walk, he breakfasted, and his breakfast wasn't just two bread rolls. Then at midday he ate copiously, for he was a great eater. And thus he passed his days.

Now I want to tell you how he died. My father told me that one day Bonaccorso decided he wanted to go to the warming room [heated by hot air blown in from below or on the sides]; while there, he struck his foot on something. When he returned and saw that on account of this injury he was unable to take his usual exercise, he immediately believed he was going to die. It happened that at this time his son Filippo, who was my grandfather, was about to marry his second wife, Madona Gemma de' Pulci. That day Bonaccorso had jested a great deal, saying: "I, not my son, am the one who needs to take a wife," and many other witticisms. Lying on his bed, he decided to have himself carried to his lounging chair; so he called his grandsons—that is, my father and my uncle Gherado—and leaning his hands and arms on their shoulders, suddenly the life went out of him on account of his great age, and he died; that was in 1296.

Questions: How would you characterize the quality of life of this old man? To what extent were his activities a function of his advanced age? How did his family regard him?

83. CARING FOR THE AGED IN MEDIEVAL EXETER

There was no insurance or old-age pensions in the Middle Ages, so the aged had to rely on the care of relatives and friends if they were unable to support themselves. In northern Europe, where extended family structures were less common and family honor more diffuse, well-off burgesses not infrequently made contractual arrangements to ensure reliable care in their old age. Sometimes these contracts were made with members of their own families, and sometimes the contract arranged for retirement to a local religious house.

Source: (A) trans. M. Kowaleski, from Exeter Cathedral Library, Vicard Choral 3105; (B) trans. M. Kowaleski, from Devon Record Office, DD 6724.

(A) Retirement at Home

Grant by Ivo de Gatepath to Richard Crok, with Elena, Ivo's daughter in free marriage or dower, his tenement in the suburb outside the south gate of the city of Exeter in Cartere Street between the tenement of the vicars of the church of St. Peter and the tenement of Peter Beyvin ... for Richard and Elena and their issue to hold after the death of the grantor along with its utensils and furniture. During the life of the grantor, he is to be the sole owner of the house and goods, and Richard and Elena are to be like members of his household. Ivo and Richard will each provide for themselves and their families and share expenses. If Richard and Elena or either of them prove ungrateful, or do damage to Ivo's goods or manifest other ingratitude towards him, he may revoke this gift and expel them from his house. In this case, after Ivo's death, Richard and Elena should have the tenement, but the goods and furniture should be disposed of as he wishes in his will. If Elena dies without issue or has children who die before coming into the inheritance, the tenement should revert to the nearest heirs of Ivo.... Dated at Exeter ... 1313.

(B) Retirement to a Religious House

Indenture made between John Tetteforde, prior of St. James near Exeter, on one part, and Thomas Stur on the other, witnessing that Thomas gave and delivered goods and chattels, alive and dead, to the value of 8 marks to the prior for the use of the prior. For this the prior agreed that Thomas could live for his life in the priory and have daily food and drink and a chamber for his bed if he should wish to remain there during his life. Dated at the priory, 3 May 1404.

Questions: What do these documents tell us about the quality of retirement for these elderly Exeter men? How did Ivo in doc. A seek to retain some power and control over his estate during his retirement? How did their experience in old age compare with that of the well-off Florentine in doc. 82?

84. FAMILY AND HOUSEHOLDS: A DEMOGRAPHIC PERSPECTIVE

Historical demography applies quantitative methods to study past populations, especially their size and composition (such as age, sex, and marital status). Because medieval taxes assessed people by households, they often provide this type of information. The English poll tax of 1377, for instance, which taxed all adults over the age of fourteen 4 pence each, was often recorded in a way that allows us to see the membership of individual households (which could include servants, lodgers, and extended family members). Table A shows data collected from this tax that compares rural and urban households in terms of their average size (after a 1.65 multiplier is added to account for evasion and children under the age of 14) and composition. Tables B and C are drawn from data in the Florentine catasto *(see doc. 66), which taxed not only the households of the city of Florence, but also those in the towns and villages in its* contado.

Source: (A) and (B): calculated by M. Kowaleski from data in *The Poll Taxes of 1377, 1379 and 1381*, ed. C. Fenwick, 2 vols. (London: British Academy, 1998–2001), vol. 2, pp. 267–71 (Northumberland), 316–19 (Oxfordshire), 355–73 (Rutland); the urban data are from P.J.P. Goldberg, *Women, Work and Life Cycle in a Medieval Economy: Women in York and Yorkshire c. 1300–1520* (Oxford: Clarendon Press, 1992), pp. 161, 306, 310, 370, 372, and J.C. Russell, *British Medieval Population* (Albuquerque: University of New Mexico Press, 1948), p. 27. (C) and (D): data are drawn from D. Herlihy and C. Klapisch-Zuber, *Tuscans and Their Families: A Study of the Florentine* Catasto *of 1427* (New Haven, CT: Yale University Press, 1985), (C) p. 87; (D) pp. 90, 91, 288 n. 13, 308, 334.

(A) Table 6.1: The Size and Composition of Urban and Rural Households (HH) in England, 1377

Place	Total population	Mean HH Size	% of HH headed by women	Adult sex ratio (# men to 100 women)
Rural households in the poll taxes				
Oxfordshire, 12 vills	438	3.74	12.4%	118.5
Northumberland, 38 vills	1276	3.50	10.6%	107.5
Rutland, 41 vills	3595	3.53	14.5%	103.0
Urban households in the poll taxes				
Dartmouth	512	3.76	15.4%	87.6
Carlisle	661	3.83	23.9%	89.7
Northampton★	672	4.18	8.0%	93.4
Oxford, St. Mary par.	295	3.96	8.9%	98.0
Oxford, St. Peter par.	177	4.10	16.7%	98.9
Hull	1557	3.71	23.4%	92.7
Colchester	2912	3.50	19.3%	100.0
York★	1934	4.12	19.3%	90.5

Note: ★=partial or damaged return. For rural vills, only fully nominative returns were employed. The mean household size has been calculated by using a multiplier of 1.65 to account for children under 14 and others who evaded the tax.

(B) Table 6.2: Servants in Urban and Rural Households (HH) in England, 1377

Place	Total population	% of HH with servants	% in service	Servant sex ratio (# men to 100 women)
Rural households in the poll taxes				
Oxfordshire, 12 vills	438	16.1%	11.9%	188.9
Northumberland, 38 vills	1276	12.1%	7.8%	316.7
Rutland, 41 vills	3595	15.3%	10.2%	157.3
Urban households in the poll taxes				
Dartmouth	512	30.3%	20.5%	–
Carlisle	661	23.9%	17.1%	113.2
Northampton★	672	36.2%	30.2%	–
Oxford, St. Mary par.	295	26.8%	24.4%	89.5
Oxford, St. Peter par.	177	29.2%	27.7%	145.0
Hull	1557	14.8%	22.8%	119.1
Colchester	2912	–	15.5%	137.9
York★	1934	38.4%	31.9%	–

Note: ★=partial or damaged return. For rural vills, only fully nominative returns were employed. Note that the Dartmouth, Northampton, and York returns do not name the servants and so their sex cannot be determined.

(C) Table 6.3: Age at Marriage in Tuscany

Place	Men		Women	
	1427	1470–80	1427	1470–80
Rural residents in Florentine *contado*	25.7	27.7	18.4	21.0
Urban residents				
Florence	30.3	31.4	17.6	20.8
Prato	26.9	29.6	17.6	21.1

Note: The data for Florence comes from the 1427 and 1480 *catasti*; the data for the *contado* and Prato comes from the 1427 and 1470 *catasti*. The figures for 1470–80 are based on a sample of 10% of households.

(D) Table 6.4: Household (HH) Composition in Tuscany, by Percentages, 1427–1480

Place	N=	Year	Mean HH Size	% Single	% HH Headed by Women
Rural households	37,029	1427	4.74	10.9%	9.0%
(of *contado*)		1470		8.8%	
Urban households					
Florence	9,821	1427	3.78	20.1%	16.5%
		1458	4.72		
		1480		14.8%	
Prato	943	1427	3.73	17.2%	15.6%
		1470	4.26	20.9%	

Notes: The figures for households in the *contado* in 1470, in 1480 Florence, and 1470 Prato are based on a sample of 10% of households. The figures for the % of households headed by women for 1427 Florence are based on all urban households in Florence and its *contado*.

Questions: *What were the major differences between English urban and rural households in terms of their size, gender composition, and servant residents? What accounts for these differences? Did similar differences exist between the Tuscan urban and rural populations? How might we interpret the changes that occurred in the household composition of Tuscan households over time? Why would urban men marry so late and urban women marry so early in the Tuscan cities? What impact could the large spousal age gap have had on Italian urban marriages?*

CHAPTER SEVEN

WOMEN

Figure 7.1
Women at Work in the Marketplace
An official exacts a market toll from a woman trader while other women hawk their own wares
and yet others (carrying baskets) do their household shopping. The town market was a place for
women to congregate and exchange gossip as well as wares. From one of the painted windows of the
Cathedral of Tournai (fifteenth century). Reproduced from Paul LaCroix, *Manners, Customs, and Dress
During the Middle Ages and During the Renaissance Period* (London: Bickers and Son, 1870), fig. 260.

85. PROPER BEHAVIOR FOR A YOUNG TOWNSWOMAN

These extracts come from a Middle English poem, "How the Good Wife Taught Her Daughter," which is part of a long tradition of didactic works ostensibly written as parental instructions. Although presented as a mother's advice to her daughter, this poem was probably written by a cleric who used maternal authority to get across lessons about how a good young woman should behave. The early stanzas, for example, exhort young women to attend church regularly, pay tithes, and not to chatter in church. The later stanzas offer advice to newly married women. References in the poem, however, indicate that it was directed toward middle-class urban women, thus offering us some idea of the attitudes toward and expectations of townswomen, at least from the viewpoint of the Church. In so doing, moreover, the poem also relates aspects of the everyday life of a young woman in a fourteenth-century English town.

Source: trans. E. Rickert, *The Babees' Book: Medieval Manners for the Young* (London: Ballantyne Press, 1908; rpt. London: Chatto and Windus, 1923), pp. 31–42, selections, modernized.

The good wife taught her daughter,
Full many a time and often,
A full good woman to be;
For said she: "Daughter to me dear,
Something good now you must hear,
If you will prosper thee....

The man that shall wed you before God with a ring,
Love you him and honor most of earthly thing.
Meekly you answer him and not as a shrew,
So you may calm his mood, and be his dear darling.
A fair word and a meek, does anger slake,
My dear child....

Don't go into the town, as if you were gawking,
From one house to another, seeking to be amazed;
Nor go to market to sell your russet cloth,
And then to the tavern to bring your reputation low.
For they who taverns haunt, from thrift soon come to want,
My dear child.

And if you be in any place where good ale is aloft,
Whether you are served or that you sit soft,
Take moderately so that you fall in no blame,

For if you are often drunk, it falls to your shame.
For those that are often drunk, thrift is from them sunk,
My dear child.

Do not go to see wrestling, or shooting at the cock,
As if you were a strumpet or a giggling girl;
Dwell at home, daughter, and love your work much,
As so you shall, my dear child, soon grow rich.
A merry thing it is evermore, for a man to be served of his own thing,
My dear child.

Aquaint you not with each man that travels the street,
If any man speak to you, swiftly greet him;
Do not stand by him, but let him his way depart,
Lest he by his villainy should tempt your heart.
For all men are not true, who fair words can show,
My dear child.

Also beware for covetousness gifts to take;
Unless you know another reason, quickly them forsake;
For with gifts may men soon women overcome,
Though they were as true as steel or as stone.
Bound forsooth is she, who takes of any man a fee,
My dear child.

And wisely govern your house, and serving maids and men,
Don't be too bitter or too debonaire with them;
But look at what most needs to be done,
And set your servants to it, both quickly and soon.
For ready is at need, a foredone deed,
My dear child.

And if your husband be from home, let not your servants do ill,
But look who does well and who does nil,
And he that does well, pay him well his while,
But he that does otherwise, treat him as vile.
A foredone deed, will another speed,
My dear child....

And if your children are rebellious and will not bow down low,
If any of them misbehave, neither curse them nor scold;

But take a smart rod and beat them in a row,
Till they cry mercy and their guilt well know.
Dear child, by this lore, they will love you evermore,
My dear child.

And look to your daughters that none of them be lost,
From the very time that they are of you born,
Busy yourself and collect fast for their marriage,
And get them espoused, as soon as they are of age.
Maidens be fair and amenable, but in their love full unstable,
My dear child....

Questions: What types of activity were young English townswomen doing? Which of these activities were frowned upon? What can this poem tell us of attitudes toward women, or of relations between women and men?

86. WOMEN AND GOSSIP

In late medieval England, there was a growing concern about women's talk or chattering, an anxiety that was expressed in a new type of indictment against "scolds" in many town courts (see also the last entry in doc. 72). The first passage contains selections from the borough courts of the town of Exeter, where these indictments were listed some four or five times a year. The second extract shows the concern about defamation and the harm it could do in a case tried before the church court of York. The "articles" refer to a specific set of questions that each witness was required to answer.

Source: (A) trans. M. Kowaleski, from Devon Record Office, Exeter Mayor's Court Rolls, 1390/1, m. 38d; 1392/3, m. 23d; 1463/4, mm. 14d, 42; (B) trans. P.J.P. Goldberg, *Women in England c. 1275–1525: Documentary Sources* (New York: St. Martin's Press, 1995), pp. 230–31.

(A) Exeter Borough Courts

Mayor's Court, 1390/91. The jurors [named] present that Mabillia, wife of John Payn scolded John, rector of St. Keran's church and with William Wymark and his wife on Saturday in the Feast of the Nativity of St. John [24 June] in 1391 and she is a common scold and perturbs the king's peace. They also say that Joan, wife of Gervase Baker, scolded John Brige, weaver, on the Feast of St. Barnabas [11 June] in 1391 and is a common scold.... [An inquisition is ordered on both charges.]

Mayor's Court, 1392/93. The jurors [named] present that ... Alicia, servant of Galfrid Coyl, scolded Agnes Baylesford and Mabilla Baillesford at Exeter on Friday and is a common scold.... Joan, wife of Thomas May, Alicia Laverantz (denies the charge and finds pledges to defend herself), and Joan, wife of John Jolyf, gossip and scold with each other and others and perturb the peace....

Mayor's Court, 1463/64. The alderman of the North Gate suburb presents that Katerina Swell on 17 December 1463 scolded Margery, wife of John Brian, and Rosa Brian, calling them whores in perturbing the peace of the king, so they are attached.... The jurors [named] present that ... Isabella, wife of John Rondell of Exeter (fined) on 2 July with force and stones assaulted John Lewis of Exeter and his wife, Willemina, calling them thief and whore and Isabella is a common sower of lies and foments discord amongst her neighbors against the peace....

(B) York Church Court, 1422

Sir Ralph Amcotes of the parish of Holy Trinity, King's Court, chaplain [priest], aged 50 years [is questioned]....

Asked on the first article he says he knew Agnes, about whom this cause is concerned, for the past twelve years and more and that during that time he never told or heard say other than that Agnes was a trustworthy woman of good reputation and of honest conversation....

Asked about the second, third, fourth, fifth, sixth, seventh, and eighth articles read out to him separately, he says that on Sunday last of the present month, immediately after vespers had been sung in the parish church of Holy Trinity and at the time when the parishioners of the same church were returning to their homes in great number, this witness was present in person in the cemetery of the parish church. He heard Emmot, about whom this cause is also concerned, publicly and in a loud voice call out and name the said Agnes as she was going from the vespers and the cemetery to her own home in Colliergate, York, which was right by the cemetery and the church, "old whore of monks and friars," in English "ald munkhore and ald frerehor," and "thief and attainted thief," in English "ald rank tayntydthefe." The said Emmot at that time and place in the presence, as he believes, of sixty men and women returning from the parish church and vespers, as stated before, and many other men and women of other parishes and places present there in many various places repeated and publicly proclaimed these words with great spirit and great malice out of wickedness and hatred with the intention of publicly defaming Agnes, so that by the pronouncement of these words and Emmot's malice all who heard and saw Emmot knew and would clearly be able to know that Emmot, although she appeared somewhat infirm in body, had a tongue flexible and vigorous for articulating her talkativeness, and a spirit full of malice and irascibility because Emmot purposed and desired to hit the same Agnes with a club which she then had and held in her hand had she not gone back into her home more quickly. Because of the defamatory words, Agnes's character was besmirched and her standing, esteem, and reputation gravely and abusively defamed and injured. Because of these defamatory words to the knowledge and hearing of this witness, certain of Agnes's neighbors refused [gap in the manuscript] with Agnes as they used to, and the husband of the same Agnes would have driven her from his society and his home were it not for the special request and entreaty of his neighbors....

[Three further depositions offer similar accounts.]

William Baker of the parish of Holy Trinity, King's Court, tailor, aged 50 years and more ... [he knew Agnes sixteen years].

Alice, wife of John Rode, goldsmith, of the parish of Holy Trinity, King's Court, aged 20 years and more ... [knew Agnes ten years and more].

Isabel Cook of the parish of Holy Trinity, King's Court, aged 40 years and more ... [knew Agnes sixteen years and more].

Questions: Why were women charged in court so much more often than men for scolding? What type of women seems to have been presented for this offense? Why would male authorities be so anxious to criminalize women's speech?

Figure 7.2
Women Gossiping
This group of women talk among themselves while watching a tournament. From a manuscript with the story of St. Graal and Lancelot, reproduced from Thomas Wright, *The Archaeological Album* (London: Chapman and Hall, 1845), p. 77.

87. WOMEN AND FASHION

Sacchetti (c.1335–c.1400) was a poet and storyteller who also served Florence in the office of prior. His extant stories tell us much about everyday life in fourteenth-century Florence. These extracts focus on women's fashions and the futile effort to enforce the sumptuary laws, which were meant to control the extravagant excesses of fashionable clothing and runaway costs, as well as to make sure that lower social orders did not ape fashions considered suitable only for the wealthy elite. The Florentine sumptuary laws, moreover, restricted women's dress more than men, who were given leeway to wear, for example, as many buttons and other ornamentations as they wished. For examples of the different fashions worn by men and women, see figures 12.3 to 12.7.

Source: trans. M.G. Steegman, *Tales from Sacchetti* (London: J.M. Dent and Sons, Ltd., 1908), pp. 116–19, 200–02, revised.

Evading the Sumptuary Laws

... In this story I will show how women's laws have vanquished learned doctors and how they can be very great logicians when they want to be. Not a long time ago, while I was (although unworthy) one of the priors of our city [Florence], there came a judge whose name was Messer Amerigo degli Amerighi, from Pesaro, a very handsome man, and very able in his business. Presenting himself at the place of our office upon his arrival, with all due solemnity and speeches, he began his term of office. New laws on the ornaments of women had been passed, so he was sent for within a few days and reminded to carry out these orders with all the solicitude possible, and he replied that he would do so. He returned home, looked over these ordinances, and for many days his sergeants went about making the necessary inquisition [seeking those disobeying the ordinances]. But when the notary who accompanied them returned, he told him that whenever he found a woman disobeying the law and wished to write down her name, she began to argue with him, and the notary was almost out of his mind. Messer Amerigo had noted and considered all his notary's reports.

It happened by chance that certain citizens, seeing how women wore whatever they liked without any restriction, and hearing of the law which had been passed, and also that a new officer had arrived, went to the Signori [the city rulers] and said that the new officer did his work so well that never before had the women had so much liberty in their dress as at the present time. So the Signori sent for the judge and told him that they marveled at the negligent manner in which he carried out the orders concerning the women. Messer Amerigo answered as follows:

"My lords, I have studied all my life to learn law, and now, when I thought that I knew something, I find that I know nothing. For, when searching for ornaments forbidden to your women according to the ordinances you gave me, I have never before found in any law such arguments as they made in their defense. From among them I would like to mention a few. A woman came with the long peak of her hood fringed and twisted around her head. My notary said: 'Tell me your name, because the peak of your hood is fringed.' The good woman took down the peak, which was fastened to the hood with a pin, and holding it in her hand, she told the notary that it was only a wreath. Later on, he met a woman wearing many buttons in front of her dress. He said to her: 'You cannot wear those buttons,' and she answered, 'Yes, Messere, I can for these are not buttons, they are beads, and if you do not believe me, look at them; they have no hanks, nor do they have any button-holes.' The notary met another who was wearing ermine [an expensive fur] and wondered, 'What will she have to say?' 'You are wearing ermine,' he said, and was about to write down her name, but the woman answered, 'Do not put down my name, for this is not ermine, this is the fur of a suckling.' The notary asked, 'What is this suckling?' and the woman answered, 'It is an animal.' And my notary is stuck like an animal! ...

Said one of the Signori: 'We are only knocking our heads against a wall.'

Another said: 'We had best attend to business of greater import.'...."

And thus, one alleging one thing and another something else, all the officers advised Messer Amerigo to do the best he could and leave the rest alone. And this was said at that time and on that occasion, so that after this hardly any officer carried out his orders or gave himself any trouble, but allowed the peaks to pass for wreaths and meddled not with the false buttons and the suckling's fur and the belts....

Fashion in the Italian Cities

How many fashions have been altered in my time by the changeableness of those persons now living, and especially in my own city! Formerly the women wore their bodices cut so open that they were uncovered to beneath their armpits! Then, with one jump, they wore their collars right up to their ears! And these are all outrageous fashions. I, the writer, could recite as many more of the customs and fashions which have been changed in my days as would fill a book as large as this whole volume. But although they were constantly changing in this city of ours, they were not invariable either in most of the other great cities of the world. And although formerly the Genoese never altered the fashion of their dress, and neither the Venetians nor the Catalans altered theirs, nor did their women either, nowadays it seems to me that the whole world is united in having but little firmness of mind; for the men and women of Florence, Genoa, Venice, Catalonia, indeed of all the Christian world, go dressed in the same manner, not being able to distinguish one from another: And would to Heaven they all remained fixed upon the same manner, but quite the contrary! For if one jay does but appear with a new fashion, all the world copies it. So that the whole world, but most especially Italy, is variable and hastens to adopt the new fashions.

The young maidens, who used to dress with so much modesty, have now raised the hanging ends of their hoods and have twisted them into caps, and they go attired like common women, wearing caps, and collars and strings round their necks, with diverse kinds of beasts hung upon their breasts. And what more wretched, dangerous, and useless fashion ever existed than that of wearing such sleeves as they do, or great sacks, as they might rather be called? They cannot raise a glass or take a mouthful without soiling both their sleeves and the tablecloth by upsetting the glasses on the table. Likewise youths wear these immense sleeves, but still worse is it when even sucklings are dressed in them. The women wear hoods and cloaks. The young men for the most part go without cloaks and wear their hair long; they only have to but divest themselves of their breeches and they will then have left off everything they can, and truly these are so small that they could easily do without them. They put their legs into tight socks and upon their wrists they hang a yard of cloth; they put more cloth into the making of a glove than into a hood. Perchance they will thereby all do penance for their many vanities. For whoever lives but one day in this world changes his fashions a thousand times; each one seeks liberty and yet deprives himself of it. The Lord created our feet free, yet many persons are unable to walk on account of the long points of their shoes. He created legs with joints, but many have so stiffened them with strings and laces that they can scarcely sit down; their bodies are drawn in tightly, their arms are burdened with a train of cloth, their necks are squeezed into their hoods and their heads into a sort of nightcap, whereby all day they feel as though their heads were being sawn off. Truly there would be no end to describing the women's attire, considering the extravagance of their dress from their feet up to their heads, and how every day they are up on the roofs, some curling their hair, some smoothing it, and some bleaching it, so that often they die of the colds they catch!

Questions: What do these tales tell us about attitudes toward women? Was there a gap between male expectations of women and how they actually behaved? What female fashions does Saccheti find objectionable? Why would the Florentine rulers have felt compelled to create "fashion police" to discover, report on, and fine those breaking the sumptuary laws?

88. SINGLEWOMEN IN COVENTRY, 1492–95

The northern English town of Coventry reacted to a severe economic crisis by imposing a series of reforms on the citizenry that had a strongly moralizing tone and included a concerted effort to stamp out prostitution. These extracts represent some of the reform ordinances that dealt specifically with singlewomen, most of whom had probably migrated to Coventry and were working at various low-paid jobs in the city. Indeed, the poor state of the city's economy appears to have driven many able-bodied working men out of the city in search of work.

Source: modernized M. Kowaleski, from *The Coventry Leet Book*, vol. II, ed. M.D. Harris (Early English Text Society, original series, vol. 135, 1907), pp. 545, 568.

1492. Also that no person within this city from henceforth to keep, hold, receive, or favor any tapster [a barmaid, or someone who retails ale], or woman of evil name, fame, or condition with whom any contact is inclined to be sinful, pertaining to lechery, upon the penalty that every such household lose 20 shillings for every offense. And that every person that has such a tenant, keeping such suspect persons within his house after such warning by an officer, unless he evicts such a tenant, is to lose 40 shillings.

1492. Also that no singlewoman, being in good health and strong enough body to work, under the age of 50 years, may henceforth take or keep houses or rooms by themselves, nor may they rent any room with any other person, but they should go into service [that is, domestic service] until they are married. Whoever does to the contrary to lease [a room] at the first default [is to pay] 6 shillings 8 pence and at the second default to be committed to prison, there to abide until they fine surety to go into service. And that every such person who receives such women, or sets them any house or room to lease, [is to pay] 20 shillings at the first default and 40 shillings at the second default, and to be committed to prison at the third default, there to remain until he finds surety to conform himself to this ordinance.

1495. And also that every maiden and singlewoman, under the age of 40 years old, who keeps any house alone by herself, should take a room with an honest person, who shall answer for her good behavior, or else [she] is to go into service between this Feast of All Hallows [1 November] and the next coming, upon pain of imprisonment, there to abide until the time that she finds surety to do so, or else to vacate the city. And that the sheriffs should weekly make a search and do execution of and in the premises, upon the pain of losing 100 shillings every time that they be found lax in making searches and not executing [the order] on the premises. That fine is to be levied by the mayor for the time being to the use of the city.

Questions: What limits are put on the activities of singlewomen? What anxieties do these ordinances reflect about young singlewomen? What did the civic elite fear about these women?

89. WOMEN IN THE PARISIAN CRAFT GUILDS, c. 1270

The collection of guild regulations in Paris compiled around 1270 listed over one hundred guilds, seven of which were exclusively female or female-dominated. The female guilds specialized in detailed handwork and luxury textiles, such as spinning silk, weaving silk ribbons, and producing fancy head-gear and purses decorated with silk, gold thread, and pearls. The membership lists of these guilds indicate that most of the women were working independently of their husbands or male relatives, and could become guild masters regardless of their marital status. Arrangements for governing the guilds, however, tended to vary widely in the degree of authority enjoyed by the female members.

Source: (A-C) trans M. Kowaleski, from *Métiers et corporations de la ville de Paris, XIIIe siècle, Le Livre des Métiers d'Étienne Boilieau*, ed. R. de Lespinasse and F. Bonnardot (Paris: Imprimerie Nationale, 1879), pp. 68–70, 74–75, 83–84; (D) trans. M. Kowaleski, from *Réglements sur les arts et métiers de Paris rédigés au XIIIe siècle, et connu sous le nom du Livre des Métiers d'Étienne Boileau*, ed. G.B. Depping (Paris: Imprimerie de Crapelet, 1837), pp. 379–82.

(A) The Silk Spinners on Large Spindles

1. Anyone who wishes to be a silk spinster on large spindles in Paris, namely to be able to reel, spin, double, and retwist, may freely do so, provided she works according to the following customs and usages of the craft:

2. No spinster on large spindles may have more than three apprentices, unless they be her own or her husband's children born in true wedlock. Nor may she contract with them for an apprenticeship of less than seven years or for a fee of less than 20 Parisian shillings to be paid to her, their mistress, or for eight years if no fee is paid. But she may accept more money and more service if she can get them....

4. No woman of the craft may hire any other apprentice or journeywoman before she herself has completed her years of service with the mistress to whom she was apprenticed.

5. If any [spinster] has taken on an apprentice in this craft, she may not take on another before the first has completed her seven years, unless the apprentice die or forswear the craft forever.

6. If an apprentice buys her freedom before serving the said seven years, she may not take on an apprentice until she herself has practiced the craft for seven years.

7. If any spinster sell her apprentice, she should owe 6 pence to the guardians appointed in the king's name to safeguard the [standards of the] craft. And she must make this agreement before the two guardians; and she owes 6 pence to the guardians.

8. If any journeywoman comes to Paris from outside of Paris and wishes to work in this craft, she must swear before two guardians of the craft that she will practice the craft well and loyally and she will conform to its customs and usages....

9. If any woman of this craft takes silk to spin from anyone and she pawns this silk and the owner of the silk complains, the fine is 5 Parisian shillings to the king....

10. No journeywoman should farm out another's silk to be worked upon outside her own workshop.

11. The said craft has as guardians two men of good standing sworn on the king's behalf whom the provost of Paris may appoint and change at his will. They swear an oath before the provost of Paris that they will guard the said craft well and loyally to their utmost and that they will inform the provost of Paris or his representative of all malpractices that they discover, as soon as they reasonably can.

12. Any woman who infringes any of these regulations owes 5 Parisian shillings to the king each time she is reprimanded. From these 5 shillings the guardians should have 12 pence for their costs and their trouble in pursuing the fines. And the guardians are quit of watch [guard-duty in the city] for their effort and work that they do for this craft as guardians on behalf of the king.

(B) The Makers of Silk Fabric

1. No journeywoman maker of silk fabric may be a mistress of the craft until she has practiced it for a year and a day in residence on the job, for then she will have done her term [of apprenticeship], because she will be more competent to practice her craft.

4. No mistress of the craft may, nor must they, weave ordinary thread with silk, or foil with silk, because such work is counterfeit and wicked and it must be burnt if it is discovered.

5. No mistress or journeywoman of this craft may, nor must they, make counterfeit raised embroidery, either of ordinary thread or foil, nor may she do raised work of ordinary thread or foil. And if such work is discovered, it must be burned, because it is false and bad.

7. It is ordered regarding this craft that all the mistresses of the craft who send their work outside the town to be done must show it to those women who are designated to watch over the craft, along with the work of their workshop, to make sure there are no mistakes [on the work done outside the workshop].

8. And anyone who infringes on any of these regulations must pay 8 Parisian shillings each time she is found at fault. Of these 8 shillings, the king will have 5 shillings, and the confraternity of the craft 12 pence, and 2 shillings for the masters who oversee the craft for their pains and the work they do in overseeing the craft.

9. To safeguard this craft in the manner described above, there should be established three masters and three mistresses, who will swear by the saints that they will make known to the provost of Paris or to his representative all the infringements of the regulations, to the best of their ability.

(C) The Weavers of Silk Kerchiefs

1. Any woman who wishes to weave silk kerchiefs in Paris may do so, provided she knows how to practice the craft well and truly, according the following usages and customs....

   [The eight regulations that follow are similar to those of the other crafts, including ordinances about the number of journeywomen and apprentices, working conditions, fines for disobedience, etc.]

10. The said craft has three good women and true who will oversee the craft on behalf of the king, sworn and pledged at the Châtelet, who will make known all infringements against the craft, whenever they discover them. [added later in the margin:] Johana la Pie in the street of the Watch; Hondée de Fosses, Aelesia de Meldis ... are the guardians of this craft on the Wednesday after the [feast] of the Magdalene [25 July] in the year 1296.

(D) The Embroiderers

To all those who see these letters, greetings from Guillaume de Hangest, warden of the prevostship of Paris. Know all that [these regulations] have been agreed and ordered by all the male and female embroiderers of the town of Paris, especially by Jeanne, wife of Jean de Meudon; Ameline la Brouderesse, called la Parquière; Jeanne, daughter of Giles the Mercer; Jeanne de Braye; Benoite d'Arraz; Marie, daughter of Estienne the Skinner; Mabile du Perche; Belon, daughter of Michel le Convert; Jeanne, wife of Sanguin the Goldsmith; Aalis, wife of Jean du Bongenoul ... [a total of 12 male and 83 female members are listed; of the women members, 16 are termed daughters (5 of these were daughters of female members), 2 are identified as sisters of other female members, 24 are identified as wives (none had husbands in the craft), and 44 are identified simply by their own surname] and by all others in the craft, and for the common profit of the town of Paris and all other good people, with the consent and assent of the provost of Paris.

[1.] First, it is ordered that whoever wishes to be an embroiderer in Paris, male or female, may do so provided he knows how to practice the craft of embroiderer according to the following usages and customs of the craft:

[2.] First, it is ordered that from now on no man or woman of the craft may take on another male or female apprentice until the previous apprentice is in his last year of service, taking all absences into account.

[3.] Moreover, from now on a man or woman of the craft may have only one male or female apprentice together. Nor may any one take on another until the male or female apprentice is in the last year of their service, as stated above.

[4.] Moreover, from now on no man or woman of the craft may take on a male or female apprentice without at least eight years of service, even if they have the money [to support the apprentice], but after serving the entire term they may hire him, if they like.

[5.] Moreover, no man or woman may work at this craft at night, but only by the light of day, because the work done at night is not as good or sufficient as the work done during the day.

[6.] Moreover, whoever is discovered working during the night, should pay a fine of 2 shillings; that is, 12 pence to the king and 12 pence to the guardians of the craft.

[7.] Moreover, no man or woman of the craft should work in the craft on Sunday or the four feasts of Our Lady, nor on the six feast-days of the apostles. And whoever is discovered working on any of these days should pay a fine of 2 shillings, of which 12 pence should go to the king and the other 12 pence to the guardians of the craft.

[8.] Moreover, no man or woman may take on a male or female apprentice if they do not maintain a workshop, or if they themselves are not workers in the craft....

[10.] Moreover, it is ordered that no man or woman should be able to go to work in the house of anyone who is not a member of the craft because it is not good when workers work with those who know nothing of the craft. And it becomes a problem when masters have made contracts with rich customers to do their gold embroidery but cannot find their workers because they have gone elsewhere than to those who know the craft, and they cannot keep the contract with rich customers by their own default. And whoever goes to work like this should pay a fine of 2 shillings: 12 pence to the king and 12 pence to the masters....

[12.] This craft should have four trustworthy and sufficient men, sworn to uphold the ordinances of the craft, whom the provost of Paris may appoint or change at his will. These guardians are to report well and truly the infringements that they find in the craft, and what they say under oath will be taken as either full proof, three-quarters of a proof, or half of a proof [their evidence will be assigned a certain percentage depending on their status and quality of the evidence; the idea was to add up the proofs offered until it came to 100.]

Questions: What do these regulations tell us about the tasks, status, working environment, and organizational profile of wage-earning women in medieval Paris? What measure of authority do you think these women gained from their work and membership in an officially sanctioned guild?

Figure 7.3

Women Carding and Spinning

These women are engaged in the low-end occupations of carding and spinning wool, neither of which was ever organized into a guild. Spinning in particular was carried on by many women, often on a part-time basis in between other domestic and craft duties, sometimes for profit, but probably more often simply to make yarn to use in weaving wool clothing for their families. Reproduced from Charles Knight, *Old England: A Pictorial Museum of Regal, Ecclesiastical, Municipal, Baronial and Popular Antiquities,* 2 vols. (London: James Sangster and Co., 1850), fig. 803.

90. LIMITS ON EMPLOYING WOMEN AS WEAVERS IN BRISTOL, 1461

When times were tough—as they were in the port town of Bristol during the "depression" of the mid-fifteenth century—the secondary status of women in craft guilds made them vulnerable to rules designed to create more employment for able-bodied men, who were seen as more worthy of full-time work.

Source: modernized M. Kowaleski, from *The Little Red Book of Bristol*, vol. 2, ed. F.B. Bickley (Bristol: W. Crofton Hemmons, 1900), pp. 127–28.

Also, it is agreed, ordained, and assented by William Canynges, mayor of the town of Bristol, Thomas Kempson, sheriff of the same, and all the Common Council of the town of Bristol held in the Guildhall there the 24th day of September ... that for as much as various persons of the weavers' craft of the town of Bristol employ, occupy, and hire their wives, daughters, and maids, some to weave on their own looms and some to hire them to work with other persons of the craft, whereby many and various of the king's liege people, likely men liable to do the king service in his wars and in defence of this his land, and sufficiently learned in the craft, go vagrant and unemployed, and may not have work for their livelihood. Therefore, no person of the craft of weavers within the town of Bristol from this day forward may set, employ, or engage his wife, daughter, or maid for any weaving work at the loom with himself or with any other person of the craft within the town of Bristol, and that upon pain of losing at every time ... 6 shillings 8 pence to be levied, half to the use of the Chamber of Bristol, and half to the contribution of the craft, provided always and except that this act does not pertain to the wife of any man of the craft of weavers now living at the making of this act, but they may employ their wives during the natural life of the said women in manner and form as they did before the making of this act, etc.... [In the following year, the town passed a similar ordinance forbidding the employment of strangers and foreigners as weaving because they too were taking away jobs from able-bodied citizens.]

Questions: Why would weavers prefer to hire their wives, daughters, and maids to work in their business? What do the exceptions to the new regulations tell us about wives and work?

91. ADVICE ON HIRING MAIDSERVANTS, c. 1393

This extract comes from an advice book written by a wealthy, middle-aged Parisian for his new teenaged wife. Although the work is highly prescriptive in that it views women's role in the household as it ought to be, the very practical nature of much of the advice (including recipes and much detailed information on keeping things clean) means that we also obtain a glimpse into everyday household management. In this extract, the husband's advice about hiring chambermaids not only offers us an idea of their working conditions, but also suggests that there might have been a fairly rapid turnover in these waged positions.

Source: trans. E. Power, *The Goodman of Paris* (London: George Routledge & Sons, Ltd., 1928), pp. 208–11, 213–14, 218–19, abridged and revised.

And know that of those chambermaids who need a job, there are many who offer themselves and clamor and seek urgently for masters and mistresses. And of these, take none until you first know where their last place was, and send some of your people to learn their character, to wit whether they chattered or drank too much, how long they were in that place, what work they have been accustomed to do and know how to do, whether they have homes or friends in the town, from what manner of folk and what part of the country they come, how long they were there and why they left. And by their work in the past you shall find out what hope or expectation you may have of their work in the future. And know that oftentimes such women from distant parts of the country have been blamed for some vice in their own district and that is what brings them into service at a distance. For if they were without fault they would be mistresses, not servants; and of men I say the same. And if you find from the report of her master and mistress that a girl is what you need, find out from her and cause Master Jehan to register in his account book in her presence, on the same day whereon you engage her, her name and the names of her father and mother and some of her kinsfolk, and the places where they live and her birthplace and her references. For servants will fear the more to do wrong if they know that you are recording these things, and that if they leave you without permission, or be guilty of any offence, you will write and complain to the justice of their country and to their friends. And, notwithstanding, bear in mind the saying of the philosopher called Bertram the Old, who said that if you engage a maid or man of high and proud answers, you shall know that when she leaves she will miscall you if she can; and if, on the contrary, she be flattering and full of blandishments, trust her not, for she seeks in some other way to trick you; but if she blushes and is silent and shamefast when you correct her, love her as your daughter.

… After your husband, you should be mistress of the house, the giver of orders, visitor, ruler, and sovereign administrator, and it is for you to keep your maid-servants in subjection and obedience to you, teaching, correcting, and chastising them; wherefore forbid them all excess and gluttony of life.

Also forbid them to quarrel with each other or with your neighbors; forbid them to speak ill of others, save only to you and in secret, and in so far only as the misdeed concerns your profit, and to save harm from befalling you and not otherwise. Forbid them to lie, to play at forbidden games, to swear foully and to utter words that smell of villainy, unseemly words or ribald, like to certain or ill-bred persons….

… And bid dame Agnes the Béguine [the housekeeper] see that what you desire to be done [is] at once begun before her eyes. And first, let her bid the chambermaids very early to sweep out and clean the entrances to your house, with the hall and other places whereby people enter and stay to speak in the house, and let them dust and shake out the covers and cushions which be on the benches; and afterwards let the other rooms be likewise cleaned and tidied for the day….

… Now let me return to the subject of how you shall set your folk to work, you and the Béguine, at fit times and shall cause your women to air and go over your sheets, coverlets, dresses and furs, fur coverlets, and other things of the sort …

… At times fitting, cause them to be seated at a table, and give them to eat one kind of meat only, but good plenty thereof, and not several varieties, nor dainties and delicacies. And order them one drink nourishing but not intoxicating, be it wine or something else, and not several kinds. And do you bid them to eat well and drink well and deeply for it is reasonable that they should eat at a stretch, without sitting too long over their food and without lingering over their meat, or staying with their elbows on the table. And as soon as they shall begin to tell tales and to argue and to lean upon the table, order the Béguine to make them rise and remove their table … And after their afternoon's work, and upon feast days, let them have another meal, and after that, to wit in the evening, let them be fed abundantly and well as before, and if the weather be cold let them warm themselves and take their ease.…

Questions: What was the experience of female servants who worked in the households of the urban elite? Was there any type of hierarchy among the servant class? Does this passage tell us anything about the relationship between the wealthy mistress of the establishment and those she employed?

92. FEMALE SERVANTS AND PROSTITUTION

Young women who came to big towns found work easily, but they were often vulnerable to exploitation if they were far from family and friends. This London court case tells the story of one such young woman, whose new employer turned out to be a procuress. For a similar tale of prostitution, see doc. 136.

Source: trans. H.T. Riley, *Memorials of London and London Life in the XIIIth, XIVth and XVth Centuries* (London: Longmans, Green, and Co., 1868), pp. 484–86, revised.

Elizabeth, the wife of Henry Moring, was brought before Nichols Brembre, knight, the mayor, aldermen, and the sheriffs of London, in the Guildhall because, at the information of diverse persons and upon the acknowledgment and confession of one Johanna, her servingwoman, the mayor, aldermen, and sheriffs were given to understand that Elizabeth, under color of the craft of embroidery, which she pretended to follow, took in and retained Johanna and diverse other women as her apprentices and bound them to serve her after the manner of apprentices in such art. Whereas, the truth of the matter was that she did not follow that craft, but that, after retaining them, she incited Johanna and the other women who were with her, and in her service, to live a lewd life and to consort with friars, chaplains [priests], and all other such men as desired to have their company, as well in her own house, in the parish of All Hallows near the wall in Broad Street Ward in London, as elsewhere. And she used to hire them out to friars, chaplains, and other men for such stipulated sum as they might agree upon, as well in her own house as elsewhere, she retaining in her own possession the sum so agreed upon.

And, in particular, on Thursday, May 4th last past, by the compassing and procuring of Elizabeth and of a certain chaplain whose name is unknown, she sent Johanna and ordered her to accompany this chaplain at night so that she might carry a lantern before him to his chamber, but in what parish is likewise unknown. It was her intention that Johanna should stay the night there with the chaplain, of their own contriving, while Johanna herself, as she says, knew nothing about it. Still, she remained there with the chaplain the whole of that night. When she returned home to her mistress on the morrow, Elizabeth asked if she had brought anything with her for her work that night, to which she made answer that she had not. Whereupon, Elizabeth used words of reproof to her, and ordered her to go back to the chaplain on the following night, and whatever she should be able to lay hold of, to take the same for her trouble, and bring it to her. Accordingly, Johanna by her command went back on the following night to the chaplain at his chamber and again passed the night there. And on the morrow she rose very early in the morning and bearing in mind the words of her mistress, and being afraid to go back without carrying something to her mistress, she took a portifory [breviary] that belonged to the chaplain and carried it off, the chaplain himself knowing nothing about it. Which portifory she delivered to Elizabeth who took it, well knowing how and in what manner Johanna had come by it. And after this, Elizabeth pledged this portifory for 8 pence to a man whose name is unknown.

And many other times Elizabeth received the like base gains from Johanna and her other servingwomen, and retained the same for her own use, living thus abominably and damnably, and inciting other women to live in the same manner, she herself being a common harlot and procuress.

Whereupon, on this day, Elizabeth was asked by the Court how she would acquit herself of this, to which she made answer that she was in no way guilty, and put herself upon the country [that is, she asked for a jury trial]. Therefore the sheriffs were instructed to summon twelve good men of this venue to appear here on the 28th day of the month to make a jury thereon, and Elizabeth was in the meantime committed to prison.

Upon which day the good men of the venue appeared … who declared upon their oath that Elizabeth was guilty of all the things imputed to her, and that she was a common harlot and a common procuress. And because many scandals had befallen the city through such women and similar deeds, and great peril might arise in the future through such transactions, therefore, according to the custom of the city of London provided for such cases, and in order that other women might beware of doing the like, it was adjudged that Elizabeth should be taken from the Guildhall to Cornhill, and be put upon the *thew* [a type of pillory mainly used for women] there to remain for one hour of the day, the cause thereof being publicly proclaimed. And afterwards she was to be taken to some gate of the city and there be made to forswear the city and its liberty to the effect that she would never again enter it on pain of imprisonment for three years and the punishment of the *thew*, at the discretion of the mayor and aldermen for the time being, so often as it should please them that she should suffer such punishment.

Questions: Why do you think that Johanna went along with Elizabeth's plans? Who was considered in the wrong, and who was punished? What were the intentions of the city officials in choosing the particular punishment they did?

CHAPTER EIGHT

RELIGION, PIETY, AND CHARITY

Figure 8.1

Friar Preaching

Franciscan and especially Dominican friars were famous for their preaching in towns (see doc. 99), which they usually did out of doors. Note the humble dress and bare feet of the preacher and the presence of both men and women in the audience. Drawn from a medieval manuscript illustration. Reproduced from Charles Knight, *Old England: A Pictorial Museum of Regal, Ecclesiastical, Municipal, Baronial, and Popular Antiquities*, 2 vols. (London: James Sangster and Co., 1850), fig. 1333.

93. THE BISHOP OF SPEYER GIVES THE JEWS OF THE CITY A CHARTER, 1084

In this charter, the bishop of Speyer, who is lord of the town, grants various rights to Jews to encourage them to settle in his new town. The charter also provides details concerning their relationship with local Christians, their quarter in the city, their way of living, and their occupational pursuits.

Source: O.J. Thatcher and E.H. McNeal, *A Source Book for Mediaeval History* (New York: Charles Scribner's Sons, 1905), pp. 577–78.

1. In the name of the holy and undivided Trinity. I, Rudeger, by cognomen Huozman, humble bishop of Speyer, when I wished to make a city of my village of Speyer, thought that it would greatly add to its honor if I should establish some Jews in it. I have therefore collected some Jews and located them in a place apart from the dwellings and association of the other inhabitants of the city. And that they may be protected from the attacks and violence of the mob, I have surrounded their quarter with a wall. The land for their dwellings I had acquired in a legal way; for the hill [on which they are to live] I secured partly by purchase and partly by trade, and the valley [which I have given them] I received as a gift from the heirs who possessed it. I have given them this hill and valley on condition that they pay every year £3 ½ of money coined in the mint of Speyer, for the use of the brothers [monks of some monastery which is not named here].

2. I have given them the free right of changing gold and silver coins and of buying and selling everything they wish within their own walls and outside the gate clear up to the boat-landing [on the Rhine] and also on the wharf itself. And they have the same right throughout the whole city.

3. Besides, I have given them a piece of the land of the church as a burial-ground. This land they shall hold forever.

4. I have also granted that, if a Jew comes to them from some other place and is their guest for a time, he shall pay no tolls [to the city].

5. The chief priest of their synagogue shall have the same position and authority among them as the mayor of the city has among the citizens. He shall judge all the cases which arise among them or against them. If he is not able to decide any case it shall be taken before the bishop or his chamberlain.

6.   They are bound to watch, guard, and defend only their own walls, in which work their servants may assist them.

7.   They may hire Christian nurses and Christian servants.

8.   The meats which their law forbids them to eat they may sell to Christians, and the Christians may buy them.

9.   To add to my kindness to them I grant them the most favorable laws and conditions that the Jews have in any city of the German kingdom....

Questions: Why did the bishop of Speyer wish to attract Jews to his new town, and what measures did he take to entice Jewish settlers? What sense does this document give you of the relations between Jewish and Christian town dwellers?

94. RESTRICTIONS ON JEWISH COMMUNITIES IN ENGLISH TOWNS

The Jews of England were under the special protection of the king, who in return felt free to tax them at will. He also restricted them to towns (numbering seventeen by 1221) that possessed an archa, *or office for the registration of Jewish bonds. Restrictions on what Jews could own or the types of occupations they could practice ended up channeling many Jews into moneylending, an occupation that often provoked resentment by debtors whose property or goods were confiscated to pay off their bad debts. The rise of crusading in the twelfth century also fostered anti-Semitism that reached fever pitch in the massacres of the Jewish communities at York in 1190 and pogroms against the Jews in London and other towns during the thirteenth century. Eventually King Edward I expelled all the Jews from England in 1290, profiting from their departure when he took over all of the debts owed to them.*

Source: trans. J.M. Rigg, *Select Pleas, Starrs, and Other Records from the Rolls of the Exchequer of the Jews A.D. 1220–1284* (Selden Society, vol. 15, 1902), pp. xlix, l, 85, revised.

Ordinances of 1253 Restricting Jews to Certain Towns
The king has provided and decreed, etc., that no Jew should dwell in England unless he does service for the king, and that as soon as a Jew is born, whether male or female, in some way he should serve the king. And there should be no communities in England except in those places where such communities were in the time of the lord king John, the king's father. And that in their synagogues the Jews, one and all, should worship in subdued tones according to their rite, so

that the Christians will not hear it. And that all Jews should answer to the rector of the parish in which they dwell for all parochial dues owed from their houses. And that no Christian nurse hereafter should suckle or nourish the male child of any Jew, and that no Christian man or woman should serve any Jew or Jewess, nor eat with them, nor dwell in their house. And that no Jew or Jewess should eat or buy meat in Lent. And that no Jew should disparage the Christian faith, nor publicly dispute anything about it. And that no Jew should have secret intercourse with any Christian woman, nor any Christian man with a Jewess. And that every Jew should wear on his breast a conspicuous badge. And that no Jew should enter any church or chapel except in passing through, nor staying in it, to the dishonor of Christ. And that no Jew should in any way hinder another Jew willing to be converted to the Christian faith. And that no Jew should be received in any town without the special license of the king, except in those towns where the Jews are accustomed to dwell.

And the justices appointed to the guardianship of the Jews are commanded to cause these provisions to be carried out and strictly kept on pain of forfeiture of the goods of the Jews.

Ordinances of 1271 Restricting Property Ownership of Jews in London
Greetings from the king to his beloved and trusty men, his mayor and sheriffs of London, and to all his bailiffs and trusty men to whom [these present letters shall come]. Know that for the honor of God and the Church Universal, and for the improvement and profit of our land and the relief of Christians from the damages and burdens which they have borne on account of the freeholds which the Jews of our realm claim to have ... we have ordained and decreed for us and our heirs that no Jews should have a freehold in any manors, lands, tenements, fees, rents, and holdings by charter, gift, feoffment, confirmation, or any other obligation.... However, they may dwell hereafter in their houses in which they themselves reside in cities, boroughs, or other towns, and may have them as they have been accustomed to have them in times past. And also they are allowed lawfully to lease their other houses only to Jews and not to Christians.... It is not lawful for our Jews of London to buy or in any way purchase more houses than they now have in our city of London, because the parish churches of the city or their rectors may incur loss. Nevertheless, the Jews of London should be able to repair their ancient houses and buildings formerly demolished or destroyed, and restore them at their will to their former condition.... Regarding lands and holdings, however, of which the Jews were enfeoffed [had possession] and still hold before the present statute, we wish such infeudations and gifts to be totally annulled and that the lands and tenements remain to the Christians who demised [sold or leased] them to the Jews. But the Christians should satisfy the Jews of the money or chattel specified in their charters and bonds which the Jews gave

to the Christians in exchange for these gifts and infeudations, without interest, with the condition that if those Christians cannot satisfy them forthwith, it is lawful for the Jews to demise those tenements to other Christians until they [can be reimbursed], as long as the Jew receives his money or chattel by the hands of Christians and not of Jews.

Removal of Jewish Communities to Other Towns, 1275
By writ of the lord the king directed to the justices in these words: Whereas by our letters patent we have granted to our dearest mother, Eleanor, queen of England, that no Jew should dwell or stay in any towns which she holds ... and for this reason we have provided that the Jews of Marlborough be transferred to our town of Devizes, the Jews of Gloucester to our town of Bristol, the Jews of Worcester to our town of Hereford, and the Jews of Cambridge to our city of Norwich, with their chirograph chests [*archa*], and with all their goods, and that henceforth they should dwell and stay in these towns and city among the rest of our Jews there. We command you to cause these Jews of Marlborough, Gloucester, Worcester, and Cambridge to be removed from those towns, without doing any damage to them in respect of their persons or their goods, and to transfer them to these other places with their chirograph chests, as safely to our use as you shall think it may be done. Witnessed myself at Clarendon on the 16th day of January in the third year of our reign.

Questions: What were the specific restrictions placed on Jews in England during this period, and how would these restrictions affect the daily life of Jews living in English towns? What accounts for the different treatment of Jews by the bishop of Speyer (doc. 93) and Jews in English towns?

95. PERSECUTION OF THE JEWS IN STRASBOURG AND GERMAN TOWNS, 1349

Resentment against the Jews could rise at times of crisis, such as the devastating Black Death of 1348–49, when people were looking for a scapegoat to blame. This extract describes why and how the townspeople of Strasbourg blamed the Jews for the terrible loss of life during the plague. Not all townspeople joined in this persecution, and many even sought to protect the Jews, but in the end, the will of the mob prevailed.

Source: trans. J.R. Marcus, *The Jew in the Medieval World: a Source Book, 315–1791* (repr. Philadelphia: Jewish Publication Society, and New York: Meridian Press, 1960; first published 1938), pp. 45–47.

In the year 1349 there occurred the greatest epidemic that ever happened. Death went from one end of the earth to the other, on that side and this side of the sea....

And as to from what this epidemic came, all wise teachers and physicians could only say that it was God's will. And as the plague was now here, so was it in other places, and lasted more than a whole year. This epidemic also came to Strasbourg in the summer of this year, and it is estimated that about 16,000 people died.

In the matter of this plague the Jews throughout the world were reviled and accused in all lands of having caused it through the poison which they are said to have put into the water and the wells—that is what they were accused of—and for this reason the Jews were burnt all the way from the Mediterranean into Germany, but not in Avignon, for the pope protected them there.

Nevertheless they tortured a number of Jews in Berne and Zofingen [Switzerland] who then admitted that they had put poison into many wells, and they also found the poison in the wells. Thereupon they burnt the Jews in many towns and wrote of this affair to Strasbourg, Freiburg, and Basel in order that they too should burn their Jews. But the leaders in these three cities in whose hands the government lay did not believe that anything ought to be done to the Jews. However, in Basel the citizens marched to the city hall and compelled the council to take an oath that they would burn the Jews, and that they would allow no Jew to enter the city for the next two hundred years. Thereupon the Jews were arrested in all these places and a conference was arranged to meet at Benfeld [Alsace, 8 February 1349]. The bishop of Strasbourg [Berthold II], all the feudal lords of Alsace, and representatives of the three above-mentioned cities came there. The deputies of the city of Strasbourg were asked what they were going to do with their Jews. They answered and said that they knew no evil of them. Then they asked the Strasbourgers why they had closed the wells and put away the buckets, and there was a great indignation and clamor against the deputies from Strasbourg. So finally the bishop and the lords and the imperial cities agreed to do away with the Jews. The result was that they were burnt in many cities, and wherever they were expelled they were caught by the peasants and stabbed to death or drowned....

[The town-council of Strasbourg which wanted to save the Jews was deposed on 9–10 February, and the new council gave in to the mob, who then arrested the Jews on Friday, 13 February.]

On Saturday—that was St. Valentine's Day—they burnt the Jews on a wooden platform in their cemetery. There were about two thousand of them. Those who wanted to baptize themselves were spared. [Some say that about a thousand accepted baptism.] Many small children were taken out of the fire and baptized against the will of their fathers and mothers. And everything that was owed to the Jews was canceled, and the Jews had to surrender all pledges and notes that they had taken for debts. The council, however, took the cash that the Jews possessed and divided it among the working-men proportionately. The money was indeed the thing that killed the Jews. If they had been poor and if the feudal lords had not been in debt to them, they would not have been burnt. After this wealth was divided among the artisans some gave their share to the cathedral or to the church on the advice of their confessors.

Thus were the Jews burnt at Strasbourg, and in the same year in all the cities of the Rhine, whether free cities or imperial cities or cities belonging to the lords. In some towns they burnt the Jews after a trial, in others, without a trial. In some cities the Jews themselves set fire to their houses and cremated themselves.

It was decided in Strasbourg that no Jew should enter the city for a hundred years, but before twenty years had passed, the council and magistrates agreed that they ought to admit the Jews again into the city for twenty years. And so the Jews came back again to Strasbourg in the year 1368 after the birth of our Lord.

Questions: Why did these townspeople blame the Jews for their suffering during the epidemic of the Black Death? Is there any evidence of how the Jews reacted to this persecution? Why would the Jews return to Strasbourg?

96. PROBLEMS AMONG THE CLERGY OF ROUEN CATHEDRAL, 1248

Bishops had the right to visit monasteries and other religious houses in order to ensure the clergy were abiding by their religious rule and to correct abuse. This extract reveals what the great reforming bishop of Rouen, Eudes de Rigaud, discovered when he made a formal visit or inquiry at the chapter of clergy attached to the cathedral in the northern French city of Rouen. Note that "Sir" is the usual title given to priests, while the title "Master" means the person had a master's degree from a university.

Source: trans. G.G. Coulton, *A Medieval Garner: Human Documents from the Four Centuries Preceding the Reformation* (London: Constable and Co., 1910), pp. 311–12.

We visited the chapter of Rouen, and found that they talk in choir contrary to rule. The clergy wander about the church, and talk in the church with women during the celebration of divine service. The statute regarding the entrance [of lay folk] into the choir is not kept. The psalms are run through too rapidly, without due pauses. The statute concerning going out at the Office of the Dead is not kept. In asking to go outside, they give no reason for so going. Moreover, the clergy leave the choir without reason, before the end of the service already begun; and, to be brief, many other of the statutes written on the board in the vestry are not kept. The chapter revenues are mismanaged.

With regard to the clergy themselves, we found that Master Michael de Bercy is ill-famed of incontinence; also, Sir Benedict, of incontinence; also, Master William de Salemonville of incontinence, theft, and manslaughter; also, Master

John de St. Lô, of incontinence. Also, Master Alan, of tavern-haunting, drunkenness, and dicing. Also, Peter de Auleige, of trading. Master John Bordez is ill-famed of trading; and it is said that he gives out his money to merchants, to share in their gain. Of our own free will we have denounced these persons aforesaid to the archdeacons of Greater and Lesser Calais; and the chapter is bound to correct these offenses through the aforesaid archdeacons, or through other officials, before the Assumption of the Blessed Virgin [15 August]; otherwise (we said), we ourselves would forthwith set our hands on the business, as we have notified to them by letter; and it is for them to let us know how the corrections have been made.

Questions: What impression does this inquiry give us of the activities of the cathedral clergy within the town of Rouen? What were considered the right relations between the clergy and townspeople?

97. THE BEGUINES OF GHENT, 1328

"Beguine" was a name applied to women who wished to devote their lives to God without becoming nuns. Unlike nuns, who were cloistered and subject to a monastic rule, Beguines lived in the world, usually working to support themselves. Beguines were found primarily in northern European towns, particularly in Flanders and the Rhineland. Many lived together in "Beguinages" such as the one founded in the large Flemish city of Ghent. This extract is from a Ghent inquiry into Beguine activities, which were the focus of increasing anxiety by the established Church, which worried about the orthodoxy of unsupervised religious women.

Source: trans. E.A. Amt, *Women's Lives in Medieval Europe: A Sourcebook* (New York: Routledge, 1993), pp. 263–67.

Why the Beguinage Was Founded

Those ladies of good memory, Joanna and her sister Margaret, successive countesses of Flanders and Hainault, notice that the region was greatly abounding in women for whom, because of their own position or that of their friends, suitable marriages were not possible, and they saw that the daughters of respectable men, both nobles and commoners, wished to live chastely, but could not easily enter a monastery because of the great number of these girls and the poverty of their parents, and that respectable and noble but impoverished damsels had to go begging or shamefully support themselves or seek support from their friends, unless some solution could be found. Then by divine inspiration, as it is piously believed, having first obtained the advice and consent of respectable men of the diocese and elsewhere, in various parts of Flanders they set up certain spacious places which are called Beguinages, in which the aforesaid women, girls and damsels were received, so that living in common therein, they might preserve their chastity, with or without taking vows, and where they might support and clothe themselves by suitable work, without shaming themselves or their friends.

The Beguinage of Saint Elizabeth

Among these Beguinages, they founded one in Ghent, which is called the Beguinage of Saint Elizabeth, which is encircled by ditches and walls. In the middle of it is a church, and next to the church a cemetery and a hospital, which the aforesaid ladies endowed for the weak and infirm of that same Beguinage. Many houses were also built there for the habitation of the said women, each of whom has her own garden, separated from the next by ditches or hedges; and two chaplains were established in this place by the same ladies.

The Manual Work Which They Do

In these houses, indeed, many dwell together communally and are very poor, having nothing but their clothing, a bed and a chest, nor are they a burden to anyone, but by manual work, washing the wool and cleaning the pieces of cloth sent to them from the town, they earn enough money daily that, making thereby a simple living, they also pay their dues to the church and give a modest amount in alms. And in each convent there is one who is called the mistress of work, whose duty is to supervise the work and the workers, so that all things are faithfully carried through according to God's will.

Their Way of Working and Praying

On work days they hold to the practice of rising early in the morning and coming together in the church, each going to her own place, which she has specially assigned to her, so that the absence of anyone be more easily noticed. After they have heard the Mass and said their prayers there, they return to their houses, working all day in silence, in which thing they are considered very useful to the whole country. And while working thus, they do not cease from prayer, for in each convent the two women, who are best suited for this recite clearly the psalm "Miserere" and other psalms which they know, and the "Ave Maria," one singing one verse, the other the next, and the rest recite silently with them, or diligently listen to those who are reciting. Late at night, after Vespers, they go into the church, devoting themselves to prayers and meditations, until the signal is given and they go to bed. On Sundays and holy days, with masses and sermons, prayers and meditations, they devote themselves to the Lord's service in all things; nor may anyone leave the Beguinage on these days without special permission from the principal mistress.

The Severity of Their Life

We shall not say much of their abstinence from food and drink but this: that many of them are satisfied for the whole day with the coarse bread and pottage which they have in common in each convent, and with a drink of cold water they lessen their thirst rather than increase their appetite. And many among them are accustomed to fast frequently on bread and water, and many of them do not wear linen on their bodies, and they use straw pallets instead of beds.

Their Training in Manners

And in all these things, they have such respectable manners and are so learned in domestic affairs that great and respectable persons often send them their daughters to be raised, hoping that, to whatever estate they may later be called, whether in the religious life or in marriage, they may be found better trained than others. Their way of living, in fear of God and in obedience to the holy Mother Church, has been such that nothing unusual or suspect has ever been heard concerning their congregation.

Their Prayers for the Dead

When any one of them dies, each member of the convent visits the corpse individually, with devout prayers and intercessions, and each, according to her obligation, devoutly performs fasts, vigils, psalms and prayers for the one who has died.

The Color and Form of Their Clothing

All wear the same color and style of clothing, so that they may thereby very strictly avoid anything that might distinguish them from the others or be suspect. For they wear a habit which is grey in color, humble, and of a coarse shape, and none may have anything which is unusual or suspect in its shape, sewing or belting, or in the way of nightcaps, hoods, gloves, mitts, straps, purses and knives.

Government and Correction

One woman, nominated by the conventual mistresses, rules the previously mentioned hospital. She is called the principal mistress of the Beguinage, or the great mistress, and each year, after the accounts are rendered, it is customary for her to be retained in or removed from this office according to the will of the aforementioned conventual mistresses. And she appoints the mistresses in the individual convents, with the advice and consent of the convents and of respectable men; and only with the permission and at the will of the said principal mistresses is anyone permitted to build or to tear down in that place, or to give or assign a place in the convent. To her also falls the correction of those who transgress against the praiseworthy rules of the said place, so that she may combat vices through restraint within the Beguinage, or by the transfer of a person from one convent to another, or by other similar penalties, or she may, through the complete expulsion of the rotten member from the Beguinage, preserve the body of the rest from shame and decay. And no one may be away from the Beguinage for long or spend the night in the town without her permission. Nor may anyone leave the Beguinage for an hour, without the special permission of the conventual mistress; and she who has that permission may not go alone but must have one or more companions, taken only from her own convent. Those who go out are required to avoid anything suspect in all their movements, and in the places they go, and in the persons they meet; those who do otherwise are warned about these matters, and unless they immediately desist they are deprived of the consolation of the Beguinage.

The Fame of the Place

That benevolent confessor, the most pious king Saint Louis, personally visited this place in devotion, and, pleased with the zeal of these women, arranged with the venerable father, the lord bishop of Tournai, that a church should be consecrated for them, and acquired and conferred on them many privileges and liberties for their devotion, and he established and endowed a Beguinage like this one at Paris, and others in various places. There is also another Beguinage in Ghent, which is called "Oya," and many houses throughout the town where women dwell in a similar situation.

Questions: Is there any evidence of why so many urban women were drawn to the Beguine movement? To what extent did Beguines participate in town life? Is there any evidence of how the townspeople might have viewed these religious women who lived in the world, rather than in a convent?

98. THE GOOD CANON OF COLOGNE

This description of the virtues of a highly placed canon (a priest who lived in a community and abided by a religious rule) of Cologne was written by a Cistercian monk, Caesarius of Heisterbach, as part of an effort to train young novices. It very much reflects twelfth-century concerns for the poor, but it also gives considerable details about the interaction of the urban laity and the cathedral clergy.

Source: trans. G.G. Coulton, *A Medieval Garner: Human Documents from the Four Centuries Preceding the Reformation* (London: Constable and Co., 1910), pp. 244–51, revised and abridged.

Ensfrid, dean of St. Andreas at Cologne, was born in that same bishopric, a simple and upright man and foremost in works of mercy. What his life was before his ordination to the priesthood or what he did in his youth I know not; but that mercifulness grew and increased with him I gather from his later acts. That he was of docile mind and eager to learn was shown by the effect; for even in his boyish years he laid so good a foundation of learning that, as I have heard from his own mouth, he became master of the schools as a mere youth, and instructed many both in word and in example, not only to learn but, what is more, to live well. Having been ordained a priest, he received the rectory of a church at Siegburg, a good parish that is rich in oblations, where he put his learning to effect. The pilgrim remained not without, for his door was open to the wayfarer. He was the father of widows, the consoler of orphans, the rebuker of sinners. He nourished many scholars in his house; and, being of a dove-like simplicity, at that season when the cherries were ripe he said to his cellarer: "Good man, give the boys leave to climb the trees, that they may eat of cherries as many as they will and as they can; then you need to give them no other food; for there is no other food wherein they take such delight." This he said not as a niggard, but from the abundant kindliness of his heart. When therefore they had done this for some days, and the freedom given to the boys pleased their boyish hearts, the cellarer said to Ensfrid: "Of a truth, my lord, unless these boys eat other food also, they will soon fail." He thus straightway allowed himself to be persuaded.

After this he was made canon of the church of St. Andreas in Cologne; and not long after, for the goodness of his life, he was raised to the deanery, where, although he was of blameless life and strong in the virtue of chastity, yet he was especially fervent in works of mercy. In the parish of St. Paul, which adjoins the church of St. Andrew, there was no poor widow whose cottage he knew not, and whom he failed to visit with his alms. So much bread was given from his table to those who begged from door to door, so much money passed from his hands into Christ's treasury—that is, into the hands of the poor—that many who knew his annual revenues marveled at it....

... For these and other like deeds some said that they had never read of a man who was so compassionate, so merciful, and so pitiful to the poor.... On a certain solemn festival when the lord Adolf, Dean of the cathedral church and afterwards archbishop, had invited him to his feast, Ensfrid refused, saying that he had noble guests. So, when mass had been said and the blessed man was hastening homewards, then Gottfried, his fellow canon and notary of the cathedral deanery (who told me this story himself), looked out from the window of the upper chamber of the clergy house and saw many poor following him. Some were lame and others blind, and since they could not cross the stepping-stones which there divide the square, he, aged and decrepit as he was, was giving his hand to each in turn. Right away the clerk called his master to the window and said: "Behold, lord, these are the noble guests whom our friend the dean said that he had invited," and both were much edified.

I myself have seen another like work of his mercy. On the anniversary of the lord Bruno, archbishop of Cologne, when all the chapters [groups of clergy] of the conventual churches flocked together to the church of St. Pantaleon which Bruno had built, after mass had been said for his soul, and the priors as had been ordained were entering the refectory, I know not how many poor folk followed the lord Ensfrid to the very refectory door. When the refectorer went to admit him and cast out the poor, he was moved with indignation and cried: "I will not enter today without them": for, as a most prudent man, he knew that the poor are God's friends and door-keepers of heaven, and he kept well in his memory that counsel of the Son of God: "Make unto you friends of the mammon of iniquity, that when you shall fail they may receive you into everlasting dwellings." Hence one day when he had been set to stand beside the relics and to warn those who came in to give alms for the building of that church of which he was then guardian, he spoke to the people in these words: "Good folk, see well what noble buildings stand here around you! You will do well indeed in giving your alms to them, yet expend them better and more safely on the poor." ...

A certain citizen of Cologne, named Lamprecht, was his familiar friend and near neighbor who, sitting one day with Gottfried the notary, as they spoke together of the lord Ensfrid's almsgivings, said in my hearing: "I will tell you how he treated me. One day he had invited me and my wife to sup with him. We sat down to table with him and waited long in expectation that some meat would be set before us, for nothing was there but dry bread. Then I, knowing well his ways, called one of the servants and whispered in his ear: 'Tell me, good fellow, shall we have anything to eat?' The man answered: 'We have nothing, for a goodly repast had been prepared for you, but my master entered the kitchen before the hour of supper and divided among the poor all that we had prepared, in spite of all our cries.' Then I smiled and sent the same servant to my own house, and he brought enough meat to suffice for all our guests. Another day I came into his kitchen and saw I know not how many geese roasting on the spit; then said I in my heart: 'Of a truth this dean nourishes his household well!' But when the geese were roasted he himself came in and cut them down, and dividing them plate by plate, sent them round to the widows and poor even unto the last fragment...."

A certain citizen of Cologne, as one of the priests of St. Andreas related to me, loved his own wife little and afflicted her often, so she stole much money from him. When her husband accused her and she stoutly denied, then, fearing to be caught by him, she cast the money into the cesspool. After this, grieving at that which she had done, she came to the dean and told him, under seal of confession, of her theft and its cause. And I think that the holy man must have persuaded her to bring the money back to her husband, but she, because she had denied the deed to him with an oath, dared not do this, fearing that he [her husband] should afflict her all the more on this account. The dean therefore answered her: "If I may get the money secretly, will you give it to the poor?" "Yes," said she, "that is all my desire." Thus, a few days afterwards, the dean said to this citizen: "Will you give me leave to cleanse your cesspool and take from it whatsoever the Lord shall give me there?" He, knowing the dean to be a holy man, and thinking moreover that God had revealed something to him, gave him leave. The place was purged, the money was found, and within a few days was spent among the poor by the hands of this man of God....

... He never returned evil for evil, for the simplicity of a dove reigned in him; but, though he was so exceeding merciful, as I have said, yet he burned with the zeal of justice. One day he met the abbess of the Holy Eleven Thousand Virgins [a local convent]. Before her went her clerks, wrapped in mantles of gray fur like the nuns, behind went her ladies and maid-servants, filling the air with the sound of their unprofitable words, while the dean was followed by his poor folk who beseeched him for alms. This righteous man, burning with the zeal of discipline, cried aloud in the hearing of all: "Oh, lady Abbess, it would better befit your profession, it would better adorn your religion, if you, like I, should be followed not by buffoons but by poor folk!" At this she was much ashamed, not presuming to answer so worthy a man....

Questions: What types of social, religious, and charitable interactions did the canon have with the townspeople of Cologne? What does the passage tell us about attitudes towards the poor? Why does the canon criticize the abbess, and how does his concern compare to the complaints of the reforming bishop of Rouen in doc. 96?

99. A POPULAR FRANCISCAN PREACHER IN PARIS, 1429

We can get some idea of the powerful sway of a charismatic preacher from this description, by an unidentified bourgeois of Paris during the tumultuous years of the Hundred Years War, of the impact of a visiting Franciscan.

Source: trans. J. Shirley, *A Parisian Journal 1405–1449* (Oxford: Clarendon Press, 1968), pp. 230–35.

1429. Also, the duke of Burgundy returned to Paris April 4th, St. Ambrose's day, with a splendid company of knights and squires. About a week later a grey friar [a Franciscan] called Brother Richard arrived in Paris. He was a man of great judgment, wise in prayer, a sower of sound doctrine for his neighbor's edification. He worked tremendously at this task; one could scarcely believe it without having seen it all—all the time he was in Paris, he preached every single day except one. He began on Saturday, 16 April 1429, at St. Geneviève, and the next Sunday and the week after, that is, Monday, Tuesday, Wednesday, Thursday, Friday, Saturday,

Sunday, at the [church of] the Innocents. He would begin about five o'clock in the morning and go on till between ten and eleven o'clock and there was always five or six thousand persons listening to him. He preached from a high platform—it was nearly one and a half *toises* high—with his back to the charnel-houses opposite the Charronerie near the Danse Macabré....

The grey friar mentioned earlier preached on St. Mark's day at Boulogne-la-Petite and there were great crowds there, as is said above. Indeed, when they came away from the sermon that day, the people of Paris were so moved and so stirred up to devotion that in less than three or four hours' time you would have seen over a hundred fires alight in which men were burning chess and backgammon boards, dice, cards, balls and sticks, *mirelis* [a board game], and every kind of covetous game that can give rise to anger and swearing. The women too, this day and the next, burned in public all their fine head-gear—the rolls and stuffing, the pieces of leather or whalebone that they used to stiffen their headdresses or make them fold forwards. Noblewomen left off their horns, their trains, and many of their vanities. Indeed, the ten sermons he preached in Paris and one at Boulogne did more to turn people towards piety than all the preachers who had preached in Paris for the past hundred years....

... on that Tuesday when Brother Richard finished his last sermon, the tenth, because he had not got permission to preach in Paris any more, when he said goodbye and commended the people of Paris to God and they should pray for him and he would pray to God for them, everyone, great and small, cried bitterly and as feelingly as if they had been watching their dearest friends being buried, and so did he too, This good man intended to have set off that day or next for Burgundy, but his brothers managed to persuade him to stay in Paris and confirm by further preaching the good beginning he had made....

Brother Richard now went away. On the Sunday before he was to go it was said all over Paris that he was going to preach at or near the place where the glorious martyr St. Denis was beheaded, and many other martyrs. Over 6,000 people therefore went there from Paris, most of them leaving in great crowds on the Saturday night so as to have better places in the morning. They slept in the open country in old shacks or wherever they could, but the sermon was canceled. Why this was I shall not say, but he did not preach, at which the good people were much upset. He preached no more in Paris at this time and had to go away. [Later on it turns out he was on the side of the Armagnacs, the enemies of the Parisian partisans of the duke of Burgundy.]

Questions: What does this passage tell us about sermonizing and its impact in medieval towns? Why were people compelled to attend these long sermons? How did those most influenced by the sermons react and why did they take the actions they did?

100. LAY PIETY AND REFORM: PETER WALDO OF LYONS

Dissatisfaction with the established church flared up in the central Middle Ages, aimed in part against what was perceived to be the clergy's worldly concern with wealth and power. Dissatisfied laity sought alternative paths of religious expression that the Church eventually condemned as heretical. One of the main heretical sects, called the "Poor of Lyons," grew up around Peter Waldo, a merchant of the French city of Lyons who renounced his wealthy lifestyle to take up a life of apostolic poverty. The passage from an anonymous chronicle describes Peter Waldo's initial "conversion" to a reformed way of life.

Source: trans. J.H. Robinson, *Readings in European History* (Boston: Ginn, 1906), I, pp. 170–71.

And during the same year, that is the 1173rd since the Lord's Incarnation, there was at Lyons in France a certain citizen, Waldo by name, who had made himself much money by wicked usury. One Sunday, when he had joined a crowd which he saw gathered around a troubadour, he was smitten by his words and, taking him to his house, he took care to hear him at length. The passage he was reciting was how the holy Alexis died a blessed death in his father's house. When morning had come the prudent citizen hurried to the schools of theology to seek counsel for his soul, and when he was taught many ways of going to God, he asked the master what way was more certain and more perfect than all others. The master answered him with this text: "If thou wilt be perfect, go and sell all that thou hast," etc.

Then Waldo went to his wife and gave her the choice of keeping his personal property or his real estate, namely, what he had in ponds, groves and fields, houses, rents, vineyards, mills, and fishing rights. She was much displeased at having to make this choice, but she kept the real estate. From his personal property he made restitution to those whom he had treated unjustly; a great part of it he gave to his two little daughters, who, without their mother's knowledge, he placed in the convent of Font Evrard; but the greatest part of his money he spent for the poor. A very great famine was then oppressing France and Germany. The prudent citizen, Waldo, gave bread, with vegetables and meat, to everyone who came to him for three days in every week from Pentecost to the feast of St. Peter's bonds.

At the assumption of the blessed Virgin, casting some money among the village poor, he cried, "No man can serve two masters, God and mammon." Then his fellow citizens ran up, thinking he had lost his mind. But going to a higher place, he said: "My fellow citizens and friends, I am not insane, as you think, but am avenging myself on my enemies, who made me a slave, so that I was always more careful of money than of God, and served the creature rather than the Creator. I know that many will blame me that I act thus openly. But I do it both on my own account and on yours; on my own, so that those who see me henceforth possessing any money may say that I am mad, and on yours, that you may learn to place hope in God and not in riches."

On the next day, coming from the church, he asked a certain citizen, once his comrade, to give him something to eat, for God's sake. His friend, leading him to his house, said, "I will give you whatever you need as long as I live." When this came to the ears of his wife, she was not a little troubled, and as though she had lost her mind, she ran to the archbishop of the city and implored him not to let her husband beg bread from any one but her. This moved all present to tears.

[Waldo was accordingly conducted into the presence of the bishop.] And the woman, seizing her husband by the coat, said, "Is it not better, husband, that I should redeem my sins by giving you alms than that strangers should do so?" And from that time he was not allowed to take food from any one in that city except from his wife.

Questions: Why did the reforming message of apostolic poverty strike such a chord with Waldo and other urban residents? Why did the bishop eventually forbid Waldo from taking food from anyone but his wife?

101. THE PROCESSIONS OF THE FLAGELLANTS, 1349

The severity and devastation of the Black Death in 1349 was widely seen as God's punishment for sinning behavior. Atoning for these sins was the major impetus of the penitential movement of the late Middle Ages, which, in one of its more severe manifestations, included ritual self-flagellation, such as described here.

Source: trans. D. Hughes, *Illustrations of Chaucer's England* (London: Longmans, Green and Co., 1918), pp. 192–93, revised.

In the year 1349, about Michaelmas, more than 120 men, natives, for the most part, of Holland and Zeeland, came to London from Flanders. And twice a day, barefoot in procession one after another, holding a scourge with three thongs having each a knot through which sharp points were fixed, they scourged their bare and bleeding bodies, sometimes in the church of St. Paul, sometimes in other places of the city, in sight of all the people. And they were covered with a linen cloth from the thighs to the heels, the rest of the body left bare, and each wearing a cap marked before and behind with a red cross. Four of them would sing in their own tongue, in the manner of litanies sung by Christians. Three times in their procession they would all together fling themselves upon the ground, their hands outspread in the form of a cross, continually singing, and beginning with the last, one after another, as they lay, each in turn struck the man before him with his flail; and so from one to another, each performed the same rite to the last. Then each resumed his usual garments, and still wearing their caps and holding their flails, they returned to their lodging. And it was said that they performed the same penance every evening.

Question: What impact do you think these processions had on the townspeople who witnessed them?

102. THE RELIGIOUS FRATERNITY OF ST. KATHARINE AT NORWICH, 1389

Religious guilds, such as that dedicated to St. Katharine in the English city of Norwich, provided a range of spiritual and practical benefits to members, who pooled their resources to pay for such things as candles to light at the altar of their patron saint in the parish church or for a priest to say masses for recently deceased members. Dirige *referred to the prayers said at Matins (the morning) for the Office of the Dead, from the first word of the first antiphon recited);* placebo *referred to the prayers said at Vespers (the evening service) for the Office of the Dead, from the first word in the first antiphon recited.*

Source: trans. M. Kowaleski, from *English Gilds,* ed. T. Smith and L.T. Smith (Early English Text Society, original series, 40, 1870; reprinted 1963), pp. 19–21, modernized.

… Our fraternity was founded in the year 1307, by certain parishioners of the church [of Sts. Simon and Jude in Norwich] and by others devoted to God, to the honor of the Holy Trinity, and of the most blessed Virgin Mary, and of St. Katharine the virgin and martyr, and of all saints, and for maintaining the light [candles] in the church, under certain ordinances made and issued with common consent of the brothers and sisters of the fraternity. The tenor of these ordinances follow in these words.

In the beginning with one assent it is ordained that all brothers and sisters of this guild should come together to the parish church of St. Simon and St. Jude in Norwich, on the [feast] day of St. Katharine, to go in the procession with their candle, which is borne before them, and to hear the mass of St. Katharine in the church. And at that mass every brother and sister should offer ½ penny.

And also it is ordained that any brother or sister absent from this procession, or at mass, or at offering, should pay 2 pounds of wax to the fund of the guild, but he may be excused reasonably.

And also it is ordained that when a brother or sister dies, every brother and sister should come to *Dirige* and to mass, and each should offer ½ penny and give ½ penny to alms, and 1 penny for a mass to be sung for the soul of the dead. And at the *Dirige,* every brother or sister who is literate should say *placebo* and *Dirige* for the dead in the place where they come together. And every brother and sister who is not lettered should say the Our Father twenty times with the Hail Mary. And the fund of the guild should provide two wax candles, of 16 pounds weight, set around the body of the deceased.

And also it is ordained that if any brother or sister die within eight miles of the city of Norwich, six of the brethren that are keepers of the goods of the guild [that is, the officers] should go to that brother or sister who is dead, and if it be lawful, they should carry it [the body] to Norwich, or else it should be buried there. And if the body is buried outside of Norwich, all the brothers and sisters should be warned to come to the church of Sts. Simon and Jude, and there should be done for the soul of the dead all the service, lights, and offerings as if the body were present. And if any brother or sister is absent at *placebo* and *Dirige*, or at mass, he should pay 2 pounds of wax to the fund of the guild, but he may reasonably be excused. And nevertheless, he should do for the dead as it is said before.

And also it is ordained that, on the day after the guild day, all the brothers and sisters should come to the church and there sing a mass of requiem for the souls of the brothers and sisters of this guild, and for all Christian souls, and each should offer ¼ penny. And whoever is absent should pay one pound of wax.

And also it is ordained that if any brother or sister fall into poverty, through adventure of the world, his estate should be helped by every brother and sister, with ¼ pence each week.

And also it is ordained by common assent that if there is any discord between brothers and sisters, that discord should first be revealed to other brothers and sisters of the guild, and they should help make an accord if it can be done skillfully. And if they cannot be brought to an agreement, it is lawful for them to go to the common law, without any maintenance. And whoever goes against this ordinance should pay 2 pounds of wax to the light.

Also it is ordained by common assent, that if any brother of this guild is chosen for office and refuses it, he should pay 2 pounds of wax to the light of St. Katharine.

Also it is ordained, by common assent, that the brothers and sisters of this guild, in the worship of St. Katharine, should have hoods as a livery suit [a common uniform], and eat together on their guild day at their common cost. And whoever fails [to do so] should pay 2 pounds of wax to the light.

Also it is ordained by common assent, that no brother or sister should be received into the guild except by the alderman and twelve brethren of the guild.

And as to the goods and chattels of the fraternity ... we the guardians have in our custody 20 shillings of silver for the use of the guild.

Questions: Why would townspeople wish to join this guild? What services or benefits did it have to offer? How did the guild help ensure a sense of solidarity among its members?

Figure 8.2

A Burial Service

This miniature depicts a burial service. The corpse is wound tightly in a shroud and placed in the grave without a coffin. The figures in black are mourners, seemingly women with their black veils drawn over their faces. To the right of the priest performing the ceremony is a man with a bucket of holy water, for blessing the grave. From a breviary. Reproduced from Thomas Wright, *The Archaeological Album* (London: Chapman and Hall, 1845), p. 90.

103. THE ACCOUNTS OF THE CHURCHWARDENS IN CANTERBURY, 1485–86

By the late fourteenth century, parishioners were taking a more active role in the life of their parish, spurred on by rising literacy and learning among the laity, as well as by their responsibility for maintaining the church and its furnishings. Repairs, as well as new decorative schemes or the enlargement of the church, required funds, which were largely raised and spent by elected church officials—called churchwardens— thus giving rise to churchwardens' accounts, such as those printed here for the parish of St. Andrew in the small city of Canterbury in eastern England. The revenues associated with the second Monday and Tuesday after Easter—called Hocktide— were sums raised by parishioners from different charitable events (like bake sales today). Note too that the first section on Receipts was written in Latin, but the second, longer section on expenses was written in Middle English.

Source: trans. M. Kowaleski, from "The Churchwardens' Accounts of the Parish of St. Andrew, Canterbury, 1485 to 1625," by C. Cotton, *Archaeologia Cantiana* 32 (1917), pp. 211–14.

The account of Edmund Mynot and Robert Bone, wardens of the goods, works, and chattels of the parishioners of the parish church of St. Andrew in the city of Canterbury, from the Feast of St. Michael the Archangel in the first regnal year of King Henry VII to the Feast of St. Michael the Archangel in the following year, namely for one whole year [29 September 1485 to 29 September 1486].

[Receipts]
First they account for receiving the waste of 4 mortuary candles at different times, 28 pence [the value of leftover wax from candles used during burial services].

And they received from John Berkevile for the lease of one pasture in the parish of St. Paul near the lane called Ivy Lane, at the Feast of St. Michael in 1485, 3 shillings 4 pence.

They also received from the widow of William Goldsmyth from William's will, 13 shillings 1 pence.

They also received from the widow of James Willelm for the rent of one tenement in the parish of Blessed Mary in Northgate in the city of Canterbury, at the same Feast of St. Michael, 2 shillings 6 pence.

They also received from Robert Feraf for the arrears of rent owed on the same tenement in Northgate, 3 shillings 4 pence.

They also received from Richard Grene for the rent owed on one tenement in Northgate at the same Feast of St. Michael, 14 pence.

They also received from diverse persons for the repair of the clock, 17 pence.

They also received from the parishioners at Easter, 20 shillings 6 pence.

They also received on Hokemonday by the hand of a woman, 9 shillings 6 pence.

They also received on Hoketuesday from women, 2 shillings 4 pence.

They also received from rents owed [on property] in Sandwich [a nearby town] at the same Feast of St. Michael, 6 shillings 8 pence.

They also received from arrears of rent of [Nicholas] Durbourne for a tenement in the parish of Blessed Mary in Northgate at the same Feast of St. Michael, 2 shillings 6 pence.

They also received from John Kent the arrears of rent of one garden in the parish of St. Paul, Canterbury, 2 shillings 4 pence.

They also received for a bit of one piece of silver weighing ½ penny, ½ pence.

They also received for one donated silver ring weighing 2 pennies, 2 pence.

They also received money from a certain woman, 6 shillings 8 pence.

Sum total, £4, 4 shillings 8½ pence.

[Expenses]

Payments made by the wardens during this time at diverse times as appears in the particulars below.

First, paid to Robert Martyn, waxchandler, for striking [making new or building up old candles by adding additional wax when they burned down] the stock of the lights of St. Andrew and for 3¼ pounds of wax applied to the same stock, 2 shillings 2½ pence.

Also paid to the same Robert for newly striking 3 mortuary candles and for 3 pounds of wax put on them, 28½ pence.

Also paid to John Curteys, carpenter, for making the chest that stands before St. Andrew in the choir for storing vestments and books, 7 shillings.

Also paid for broad-nails, nails, and hinges and keys for the chest, 20 pence.

Also paid for the mending of surplices [knee-length vestment of white linen] and vestments and for [...illegible] of albs [full-length vestment of white linen] and frontel cloths [a decorative hanging for the altar] after washing, 3 shillings 2 pence.

Also paid for making a new surplice, 2 shillings.

Also paid for a surplice purchased from the wife of Peter Broiderer, 16 pence.

Also paid to Thomas for maintaining the clock for one whole year, except for one-fourth of the year, 4 shillings.

Also paid to the same Thomas for making and striking 3 tapers and for waste of wax burned before the Cross, 11 pence.

Also paid to John Kemsyn for binding this book in which the inventory of church goods is to be written, 16 shillings [the inventory appears in the section before these accounts].

Also paid to the locksmith for 1 pair of hinges, 1 lock, 1 key, and 2 staples for a chest in the church, 10 pence.

Also paid to John Martyn, waxchandler, for striking the 3 tapers before the Cross and for waste of the wax [used at] the Feast of St. Matthew [21 September], 9½ pence.

Also paid for washing the surplices, albs, altar-cloths, towels, and other napery of the church at diverse times during this period, 17 pence.

Also paid to Robert Martyn, waxchandler, for striking 33¾ pounds of wax for the lights at the Cross during Easter time, 16¾ pence.

Also paid to the same Robert for 12¼ pounds of new wax used for the lights before the Cross during Easter time, at the price of 9 pence per pound, sum of 9 shillings 2 pence.

Also paid to the same Robert for striking of the Pascal [candle] weighing 8 pounds, 4 pence.

Also paid to the same Robert for 1 pound of wax put on the same Pascal, 9 pence.

Also paid for the font taper weighing 1½ pounds, at the price of 13½ pence.

Also paid to the Registrar [the bishop's clerk] at the visitation of [the bishop to] St. George's Church in Canterbury, 3 pence.

Also paid for 2 tapers before the Cross during the Feast of St. George [23 April], 13 pence.

Also paid for one rope for the clock, 5 pence.

Also paid for a red skin for the book called "*le graill*," [a liturgical book: a graduale], 4 pence.

Also paid for a buck skin for the same book and for binding it, 4 shillings.

Also paid for a new torch weighing 22 ½ pounds purchased from Robert Martyn, at the price of 7 shillings 4 pence.

Also paid for another torch weighing 20 pounds purchased from Clement Hamon, 6 shillings 8 pence.

Also paid to Nicholas Bekelys for mending the iron work of the clock, 21 pence.

Also paid to Thomas Cook for 3 new tapers before the Cross at the time of the Feast of St. John the Baptist [24 June], 12 pence.

Also paid to John Kemsyn for mending the second mass-book and for binding it and for setting in it the whole service of the visitation of St. Elizabeth, 3 shillings 8 pence.

Also paid to Master Hikson for writing down this whole service, 7 shillings 8 pence.

Also paid for a red skin for [the binding] of the third mass-book, 4 pence.

Also paid for writing the whole sequence for the third mass-book, 6 shillings 8 pence.

Also paid to John Kemsyn for mending and binding this third mass-book, 2 shillings.

Also paid for a red skin for [the binding] of the book, 4 pence.

Also paid to Nicholas Bekelys for maintaining the clock for one-quarter of the year, 20 pence.

Also paid to the widow of William Golesmith for lamp oil, 2 shillings 8 pence.

Also paid to Thomas Petyt for lamp oil, that is for 7¾ flagons, 10 shillings.

Also paid to John Martyn for 3 tapers placed before the Cross, 12 pence.

Also paid to the same Martyn for 3 tapers placed before the Cross another time, 12 pence.

Sum, 100 shillings ¾ pence.

Questions: Where did the churchwardens obtain and expend their funding and in what did they involve other parishioners? What can we discern about the appearance of the interior of the church from these accounts? About the religious practices of the parishioners?

104. RELIGION, MORALITY, AND POLITICS: SAVONAROLA'S INFLUENCE OVER THE FLORENTINES

One of the most influential medieval preachers was Girolamo Savonarola, a Dominican prior in Florence during the late fifteenth century. These excerpts from the diary of Luca Landucci show the powerful impact that Savonarola's preaching had on the Florentine populace around the time when the tyrant, Piero de Medici, had been expelled by the populace. As Landucci's reports make clear, Savonarola's exhortations touched not only moral and religious issues, but also extended to strong comments on the current political situation. Savonarola's attacks on the ecclesiastical establishment (especially the pope) and his strong political views eventually led to his downfall; he was arrested, tortured to extract a confession that his prophecies were not divinely inspired, and burned to death in the Piazza della Signoria in 1498.

Source: trans. A. de Rosen Jervis, *A Florentine Diary from 1450 to 1516*, by Luca Landucci (New York: E.P. Dutton & Co., Inc., 1927), pp. 74–75, 76, 79, 80, 85, 101–02.

1494 …

6th December (Saturday). Fra Girolamo preached, and ordered that alms should be given for the *poveri vergognosi* [the honorable poor] in four churches: Santa Maria del Fiore, Santa Maria Novella, Santa Croce, and Santo Spirito; which were collected on the following day, Sunday. And so much was given that it was impossible to estimate it: gold and silver, woollen and linen materials, silks and pearls and other things; everyone contributed so largely out of love and charity.

7th December (Sunday). The said offering was made. And he preached again in Santa Maria del Fiore, and ordered that a procession should be made, in order to thank God for the benefits received.

8th December (Monday). The procession was made, and more offerings were given for the *poveri vergognosi*, without stint. It was a marvelous procession, of such a number of men and women of high estate, and carried out with perfect obedience to the *Frate* [Savonarola], who had ordered that no woman should stand upon the stone seats along the walls, but that they should stay inside their houses with the door open, if they wished. Not a single woman was seen standing on the stone seats or elsewhere. Such devotion was shown as perhaps will never happen again. The alms given were not less than on the previous day. I did not hear the exact amount, but it must have been thousands of florins.

... 14th December (Sunday).... Fra Girolamo did his utmost in the pulpit to persuade Florence to adopt a good form of government; he preached in Santa Maria del Fiore every day, and today, which was a Sunday, he wished that there should be no women, but only men; he wished that only the gonfaloniers [heads of the political wards] and one of the Signori [the ruling council] should remain in the Palazzo, and that all the officers of Florence should be there; and he preached much about state matters, and that we ought to love and fear God, and love the common weal; and no one must set himself up proudly above the rest. He always favored the people and he insisted that no one ought to be put to death, but there must be other forms of punishment; and he continued to preach in this manner every morning. Many forms were drawn up, and there was much controversy among the citizens, so that every day it was expected that the bell would be rung for a *parlamento* [a meeting of the people].

... 1495

1st January. The new Signori entered into office, and it was a great joy to see the whole piazza filled with citizens, quite different from other times, as a new thing, thanking God who had given this impartial government to Florence, and delivered us from subjection. And all this had been done at the instigation of the *Frate*.

... 11th January (Sunday). Fra Girolamo preached, and spoke much concerning the reforms of the city; and exculpated himself from various accusations, saying that there were devils who disturbed the life of the commune; and that they wrote forged letters, which made it appear as if the *Frate* had given Piero de' Medici hopes of returning, in order to make the people turn against him. But nevertheless all this was untrue; he was entirely for the people and the common weal....

... 17th January (Saturday). Fra Girolamo preached; and concerned himself much about this peace and union of the citizens; and many of them grew angry with him, saying ... "This wretched monk will bring us ill-luck."

... 1st April. Fra Girolamo preached, and said and testified that the Virgin Mary had revealed to him, that after going through much trouble, the city of Florence was to be the most glorious, the richest, and the most powerful that ever existed; and he promised this absolutely. All these things he spoke as a prophet, and the greater part of the people believed him, especially quiet people without political or party passions.

... 1496

... 7th February. Some boys took away a girl's veil-holder in the Via de' Martegli, and her people made a great disturbance about it. This happened because Fra Girolamo had encouraged the boys to oppose the wearing of unsuitable ornaments by women, and to reprove gamblers, so that when anyone said, "Here come the boys of the *Frate!*" every gambler fled, however bold he might be, and the women went about modestly dressed. The boys were held in such respect that everyone avoided evil, and most of all the abominable vice. Such a thing was never spoken of by young or old during this holy time; but it did not last long. The wicked were stronger than the good. God be praised that I saw this short period of holiness. I pray Him that He may give us back that holy and pure life. And in order to realize what a blessed time it was, you have only to consider the things that were then done.

16th February. The Carnival. Fra Girolamo had preached a few days before that the boys, instead of committing follies such as throwing stones and making huts of twigs, should collect alms for the *poveri vergognosi*; and as it pleased the divine grace, such a change took place that instead of senseless games, they began to collect alms several days beforehand; and instead of barriers in the streets, there were crucifixes at each corner, in the hands of holy innocents. On this last day of Carnival, after vespers, these troops of boys assembled in the four quarters of Florence, each quarter having its special banner. The first was a crucifix; the second was an image of Our Lady, and so on; and with them went the drummers and pipers, the mace-bearers and servingmen of the *Palagio*, the boys singing praises to Heaven, and crying ... "Long live Christ and the Virgin Mary our queen!" all with olive-branches in their hands, so that good and thoughtful people were moved to tears, saying: "Truly this change is the work of God. These lads are those who will enjoy the good things which the *Frate* promised." And we seemed to see the crowds of Jerusalem who preceded and followed Christ on Palm Sunday, saying: "Blessed art thou who comest in the name of the Lord." ... And observe that there were said to be 6,000 boys or more, all of them between five or six and sixteen years of age. All the four troops united at the *Servi*.... They then took the way of all processions; they crossed the Ponte a Santa Trinita (and went round over the Ponte Vecchio) into the Piazza [della Signoria], and so to Santa Maria del Fiore, the church being crowded with men and women, divided, the women on one side and the men on the other; and there the offering was made, with such devotion and tears of holy emotion as was never seen. It was estimated that there were several hundred florins. Many gold florins were put into their collecting bowls, but the greater part consisted in *grossi* [copper coins] and silver. Some women gave their veil-holders, some their silver spoons, kerchiefs, and many other things. All was given without grudging. It seemed as everyone wished to make an offering to Christ and His Mother. I have written these things which are true, and which I saw with my own eyes, and felt with so much emotion; and some of my sons were amongst those blessed and pure-minded troops of boys....

Questions: What moralizing messages did Savonarola preach about the treatment of the poor and the behavior of women? What was the point of the religious and political content of his preaching? What evidence is there that the Florentines were inspired by his preaching? How did the reaction of the Florentines compare to the behavior of the Parisians in doc. 99?

105. A *MAISON-DIEU* IN PONTOISE, C. 1265

Maison-Dieu translates roughly as "house of God," a reference to the charitable impulses behind their foundation and support by the urban populace. These hospitals took in the desperately ill, poor, and pregnant, who had nowhere else to go. Like most such establishments, the Maison-Dieu in the northern French city of Pontoise was governed by statutes, which are translated in the extract below. This comes from a long set of regulations or statutes that set out how the hospital should be run; the number and duties of the brothers and sisters who lived in and ran the hospital; who should be admitted; and much on the religious life of the brothers, sisters, and hospital inmates.

Source: trans. M. Kowaleski, from *Statuts d'hôtels-Dieu et de léproseries; recueil de textes du XIIme au XIVme siècle*, ed. L. Le Grand (Paris: Picard, 1901), pp. 129, 132–35, 136, 137–39, selections.

... the number of brothers should not be more than seven, of which five should be clerics, and of these five clerics, at least three should be priests, and the other two lay brothers. And [there should be] thirteen sisters and no more should be professed.... Both the sisters and brothers owe all obedience to the prior....

[Then follow statutes setting out the liturgy to be celebrated in the hospital church.]

All the brothers and sisters should confess at least once every other week. The confessions should be heard in an honest and common place [medieval confession was said in public, not in private] between the sun rising and the sun falling, and if necessary, can be heard in the infirmary for the sisters who are ill.... When anyone visits the ill sisters, there should always be someone who can see them talking together....

The sisters cannot grow their hair long, but should have it shaved or cut at least every month. The tonsure of the brothers should be done above the ears;

the haircut of the clerics should be done beneath, not too short, so that it doesn't come more than three fingers length below the ears. From Easter to the Exaltation of the Cross [14 September], they should have it cut about every other week, and from the Exaltation of the Cross to Easter, every third week....

The sisters should keep silent in their oratory, in the refectory [where they ate] and in the dormitory. If by chance, when they do not have a sign for something, they can speak a word or a prayer, briefly and quietly.... The sisters should not talk to men of the household unless for a special reason.... The brothers should keep silent in their dormitory and refectory. If by chance they have to talk for something necessary, they should do so briefly and quietly....

The brothers and sisters going into town cannot eat or drink outside the hospital, nor can the sisters go out by themselves. When they go out, the first one in the order should be the first to go out, if the prior of the hospital has not ordered otherwise. Without licence, no brother or sister can go outside the hospital except with the licence of their sovereign.

The clerical and lay brothers who reside in the town can eat and drink outside the hospital, or with the bishop or abbot, but not a lot and with the licence of their sovereign....

Before the ill person can be received, he should confess his sins and, if there is need, should devoutly and honestly receive communion. After this, he should be carried to bed and there, as if he was lord of the house, be treated charitably and reverently. Each day, before the brothers and the sisters eat, charitably satisfied with any meat and drink that he might demand to be given to him, according to the wealth of the house and his profit.

And if he arrives with a great infirmity ... such that he must be removed from the common company of the patients, he should be put in the infirmary with the most gravely ill ... and diligently visited by confessors....

And when he should recover health, he should be kept in the hospital for seven days, so that he will not relapse....

The prioress should assign at least three sisters by day and two at night with two or more chamber-maids, when there is need, to look after the patients, for their sustenance and their comfort.

If something is sent or given to the poor patients ... it should be distributed to them just as the donor or sender has ordered....

Pregnant women who will be received into the house, after giving birth, can be cared for for three weeks, or for however long they wish to be there. Everything that needs to be done to ensure the baptism of the child ... should be at the expense of the house; and what is given to the child at his baptism should belong to the child and will be given to the mother when she wishes to leave. If the mother dies at the house, the child should be nourished likewise in the house if there is no father....

[Most of the remaining statutes treat the entry of brothers and sisters into the order, novices, their religious and moral behavior, and the entry of young women into the order.]

Questions: What types of patients entered this "hospital"? What rules did the statutes impose on the patients and upon the hospital administration? Why is there such an emphasis upon the religious and moral behavior of the brothers and sisters of the hospital order, as well as of the patients?

106. THE DISTRIBUTION OF ALMS IN FLORENCE, 1356

The Orsanmichele was the wealthiest charity of Florence. This list of its charitable distributions offers us some idea of who was considered worthy of help and for what reasons. To give some idea of the amount of money involved, note that an unskilled laborer made about 7–10 shillings a day.

Source: trans. G. Brucker, *The Society of Renaissance Florence: A Documentary Study* (New York: Harper and Row Torchbooks, 1971), pp. 23–33.

Alms distributed in the quarter of S. Spirito through the month of October [1356, by the society of Orsanmichele]. To Monna Francesca, who has broken her arm and has four children. She lives near Pino's cell. She had 5 shillings on September 2nd.

To Monna Giovanna, who is pregnant and lives with Madonna Lapa in the Borgo Vecchio of S. Maria Novella. She received 10 shillings on September 5th. Buoso [a servant] delivered it.

To Monna Caterina, a foreigner who is pregnant. She lives in the parish of S. Frediano in the Via del Fielo. Buoso delivered 10 shillings.

To Monna Fiora, pregnant, whose landlord is the church of S. Apollinare. Buoso gave her 10 shillings.

To Madonna Bella, who lives in the Borgo S. Croce and is very ill, Buoso delivered 10 shillings.

To Nezetta, who is old and sick and lives in the Via S. Gallo.... Buoso gave her 20 shillings.

To Madonna Bartolomea di Piero, a widow, with four children; her landlord is the prior of S. Romolo. Francesco brought her 10 shillings....

To Madonna Fiora di Lapo, who is blind and pregnant; she lives in the parish of S. Felice in Piazza. Buoso gave her 10 shillings.

To Madonna Simona di Puccino, pregnant, of the parish of S. Frediano, Buoso delivered 6 shillings.

To Madonna Giovanna, wife of Giovanni, a soldier from Genoa, living in the parish of S. Giorgio, who is ill without her husband, 6 shillings.

To Piera, Elizabeth, Angela, and Caterina, poor women who are cloistered on the Rubaconte bridge, 8 shillings. To Santa, Nucca, and Caterina, also cloistered on that bridge, 6 shillings. To Jacopa and Giovanna, poor recluses on the Rubaconte bridge, 5 shillings.

To Madonna Agnese, a poor and infirm woman who lives in the house of Giovanni di Monna Nella, 5 shillings.

To Monno Bice, whose landlord is Priorazzo in [Via] S. Niccolo, and who is poor, old, and infirm, 3 shillings....

To Monna Dea, who lives with two children in S. Niccolo del Borgo, 4 shillings.

To Caterina, a girl whose host provides for her for the love of God, in S. Niccolo del Borgo, 3 shillings.

To Monna Lippa, a poor and sick market peddler in the parish of S. Ambrogio, 3 shillings.

To Monna Margherita, widow of Giovanni, who lives with two children ... in the parish of S. Lucia dei Magnoli, 4 shillings.

To Monna Diana di Bartolomeo, a poor woman in the Chiasso of Francesco Forzetti, 2 shillings.

To Stefano, orphaned son of Antonio, whose host provides for him for the love of God, 2 shillings.

To Lisa, widow from Pistoia, who now lives in Florence in the parish of S. Lorenzo with two small children, 2 lire, which the captains [of the society] decided to grant her.

To Monna Isabetta, from the Valdisieve, who is pregnant and in prison, 15 shillings....

To Buona di Rosso, a poor abandoned girl who lives in the Via Ghibellina, 2 lire, which the captains decided to give her.

To Gherardo, a poor sick boy from the Mugello, 12 shillings.

To Monna Dolce, a poor, old, and infirm woman who lives in the Piazza d'Ogni Santi, and who takes care of a girl who was recommended to her by the society, 15 shillings.

Questions: Who—in terms of gender, maritial status, and age—was most likely to receive help from this private charity? What were the circumstances of most receipents of charity?

107. CHARITABLE BEQUESTS IN SIENA, 1300–25

The relative prosperity of Siena during the early fourteenth century is reflected in will-mak-ers' interest in funding ambitious projects that embodied civic and religious pride. These wills also show the charitable impulses of urban citizens, who—in following the church's strictures to leave one-third of their estate to "God's work"—made choices about where to disburse their money, including local religious institutions, charitable causes, and particular individu-als in need. In the absence of large-scale charitable institutions, these bequests provided the bulk of charitable funding in medieval towns. Most of these testators were well-off, although Lady Maria's residence in one of the city's poorer neighborhoods and her fewer bequests sug-gest she was not wealthy. Note that the wills tend to use the term "monastery" for female religious houses of nuns, and the word "convent" or "friary" for the mendicant male religious groups. The honorifics "Lady" and "Lord" are not noble titles, but an indication of respect-ability and high status. "Ser" was used to designate someone of means in the professional class. To put the amounts noted in perspective, note that in c. 1300 a day's wage for an un-skilled laborer was about 7 shillings.

Source: (A) trans. A. Clark, from Archivio di Stato di Siena: Archivio Generale dei Contratti, Diplomatico, 17 October 1300; (B) trans. A. Clark, from Archivio Spedale, Diplomatico, 11 July 1311; (C) trans. A. Clark, from Archivio Spedale, Diplomatico, 12 December 1320; (D) trans A. Clark, from Archivio di Stato di Siena: Archivio Generale dei Contratti, Diplomatico, 5 June 1325.

(A) Will by Lady Maria

In the year of our Lord 1300, the seventeenth day of the month of October. I, Lady Maria, widow of Lord Sygherius of the Gallerani family, daughter of the now-deceased Lord Renaldus Schanna from Rome, of the neighborhood of St. Peter of Ovile of Siena. With an infirm body, but a healthy mind and spirit, I wish and intend to distribute my goods and property and make my will. Firstly, I declare openly that my body is to be buried at the Franciscan friary in Siena, and at this location I elect to be buried. And for my soul and for the remission of my sins I declare openly and bequeath to the Franciscans one *modium* [about 24 bushels] of grain. Also to Friar Ildobrandino of the community of St. Reale, my confessor, 40 shillings. And to the Dominicans of Siena, 100 shillings. And to the Augustinians of Siena, 40 shillings. And to the Servites of St. Maria, 10 shillings. And to the Friars of St. John the Baptist of Siena, 40 shillings. And to the Lady Abbess of the Ladies of Penitence of the city of Siena, the third order of St. Francis, 10 lire, which they must spend distributing to the poor for the salvation of my soul. And to the Ladies of St. Lawrence of Siena, 20 shillings. And to the Ladies of St. Prospero of Siena [blank]. And to Sister Bellina of the monastery St. Prospero, 20 shillings. And to Sister Thomassina of the monastery of St. Maria Novella, daughter of Ser Maichenghi, 20 shillings. And to Friar Renaldo, son of said Ser Maichenghi, 20 shillings. And to the Sisters Lucia and Palmieria enclosed in cells outside of the Gate of Camollia, 20 shillings. And to Ser Taurello, notary, 50 lire ... [then follow legacies to family members].... And to the hospital of Lady Agnese of Siena, 40 shillings. And to the church of St. Peter of Ovile, 40 shillings. And to the Lord Bishop of Siena, 5 shillings ... [more family legacies follow, including money for her sons] who must every year while they live have performed and sung a conventual mass at the Franciscan church for my soul and the soul of Lord Sygherius.... And this is my testament and last will and disposition.

[Appendix to the will, written on the same page.] In the year of the Lord 1300, the twenty-third day of the month of October. I, Lady Maria widow of Lord Sygherius of the Gallerani family, daughter of the now-deceased Lord Renaldus Schanna from Rome, of the order of the Ladies of Penitence, third order of St. Francis of Siena. With an infirm body, but sound in mind and spirit, wanting to amend my testament ... in this way. And I declare openly and bequeath to the Franciscans of Siena, 4 lire which the executor of my will should give to them every year....

(B) Will by Ser Taurello

In the name of the Lord, amen. I, Taurello Baccelliere, notary, of the neighborhood of St. Bartholomew of Siena, thanks to Jesus Christ, of sound mind and body ... [make my last will and testament] ... I declare openly and bequeath my land and vines and woods located at Montecellesi ... to the hospital of St. Croce [he had founded this hospital] located in the Castellaccia of Camollia next to the gate of the city of Siena, which cannot be sold to anyone ... I declare openly and bequeath to this hospital of St. Croce annually in perpetuity 10 lire for masses celebrated in the chapel of this hospital ... for my soul and that of my family. And I bequeath to the church of St. Bartholomew of Siena annually in perpetuity a candelabrum of candles worth 5 lire which should be used during the administration of the body of our Lord Jesus Christ, when it is raised on the altar in this church. And I bequeath to the monastery of St. Petronilla annually in perpetuity, 10 shillings. And I bequeath to the monastery of the Holy Spirit annually in perpetuity, 10 shillings. And I bequeath to the Abbey of Montecellesi annually in perpetuity, 5 shillings for the Feast of St. Nicholas. And I bequeath to the monastery of Vico near Siena annually in perpetuity, 3 shillings. And I bequeath to Sisters Lucia and Palmiera, 5 shillings every year while they are living. And I bequeath to the convent of the Umiliati friars of Siena annually in perpetuity, 3 shillings. And I bequeath to the monastery of St. Lorenzo of Siena annually in perpetuity, 3 shillings. And I bequeath to the convent of the Dominicans annually in perpetuity, 10 shillings. And I bequeath to the House of Mercy of Siena annually in perpetuity, 10 shillings. And I bequeath to the convent of the Franciscans annually in perpetuity, 10 shillings. And I bequeath to the convent of the Hermits of St. Augustine of Siena annually in perpetuity, 10 shillings. And I bequeath to the monastery of the Brothers [a female monastery] near Siena annually in perpetuity, 5 shillings. And I bequeath to the convent of the Friars of the Servites of St. Maria of Siena annually in perpetuity, 5 shillings. And I bequeath to the monastery of St. Benedict annually in perpetuity, 2 shillings. And I bequeath to the Ladies of St. Margaret annually in perpetuity, 2 shillings. And I bequeath to the Friars of the order of St. Maria of Mount Carmel annually in perpetuity, 2 shillings. And I bequeath to the new fraternity which calls itself the fraternity of the Blessed Virgin Mary annually in perpetuity, 10 shillings. And I bequeath to the Hospital of St. Maria of the Scale annually in perpetuity, 10 shillings. And I bequeath to the hospital of Lady Agnese annually in perpetuity, 5 shillings. And I bequeath to each fraternity of priests in the city of Siena annually in perpetuity, 5 shillings. And I bequeath to each fraternity in the city of Siena annually in perpetuity, 2 shillings. And I bequeath to every hermit, both male and female, in the city of Siena and near the city up to a mile, annually in perpetuity, 12 pence....

(C) Will by Lady Mita

In the year of our Lord 1320, the twelfth day of the month of December ... I, Lady Mita, widow of Meo Compagno, living in the neighborhood of St. Quirico in Castelvecchio in Siena, want to make my testament and distribute my goods in this manner. Firstly, I declare openly that my body is to be buried in the church of St. Quirico, to which church I bequeath 30 shillings. And I bequeath to the Friars of St. Augustine 20 shillings. And I bequeath to each convent of friars of the city of Siena 6 shillings. And to each church and hospital of the city of Siena, 12 pence. And I bequeath to the hospital of Ser Gori a bed of the value of 8 lire ... [she then recites family legacies including household goods to her two daughters and a piece of land to her son]....

(D) Will by Lady Lagia

In the year of our Lord, the fifth day of the month of June ... I, Lady Lagia of the Palmieri family, wife of Vitalis Corari of the neighborhood of St. Pellegrino. Sane in mind and spirit thanks to God ... and with a healthy body ... I want to make my last will and testament.... Firstly, I recommend my soul to God, and my body I declare openly and bequeath to be buried in the cemetery of the church of St. Martin of Siena and there I elect my body to be buried. And I bequeath of my goods 10 lire to this church for my soul. And to the church of St. Pellegrino I give of my goods 3 lire. And to the Lord Bishop of Siena, 5 shillings for my soul. And to the church of St. Pellegrino, and the Franciscans of Siena, and the Dominicans of Siena, and the hermits of St. Augustine, I bequeath of my goods for my soul, for each of them a candelabrum of candles of the cost and value of 40 shillings for the purpose of illuminating the body of my lord Jesus Christ when it is elevated in these places and churches. And I bequeath of my goods for masses sung and given for my soul 10 lire to each presbytery and religious place which my executor decides upon. And to the convent of St. Petronilla, and the convent of St. Maria Novella next to the Gate of Camollia of the city of Siena, and to the convent of the Ladies of St. Prospero, and the convent of St. Lawrence, and the convent of the Ladies of St. Clare, and a convent which calls itself Melianda which lies next to the Gate of Uliviera of the city of Siena [she then lists five more female convents] to each of them of my goods I bequeath for my soul, 2 shillings. And to the hospital of Lady Agnese of my goods for my soul I bequeath 10 shillings. And to the hospital of Lady Santuccia of Maciareto I bequeath of my goods for my soul, 10 shillings; [she then lists 12 more hospitals in the city of Siena] to each of them I bequeath of my goods for my soul, 2 shillings. And I bequeath of my goods for my soul 20 tunics of the cost and value of 20 shillings of each of them, which are to be distributed to the poor ... [she goes on to list legacies to individual friars].... And to the fraternity of the house of St. Maria, and the fraternity of St. Maria of Carmelo, and to the fraternity of Camporeggio [area of city where the Dominican friary was located], and the fraternity of Ovile [area of the city where the Franciscan friary was located], and the fraternity of St. Augustine, and the fraternity of the Servites of St. Maria, to each of them I bequeath of my goods for my soul 2 shillings. And I bequeath for my soul 12 pence to each male hermit or female hermit living at the cell of Friar Geri near the gate of Castel Montone of the city of Siena, and those living at the monastery of St. Petronilla near the hospital of St. Croce, and those living at the Gate of Laterano of the city of Siena from the road up to the monastery of St. Catherine which is in this neighborhood....

Questions: What were the types of religious orders, institutions, and individuals who were included in the bequests of these four Siennese citizens? What differences and similarities do you see between the choices made by the testators in deciding who the beneficiaries of their charity would be and how much they received? What do the testators' choices of burial tell you about their religious affiliations? Which religious groups tended to receive larger or smaller amounts of money? What do the nature of these legacies—some in cash, and some not—indicate about medieval urban religiosity?

CHAPTER NINE

EDUCATION

Figure 9.1
Seal of Oxford University
Universities, like communes (figs. 2.2, 2.3) and guilds, also had seals they used to seal official documents. This is the seal of Oxford University, founded c. 1200. Reproduced from Paul LaCroix, *Science and Literature in the Middle Ages and at the Period of the Renaissance* (New York: D. Appleton and Co., 1878), fig. 29.

108. THE COST OF SCHOOLING, 1394–95

The following account lists what Gilbert Maghfield, a wealthy London merchant, paid for educating two young boys (one his ward, the other his son). The boys were sent to live with the vicar of Croydon, a village to the south of London. The costs included room and board ("the commons"), shoes and stockings, and a variety of other expenses. The low salary paid to the schoolmaster suggests that he was a clerk hired by the vicar to school the boys.

Source: trans. M. Kowaleski, from "Documents and Records: Extracts from a Fourteenth-Century Account Book," by E. Rickert, *Modern Philology* XXIV (1926–1927): 251–52.

In the seventeenth year [of the reign of Richard II], the month of May, John Frogenhale and William Maghfield were sent to Croydon to school on the Eve of St. Dunstan [18 May 1394], paying by the week, 2 shillings.

Also, paid on the Eve of St. Michael [18 September] in the 18th year [1394] for 19 weeks: 38 shillings.

Also given to their master for their schooling: 3 shillings 4 pence.

Also, given to him the same day for stockings: 2 shillings.

Also, paid upon the Eve of Christmas for 12 weeks: 24 shillings.

Also, for 4 pairs of shoes: 16 pence.

Also, for 2 pairs of stockings: 16 pence.

Sum, 26 shillings 8 pence.

Also, delivered at Christmas a book called "Este" which cost: 7 shillings.

Also, given to the master for their schooling: 3 shillings 4 pence.

Also for 2 pairs of stockings for both of them: 16 pence.

Also, given to the vicar of Croydon, a cade [a barrel holding about 600] of herrings, price: 6 shillings; and a small basket of figs: 16 pence....

Also paid for 14 weeks, that is, from Epiphany to Easter in the 18th year [1395]: sum, 28 shillings.

Also, for 4 pairs of shoes: 16 pence.

Also, given to the servants in the vicar's household: 20 pence.

Also, for expenses of myself and my horses to Croydon: 15 pence.

Also, paid to the schoolmaster for his salary: 40 pence.

Also for 1 pair of stockings: 12 pence.

Sum, 4 shillings 4 pence.

Also, given to the master for 1 pair of stockings: 20 pence.

Also, on the morrow of St. John the Baptist [25 June 1395] paid to the schoolmaster: 3 shillings, 4 pence.

Also, the same time to the two children: 8 pence.

Also, paid for their commons for 11 weeks, that is, until July 8 in the 19th year [1395]: 22 shillings.

Also, for their shoes: 16 pence.

Also, for the washerwoman for washing their clothes: 16 pence.

Also, expended by Frogenhale on two occasions: 15 pence....

Also, paid for 12 weeks from the day of St. Thomas Martyr [7 July] until St. Michael [29 September]: 24 shillings.

Also, to the master for his salary: 40 pence.

Also, to him for one pair of stockings: 20 pence.

Also, for the children, 4 pairs of shoes: 16 pence.

Also, 4 pairs of stockings: 2 shillings, 3 pence.

Also, for the washerwoman: 6 pence....

Also, given to the master one coat of my livery, furred, against Christmas in the 19th year [1395]: at the price of 11 shillings, 8 pence.

Questions: What does this expense account tell us about the life of these two well-off children in school, and about the nature of their education and upkeep?

109. NICCOLO MACHIAVELLI AS A YOUNG STUDENT

This extract from the ricordi of Bernardo Machiavelli, a Florentine jurist and merchant, describes what he spent on educating his sons, Niccolo, who was born in 1469, and Totto, his younger son. Note the care that Bernardo took in choosing good teachers and ensuring his son Niccolo had the best books available. Niccolo became an influential member of the Florentine government, but he lost his position in 1512 when the republic was replaced by the Medici regime. He went into exile, where he wrote his most famous work, The Prince, *a treatise of political advice to a new ruler.*

Source: trans. M. Baca, *Merchant Writers of the Italian Renaissance from Boccaccio to Machiavelli*, ed. Vittore Branca (New York: Marsilio Publishers, 1999), pp. 149–52.

I record that on this 6th day of May 1476, my son Niccolo began to go to Maestro Matteo, the grammar master who lives at the foot of this side of the Santa Trinita bridge, to learn to read the *Donatello* [an abridged version of Donatus's *Ars grammatica*] and to pay for this teaching I must give him 5 shillings per month, plus 20 at Eastertide....

I record that on this 8th day of May my son Niccolo brought 5 shillings to Maestro Matteo who teaches him, as his salary for this month....

I record that on this fifth day of July 1476 I brought to Maestro Niccolo Tedesco, the priest and astrologer, twelve *quinterni* [a gathering of five folios of paper or parchment] of quarto size, on which I had written all of the cities and provinces, islands, and mountains that are mentioned in Livy's *Decades* [Livy was an ancient Roman historian], with their addenda according to the books of each of the *Decades* in which Livy mentions them and he wrote them out for me in Latin, for which he declared himself to be content and satisfied. I had purchased the 3 *Decades* in print from the stationer Zanobi, as we had agreed and as I recorded on folio 4 of this same book, and we also agreed that as a reward for my labors he would bind them for me.

I record that on 20 March 1476 my son Niccolo began to go to Ser Battista di Filippo da Poppi to learn the *Donatello*. Ser Battista gives lessons in the church of San Benedetto in the area of San Giovanni....

I record that on this 3rd day of November 1477 I purchased from Francesco Bartoli and company, cloth cutters, 5½ *braccia* [a unit of measurement of about 60 cm.] of reddish-brown dyed wool cloth from Garbo to make a little tunic and cloak for Niccolo. It came to 10 lire and 15 shillings. I gave them nine lire in cash: 15 shillings in a Sienese half florin and 6 lire and 18 shillings in small change. I still owe them 20 shillings. Their boy took the cloth to Leonardo the cloth cutter to have it cut, and left it with his son-in-law Girolamo. He promised me that I could have it back next Thursday morning.

Later I gave them the remaining 20 shillings....

I record that on this 3rd day of January 1479 I put my son Niccolo to board with Piero Maria, the master of arithmetic and bookkeeping, and we agreed that I would pay him for all this teaching as follows: a half florin when Niccolo begins to study the rudiments of arithmetic, and another later on in the teaching.

On the same day I set Totto to learning the alphabet.... I record that on the 5th day of November 1481 my sons Niccolo and Totto began to study with Maestro Pagolo da Ronciglione, the grammar master. Niccolo is doing the Latin classics, and Totto is learning Donatus; I don't yet have an agreement with Maestro Pagolo about the payment.

I record that on this 21st day of June 1486 I gave to Francesco d'Andrea di Bartolomeo, the stationer at San Giorgio in Florence, a printed version of a reading of the Abbot of Sicily [Nicolaus de Tedeschi, d. 1445] on the 4th and 5th Decretals [a canon law text], in folio, as well as the three *Decades* with the epitome of the 40 books of Livy, printed, also in folio. He is going to bind them well for me, with half-leather boards and two clasps each, and I have agreed to give him 4 lire and 5 shillings for binding both volumes. I also agreed to sell him some red wine that he tasted for 50 shillings per barrel. He took the books away with him, and promised to bring them back within eight days. On the same day, in the evening after the 24th hour he came with a porter and took away a barrel of red wine for 50 shillings, as we had agreed above.

On the 27th of June I gave him Giovanni d'Andrea's gloss on the sixth Decretal to bind; I bought this from Bartolo di Fruosino, a bookseller in the Garbo, and then Francesco d'Andrea took it to bind it along with the *Mercuriali*, for which he promised to come here this evening when he leaves his shop. On the same day, at the hour of the Ave Maria, Francesco came here, and I gave him Giovanni Andrea's *Mercuriali* [a law text] to bind, and we agreed that he would bind them together with the *Novellina* [a law text] in a single volume with half-leather boards and 2 clasps, for 40 shillings. I agreed to give him wine at 50 shillings per barrel as above.

I record that on the first of July my son Niccolo gave the stationer Francesco d'Andrea, to whom I had given these books to bind, as is recorded in the preceding page, a barrel of red wine for 50 shillings.

On the 4th he gave him 20 shillings in cash; for Francesco had said that he couldn't bind the books without 20 shillings to buy the leather. On the 8th of July Niccolo gave Francesco d'Andrea 3 flasks of red wine and a flask of vinegar, which he came to pick up. So he no longer owed him 5 shillings. On the same day, Francesco delivered the bound books. One, the abbot's reading of the sixth Decretals, was well bound, as we had agreed; the other two were poorly bound and didn't live up our agreement. He did this because I was away in the country.

Questions: What can we find out about the identity, expertise, and remuneration of teachers in late medieval Florence? What were the experiences of Florentine students in terms of where they attended school, what they studied, and how their lessons progressed as they grew older? Do you see any parallels in the educational experience of these Florentine boys and the English boys in doc. 108? How did the father shape the education of his sons?

Figure 9.2

A Student is Punished

This image depicts an urban school of mendicant friars, with a student being switched in the foreground. Most medieval educational institutions were under the auspices of the Catholic church. Reproduced from Paul LaCroix, *Science and Literature in the Middle Ages and at the Period of the Renaissance* (New York: D. Appleton and Co., 1878), fig. 14.

110. PRIVILEGES GRANTED TO MASTERS AND STUDENTS AT THE UNIVERSITY OF PARIS

Monarchs and ecclesiastical authorities often gave special privileges to the teachers and students attending universities that tended to put limits on the townspeople's ability to deal with members of the university, who were usually from outside of the city. The privileges granted by the French monarch in the first extract followed a brawl between some German students and local Parisians in which five students were killed. Because the city provost took the side of the citizens, the students appealed to the king, who responded with this grant of privileges to assuage the students and stop them from leaving Paris. Note, however, that the students' disputes with the provost continued and reached such a bad state in 1229 that the University of Paris suspended lectures for two years. Since the university bolstered the town's economy, and since the king needed well-educated clerks to run an effective government, the university continued to demand and receive privileges, including complete exemption from local taxation in 1340, in the second extract.

Source: (A) trans. D.C. Munro, "The Medieval Student," *Translations and Reprints from the Original Sources of European History*, vol. 2, no. 3 (Philadelphia: University of Pennsylvania Press, n.d.), pp. 4–5, revised; (B) trans. A.O. Norton, *Readings in the History of Education: Medieval Universities* (Cambridge, MA: Harvard University Press, 1909), p. 89.

(A) Royal Privileges Granted by King Philip Augustus, 1200

In the name of the sacred and indivisible Trinity, amen. Philip, by the grace of God, king of the French. Let all men know, now and in the future, that for the terrible crime owing to which five of the clergy and laity of Paris were killed by certain malefactors, Thomas, then provost [of the city], about whom the students have complained more than all others, because he denied the deed, we consign to perpetual imprisonment ... unless he chooses to undergo the ordeal of water at Paris.... Moreover, concerning the others who are in prison for the same crime ... we will detain them in perpetual imprisonment, in our custody, unless they prefer to undergo the ordeal by water and to prove their innocence by God's witness....

Also, concerning the safety of the students at Paris in the future, by the advice of our subjects, we have ordained as follows. We will cause all citizens of Paris to swear that if anyone sees an injury done to any student by any layman, he will testify truthfully to this, nor will anyone withdraw in order not to see [the act]. And if it happens that anyone strikes a student, except in self-defense, especially if he strikes the student with a weapon, or a club or a stone, all laymen who see [the act] should in good faith seize the malefactor or malefactors and deliver them to our judge....

And neither our provost nor our judges should lay hands on a student for any offence whatever, nor should they place him in our prison, unless such a crime has been committed by the student that he ought to be arrested. And in that case, our judge should arrest him on the spot, without striking him at all, unless he resists, and should hand him over to the ecclesiastical judge, who should guard him in order to satisfy us and the one suffering the injury. And if a serious crime has been committed, our judge should go or should send to see what is done with the student. If, indeed, the student does not resist arrest and yet suffers any injury, we will exact satisfaction for it, according to the examination and the oath. Also our judges should not lay hands on the chattels of the students at Paris for any crime whatever. But if it seems that these should be sequestrated, they should be sequestrated and guarded after sequestration by the ecclesiastical judge, in order that whatever is judged legal by the church may be done with the chattels. But if students are arrested by our count at such an hour that the ecclesiastical judge can not be found and be present at once, our provost should cause the culprits to be guarded in some student's house without any ill-treatment, as is said above, until they are delivered to the ecclesiastical judge.

Concerning the lay servants of the students [who are not permanent residents of the city or who do not live by trade there] ... it should be as follows. Neither we nor our judge should lay hands on them unless they commit an open crime, for which we or our judges ought to arrest them....

In order, moreover, that these [decrees] may be kept more carefully and may be established forever by a fixed law, we have decided that our present provost and the people of Paris should affirm by an oath, in the presence of the scholars, that they will carry out in good faith all of the above-mentioned. And always in the future, whosoever receives from us the office of provost in Paris, among the other initiatory acts of his office, namely, on the first or second Sunday, in one of the churches of Paris—after he has been summoned for this purpose—should affirm by an oath, publicly in the presence of the scholars, that he will keep in good faith all the above-mentioned....

(B) Exemption from Taxation, c. 1340

To the Masters and Scholars [of Paris], now in attendance at the university, and to those who are hereafter to come to the same university, or who are actually preparing in sincerity so to come, also while they are staying at the university, or returning to their own homes, we grant ... that no layman, of whatever condition or prominence he may be, whether he be a private person, prefect, or bailiff, shall disturb, molest, or presume otherwise in any way whatsoever to seek to extort anything from the aforesaid masters and scholars, in person, family, or property under pretext of toll, *taille* [a type of tax], tax, customs, or other such personal taxes, or other personal exaction of any kind, while they are either coming to the university itself, or actually preparing in sincerity to come, or returning to their own homes. And their status as scholars shall be established by the proper oath.

Questions: What legal and economic privileges did the teachers and students of the University of Paris receive? What do their demands tell us about town/gown relationships?

III. TOWN/GOWN CONTROVERSIES IN OXFORD AND PARIS

The presence of large numbers of young, male students in university towns caused frequent clashes with the local townspeople, who grew weary of their raucous behavior, which was often fueled by alcohol. The scholars, for their part, thought the townspeople took advantage of them by charging high prices for food and lodging. Both sides wielded what weapons and influence they could, as these extracts from chronicles indicate.

Source: (A) trans. J.A. Giles, *Roger of Wendover's Flowers of History* (London: H.G. Bohn, 1849), II, pp. 249–50; (B) trans. A.O. Norton, *Readings in the History of Education: Medieval Universities* (Cambridge, MA: Harvard University Press, 1909), pp. 93–94; (C) trans. H.E. Salter, *Munimenta Civitatis Oxonie* (Oxford Record Society, vol. 71, 1920), pp. 127–28.

(A) Troubles in Oxford, 1209

About this same time a certain clerk, who was studying the liberal arts at Oxford accidentally killed a woman, and when he found that she was dead, he sought safety in flight. But the mayor of the city and several others, coming to the place and finding the dead woman, began to search for the murderer in his house which he had rented with three other of his fellow clerks. And, not finding the guilty man, they took his three fellow-clerks, who were altogether ignorant of the murder, and cast them into prison. And, after a few days, by the order of the king but in contempt of the rights of the church, these clerks were taken out of the city and hanged.

Whereupon some 3,000 clerks, both masters as well as pupils, departed from Oxford, so that not one of the whole university remained. Some scholars went to Cambridge and others to Reading to pursue their studies, leaving the city of Oxford empty.

(B) Troubles in Paris, 1229

In that same year, on the second and third holidays before Ash Wednesday, days when the clerks of the university have leisure for games, certain of the clerks went out of the city of Paris in the direction of St. Marcel's, for a change of air and to have contests in their usual games. When they had reached the place and had amused themselves for some time in carrying on their games, they chanced to find in a certain tavern some excellent wine, pleasant to drink. And then, in the dispute that arose between the clerks who were drinking and the shopkeepers, they began to exchange blows and to tear each other's hair, until some townsmen ran in and freed the shopkeepers from the hands of the clerks. But when the clerks resisted they inflicted blows upon them and put them to flight, well and thoroughly pummelled. The latter, however, when they came back much battered into the city, roused their comrades to avenge them. So on the next day they came with swords and clubs to St. Marcel's, and entering forcibly the house of a certain shopkeeper, broke up all his wine casks and poured out wine on the floor of his house. And, proceeding through the open squares, they attacked sharply whatever man or woman they came upon and left them half dead from the blows given them.

But the prior of St. Marcel's, as soon as he learned of this great injury done to his men [his tenants], whom he was bound to defend, lodged a complaint with the Roman [papal] legate and the bishop of Paris.... [A royal body-guard of mercenaries were sent to punish the wrongdoers, but came across clerks who had nothing to do with the previous altercations.] The police, rushing upon these men whom they saw were unarmed and innocent, killed some, wounded others, and handled others mercilessly, battering them with the blows they inflicted upon them. But some of them escaping by flight lay hidden in dens and caverns. And among the wounded it was found that there were two clerks, rich and of great influence, who died, one of them being by race a man of Flanders, and the other of the Norman nation.

But when the enormity of this transgression reached the ears of the masters of the university, they came together in the presence of the queen [of France, who was ruling while the king was away] and legate, having first suspended all lectures and debates, and strenuously demanded that justice be shown for such a wrong....

But when finally every sort of justice had been refused them by the king and legate, as well as by the bishop, there took place a universal withdrawl of the masters and a scattering of the scholars, the instruction of the masters and the training of the pupils coming to an end, so that not one person of note out of them all remained in the city. And the city which was wont to boast of her clerks now remained bereft of them.... Thus withdrawing, the clerks betook themselves practically in a body to the larger cities in various districts. But the largest part of them chose the metropolitan city of Angers for their university instruction....

At length, through the efforts of discreet persons, it was worked out that, certain things being done to meet the situation as required by the faults on both sides, peace was made up between the clerks and citizens and the whole body of scholars was recalled.

(C) Troubles in Oxford, 1335

These are the injuries done to the mayor, bailiff, and commonalty of Oxford by the scholars of the University of Oxford.

First, on Tuesday before the Feast of St. Valentine last past, there came Walter Spryngeheuse, Roger de Chesterfield, and other scholars to the tavern called Swyndolnestok and there took a quart of wine and threw the said wine in the face of John Croidon, taverner, and then with that quart pot beat John without reason. Whereupon the bailiffs came and asked them to amend and redress their trespass in good manner; but they would not amend the trespass or redress it, but they left the tavern and at once they had bows and arrows and other arms ready for ill-doing at the Carfax [central market square]. Then the bailiffs confiscated the bows and arrows, and the scholars made great noise and great debate, for which reason the mayor, bailiffs, and sergeants approached the chancellor of the University and beseeched him to have the malefactors arrested and to aid in keeping the peace on his side. And when the mayor, bailiffs, and sergeants returned from the chancellor, he doing none of those things that they had prayed, there came two hundred and more of the scholars, armed in the manner of war, and they beat and assaulted the mayor, bailiffs, and sergeants, and wounded some of them, whereby they despaired for their lives, and then they slew a child of about fourteen years and threatened to set the town on fire. And further, the next morning, when the mayor, bailiffs, and good folk of the town were gone to Woodstock to complain to the king about these injuries, these scholars came with royal power and took the wardens of the city and closed the gates and fought with shields and arms by plan and openly, and set the town on fire in diverse parts, and broke open and robbed diverse houses of lay folk, and wounded many people and killed many. By which alarm of fire and of the fighting the common people arose in aid and defense of the town.

Questions: What was the source of conflict between the town's citizens and the university students? What recourse did the citizens and then the university authorities have to address the disputes?

112. A STUDENT RIOT AT OXFORD, 1388–89

Students at medieval universities were often categorized by "nations," which reflected their ethnic origins. Disputes between these groups were common and often reached a frightening level of violence, as described here by one of the ringleaders of the Welsh "nation" at Oxford, Adam of Usk, who went on to a distinguished career in the service of two popes.

Source: trans. E.M. Thompson, *Chronicle of Adam of Usk, 1377–1421* (Royal Society of Literature, H. Frowde, 1904), pp. 109–10.

In these days there happened at Oxford a grave misfortune. For, during two whole years there was great strife between the men of the south and the men of Wales on the one side and the northerners on the other, from which arose fights, quarrels, and often loss of life. In the first year the northerners were driven clean away from the university. And they laid their expulsion chiefly to my charge. But in the second year, in an evil hour, coming back to Oxford, they gathered by night, and denying us passage from our quarters by force of arms, for two days they strove sorely against us, breaking and plundering some of the halls of our side, and slaying certain of our men. However, on the third day our party, bravely strengthened by the help of Merton Hall, forced our adversaries shamefully to fly from the public streets, which for the two days they had held as a camp, and to take refuge in their own quarters. In short, we could not be quieted before many of our number had been indicted for felonious riot. And among them I, who am now writing, was indicted, as the chief leader, and abettor of the Welsh, and perhaps not unrighteously. And so indicted we were hardly acquitted, being tried by jury before the king's judge. From that day forth I feared the king, hitherto unknown to me in his power, and his laws, and I put hooks into my jaws.

Questions: What does this passage tell us about tensions within the university community itself? How might the behavior of the students here have affected the townspeople?

113. WOOING MASTERS AND STUDENTS FROM PARIS TO THE NEW UNIVERSITY OF TOULOUSE, 1229

The economic and status benefits of hosting a university made cities eager to attract students to their university, as is seen in this over-wrought declaration of the advantages available to teachers and students who came to the university in Toulouse in southern France. After the suppression of heresy in southern France following the crusade against the Cathar heretics, the citizens of Toulouse felt the city would benefit from a university, so their local count agreed to pay the salaries of fourteen teachers, including two in theology, two in canon law, six in liberal arts, and two in grammar. This announcement of the new enterprise was made in 1229, when university students and teachers left Paris following a quarrel with the local authorities, a situation that Toulouse hoped to exploit. Current students may wish to compare the rhetoric in this plea to the content of today's college brochures.

Source: trans. L. Thorndike, *University Records and Life in the Middle Ages* (New York: Columbia University Press, 1944; repr. New York: Octagon Books, 1971), pp. 32–35.

To all Christ's faithful and especially to masters and scholars studying in any land who may see this letter, the university of masters and scholars of Toulouse, about to plant a new studium, wish continued good life with a blessed end. No undertaking has a stable foundation which is not firmly placed in Christ, the foundation of holy mother church. We therefore with this in mind are trying in Christ with all our might to lay the permanent foundation of a philosophy school at Toulouse, on which others may build with us whose good will is lighted to this by luminous rays of the Holy Spirit. For blessed Augustine says, "God prepares good will to be aided and aids it when prepared. He indeed causes the unwilling to will and aids the willing lest he will in vain." Therefore, most cherished, do what you will with us to prepare good will for the Lord which, when he finds prepared, he will lead on the holy works, so that where once swords cleaved a path for you, you shall fight with a sharp tongue; where war waged carnage, you shall militate with peaceful doctrine; where the forest of heretical depravity scattered thorns, the cedar of catholic faith shall be reared by you to the stars.

And lest the approach of so much labor terrify you, we have prepared the way for you, we have sustained the first hardships, we offer you the standard of security so that, with us preceding as your armsbearers, you soldiers of philosophy may be able to fight the more safely with the art of Mercury, the weapons of Phoebus, the lance of Minerva. That you may again have hope for the stability of the new university we have undertaken the load enjoined by authority of the church. For our Moses was the lord cardinal and legate in the realm of France, leader and protector and author after God and the pope of so arduous a beginning, who decreed that all studying at Toulouse, both masters and disciples, should obtain plenary indulgence of all their sins. Therefore for this cause and because of the continuity of lecturing and disputing which the masters exercise more diligently and frequently than they did at Paris, many scholars are flocking to Toulouse seeing that flowers already have appeared in our land and the time of putation is at hand.

Therefore let no Deidamiai detain our Achilles going forth to philosophic war, that he attain not this second Troy, of which our Toulousan Statius might sing once more:

> All honor there, there great names strive;
> Fearful mothers and groups of virgins
> With difficulty remain idle.
> Here he is condemned to many sterile years
> And hateful to God, if sluggishly
> He lets this new glory pass him by.

So let each upright man put on the warlike mien of Achilles, lest meticulous Thersites take the laurel promised to magnanimous Ajax, so that at least, the war finished, he may admire the zeal of the militant and the zeal of the philosophizing. And that the studious may more willingly know the glory of Toulouse and its university, let them know that this is the second land of promise flowing with milk and honey, green with lush pastures, where fruit trees are leafing, where

Bacchus reigns in vineyards, where Ceres rules in fields, where the temperate air was preferred by the ancient philosophers to other stations of earth. O, how incomprehensible are the greatnesses of almighty God!

> Here is peace, elsewhere Mars rages in all the world.
> But this place received Mars and death formerly.

Further, that ye may not bring hoes to sterile and uncultivated fields, the professors at Toulouse have cleared away for you the weeds of the rude populace and thorns of sharp sterility and other obstacles. For here theologians inform their disciples in pulpits and the people at the crossroads, logicians train the tyros in the arts of Aristotle, grammarians fashion the tongues of the stammering on analogy, organists smooth the popular ears with the sweet-throated organ, decretists extol Justinian, and physicians teach Galen. Those who wish to scrutinize the bosom of nature to the inmost can hear here the books of Aristotle which were forbidden at Paris.

What then will you lack? Scholastic liberty? By no means, since tied to no one's apron strings you will enjoy your own liberty. Or do you fear the malice of the raging mob or the tyranny of an injurious prince? Fear not, since the liberality of the count of Toulouse affords us sufficient security both as to our salary and our servants coming to Toulouse and returning home. But if they suffer loss of their property through the hands of brigands in the domain of the count, he will pursue our malefactors with the forces of the capitol of Toulouse, the same as on behalf of citizens of Toulouse. To what has been said we add further that, as we hope truly, the lord legate will summon other theologians and decretists here to enlarge the university and will set a time which scholars ought to spend at Toulouse to receive the indulgence, if that prevaricator envious of the human race does not impede their stay, which God forbid, that henceforth they may magnify the place and the folk of Romanus, fighting by the salubrious triumphal mystery of the cross.

As for prices, what has already been said should reassure you and the fact that there is no fear of a failure of crops. On this point you may trust both report and the nuncio and these verses:

> For a little, wine, for a little, bread is had;
> For a little, meat, for a little, fish is bought.

The courtesy of the people should not be passed over. For here is seen that courtly good humor has struck a covenant with knighthood and clergy. So if you wish to marvel at more good things than we have mentioned, leave home behind, strap your knapsack on your back, and make your motto the words of Seneca: "I shall see all lands as mine, mine as of all; I shall so live that I shall know I am known to others; for to aim high and have enlarged ideas is characteristic of a noble soul."

Questions: What rhetorical strategies did the city of Toulouse employ to convince students to come to its new university? What features of life in Toulouse and its university did the city think would be particularly attractive to students? Why was it advantageous for a city such as Toulouse to have a university despite the town/gown problems experienced elsewhere (docs. 111, 112)?

114. CONTRACT BETWEEN THE TOWN OF VERCELLI AND THE STUDENTS AT PADUA, c. 1228

Italian universities differed from their northern European counterparts in their origins (which at Bologna, for example, stemmed from the efforts of students more than masters); their greater focus on the study of law; and in particular, the more direct relationship between communal governments and the university, without the interference of kings. As in northern Europe, however, competition for the right to host a university was fierce because of the advantages a good university brought to a town. In this extract, we see the contract drawn up between the town of Vercelli and representatives of the students (rectors) at the university in neighboring Padua, who were dissatisfied with their treatment in Padua. To lure the university of Padua to its town, the proctors of Vercelli were ready to extend specific privileges to the university community, particularly financial incentives. These incentives included a willingness to recruit and subsidize well-known professors in order to attract more students. Such arrangements were the beginning of the "endowed chairs" upon which many universities today rely.

Source: trans. A.O. Norton, *Readings in the History of Education: Medieval Universities* (Cambridge, MA: Harvard University Press, 1909), pp. 99–100, revised.

... Likewise the proctors have promised in the name of the town of Vercelli that the town will loan to the scholars, and to the university of scholars, the sum of 10,000 pounds, at the [interest] rate of 2 pence for two years, and thereafter 3 pence for six years [under proper security. The customary rate seems to have been 4 pence].... Likewise, when a scholar pays the money loaned to him, the town of Vercelli will retain that amount in the common treasury as principal, and from it will help some other needy scholar under the same agreement and similar conditions.

... Likewise, the town of Vercelli will not allow provisions within the town limits to be withdrawn from their markets [in order to ensure a sufficient food supply at a reasonable price] but will cause them to be delivered in the city in good faith, and will cause them to be put on sale twice a week.... [Also 1,000 bushels of grain will be put in the city granary and sold to scholars at cost in time of need].... Likewise, the town of Vercelli will provide salaries [for professors] who shall be deemed competent by two scholars and two townsmen, and if they disagree the bishop shall decide the matter ... and these salaries should be for one theologian, three masters of laws, two decretists [canon lawyers], two teachers of natural philosophy, two logicians, and two grammarians.... [The town will send out at its own expense] trustworthy messengers under oath, who shall in good faith, and in the interests of the University of Vercelli, seek out the chosen masters and teachers, and shall use their best endeavors to bind them to lecture in the city of Vercelli. [The town will preserve peace within its borders, will consider scholars and messengers neutral in time of war, will grant them the rights of citizens, and will respect the legal jurisdiction of the rectors, except in criminal and other specially mentioned cases.]

Likewise, the town of Vercelli will provide two copyists, through whom it will undertake to furnish men able to supply to the scholars copies in both kinds of law [civil and canon] and in theology, which will be satisfactory and accurate both in text and glosses, and the students will pay for their copies [no extortionate prices but] a rate based on the estimate of the rectors [of the university].

... Likewise, the scholars or their representatives shall not pay the tributes in the district of Vercellio.... The podestà and the town itself shall be bound to send, throughout the cities of Italy and elsewhere (as shall be expedient to them), notice that a university has been established at Vercelli, and to invite scholars to come to the University of Vercelli.

Questions: What do the promises made by the town of Vercelli to the university scholars tell us about the interests of the university community? How do the attempts of Vercelli to lure university scholars compare to the efforts of Toulouse to do the same in doc. 113?

115. THE FOUNDATION OF THE UNIVERSITY OF HEIDELBERG, 1386

Universities came late to German towns, so for several centuries Germans seeking advanced learning had to go to universities in Italy, France, or England. The first university east of the Rhine was at Prague, chartered in 1348. Universities followed at Vienna (1365), Erfurt (1379), and then Heidelberg (1386). The university at Heidelberg in southern Germany started off with only two masters in 1386, but within four years had grown to include over 1,000 students and eventually became one of the most important universities in Germany. In this charter of foundation, note the conscious steps that the founder took to ensure that his new university was as much like the successful university at Paris as possible. The greater part of the grant is devoted to spelling out the legal status and privileges of students and masters in the town of Heidelberg, perhaps another reflection of the lessons learned from town/gown disputes at Paris.

Source: trans. E.F. Henderson, *Select Historical Documents of the Middle Ages* (London, 1896), pp. 262–66.

We, Rupert the elder, by the grace of God count palatine of Rhine, elector of the Holy Roman Empire and Duke of Bavaria ... do decree ... that the University of Heidelberg shall be ruled, disposed, and regulated according to the modes and manners accustomed to be observed in the University of Paris. Also that, as a handmaid of Paris—a worthy one let us hope—the latter's steps shall be imitated in every way possible; so that, namely, there shall be four faculties in it ... [theology, canon and civil law, medicine, and liberal arts]. We wish this institution to be divided and marked out into four nations, as it is at Paris; and that all these faculties shall make one university, and that to it the individual students, in whatever of the said faculties they are, shall united belong like lawful sons to one mother.

Likewise [we desire] that this university shall be governed by one rector, and that the various masters and teachers, before they are admitted to the common pursuits of our institution, shall swear to observe the statutes, laws, privileges, liberties, and franchises of the same, and not reveal its secrets, to whatever grade they may rise.... Moreover, that the various masters and bachelors shall read their lectures and exercise their scholastic functions, and go about in caps and gowns and uniform and similar nature, according to what has been observed at Paris up to this time in the different faculties.

... And we will that when the separate bodies shall have passed the statutes for their own observance, they may make them perpetually binding on those subject to them and on their successors. And as in the University of Paris the various servants of the institution have the benefit of the various privileges which its masters and scholars enjoy, so in starting our institution in Heidelberg, we grant with even greater liberality, through these presents, that all servants, i.e. its beadles, librarians, lower officials, preparers of parchment, scribes, illuminators, and others who serve it, may each and all without fraud enjoy in it same privileges, franchises, immunities, and liberties with which its masters or scholars are now or shall hereafter be endowed.

Lest in the new community of the city of Heidelberg, their misdeeds being unpunished, there be an incentive to the scholars of doing wrong, we ordain with provident counsel, by these presents, that the bishop of Worms, as a judge ordinary of the clerks of our institution, shall have and possess, now and hereafter while our institution shall last, prisons and an office in our town of Heidelberg for the detention of criminal clerks. These things we have seen fit to grant to him and his successors, adding these conditions: that he shall permit no clerk to be arrested unless for a misdemeanor; that he shall restore any one detained for such fault, or any light offense, to his master, or to the rector if the latter asks for him, a promise having been given that the culprit will appear in court and that the rector or master will answer for him if the injured parties should go to law about the matter. Furthermore, that on being requested, he will restore a clerk arrested for a crime on slight evidence, upon receiving a significant pledge—sponsors if the prisoners can obtain them, otherwise an oath if he cannot obtain sponsors—to the effect that he will answer in court to the charges against him; and that all these things there shall be no pecuniary exactions, except that the clerk shall give satisfaction, reasonably and according to the rule of the town, for the expenses which he incurred while in prison. And we desire that he will detain honestly and without serious injury a criminal clerk thus arrested for a crime where the suspicion is grave and strong, until the truth can be found concerning the deed of which he is suspected. And he shall not for any cause, moreover, take away any clerk from our town, or permit him to be taken away, unless proper observances have been followed, and he has been condemned by judicial sentence to perpetual imprisonment for a crime.

We command our advocate and bailiff and their servants in our town, under pain of losing their offices and our favor, not to lay a detaining hand on any master or scholar of our said institution, nor to arrest him or allow him to be arrested unless the deed be such that the master or scholar ought rightly to be detained. He shall be restored to his master or rector, if he is held for a slight cause, provided he will swear and promise to appear in court concerning the matter; and we decree that a slight fault is one for which a layman, if he had committed it, ought to have been condemned to a light pecuniary fine. Likewise if the master or scholar detained be found gravely or strongly suspected of a crime, we command that he be handed over by our officials to the bishop or his representative in our town, to be kept in custody.

By the tenor of these presents we grant to each and all the masters and scholars that, when they come to the said institution, while they remain there, and also when they return from it to their homes, they may freely carry with them, both coming and going, throughout all the lands subject to us, all things which they need while pursuing their studies, and all the goods necessary for their support, without any duty, levy, imposts, tolls, excises, or other exactions whatever. And we wish them and each one of them to be free from these imposts when purchasing corn, wines, meat, fish, clothes, and all things necessary for their living and their rank. And we decree that the scholars from their stock in hand of provisions, if there remain over one or two wagon loads of wine without their having practiced deception, may, after the Feast of Easter of that year, sell it at wholesale without paying impost. We grant to them, moreover, that each day the scholars, of themselves or through their servants, may be allowed to buy in the town of

Heidelberg at the accustomed hour, freely and without impediment or hurtful delay, any eatables or other necessities of life.

Lest the masters and scholars of our institution of Heidelberg may be oppressed by the citizens, moved by avarice, through extortionate prices on lodgings, we have seen fit to decree that henceforth each year, after Christmas, one expert from the university on the part of scholars and one prudent, pious, and circumspect citizen on the part of the citizens shall be authorized to determine the price of the students' lodgings. Moreover, we will and decree that the various masters and scholars shall through our bailiff, our judge, and the officials subject to us, be defended by and maintained in the quiet possession of the lodgings given to them free or those for which they pay rent. Moreover, by the tenor of these payments, we grant to the rector and the university, or to those designated by them, entire jurisdiction concerning the payment of rents for the lodgings occupied by the students, concerning the making and buying of books, and the borrowing of money for other purposes by the scholars of our institution; also concerning the payment of assessments, together with everything that arises from, depends upon, and is connected to these.

In addition, we command our officials that, when the rector requires our and their aid and assistance for carrying out his sentences against scholars who try to rebel, they shall assist our clients and servants in this matter, first however, obtaining lawful permission to proceed against clerks from the lord bishop of Worms, or from one deputed by him for this purpose.

Questions: What limits were put on the activities of the scholars and on the townspeople? What protections did the founder of the university offer to scholars? What do these protections tell us about the potential abuses of the scholars by the townspeople?

116. A SCHOLAR IN PARIS

This poem was written by Rutebeuf, a well-known French minstrel of the late thirteenth century who composed a miracle play and saints' lives as well as satires and polemical writings. He was probably born in Champagne, but spent most of his life in Paris. His name, "rude boeuf" or "rustic ox," may be a nickname given to him by fellow students in Paris. The themes of his lyric poetry include frequent references to poverty and gambling which, along with the description of a scholar's life in Paris, suggest he was very familiar with student life in the city.

Source: trans. M.E. Markley, *Legends and Satires from Medieval Literature*, by M.H. Shackford (Boston: Ginn and Company, 1913), pp. 125–27.

Much argument is heard of late,
The subject I'll attempt to state,
A question for dispute, I fear,
That will hang on for many a year.
The student-folk of Paris town
(I speak of those in cap and gown,
Students of art, philosophy, —
In short, "the University,"
And not our old-time learned men)
Have stirred up trouble here again.
Nothing they'll gain, it seems to me,
Except more bitter enmity,
Till there is no peace, day or night.
Does such a state of things seem right?

To give his son a chance to stay
In Paris, growing wise each day,
Is some old peasant's one ambition.
To pay his bills and his tuition
The poor hard-working father slaves;
Sends him each farthing that he saves,
While he in misery will stay
On his scant plot of land to pray
That his hard toil may help to raise
His son to honor and to praise.
But once the son is safe in town
The story then reads upside down.
Forgetting all his pledges now,

The earnings of his father's plow
He spends for weapons, not for books.
Brawling through city streets, he looks
To find some pretty, loitering wench,
Or idle brawl by tavern bench;
Wanders at will and pries about,
Till money fails and gown wears out. —
Then he starts fresh on the old round;
Why sow good seed on barren ground?
Even in Lent when men should do
Something pleasing in God's view,
Your students then elect to wear
For penitence, no shirts of hair,
But swaggering hauberks, as they sit
Drowning in drink their feeble wit;
While three or four or them excite
Four hundred students to a fight,
And close the University.
(Not such a great calamity!)

Yet, heavens, for one of serious mind
What life more pleasing can you find
Than earnest scholar's life may be?
More pains than precious gems has he,
And while he's struggling to grow wise,
Amusements he must sacrifice, —
Give up his feasting and his drinking,
And spend his time in sober thinking.
His life is just about as merry
As is a monk's in a monastery.
Why send a boy away to school
There to become an arrant fool?
When he should be acquiring sense,
He wastes his time and all his pence,
And to his friends brings only shame,
While they suppose him winning fame.

Questions: What does this poem tell us about student life in Paris? What are the similarities and differences between student life then and now?

CHAPTER TEN

ENTERTAINMENT AND CIVIC RITUAL

Figure 10.1

Wrestling

Wrestling matches were often organized events, providing entertainment to the audience and a chance to prove their skill to competitors. Reproduced from Charles Knight, *Old England: A Pictorial Museum of Regal, Ecclesiastical, Municipal, Baronial, and Popular Antiquities,* 2 vols. (London: James Sangster and Co., 1850), fig. 484.

117. SPORTS IN LONDON

The first extract contains a vivid description of the games enjoyed by Londoners in the late twelfth century, taken from a description of London written by William Fitzstephen, the biographer of Thomas Beckett (for his full text describing London, see doc. 151). The second extract, from a chronicle, shows how a sports competition inflamed long-standing tensions between the officials of the jurisdiction of Westminister Abbey, a suburb of London where the king's courts and palace were located, and the citizens of London.

Source: (A) trans. H. Morley, "William Fitzstephen," in *A Survay of London*, by John Stow (London: G. Routledge and Sons, Ltd., 1890), p. 75; (B) trans. J.A. Giles, *Roger of Wendover's Flowers of History* (London: H.G. Bohn, 1849), II, pp. 439–40.

(A) Sports in London, c. 1180

Furthermore, let us consider also the sports of the city since it is not meet that a city should only be useful and sober, unless it also be pleasant and merry....

London in place of shows in the theater and stage-plays has holier plays, wherein are shown forth the miracles wrought by holy confessors or the sufferings which glorified the constancy of martyrs.

Moreover, each year upon the day called Carnival—to begin with the sports of boys (for we were all boys once)—boys from the schools bring fighting-cocks to their master, and the whole forenoon is given up to boyish sport; for they have a holiday in the schools that they may watch their cocks do battle. After dinner all the youth of the city go out into the fields in a much-frequented game of ball. The scholars of each school have their own ball, and almost all the workers of each trade have theirs also in their hands. Elder men and fathers and rich citizens come on horseback to watch the contests of their juniors, and after their fashion are young again with the young; and it seems that the motion of their natural heat is kindled by the contemplation of such violent motion and by their partaking in the joys of untrammeled youth.

Every Sunday in Lent after dinner a "fresh swarm of young gentles" goes forth on war-horses, "steeds skilled in the contest," of which each is "apt and schooled to wheel in circles round." From the gates burst forth in throngs the lay sons of citizens, armed with lance and shield, the younger with shafts forked at the end, but with steel point removed. "They wake war's semblance" and in mimic contest exercise their skill at arms. Many courtiers come too, when the king is in residence; and from the households of earls and barons come young men not yet invested with the belt of knighthood, that they may there contend together. Each one of them is on fire with hope of victory. The fierce horses neigh, "their limbs tremble; they champ the bit; impatient of delay they cannot stand still." When at length "the hoof of trampling steeds careers along," the youthful riders divide their hosts; some pursue those that fly before, and cannot overtake them; others unhorse their comrades and speed by.

At the Feast of Easter they make sport with naval tourneys, as it were. For a shield being strongly bound to a stout pole in mid-stream, a small vessel, swiftly driven on by many an oar and by the river's flow, carries a youth standing at the prow, who is to strike the shield with his lance. If he break the lance by striking the shield and keep his feet unshaken, he has achieved his purpose and fulfilled his desire. If, however, he strike it strongly without splintering his lance, he is thrown into the rushing river, and the boat of its own speed passes him by. But there are on each side of the shield two vessels moored, and in them are many youths to snatch up the striker who has been sucked down by the stream, as soon as he emerges into sight or "once more bubbles on the topmost wave." On the bridge and the galleries above the river are spectators of the sport "ready to laugh their fill."

On feast-days throughout the summer the youths exercise themselves in leaping, archery, and wrestling, putting the stone, and throwing the thonged javelin beyond a mark, and fighting with sword and buckler. "Cytherea leads the dance of maidens and the earth is smitten with free foot at moonrise."

In winter on almost every feast-day before dinner either foaming boars and hogs, armed with "tusks lightning-swift," themselves soon to be bacon, fight for their lives, or fat bulls with butting horns, or huge bears, do combat to the death against hounds let loose upon them.

When the great marsh that washes the northern walls of the city is frozen, dense throngs of youths go forth to disport themselves upon the ice. Some gathering speed by a run, glide sidelong, with feet set well apart, over a vast space of ice. Others make themselves seats of ice like millstones and are dragged along by a number who run before them holding hands. Sometimes they slip owing to the greatness of their speed and fall, every one of them, upon their faces. Others there are, more skilled to sport upon the ice, who fit to their feet the shin-bones of beasts, lashing them beneath their ankles, and with ironshod poles in their hands they strike ever and anon against the ice and are borne along swift as a bird in flight or a bolt shot from a mangonel. But sometimes two by agreement run one against the other from a great distance and, raising their poles, strike one another. One or both fall, not without bodily hurt, since on falling they are borne a long way in opposite directions....

Many of the citizens delight in taking their sport with birds of the air, merlins and falcons and the like, and with dogs that wage warfare in the woods. The citizens have the special privilege of hunting in Middlesex, Hertfordshire, and all Chiltern, and in Kent as far as the river Cray.

(B) Wrestling Matches in London, 1222

... On St. James' Day [25 July], the inhabitants of the city of London met at the hospital of Queen Matilda, outside the city, to engage in wrestling with the inhabitants of the district round the city, to see which of them was possessed of the greatest strength. After they had contended for a length of time amidst the shouts of both parties, the citizens, having put their antagonists into disorder, gained the victory. Amongst others, the steward of the abbot of Westminster was defeated, and went away in deep deliberation as to how he could revenge himself and his companions.

At length he fixed on the following plan of revenge: he offered a prize of a ram on St. Peter's Day [1 August], and sent word throughout the district for all to come and wrestle at Westminster, and whoever should prove himself the best wrestler should receive the ram for a prize. He, in the meantime, collected a number of strong and skilful wrestlers, that he might thus gain the victory; but the citizens, being desirous of gaining another victory, came to the sport in great strength. The contest having been commenced by both parties, they continued to throw each other for some time. The steward, however, with his suburban companions and fellow-provincials, who sought revenge rather than sport, without any reason flew to arms, and severely beat the citizens, who had come there unarmed, causing bloodshed amongst them. The citizens, shamefully wounded, retreated into the city in great confusion. [The citizens take their revenge by destroying numerous buildings of the Westminster Abbey, but the conspirators are caught and hung or mutilated and banished by the royal justiciary.]

Questions: What different sports and games did Londoners play? Who participated? On what occasions? Where did the games occur? What problems could accompany sports competitions? How does William Fitzstephen idealize sports in the city?

Figure 10.2
Mummers
The actors in English mumming plays, all male, wore different types of disguise. These plays or ceremonies, which may have grown out of ancient rituals associated with the agricultural year, all contained elements of death and resurrection. There were several different types, including Morris dancing, which was akin to sword dancing (supposedly the enemy was the Muslim Moors in Spain) and became popular in the fifteenth century. A second type involved a hero killed in combat who was then revived by a third character. Another type included an actor disguised as a woman who was courted by a clown. Reproduced from Charles Knight, *Old England: A Pictorial Museum of Regal, Ecclesiastical, Municipal, Baronial, and Popular Antiquities*, 2 vols. (London: James Sangster and Co., 1850), fig. 1143.

118. THE START OF THE SECULAR STAGE, EXETER, 1348

Medieval drama grew largely out of liturgical performances and religious miracle plays, often performed in churches, but there was also a secular tradition that became stronger in the late Middle Ages. These types of play worried the bishop of Exeter and other ecclesiastical authorities because they often mocked or deliberately inverted religious institutions and figures of authority. The "theater" referred to in the second selection was probably not a separate building, but a moveable stage or platform set up outdoors.

Source: trans. G.G. Coulton, *Social Life in Britain from the Conquest to the Reformation* (Cambridge: Cambridge University Press, 1919), pp. 493–95, revised.

We have heard, not without grave disquietude, that a certain abominable sect of evil-minded men, named the Order (let us rather say, the Error) of Brothelyn-ghaln [a parody on the English monastic order of Sempringham, which included both men and women], has lately arisen by inspiration of him who sows all evil deeds. Which men, forming no true convent but rather a plainly unlawful and sinister conventicle, have chosen for their head a certain crazy lunatic, of temper most suitable to their evil purpose. This man they call their abbot; they dress him in monastic garb, set him up upon a stage, and adore him as their idol. Then, at the sound of a horn, which they have chosen instead of a bell, they led him not many days since through the lanes and streets of the city of Exeter, with a great throng of horse and foot at their heels; in which procession they laid hold on clergy or laity whom they found in their way—nay, they even drew some from their own houses—and held them so long in durance, with rash, headlong, and sometimes with sacrilegious spirit, until they had extorted from them certain sums of money by way of sacrifice—nay, rather, of sacrilege. And, though they seem to do this under color and cloak of play, or rather of buffoonery, yet this is beyond doubt no other than theft and rapine, since the money is taken from the unwilling....

... Although the mechanical arts, as experience ever shows us, should of necessity help one another, yet we have heard some time since that certain imprudent sons of our city of Exeter, given over to rioting and wantonness, and foolishly scorning that which had been profitably ordered for their own needs and those of the whole people, do purpose, and have banded themselves together, publicly to perform a certain noxious and blameworthy play, or rather buffoonery, in scorn and insult to the leather-dressers and their art, on this Sunday next to come and in the theater of our city of Exeter. Hence (as we are informed) there does already breed and increase a rank growth of discord, rancor, and strife between these artisans and the authors or abettors of this same play; so that (unless, led by a spirit of saner counsel, they shall altogether abstain and desist from their unlawful purpose), there must follow, alas! terrible assaults and aggressions, breaches of the peace of the king and his realm, blows and seditions, and even, by consequence, perils still more deplorable for men's immortal souls....

Questions: What aspects of this play-making did the bishop of Exeter particularly object to? Why did he want to outlaw these activities? How would the townspeople have viewed these types of play?

119. ORDER OF THE PAGEANTS OF THE CORPUS CHRISTI PLAYS IN YORK, 1415

Many late medieval towns celebrated important religious feast-days by staging a religious play. In some towns, several plays or pageants that were centered around religious themes formed a "cycle," the best known of which occurred at the Feast of Corpus Christi (which usually fell in late May or early June). In cities such as York, Coventry, and Dublin, each fraternity or craft guild had charge of one scene in the whole series and performed it on a platform on wheels, at a designated location in the city. As one pageant was completed, the actors and their wagon moved on to the next station, their place being taken by the guild in charge of the next play in the series. This selection records which guild was responsible for which play in the city of York.

Source: L.T. Smith, trans. from "English Towns and Gilds," ed. E.P. Cheyney, *Translations and Reprints from the Original Sources of European History*, vol. 2, no. 1 (Philadelphia: University of Pennsylvania Press, n.d.), pp. 29–32.

Tanners. God the Father Omnipotent creating and forming the heavens, the angels and archangels, Lucifer and the angels who fell with him into the pit.

Plasterers. God the Father in his substance creating the earth and all things which are therein, in the space of five days.

Cardmakers. God the Father forming Adam from the mud of the earth, and making Eve from Adam's rib, and inspiring them with the breath of life.

Fullers. God forbidding Adam and Eve to eat of the tree of life.

Coopers. Adam and Eve and the tree between them, the serpent deceiving them with apples; God speaking to them and cursing the serpent, and an angel with a sword driving them out of Paradise.

Armorers. Adam and Eve, an angel with a spade and distaff appointing them their labor.

Glovers. Abel and Cain sacrificing victims.

Shipwrights. God warning Noah to make an ark out of planed wood.

Fishmongers and Mariners. Noah in the ark with his wife, three sons of Noah with their wives, with various animals.

Parchment-makers and Book-binders. Abraham sacrificing his son Isaac on the altar.

Hosiers. Moses lifting up the serpent in the wilderness, King Pharaoh, eight Jews looking on and wondering.

Spicers. A doctor declaring the sayings of the prophets concerning the future birth of Christ. Mary, the angel saluting her; Mary saluting Elizabeth.

Pewterers and Founders. Mary, Joseph wishing to send her away, the angel telling them to go over to Bethlehem.

Tilers. Mary, Joseph, a nurse, the child born and lying in a manger, between an ox and an ass, and an angel speaking to the shepherds, and to the players in the next pageant.

Chandlers. Shepherds speaking to one another, the star in the East, an angel announcing to the shepherds their great joy in the child which has been born.

Goldsmiths, Goldbeaters, and Moneyers. Three kings coming from the East, Herod questioning them about the child Jesus, and the son of Herod and two counsellors and a herald. Mary with the child, and the star above, and three kings offering gifts.

(Formerly) The House of St. Leonard, (now) Masons. Mary, with the boy, Joseph, Anna, the nurse, with the young doves. Simeon receiving the boy into his arms, and the two sons of Simeon.

Marshalls. Mary with the boy and Joseph fleeing into Egypt, at the bidding of the angel.

Girdlers, Nailers, and Sawyers. Herod ordering the male children to be slain, four soldiers with lances, two counsellors of the king, and four women weeping for the death of their sons.

Spurriers and Lorimers [makers of metal spurs and harness bits]. Doctors, the boy Jesus sitting in the temple in the midst of them, asking them questions and replying to them, four Jews, Mary and Joseph seeking him, and finding him in the temple.

Barbers. Jesus, John the Baptist baptizing him, and two angels attending.

Vintners. Jesus, Mary, bridegroom with the bride, ruler of the feast with his slaves, with six vessels of water in which the water is turned into wine.

Smiths. Jesus on a pinnacle of the temple, and the devil tempting him with stones, and two angels attending, etc.

Curriers. Peter, James, and John; Jesus ascending into a mountain and transfiguring himself before them. Moses and Elias appearing, and the voice of one speaking in a cloud.

Ironmongers. Jesus, and Simon the leper asking Jesus to eat with him; two disciples, Mary Magdalene bathing Jesus' feet with her tears and drying them with her hair.

Plumbers and Patternmakers. Jesus, two apostles, the woman taken in adultery, four Jews accusing her.

Pouchmakers, Bottlers, and Capmakers. Lazarus in the sepulcher, Mary Magdalene and Martha, and two Jews wondering.

Spinners and Vestmakers. Jesus on an ass with its colt, twelve apostles following Jesus, six rich and six poor, eight boys with branches of palm, singing Blessed, etc., and Zaccheus climbing into a sycamore tree.

Cutlers, Bladesmiths, Sheathers, Scalers, Bucklermakers, and Horners. Pilate, Caiaphas, two soldiers, three Jews, Judas selling Jesus.

Bakers. The Passover lamb, the Supper of the Lord, twelve apostles, Jesus girded with a towel, washing their feet, institution of the sacrament of the body of Christ in the new law, communion of the apostles.

Cordwainers [shoemakers]. Pilate, Caiaphas, Annas, fourteen armed soldiers, Malchus, Peter, James, John, Jesus, and Judas kissing and betraying him.

Bowyers and Fletchers. Jesus, Annas, Caiaphas, and four Jews beating and scourging Jesus. Peter, the woman accusing Peter, and Malchus.

Tapestrymakers and Couchers. Jesus, Pilate, Annas, Caiaphas, two counsellors and four Jews accusing Jesus.

Listers [Dyers]. Herod, two counsellors, four soldiers, Jesus, and three Jews.

Cooks and Watercarriers. Pilate, Annas, Caiaphas, two Jews, and Judas bringing back to them the thirty pieces of silver.

Tilemakers, Millers, Furriers, Hayresters, Bowlers. Jesus, Pilate, Caiaphas, Annas, six soldiers holding spears with banners, and four others leading Jesus away from Herod, asking to have Barabbas released and Jesus crucified, and likewise binding and scourging him, and placing the crown of thorns upon his head; three soldiers casting lots for the clothing of Jesus.

Shearmen. Jesus, stained with blood, bearing the cross to Calvary. Simon of Cyrene, the Jews compelling him to carry the cross; Mary the mother of Jesus; John the apostle then announcing the condemnation and passage of her son to Calvary. Veronica wiping the blood and sweat from the face of Jesus with a veil on which is imprinted the face of Jesus, and other women mourning for Jesus.

Pinmakers, Latenmakers [makers of alloyed metal in thin sheets], and Painters. The cross, Jesus stretched upon it on the ground; four Jews scourging him and binding him with ropes, and afterwards lifting the cross, and the body of Jesus nailed to the cross on Mount Calvary.

Butchers and Poultry Dealers. The cross, two thieves crucified, Jesus hanging on the cross between them, Mary the mother of Jesus, John, Mary, James, and Salome. A soldier with a lance, a servant with a sponge, Pilate, Annas, Caiaphas, the centurion, Joseph of Arimathea and Nicodemus, placing Him in the sepulcher.

Saddlers, Glaziers, and Joiners. Jesus conquering Hell; twelve spirits, six good, and six evil.

Carpenters. Jesus rising from the sepulcher, four armed soldiers, and the three Marys mourning. Pilate, Caiaphas, and Annas. A young man seated at the sepulcher clothed in white, speaking to the women.

Winedrawers. Jesus, Mary Magdalene with aromatic spices.

Brokers and Woolpackers. Jesus, Luke, and Cleophas in the guise of travelers.

Scriveners, Illuminators, Pardoners, and Dubbers. Jesus, Peter, John, James, Philip, and the other apostles with parts of a baked fish, and a honey-comb; and Thomas the apostle touching the wounds of Jesus.

Tailors. Mary, John the evangelist, the eleven apostles, two angels, Jesus ascending before them, and four angels carrying a cloud.

Potters. Mary, two angels, eleven apostles, and the Holy Spirit descending upon them, and four Jews wondering.

Drapers. Jesus, Mary, Gabriel with two angels, two virgins and three Jews of Mary's acquaintance, eight apostles, and two devils.

Linen-weavers. Four apostles carrying the bier of Mary, and Fergus hanging above the bier, with two other Jews and an angel.

Woolen-weavers. Mary ascending with a throng of angels, eight apostles, and the apostle Thomas preaching in the desert.

Innkeepers. Mary, Jesus crowning her, with a throng of angels singing.

Mercers. Jesus, Mary, the twelve apostles, four angels with trumpets, and four with a crown, a lance, and two whips, four good spirits, and four evil spirits, and six devils.

Questions: What types of play or pageant did York townspeople see? Did the different crafts put on plays that related in any way to each craft's manufacturing focus? What types of scenery and costume might have been used? How was the city's identity or integration formed by such spectacles, and on which different levels (financial, institutional, political, religious)?

120. TROUBLE BEHIND THE SCENES IN YORK, 1420

The methods by which particular plays were assigned to specific guilds and the feelings of guild members about the play allocated to them show up in this protest filed by the masons of York. The Fergus pageant involved four apostles carrying the bier of Mary, on which Fergus and two other Jews were hanging. By 1476 the guild of linen-weavers was responsible for this play, but it was discontinued in 1485.

Source: trans. G.G. Coulton, *Life in the Middle Ages*, vol. 2 (Cambridge: Cambridge University Press, 1910), p. 141, revised.

Meanwhile, on the other hand, seeing that the masons of this city murmured among themselves concerning their pageant in the Corpus Christi play, wherein Fergus was scourged, because that pageant is not contained in Holy Scripture, and it caused rather laughter and clamor than devotion, so that strife and contentions and fights sometimes arose thence on the people's part. Seeing also that they could seldom or never produce and play this pageant in full daylight, as the preceding pageants do, therefore the masons desired with great desire to be exonerated from this their pageant, and to be assigned to some other pageant which may be in conformity with Holy Scripture, and which they will be able to produce and play by daylight.... The mayor, aldermen and council decided ... that the masons should be exonerated and quit of the Fergus pageant, and that they should take for themselves and their craft the pageant of Herod, which the goldsmiths formerly had, to be produced and played at their own expense in the play of Corpus Christi, in the most honorable fashion that befits them, to the praise of the city, as often as this play is played in the city aforesaid.

Questions: Why did the masons not want to keep on staging the play about Fergus? What does this tell us about why the craft guilds went to the trouble of staging plays?

121. FEAST AND FESTIVAL IN VENICE

Martin da Canal wrote Les estoires de Venise, *a history of the city of Venice, in the years between 1267 and 1275. He used a local variety of French called Franco-Venetian, and his work was patterned on French romance writing styles that often featured elaborate descriptions of festivals and celebrations. The following excerpts from Part 2 of his history depict how the Venetians and their secular leader, the doge, celebrated the most solemn occasions of the Venetian year, including the Feast of Saint Mark, the city's patron saint. On this day, Venetians celebrated with wine and* calzoni, *small almond-filled cookies.*

Source: trans. L. Morreale, from *Les estoires de Venise. Cronanca veneziana in lingua francese dale origini al 1275*, ed. Alberto Limnetani (Florence: Olschki, 1972), pp. 250–63.

[90] Now I would like you to know that the doge wears a crown on the eve of the Feast of St. Mark and clothes woven with gold. And at the evening service he processes underneath an umbrella preceded by standard-bearers and trumpets and cymbal players. And a host of priests and many noblemen and a group of common people accompany him. And with this solemnity, he goes to hear the mass on the day of the Feast of St. Mark; and after the mass he returns to his palace to find tables prepared and he eats with the priests from St. Mark's cathedral, and many noble men with them. And the doge celebrates both solemn and festive events in the name of St. Mark throughout the month of June, and a third event in honor of St. Mark in the month of October.

[91] I have told you about the three main feasts that the doge celebrated in honor of St. Mark, and when it is time, I will tell you about the fourth, but first I would like you to know what the doge does on Christmas. I would like you to know, gentlemen, that on the night before Christmas and the whole day before, the doge is given a tribute by those who capture birds from the river. When the birds are brought to the doge's palace, he gives them to the Venetian nobles and to leaders among the common people, and along with the river birds that the French call "malars" [wild ducks], the doge gives out to the nobles and to important commoners a good number of capons. And know also and truly that the doge gives the Venetians more than 2,000 river birds, and they take them home to their houses. On Christmas Day the doge wears a crown and clothes woven with gold, and he goes to listen to the mass in the same way that he does on other feast days. And in the evening he attends at the church of St. George, and listens to the mass as it is sung by the abbot and the monks, and many noblemen and other people go with the doge.

[92] I have told you about Christmas Day and the night before and I will tell you about the feasts that the Venetians celebrate on the last day of January—and it is in remembrance of how St. Mark first came to Venice—and about the beautiful festival that the Venetians celebrate in memory of Our Lady, blessed Mary. You should know, gentlemen, that the doge divided the districts of Venice into thirty sections, that is two districts per feast. The night before the Feast of St. Mark, a group of young men arrive in the city from the water, and once they have arrived at the palace, they go ashore and give their banners to a group of small children, and they parade, two by two, in front of the church of St. Mark. And they are followed by trumpets, and then young men who carry silver trays filled with *calzoni*, and then come others carrying silver vessels filled with wine, and cups of gold and silver; and after these come the clerics who sing and who are robed in capes made of samite [a rich silken cloth] and woven with gold. And they process, one behind the other until they reach the church of St. Maria Formosa, and they enter into the church, and there they find many noblewomen and young ladies, and they give them the *calzoni* and wine to drink, and then they give a large quantity to the priests as well. And when they have done this, they move on to another district of Venice, in the same way as I have described, and they give the *calzoni* to the noblewomen and young girls, and wine to drink, and a large amount to the priests. Now I have described to you what happens on the night before, and later I will tell you about the day of the Feast of St. Mark.

[93] You must know, dear sirs, that on the last day of January, the feast and the procession are twice as long, because the young men and the older men from one of the two districts I mentioned come by water to the doge's palace and then come ashore, giving out more than five hundred banners to the small children and then sending them, two by two, to the church of St. Mark. And behind them come larger children, holding more than one hundred silver crosses in their hands. And behind them come the clergy, all dressed in robes of samite interwoven with gold, and then the horns and cymbals come, and finally, among the crowd there is one cleric who is dressed in women's clothing, all woven with gold. And this cleric sits on a richly decorated chair supported on the shoulders of four men, and banners of gold are placed in front and to the sides of them, and the clerics proceed forth, singing. And as they advance in this manner, three clerics make their way out of the procession and when they see the doge at the window of his palace, in front of all the nobles of Venice, they jump onto a pedestal, and they sing in a loud voice all that follows:

"Christ victor, Christ leader, Christ ruler: to our lord Ranieri Zeno, who, by the grace of God, was elected doge of Venice, Dalmatia, and Croatia, and lord over one quarter and one half of the entire empire of Romania: health, honor, life, and victory. May St. Mark aid you!"

And when the praises are finished, they come down from the pedestal and the doge allows them to throw out many coins and then they return to the procession with the others, who are waiting for them. And then the cleric comes forth, who is wearing the golden crown and who is clothed so richly [in women's clothing] as I have described to you; and when he comes near the doge, he greets him, and the doge returns the greeting. And those who were carrying him on their shoulders come forth and follow the procession and enter into the church of Our Lady holy Mary and wait there until all those from the other district come in the same way, with the banners and the crosses and the priests, and three clerics sing the same praises to the doge, and the doge has them throw out coins. And you should know that the doge wears clothes that are woven with gold and a golden crown on his head. And all the noblemen of Venice, and the common people, and a great many ladies and young women come out to see the procession in honor of Our Lady, and along the route to the palace there are many spectators.

[94] When the three clerics have sung their praises to the doge in the same way as those who had done it first, they go back into the procession. And then another cleric comes forward who is sitting on a chair and is dressed in rich clothes and who resembles an angel, supported on the shoulders of four men. And when he comes before the doge, he greets him, and the doge returns his greeting. And after this he returns to the procession where the clerics were singing, and you should know that both of the processions have good organizers, both clerical and lay. And they proceed until they enter into the church of Our Lady blessed Mary, and when the cleric who was dressed as an angel enters into the church and sees the other who is dressed as the Virgin Mary, he stands up and says:

[95] "Hail Mary, full of grace, the Lord is with you, blessed are you among women and blessed is the fruit of your womb: so said our Lord." And he who was dressed as Our Lady responds and says, "How can it be, angel of God, that I will have a son, since I do not know man?" and the angel says again, "The Holy Spirit will descend upon you, Mary. Do not be afraid; you will carry the Son of God in your womb." And she responds and says, "I am the handmaiden of the Lord; let it be as you have said."

[96] What can I say? After this response everyone exits the church and goes home. After they eat, the people, both men and women, all go to the districts where they had had the procession and find twelve Marias in twelve

different houses, all of whom are clothed with such beauty and richness that it is a wonder to behold. Each of them has a golden crown on her head, decorated with precious gems, and is dressed in clothes woven with gold, and encrusted with jewels, gold, precious stones, and many pearls. The women and young ladies sit inside, dressed very luxuriously, and the men give *calzoni* to their friends and much wine to drink. And the day afterwards the same feast takes place in their friends' twelve houses. And the doge wears a crown of gold at the evening service for the Feast of Our Lady, in just the same solemn state as on the Feast of Easter. And after evening services he returns to his palace in the same way that he arrived.

[97] On the Day of Our Lady those two districts that had held the festival so beautifully and so richly, as I have described, prepare six large ships that sail from one end of the city to the other, to where the bishop of Venice lives, and decorate these six ships very luxuriously with golden cloth and tapestries. And then the women and young ladies, also dressed very richly, board the ship and place the Marias in the center of the ships. And in one of the ships there are forty well-armed men, swords unsheathed in their hands, and in another ship come clerics who are richly dressed with all of the treasures of the church, and in the other four ships are all the Marias and the women and young girls. And so the bishop comes and gives the blessing. And when the bishop has given the blessing, he boards his ship and two abbots, richly dressed and clothed in silken capes, board their large ship. And the bishop is accompanied by his canons, and the two abbots by their monks. And then the ships, decorated as I have described, move away from the bishop's ship at the shore, and advance in the water and catch up with two other richly decorated ships, who receive them so that the next year they can prepare the same festivities. In this way, they arrive just in front of the church of St. Mark and drop anchor, each ship on its own, and they stop and wait for the arrival of the doge.

[98] When the bishop and the two abbots arrive at the shore near the palace, they come on shore with those in their company and proceed to the church of St. Mark, and find the doge at mass. And after the mass they go to the ships. The doge comes, under his umbrella, with the bishop at one side and the *primicerius* of St. Mark on the other, and the two abbots before them. The doge wears a golden crown and the bishop holds his scepter and the two abbots hold theirs. The chaplains and the canons and the monks follow, singing in procession. The standard-bearers and the trumpet and cymbal players come next, and the crosses come last. In this way the doge arrives at the first ship and he comes aboard, and the nobles of Venice follow him and his judge stands at his side; and those who are carrying their swords board the ship after him.

[99] When the doge boards the first ship in the company of all the Venetian nobles as well as with many popular leaders, he sits down on a chair with the *primicerius* on one side and his judge on the other and all of the rest sit down in the ship; and the bishop and the two abbots board their ships. And so those who are in the ships lift the anchors and sail the length of city until they reach the end, and you should know that the distance is a league and a half, and even a bit more. And if you were there, gentlemen, you could see that the water is completely covered with boats carrying men and women who follow after the ships; no one could say how many. And at the windows of the palaces and on the shore along the route on both sides there are so many women and young girls who, as the city stretches out, there is nothing but ladies and maidens who are beautifully and richly dressed, in the best way that one could possibly be dressed. With such joy and celebration they continue until they reach the end of the city and then they turn back to the palace where they find the tables prepared, and they eat together with all who come with the doge in the first ship. Now I have told you about the solemn procession that the doge does in honor of our lord Jesus Christ and his sweet mother Blessed Mary and for St. Mark the Evangelist and it is done every year. And I will tell you what he has does on the first Thursday of Lent.

[100] The first Thursday of Lent, after he has eaten, the doge wears his crown and appears at the window of his palace along with the Venetian nobles, the judges, and many good men. And then all the people come to the square of St. Mark and the noblewomen come to the windows of their palaces. When everyone has arrived at the square, pigs come in, and dogs afterwards, and along with them come hunters, and they chase the pigs there where they had escaped and they bring them in front of where the doge is standing. And when someone has caught a nd captured a pig, one of the hunters comes with a naked sword in his hand and cuts off the pig's head. And then all of the others who have also caught pigs come in front of the doge and another young man comes with his sword in his hand and cuts the head off one pig, and others come forth and do the same. And so many come that, after the pigs have been killed and the chase is finished, the doge gives the meat to the noblemen of Venice and to the popular leaders, just as he gives out ducks and capons on the feast of Christmas.

[101] On Holy Thursday the doge receives fish from the sea as a tribute, and he gives twelve large fish, called turbot, to the noble councilmen, of which there are six, and the remaining fish he gives to the clergy. On Friday the doge has the precious relics of St. Mark, the blood of our Lord and the holy Cross, set out for exposition; and you should know that all the people, the ladies and the young girls, come to see. And on Saturday before Easter the Venetians baptize

their children. I have told you all that the Venetians do on the solemn feasts, and I will stop there, and take up again my narrative about the capture of the Venetians and their works, and I will begin in the following manner...

Questions: What was the relationship between the doge and members of the clergy as expressed in the urban rituals described above? What roles did different actors, including the nobles, commoners, men, women, and children, play within these same rituals? What messages might the elements of these rituals have sent to Venetians? What, for example, was the significance of the doge's gifts of food on feast days, and why would food have played such an important role in the Venetian context? Which elements of these rituals were decidedly urban, and which appear specifically Venetian?

122. THE FEAST DAY OF ST. JOHN THE BAPTIST IN FLORENCE

The full pageantry of urban life is evident in this eye-witness account of mid-summer celebrations in Florence by Goro (Gregorio) Dati, an early fifteenth-century merchant (see docs. 40 and 75) . The Feast of St. John the Baptist fell on 24 June and was the most important civic festival in Florence. The palio *(made out of a rich velvet) noted here was the first prize in a big horse race, but it eventually gave its name to similar races in other Italian cities.*

Source: trans. T. Dean, *The Towns of Italy in the Later Middle Ages* (Manchester: Manchester University Press; New York: St Martin's Press, 2000), pp. 72–75.

When springtime comes ... every Florentine begins to think of making a fine day of the Feast of St. John, which falls in mid-summer, and everyone in good time supplies themselves with garments, decorations, and jewels. Whoever is planning a wedding banquet ... postpones it until then in order to honor the feast day. Two months ahead, making of the *palio* begins, and of the servants' garments, the pennants and trumpets, as well as the *palii* that the dependant territories bring as tribute, and the candles and other things that are to be offered. [And work is begun on] inviting people, ensuring supplies for banquets, getting horses to come from everywhere to run the *palio* race, and all the city is busy preparing for the feast day.... Once the eve of St. John's day arrives, early in the morning all the guilds make a display, on the outside walls of their workshops, of all their rich things, ornaments, and jewels. As many cloths of gold and silk are displayed as would adorn ten kingdoms, and as many gold and silver jewels, rich hangings, painted panels and marvelous carvings, and things pertaining to feats of arms.... Then at around the hour of terce, a solemn procession is made by all the clerics, priests, monks, and friars ... with so many relics of saints, that it is a thing of immeasurable devotion.... With them are many companies of secular men ... dressed as angels, sounding musical instruments of many sorts; singing marvelously, and enacting the stories of those saints that each company honors.... Then in the afternoon, at around the hour of vespers, when the heat has fallen somewhat, all the citizens assemble behind the banner of their local district. There are sixteen of these, and they march one behind the other, with the citizens two by two, the worthiest and eldest at the front and so on down to the boy at the back. They march to the church of San Giovanni, each to make his offering of a 1-pound wax candle.... The streets they pass along are all decorated, the walls and seating with hangings, *spalliere* [back-rests], and bench-covers, covered in sandal [a type of silk]. And all the streets are full of young women and girls dressed in silk, and adorned with precious jewels and pearls. And this offering lasts until sunset. Once the offering has been made, every citizen and woman returns home to make arrangements for the following morning.

On the morning of St. John, whoever goes to see the Piazza dei Signori will see something magnificent, marvelous and "triumphal".... Around the piazza are one hundred towers, which seem to be of gold, some of them borne on carts, some by porters.... These are made of wood, paper, and wax, and decorated with gold, and colors and drawn figures; they are empty inside, so that men can stand inside them, and continuously make the figures go round and round. The figures are of men on horseback jousting, or of foot soldiers running with lances and shields, or young girls round-dancing.... Around the rostrum of the Palazzo there are one hundred *palii* or more, fixed on their poles with iron rings. The first are those of the principal cities who pay tribute to the commune of Florence, such as Pisa, Arezzo, Pistoia, Volterra, Cortona ... and of some of the lords of Poppi and Piombino who are allies of the commune. They are made of double velvet, some of squirrel-fur and some of silk cloth; the others are all of velvet or other fabric....

The first offering to be made in the morning is that of the Captains of the Guelf Party, with all the knights, and with foreign lords and ambassadors, and a large number of the most honorable citizens of Florence. Ahead of them the banner of the Guelf Party is carried by one of their squires on a big palfrey covered in a white cloth, bearing the arms of the party and reaching to the ground. Then follow the other *palii*, carried one by one by a man on horseback ... and they go to offer these to the church of San Giovanni. And these *palii* are given as tribute by cities acquired by Florence ... from a certain date. The wax candles, like gilded towers, however, are renders from the old territories controlled by Florence, and they proceed in order of rank, one behind the other, to offer to San Giovanni. The following day the *palii* are hung up around the inside of the church, and they remain there all year, until the next St. John's Day, when they are taken down, and they are either used to make altar covers or are auctioned off.

After this, a marvelous and countless quantity of large candles are offered, some of 100 pounds, some of 50 pounds, some more, some less, down to 10 pounds. They are carried, lit, by the peasants of the villages who offer them. After them the officials of the mint make their offering, a magnificent candle carried on a richly adorned cart pulled by a pair of oxen covered with a caparison bearing the arms of the Mint. They are accompanied by about four hundred worshipful men, members or dependants [the *sottoposti,* or laborers] of the Calimala and Cambio guilds, each with 1-pound torches in their hands. Then come the priors and their Colleges, accompanied by the judges, the podestà, captain and executor [of the Ordinances of Justice], and with such display, servants, and the sounding of trumpets and pipes that all the world seems to resonate.

When the Priors return, all the riders who have come to race for the *palio* make their offerings, and after them all the Flemings and Brabantines, weavers of woolen cloth in Florence. And then twelve prisoners are offered, who have been released from jail out of mercy and to honor St. John; and these are destitute people, imprisoned for any reason.

When the offerings are complete, everyone returns home to dine. And, as I have said, throughout the city on this day weddings and banquets are held, with so much music and singing, dancing, rejoicing, and celebration that the city seems to be paradise.

After dinner, when people have had some rest ... all the women and girls go and stand along the course of the *palio* race: the course passes straight through the middle of the city, where there are a good many homes and fine houses of the good citizens, more than in any other district. And from one end of the city to another, along this route, filled with flowers, are all the women, and all the jewels and rich decorations of the city. And there are always many foreign lords and knights who come from neighboring cities to see the beauty and magnificence of the feast day.... The horses are readied for the off and, at the sound of three tolls of the big bell of the Palazzo dei Signori, they begin to race. And at the top of the tower are boys whose support for this or that horse can be seen from their gestures. The most superior Barbary horses in the world come from all over Italy and the one that first reaches the *palio,* wins it, and is borne on triumphal four-wheeled cart, decorated with four carved lions that seem alive, one on each corner, and drawn by two horses ... the *palio* is very large and rich, of fine scarlet velvet, in two parts joined by gold trimming as wide as a man's palm, lined with squirrel belly and edged with ermine, fringed with silk and gold, and it costs in total 300 florins or more....

Questions: What happened on this feast day? Who participated in the festivities? Where did they occur? What roles did each group play in the festivities? How might the Florentines have interpreted the ritual they saw or participated in on this feast day?

123. A WAKE IN OXFORD, 1306

The coroner's inquisition following a suspicious death in Oxford reveals what went on at medieval wakes in Oxford.

Source: trans. G.G. Coulton, *A Medieval Garner: Human Documents from the Four Centuries Preceding the Reformation* (London: Constable and Co., 1910), pp. 450–52.

It happened upon the Sunday next after the Feast of the Assumption of the Blessed Virgin, in the 34th year of King Edward, that Gilbert de Foxlee, clerk, died at his lodging in the parish of St. Peter in the east about the hour of noon, and on the Monday following he was viewed by Thomas Lisewys, coroner of the lord king for the City of Oxford. He had a wound in his left leg, hard by the knee, of the breadth of four inches all around, and of the depth of an inch and a half. So an inquest was held before the said coroner by the oath of.... And [the jury] say on their oath that, on Thursday the eve of St. John last past, the tailors of Oxford and other townsfolk with them held a wake in their shops the whole night through, singing and making their solace with citherns, fiddles, and diverse other instruments, as the use and custom is to do there and elsewhere on account of the solemnity of that Feast. And after midnight, finding that no man was wandering there in the streets, they went out from their shops, and others with them, and held their dances in the High Street in front of the Cloth Hall. And as they thus played, Gilbert de Foxlee came along with a certain naked and drawn sword in his hand, and began right away to contend with them, trying by all means to break up that dance. But certain of them who were of his acquaintance, seeing this, came to him and would have led him away, and asked him to harm no man; yet for all that Gilbert would not promise, but broke away from them and came back and assaulted William de Claydon, whose hand he would have cut off with his sword as he went round in the dance, unless he had drawn suddenly back. Whereupon Henry de Beaumont Cruisor, fell upon Gilbert, together with Thomas de Bloxham, William de Leye servant to John de Leye, and William de Claydon; and Henry wounded him with a sword in the right arm, and Thomas [wounded him] with a misericorde [a dagger] in the back, and William [wounded him] upon the head, so that he fell. Then William de Leye, with a certain axe called spar-axe, struck him upon the left leg and inflicted the wound whereof he died on the Sunday aforesaid: yet he lived eight weeks and two days and a half, and had all his church rights.

Questions: What did the tailors do at this wake? Why might the victim have approached them in an angry and threatening manner?

124. PROCESSIONS FOR PEACE IN PARIS, 1412

After suffering for many years from the fighting that accompanied the Hundred Years War (1337–1453) between France and England, Paris was also plunged into the middle of a civil war due in part to the instability of the French king, Charles VI, who suffered from periods of madness. The power struggle that ensued between the Burgundians (led by the king's uncle) and the Armagnacs (the party of the duke of Orleans and duke of Berry) caused further problems. The author of this passage—an anonymous middle-class Parisian—here describes the actions of an urban populace who believe that demonstrating their religious devotion and repenting will help bring peace to their city.

Source: trans. J. Shirley, *A Parisian Journal 1405–1449* (Oxford: Clarendon Press, 1968), pp. 62–65.

As soon as people heard in Paris that the king was in his enemies' country, they arranged by common consent the most touching processions that anyone had ever seen in living memory. On Monday, the next to last day of May in the same year [1412], the people of the Palais in Paris and the mendicant orders and others all went in procession barefoot, carrying various most worthy shrines and the True Holy Cross of the Palais; also the members of the Parlement of every rank, all two by two, with some thirty thousand people following after, and all of them barefoot.

On Tuesday, the last day of May in the same year, some of the town's parishes made processions, the parishioners going around their own parishes. All the priests wore copes or surplices, each carried a candle and relics, all barefoot; the shrine of St. Blanchard, of St. Magloire, and two hundred or more little children going in front, all barefoot and each with a candle or taper in his hand. Everyone who could afford it carried a torch; all were barefooted, men and women.

On Wednesday, June 1ˢᵗ, same year, there was another procession as on the Tuesday.

The Thursday was the day of the Holy Sacrament; the traditional procession took place.

Next Friday, June 3ʳᵈ, same year, there was the most beautiful procession ever seen. All the parishes and the orders of every rank went barefoot and carrying candles or reliquaries in their devotion, as is described above. More than forty thousand ordinary people went too, all barefoot and fasting, not to mention other secret abstinences; more than four thousand torches burning. Thus they bore the holy relics to St.-Jean-en-Grève and here, with great weeping, with many tears and great devotion they took up the precious body of Our Lord....

Next Saturday, the 4ᵗʰ, same month, same year, the entire university went in procession, everyone of every rank on pain of deprivation; also the little schoolchildren, all barefoot, and everyone great and small carrying a lighted candle. They assembled thus humbly at the Mathurins and from there went to

St.-Catherine-du-Val-des-Ecoliers carrying countless holy relics. There they sang high mass and came fasting back again.

On Sunday, the 5th of the month, the people of St. Denis-en-France came to Paris, all barefoot, bringing with them seven holy bodies, the holy oriflamme [the standard of the abbey of St. Denis, where the French kings were buried; the French also carried the banner into war]—that which had been carried in Flanders—the holy nail and the holy crown, borne by two abbots, with thirteen banners in the procession. The parishioners of St. Eustace went out to meet them because St. Eustace's body was in one of the shrines. They all went directly to the Palais; there said high mass with great devotion and departed.

During the following week they took turns to make the most touching processions every day; the villages around Paris came too, barefoot, in great devotion praying God that through his holy grace peace might be made between the king and the French lords, because the whole of France was sorely distressed both for friends and for the means of livelihood. There was nothing to be found in the open country unless one took it there.

[Similar processions took place every day in the following week ...] On Friday, the 10th of the month, there was a general procession, one of the very finest ever seen. Every church, college, and parish was there, barefoot, and people past reckoning (an order had been announced the day before, every house to send one person). Many contingents came in from parishes outside Paris.... They brought all the relics they could get hold of and all came barefoot, very old men, pregnant women, little children and all with tapers or candles. [Further processions occurred in the following week.] ...

Questions: Who marched in these processions and what did the processions look like? Why did the processions keep occurring? Why did people go barefoot and carry candles and relics?

125. MAYORAL ELECTIONS IN ENGLAND

Although elected only for one-year terms, English mayors were the most important civic officials in their towns. Some of their entertainment activities on behalf of the town can be seen in the expenses for which they sought reimbursement in their annual accounts (see also doc. 65), as shown in the first extracts. The solemnity of their election is evident in the second selection, which details the religious and secular ritual surrounding the weighty business of electing a mayor in London.

Source: (A) trans. M. Bateson, *Records of the Borough of Leicester*, vol. 2 (London: C.J. Clay and Sons, 1901), pp. 11–14, abridged and revised; (B) trans. H.T. Riley, *Memorials of London and London Life in the XIIIth, XIVth and XVth Centuries* (London: Longmans, Green, and Co., 1868), pp. 565–66, abridged and revised.

(A) Extracts from the Expense Accounts of the Mayor of Leicester

[Account of 1332–33] Expenses

… He accounts for the expenses of Sir Richard of Edgbaston, and Roger of Aylesbury, the king's justices of the peace for arraying [mustering] men for [the war in] Scotland, dining with the mayor on Monday after the feast of St. Mark the Evangelist [April 27], by the consent of John Alsy and other jurats [city councilors] dining there [purchases of bread, wine, ale, large meat, geese, capons, hens, pigeons, and chickens enumerated]. Four pence for the tripe of a sheep with lord; 7 pence for two porkers; 2 pence for eggs; ½ pence for 2 loafs of wastell [the best kind of bread] and purchases of [coal, firewood, saffron, and brawn].… For the expenses of Hugh of Harborough, the steward, and of William of Bagworth, the lord [earl's] receiver, dining with the mayor on Tuesday, St. Margaret's Day [July 20, 1333]. Bread, 1 shilling ½ pence; 7 galls [for making ink] and 1 quart of wine, 7½ pence; ale, 2 shillings 4½ pence; large meat, 1 shilling 9½ pence; 6 geese, 2 shillings; 3 capons, 9 pence; 20 chickens, 1 shilling 9 pence; eggs, 4 pence. For the tripe of a sheep with lard, 3 pence; for 2½ pounds of almonds and powder of ginger, 8 pence; for mace and cloves, 4 pence. For saffron 4 pence [also purchases of coal, firewood, and brawn made].…

… The expenses of the mayor, John Alsy and other honest men of the community, treating and discussing the business of the community at the tavern after the departure of the justices, that is to say of Sir Richard of Willoughby, for wine, 10 pence. Given to Henry of Winchester for having his aid in speaking good to the lord earl [the lord of the town] and to his son for diverse causes, 6 shillings 8 pence and a pair of gauntlets for 2 pence.…

[Account of 1333–34] Expenses

… He accounts for … the expenses of the steward, William de Cloune, John Leverich, Richard Leverich, Ralph of Burton, Geoffrey of Kent, William of

Goadby and other honest men and four sub-bailiffs dining with the mayor [on election day, September 29]; purchases of [bread, wine, ale, sweet herring, hard fish, fresh-water fish, eels, apples, pears, nuts]. For the expenses of the mayor, bailiffs and many jurats dining at the tavern when the mayor was presented before the earl's court, 1 shilling....

... Given to Roger the Messenger proclaiming the mayor's [election] in the high street and claiming a reward for himself, 6 pence....

... For expenses of the steward, receiver, and jurats dining with the mayor on Tuesday before the Nativity of St. John the Baptist, 7 shillings 9 pence, as appears by particulars annexed elsewhere. Given to Richard the earl's fool, 3 pence. Given to three messengers of the king coming to the king on St. James' day, 3 pence. For 12 pullets sent to the wife of Sir William le Blount on St. James' day, 1 shilling 2 pence. For bread and wine sent to Sir Richard of Willoughby [a king's justice] coming to Leicester on Thursday before St. Bartholomew's day for delivery of the king's gaol [to preside over criminal courts].

(B) Election of Richard Whittington to his Second Mayoralty in London, 1406

On Wednesday, the feast of the Translation of St. Edward, king and confessor [13 October], in the 8th year etc., John Wodecok, mayor of the city of London, considering that upon the same day he and all the aldermen of the city, and as many as possible of the wealthier and more substantial commoners of the city, ought to meet at the Guildhall, as the usage is, to elect a new mayor for the ensuing year, ordered that a mass of the Holy Spirit should be celebrated, with solemn music, in the Chapel annexed to the Guildhall, so that the commonalty, by the grace of the Holy Spirit, might be able peacefully and amicably to nominate two able and proper persons to be mayor of the city for the ensuing year, by favor of the clemency of Our Savior, according to the customs of the city.

After the mass was solemnly celebrated in the Chapel, there was present: John Wodecok, the mayor, John Prestone, recorder, Nicholas Wottone and Geoffrey Broke, sheriffs, the Prior of the Holy Trinity, John Hadlee, William Staundone, Richard Whittington, Drew Barentyn, Thomas Knolles, John Shadworth, William Askham, William Bramptone, John Warner, William Walderne, William Venour, Robert Chychely, Thomas Fauconer, Thomas Polle, William Louthe, William Crowmere, Henry Bartone, and Henry Pountfreyt, aldermen, and many reputable commoners of the city. The mayor, recorder, sheriffs, aldermen, and commoners entered the Guildhall, where the precept of the mayor and aldermen ... was becomingly set forth and declared by the recorder to the commoners, so that the commoners should nominate unto the mayor and aldermen such able and proper persons as had before filled the office of sheriff in the city; it being for the said commoners to take no care which one of the persons so to be nominated should be chosen by the mayor and aldermen to be mayor for the ensuing year. When this was done, the mayor, recorder, sheriffs, and aldermen went up into the Chamber of the mayor's court, within the Guildhall, there to await the nomination of such two persons. Whereupon, the Commoners peacefully and amicably, without any clamor or discussion, did becomingly nominate Richard Whittington, mercer, and Drew Barentyn, goldsmith, through John Westone, common counter of the city, and presented their nominations.

And hereupon, the mayor and aldermen, with closed doors, in the Chamber chose Richard Whittington, by guidance of the Holy Spirit, to be mayor of the city for the ensuing year; after which, the mayor and aldermen, coming down from the Chamber into the Hall, to the commoners there as-sembled, as the custom is, notified by the recorder unto the same commoners, how that, by divine inspiration, the lot had fallen upon the said Richard Whit-tington, as above stated.

And further, the commoners unanimously entreated the mayor and aldermen, that they would ordain that in every future year, on the day of the Translation of St. Edward, a mass of the Holy Spirit, for the reasons before stated, should be celebrated, before the election of the mayor, in the Chapel. And hereupon, the mayor and aldermen, considering the entreaty of the commoners to be fair, reasonable, and consonant with right, and especially to the glory and laud of God, and to the honor of the said city, by assent and consent of the commoners, did ordain and decree that every year in future a solemn mass with music shall be celebrated in presence of the mayor and aldermen; the same mass, by ordinance of the Chamberlain for the time being, to be solemnly chanted by the finest singers in the Chapel, and upon that feast.

Questions: What type of entertaining did the mayor of Leicester do on behalf of the town? What type of ritual surrounded the election of the mayor in London? What were the aims or purpose of this ritual?

CHAPTER ELEVEN

THE DANGERS OF URBAN LIFE

Figure 11.1

A Town Under Siege

Towns built stone walls at great expense (see doc. 64) to protect their citizens and their wealth from the armies of other towns or nobles (docs. 132, 133). Since the town walls were so strong, it often took a long siege (with the enemy troops housed in tents outside the walls, as depicted here) to starve the townspeople into surrendering. By the late fifteenth century, however, the use of more and more powerful cannons was making it easier for opposing armies to break down parts of the wall and enter the town. From a medieval manuscript illumination, reproduced by Charles Knight, *Old England: A Pictorial Museum of Regal, Ecclesiastical, Municipal, Baronial and Popular Antiquities,* 2 vols. (London: James Sangster and Co., 1850), fig. 1252.

126. FIRES IN NOVGOROD

During the Middle Ages, Novgorod was the largest city-state in Russia, capital of the republic of Novgorod and an important kontor *of the Hanseatic League (doc. 32). Despite its wealth and independence, however, the city was very vulnerable to fire because the majority of its buildings were constructed of wood. We know that many other towns, such as London (doc. 144), took steps early on to reduce this threat with building codes and the establishment of a primitive fire brigade. These extracts from a chronicle compiled by clergy associated with the archbishop represent only a small sample of the many entries describing the destruction wrought by fire, which suggests that Novgorod had few defenses against this threat.*

Source: trans. R. Michell and N. Forbes, *The Chronicle of Novgorod 1016–1471* (Camden Society, 3rd series, vol. 25, 1914), pp. 113, 118, 134–35.

1299. On Great Saturday, 18 April, a fire broke out at 1 o'clock at night in Varangian Street [street of the Scandinavians], and for our sins a great evil happened; a storm arose with great winds and soon the fire grew so strong that all, taking what little they could, ran out of their houses; all the rest the fire took. The fire leapt from the court of the *Nemtsy* [German Hanseatic merchants] to the Nerev quarter. It broke out in Kholop Street and there still more fiercely; and amongst the Nerev residents on the other side, and the fire took the Great Bridge. And thus there was a great calamity so that only God and the good people on earth stopped it, and evil men fell to plundering. What was in the churches they took in all plunder without fear of God ... at St. Ioan's they killed the warehouse guard, at St. Yakov's the warehouse-guard was burnt. In the market quarter twelve churches were burnt; they had not time to bring out all the pictures, nor books. And in Christ Church several people were burnt, also two priests. In the Nerev quarter ten churches were burnt with many embroideries in the churches, and the good man Elferi Lazorevich was burnt. And on the morrow there was grief and lamentation....

1311 ... The same spring, on 19 May, a fire broke out at night in Yanev Street, and 37 houses were burnt and seven people. Then in the night of 28 June Glebov's house in Rozvazha Street caught fire, and the Nerev quarter was burnt, on one side so far as the ditch, and on the other beyond Borkov Street; and the church of SS. Kosma and Damian was burnt, also that of St. Sava, and 40 churches were damaged by fire and several good houses.... Then on 16 July a fire broke out at night in Ilya Street, and here likewise was a fierce conflagration with a high wind, and crashing noise. The market place was burnt, and houses up to Rogatitsa Street, and the churches burnt were seven wooden churches: St. Dmitri, St. Georgi, SS. Boris and Gleb, St. John Ishkov, St. Catherine, St Prokopi, and of Christ. And six stone churches were damaged by fire, and the seventh was the Varangian Church. And accursed men ... having no pity for their fellows, plundered other people's property....

1340 ... The same year on Tuesday in Trinity week, on 7 June, the day of the Holy Martyr Fedor, a fire broke out in Rozvazha Street, in the field beyond St. Fedor's. The Nerev quarter was burnt, even so far as St. Yakov, and hitherwards to Chudinets Street, and all the churches and houses. From there it flung itself into the town, and the Vladyka's [archbishop's] court was burnt and the church of St. Sophia; and all the houses and churches in the town, and the Lyudin quarter, up to St. Alexis' church; also churches and houses and up to the Prussian Street. For so great and fierce was the fire, with storm and gale, that they thought it was the end [of all things]. The fire went burning over the water, and many people were drowned in the Volkhov [River]. And the fire threw itself across the Volkhov to the other side [the mercantile half of the town] and there by evening service time the whole of that side rapidly burned, from the Fedor stream into Slavno and up to the fields, and stone and wooden churches, and houses. From many churches they had no time to carry out either images or books, nor from out of the houses. And whatever anyone brought out and laid either in the fields or in the gardens, or in the ditch or in boats or in canoes, all was taken by the flames. And whatever else was brough out wicked men carried it off ... and it was not only that they robbed people, their own brothers and Christians, killing some who were guarding their goods, and taking it themselves, but even in the sacred churches which every Christian ought to protect, even abandoning his own house.... In the church of the Holy Mother of God in the marketplace a priest was burnt, though others say they murdered him while guarding property because this church was entirely burnt and the icons and the books, but of the man the fire did not touch even a hair ... in the church of the Holy Friday the watchman was burnt with his son, in consequence of that fire that church collapsed ... and many people were burnt in their houses for the fire took on rapidly; and the great bridge was burnt to the water's edge.... They made a new bridge again across the Volkhov the same year.

Questions: Why were fires so common and such a hazard in medieval towns? What type of destruction did the fires and related events bring?

127. FAMINE MORTALITY IN BRUGES AND YPRES, 1316

Torrential rains throughout much of Europe caused the complete failure of the harvest in 1315 and ushered in what historians call the "Great Famine" of 1315–19, a period of bad weather, poor harvests, and widespread livestock disease. The price of grain rose astronomically to levels that most urban residents could not afford. Private charities did what they could (doc. 128), but town governments had to step in to regulate the supply and prices of grain; this regulation tended in subsequent years to soften the impact of particularly poor harvests. But in 1316 the mortality rate from famine was so high that many towns, like Bruges and Ypres in Flanders, had to pay for the removal of the corpses that had piled up on the streets. The first document shows the payments in the Ypres account for the removal and burial of the dead; the following table is compiled from the data on the numbers who died in the accounts of Ypres and Bruges. The population of Bruges in this period was probably around 35,000, and Ypres 28,000.

Source: (A) trans. M. Kowaleski, from *Comptes de la ville d'Ypres de 1267 à 1329*, 2 vols., ed. G. Des Marez and E. de Sagher (Brussels: Kiessling et cie, P. Imbreghts, 1909), v. 1, pp. 607–08; (B) trans. M. Kowaleski of data from H. van Werveke, "La Famine de l'an 1316 en Flandre et dans les régions voisines," *Revue du nord* 41 (1959): 7.

(A) Account of the City of Ypres, 1316

Summary of the dead buried in le Maselaine and Holy Cross [cemeteries]:
The [first] Saturday in May [1 May 1316]

8 shillings to William le Coletre, bell-ringer of St.-Jean, and to Jehan de le Beke, for burying all the dead, who were buried without lights [without full funeral services?], and for carrying all the dead in the streets, and also for digging in le Maselaine for three days.

Also, 4 shillings to Thieribus for burying the dead, who were buried without lights at Holy Cross, for three days....

13 shillings to brother Jake of the hospital of Notre-Dame for carrying and gathering up the dead in the streets, up to 34 dead this week....

29 shillings to those of the hospital for gathering up the dead in the streets....

Saturday on the eve of Pentecost [29 May 1316]

33 shillings 10 pence to brother Jake of the hospital for those who have gathered up the dead in the town, of which totaled 146.

20 shillings to those who buried the dead this week at le Maselaine.

10 shillings to those who buried the dead this week at Holy Cross.

Sum for this week: 3 pounds 3 shillings 10 pence

The Saturday on the eve of Trinity [5 June 1316]

19 shillings 3 pence to brother Jake of the hospital for those who gathered up the dead in the town, which totaled 101....

Saturday after the feast of St. Barnabus [12 June 1316]

20 shillings 4½ pence to brother Jake of the hospital for those who gathered up the dead in the town, which totaled 107....

Saturday before the feast of St. John the Baptist [19 June 1316]

30 shillings to brother Jake of the hospital for those who gathered up the dead in the town, which totaled 157....

(B) Table 11.1: Corpses Collected at the Expense of the Towns of Bruges and Ypres in 1316

Bruges		Ypres	
Week finishing	No.	Week finishing	No.
30 April		1 May	54
14 May	116	15 May	?
21 May	165	22 May	173
28 May	145	29 May	146
4 June	128	5 June	101
11 June	156	12 June	107
18 June	135	19 June	157
25 June	150	26 June	149
2 July	136	3 July	155
9 July	140	10 July	167
16 July	135	17 July	158
23 July	124	24 July	172
30 July	95	31 July	190
6 August	85	7 August	191
13 August	59	14 August	130
20 August	54	21 August	140
27 August	30	28 August	148
3 September	28	4 September	138
10 September	19	11 September	124
17 September	22	18 September	115
24 September		25 September	37
1 October	16	2 October	27
8 October		9 October	15
Total	1,938		2,794

Note: The accounting week ended on Friday in Bruges and on Saturday in Ypres.

Questions: Does the account give any idea of how the city handled the large number of people dying each week during the famine? How did the death rates in the two cities compare in terms of timing and severity? Who were the most likely victims of the famine based on the experience of Siena in 1329 (doc. 128)? What factors might explain when the death rate peaked and fell when it did?

128. DISCRIMINATION AGAINST THE POOR IN SIENA DURING THE FAMINE OF 1329

The large numbers of urban poor living at the edge of subsistence made grain shortages and pestilence particular concerns of town rulers who were worried not only by the human toll such crises exacted, but also by the specter of civil disorder such problems could generate. The following extract, taken from the private diary or ricordi *(see doc. 40) of Domencio Lenzi il Biadaiolo, a Florentine merchant ("il Biadaiolo" means "seller of fodder" but he mainly dealt in grain), shows the different strategies discussed by various governing constituencies to mitigate the impact of these problems on the* popolo minuto, *which was made up of poor laborers and the indigent. His description of Siena's treatment of its poor during this crisis was, however, also influenced by the long-standing animosity between Siena and Lenzi's home town of Florence.*

Source: trans. M. Baca, *Merchant Writers of the Italian Renaissance from Boccaccio to Machiavelli*, ed. Vittore Branca (New York: Marsilio Publishers, 1999), pp. 37–41.

How there was a great famine in Florence and in other parts of the world and how the Sienese expelled all the poor people from their city, and the Florentines received them.

Such a cruel famine and shortage of food went on here in Florence [1328–30] that you who read this account surely must know that other parts of the world were affected as well. According to reliable eyewitnesses, it was felt so cruelly and harshly that the poor had nothing to eat but plant roots and fruits of trees, and meats disgusting not only to the mouth, but to the nose as well. Italy, and especially Tuscany, was more overwhelmed by this pestilence than any other place. But I can say that during this time of famine my fatherland, Florence—whose countryside does not produce enough grain to support it for 5 months, and where victuals are always more expensive than in any other part of Italy—by itself supported half of the poor of Tuscany through the providence and aid of the good wealthy people and their money. Thus it might be said, and indeed is true, that the poor, having been expelled from the grain-rich surrounding lands for fear they might seize them, and having been deprived of the remedies offered to assist them, could only turn to Florence as a trusted port of consolation. During the aforementioned famine Florence not once but many times graciously sustained the poor and others, each in his own degree.

Now, I certainly would prefer to remain silent about such events as now occur to my mind; but I cannot suffer that such cruel insolence and miscarriage of mercy as that which the decadent, perverse, cruel, insane Siena showed during this famine should go untold. For Siena was so insolent and presumptuous as to blindly act against the disinherited poor when they were all cruelly bereft of benevolent mercy, giving full rein to her impious cruelty. Would that those perfidious citizens of the city of the she-wolf had not been borne and suckled by their mother, who not only devours flesh, but swallows up even the earth, and viciously assails the winds with all her cruel forces.

But, sirs, I know not whether to prove they are made of different stuff, or to bring down greater and more cruel judgment of their evils by Him who is the height of compassion; at first there had been someone in Siena, the minister of the Hospice of Santa Maria della Scala, who was willing to give so many alms to the poor that it seemed that all of God's power were intervening. To everyone—women, men, children and adults—was given a loaf of bread weighing 14 *once;* if a woman was with child, she was given two loaves. Such great and open charity attracted the poor, who came from near and far. But the alms did not run out even though the number of hungry people increased, for a way was found to replenish them by having everyone contribute to such a good cause. Thus, as can be seen in the painting on the next pages [the Siena accounts are famous for its painted illustrations], this was how it was organized: alms were distributed three days of the week—that is, Monday, Wednesday, and Friday—to as many poor as came to the Hospice of la Scala for that reason. All of the poor people would enter, and then three doors were left open through which they left the building; one was for men, the other was used by the women, and the third was for little children, who streamed out continuously. At each of the doors were positioned two very worthy members of the Hospice, who distributed the alms to the people as they emerged.

Oh! Great God, You should grant your grace directly to that house! But we know that only from you, O Lord, does good proceed, and that whoever out of love for you imparts his goods to your ambassadors the poor, by your virtue and power that good will abound in his house without discord.

But, dear readers, regard this "Mirror" entitled "Mirror of Humanity," which recounts such godless behavior, heeding God who gave himself to so much goodness. The city of Siena became envious, and in her insane iniquity clandestinely opposed what Messire Giovanni was doing. The Council of Nine sent for Messire Giovanni; when he came into their presence, he asked what they wished of him. O prideful Siena, let the whole world hear what you are! They replied that under pain of death by fire this almsgiving should not continue thenceforward. Take heed, all men! These people were not only ordering that an injury be done to

God; but that all those to whom only God is a brother should be allowed to die of hunger, in a prosperous city that had plenty of food. For I say, sirs, that these men were well brought up and trained by their mother the she-wolf; let this argument alone be brought against them, without any other syllogisms.

But even if this helps no one else, listen to how this evil went forward; now I shall recount how they went on. Having given this grim order, that city continued thus:

The next day the poor returned to the Hospice, their accustomed refuge, believing that they would receive the usual charity and relief, and that when they heard the word "Enter," they would all be comforted. But that sweet greeting became an ill-fortuned dismissal, for this is what they heard instead: "Go away, you hungry beggars, to perish along with your wants, for the lords of this city have ordered that you be left to perish in your misery; otherwise both we and our houses and possessions will be consumed by fire. We have no more charity in us." At this cruel, arrogant reply, there arose infinite cries and sounds of hands striking, shouts, and crying, and people clawing their faces so deeply that they seemed to bear the marks of nails. Throughout the entire city, countryside, castles, and fortresses could be heard the voices of people crying for someone in their family who had died. And thus the poor ran desperately in infinite numbers toward the public palace whence those orders had emanated, crying out "Have mercy!" or "Fire!" or "Die!" All this noise brought the people of the city running, armed with whatever they could find. Armed guards emerged from the public palace to put down the uprising, but to little avail; for the poor, striking with stones and sticks, stormed the palace, driving back the guards, who were fearful of greater injury.

At this Guido Ricci da Reggio, the captain of the army of that city, came running into the fray. One of the guards, carrying a staff and caring nothing for death, came up and struck him a blow on the lower back, knocking him off his feet; and if it hadn't been for the strong armor he was wearing, he might have died. There was great confusion, and many on all sides were gravely wounded. If it hadn't been that God did not wish it, that day Siena might have been properly paid back for her thieving, evil ways, providing a fearful reminder for all ages.

Several days after the uprising had quieted down, there began an intense search for whoever had incited or consented to so much violence and turmoil. In one night, no fewer than 60 men were taken from their beds, and as many were tortured as were hanged by the neck, including the man who had felled the captain. And there may have been men among those who were hanged who had never even heard about the uprising. More than a hundred men were exiled at that time; but that's the way that city is! The others remained in prison for several days.

But this did not end the cruel assaults of fiery Siena; for at a public council it was voted that the poor should be driven out of Siena and that no further succor for the love of God was to be given them.

"Oh! Cruel earth, why did you not open up?" [he is here quoting Dante's *Inferno*, XXXIII, 66]

There came the blare of a trumpet and then a human voice declared that under pain of death, every poor stranger should leave the city within three days' time. Police squadrons went around with clubs and stones, cruelly driving people out of the city gates, caring not if they were children or adults, women or men, with child or not. Those who had been driven out of Siena turned to Florence as their certain source of relief and mercy; they were well received and well treated there. And giving thanks to God, they devoutly prayed that He would keep Florence in His blessed peace and that she and her citizens be worthily praised....

Questions: What caused the famine? Why did the poor of Siena rise up and riot? What steps did the city government take to control alms to the poor? Why did the city government take these steps? Does Domencio's moral reading of events obscure a clear analysis of causes and events?

129. THE BLACK DEATH IN FLORENCE, 1348

Giovanni Boccaccio, one of the greatest writers of the medieval period, described the impact of the Black Death of 1348 in his home town of Florence. The Black Death was the most devastating plague of the medieval period, reducing the population of Florence and many other cities by almost half. Recurring visitations of plague continued in the following centuries, but none was as severe as what came to be called the "Black Death."

Source: trans. J.M. Rigg, *The Decameron*, by Boccaccio (London: David Campbell, 1921), I, pp. 5–11, revised.

I say, then, that the years of the beatific Incarnation of the Son of God had reached the tale of 1348. The mortal pestilence then arrived in the excellent city of Florence, which surpasses every other Italian city in nobility. Whether through the operations of the heavenly bodies, or sent upon us mortals through our wicked deeds by the just wrath of God for our correction, the plague had begun some years before in Eastern countries. It carried off uncounted numbers of inhabitants, and kept moving without cease from place to place. It spread in piteous fashion towards the West. No wisdom or human foresight worked against it. The city had been cleaned of much filth by officials delegated to the task. Sick persons were forbidden entrance, and many laws were passed for the safeguarding of health. Devout persons made to God not just modest supplications and not just once, but many, both in ordered processions and in other ways. Almost at the beginning of the spring of that year, the plague horribly began to reveal, in astounding fashion, its painful effects.

It did not work as it had in the East, where anyone who bled from the nose had a manifest sign of inevitable death. But in its early stages both men, and women too, acquired certain swellings, either in the groin or under the armpits. Some of these swellings reached the size of a common apple, and others were as big as an egg, some more and some less. The common people called them plague-boils. From these two parts of the body, the deadly swellings began in a short time to appear and to reach indifferently every part of the body. Then, the appearance of the disease began to change into black or livid blotches, which showed up in many on the arms or thighs and in every other part of the body. On some they were large and few, on others small and numerous. And just as the swellings had been at first and still were an infallible indication of approaching death, so also were these blotches to whomever they touched. In the cure of these illnesses, neither the advice of a doctor nor the power of any medicine appeared to help and to do any good. Perhaps the nature of the malady did not allow it; perhaps the ignorance of the physicians (of whom, besides those trained, the number had grown very large both of women and of men who were completely without medical instruction) did not know whence it arose, and consequently did not take required action against it. Not only did very few recover, but almost everyone died within the third day from the appearance of these symptoms, some sooner and some later, and most without any fever or other complication. This plague was of greater virulence, because by contact with those sick from it, it infected the healthy, not otherwise than fire does, when it is brought very close to dry or oily material.

The evil was still greater than this. Not only conversation and contact with the sick carried the illness to the healthy and was the cause of their common death. But even to handle the clothing or other things touched or used by the sick seem to carry with it that same disease for those who came into contact with them. You will be amazed to hear what I now must tell you. If the eyes of many, including my own, had not seen it, I would hardly dare to believe it, much less to write it, even if I had heard it from a person worthy of faith. I say that the character of the pestilence we describe was of such virulence in spreading from one person to another, that not only did it go from man to man, but many times it also apparently did the following, which is even more remarkable. If an animal outside the human species contacted the belongings of a man sick or dead of this illness, it not only caught the disease, but within a brief time was killed by it. My own eyes, as I said a little while ago, saw one day (and other times besides) this occurrence. The rags of a poor man dead from this disease had been thrown in a public street. Two pigs came to them and they, in their accustomed manner, first rooted among them with their snouts, and then seized them with their teeth and tossed them about with their jaws. A short hour later, after some staggering, as if the poison was taking effect, both of them fell dead to earth upon the rags which they had unhappily dragged.

Such events and many others similar to them or even worse conjured up in those who remained healthy diverse fears and imaginings. Almost all were inclined to a very cruel purpose, that is, to shun and to flee the sick and their belongings. By so behaving, each believed that he would gain safety for himself. Some persons advised that a moderate manner of living, and the avoidance of all excesses, greatly strengthened resistance to this danger. Seeking out companions, such persons lived apart from other men. They closed and locked themselves in those houses where no sick person was found. To live better, they consumed in modest quantities the most delicate foods and the best wines, and avoided all sexual activity. They did not let themselves speak to anyone, nor did they wish to hear any news from the outside, concerning death or the sick. They lived amid music and those pleasures which they were able to obtain.

Others were of a contrary opinion. They affirmed that heavy drinking and enjoyment, making the rounds with singing and good cheer, the satisfaction of the appetite with everything one could, and the laughing and joking which derived from this, were the most effective medicine for this great evil. As they recommended, so they put into practice, according to their ability. Night and day, they went now to that tavern and now to another, drinking without moderation or measure. They did even more in the houses of others; they had only to discern there things which were to their liking or pleasure. This they could easily do, since everyone, as if he was destined to live no more, had abandoned all care of his possessions and of himself. Thus, most houses had become open to all, and strangers used them as they happened upon them, as their proper owner might have done. With this inhuman intent, they continuously avoided the sick with all their power.

In this great affliction and misery of our city, the revered authority of both divine and human laws was left to fall and decay by those who administered and executed them. They too, just as other men, were all either dead or sick or so destitute of their families, that they were unable to fulfill any office. As a result everyone could do just as he pleased.

Many others held a middle course between the two mentioned above. Not restraining themselves in their diet as much as the first group, nor letting themselves go in drinking and other excesses as the second, they satisfied their appetites sufficiently. They did not go into seclusion but went about carrying flowers, fragrant herbs, and various spices which they often held to their noses, believing it good to comfort the brain with such odors since the air was heavy with the stench of dead bodies, illness, and pungent medicines. Others had harsher but perhaps safer ideas. They said that against plagues no medicine was better than or even equal to simple flight. Moved by this reasoning and giving heed to nothing but themselves, many men and women abandoned their own city, their houses and homes, their relatives and belongings in search of their own country places or those of others. Just as if the wrath of God, in order to punish the iniquity of men with the plague, could not pursue them, but would only oppress those within city walls! They were apparently convinced that no one should remain in the city, and that its last hour had struck.

Although these people of various opinions did not all die, neither did they all live. In fact many in each group and in every place became ill, but having given example to those who were still well, they in turn were abandoned and left to perish.

We have said enough of these facts: that one townsman shuns another; that almost no one cares for his neighbor; that relatives rarely or never exchange visits, and never do they get too close. The calamity had instilled such terror in the hearts of men and women that brother abandoned brother, uncle nephew, brother sister, and often wives left their husbands. Even more extraordinary, unbelievable even, fathers and mothers shunned their children, neither visiting them nor helping them, as though they were not their very own.

Consequently, for the enormous number of men and women who became ill, there was no aid except the charity of friends, who were few indeed, or the avarice of servants attracted by huge and exorbitant stipends. Even so, there weren't many servants, and those few men and women were of unrefined capabilities, doing little more than to hand the sick the articles they requested and to mark their death. Serving in such a capacity, many perished along with their earnings. From this abandonment of the sick by neighbors, relatives and friends and from the scarcity of servants arose an almost unheard-of custom. Once she became ill, no woman, however attractive, lovely or well-born, minded having as her servant a man, young or old. To him without any shame she exhibited any part of her body as sickness required, as if to another woman. This explains why those who were cured were less modest than formerly. A further consequence is that many died for want of help who might still be living. The fact that the ill could not avail themselves of services as well as the virulence of the plague account for the multitude who died in the city by day and by night. It was dreadful to hear tell of it, and likewise to see it. Out of necessity, therefore, there were born among the survivors customs contrary to the old ways of the townspeople.

It used to be the custom, as it is today, for the female relatives and neighbors of the dead man to gather together with those closest to him in order to mourn. Outside the house of the dead man his friends, neighbors and many others would assemble. Then, according to the status of the deceased, a priest would come with the funeral pomp of candles and chants, while the dead man was borne on the shoulders of his peers to the church chosen before death. As the ferocity of the plague increased, such customs ceased either totally or in part, and new ones took their place. Instead of dying amidst a crowd of women, many left this life without a single witness. Indeed, few were conceded the mournful wails and bitter tears of loved ones. Instead, quips and merrymaking were common, and even normally compassionate women had learned well such habits for the sake of their health. Few bodies had more than ten or twelve neighbors to accompany them to church, and even those were not upright citizens, but a species of vulture sprung from the lowly who called themselves "grave-diggers," and sold their services. They shouldered the bier and with hurried steps went not to the church designated by the deceased, but more often than not to the nearest church. Ahead were four or six clerics with little light or sometimes none, who with the help of the gravediggers placed the dead in the nearest open grave without straining themselves with too long or solemn a service.

Much more wretched was the condition of the poor people and even perhaps of the middle class in large part. Because of hope or poverty, these people were confined to their houses. Thus keeping to their quarters, thousands fell ill daily and died without aid or help of any kind, almost without exception. Many perished on the public streets by day or by night, and many more ended their days at home, where the stench of their rotting bodies first notified their neighbors of their death. With these and others dying all about, the city was full of corpses. Now a general procedure was followed more out of fear of contagion than because of charity felt for the dead. Alone or with the help of whatever porters they could find, they dragged the corpses from their houses and piled them in front so, particularly in the morning, anyone abroad could see countless bodies. Biers were sent for and when they were lacking, ordinary planks carried the bodies. It was not an isolated bier which carried two or three together. This happened not just once, but many biers could be counted which held in fact a wife and husband, two or three brothers, or father and son. Countless times, it happened that two priests going forth with a cross to bury someone were joined by three or four biers carried behind by bearers, so that whereas the priests thought they had one corpse to bury, they found themselves with six, eight, or even more. Nor were these dead honored with tears, candles, or mourners. It had come to such a pass that men who died were shown no more concern than dead goats today.

All of this clearly demonstrated that although the natural course of events with its small and occasional stings had failed to impress the wise to bear such trials with patience, the very magnitude of evils now had forced even the simple people to become indifferent to them. Every hour of every day there was such a rush to carry the huge number of corpses that there was not enough blessed burial ground, especially with the usual custom of giving each body its own place. So when the ground was filled, they made huge trenches in every churchyard, in which they stacked hundreds of bodies in layers like goods stowed in the hold of a ship, covering them with a bit of earth until the bodies reached the very top.

And so I won't go on searching out every detail of our city's miseries, but while such hard times prevailed, the surrounding countryside was spared nothing. There, in the scattered villages (not to speak of the castles which were like miniature cities) and across the fields, the wretched and impoverished peasants and their families died without any medical aid or help from servants, not like men but like beasts, on the roads, on their farms, and about the houses by day and by night. For this reason, just like the townspeople, they became lax in their ways and neglected their chores as if they expected death that very day. They became positively ingenious, not in producing future yields of crops and beasts, but in ways of consuming what they already possessed. Thus, the oxen, the asses, sheep, goats, pigs, and fowl and even the dogs so faithful to man, were driven from the houses, and roamed about the fields where the abandoned wheat grew uncut and unharvested. Almost as if they were rational, many animals having eaten well by day returned filled at night to their houses without any shepherding.

To leave the countryside and to return to the city, what more can be said? Such was heaven's cruelty (and perhaps also man's) that between March and the following July, the raging plague and the absence of help given the sick by the fearful healthy ones tore from this life more than one hundred thousand human beings within the walls of Florence. Who would have thought before this deadly calamity that the city had held so many inhabitants? Oh, how many great palaces, how many lovely houses, how many noble mansions once filled with families of lords and ladies remained empty even to the lowliest servant! Alas! How many memorable families, how many ample heritages, how many famous fortunes remained without a lawful heir! What number of brave men, beautiful ladies, lively youths, whom not only others, but Galen, Hippocrates, and Aesculapius themselves would have pronounced in the best of health, breakfasted in the morning with their relatives, companions and friends, only to dine that very night with their ancestors in the other world!

Questions: What were the reactions of townspeople to this great plague? What impact did the Black Death have on urban society and economy? Did disease and death come to be particularly associated with towns?

CHAPTER ELEVEN: THE DANGERS OF URBAN LIFE

130. THE PLAGUE IN EDINBURGH, 1498–99

*Many late medieval towns tried to halt the devastating impact of plague by passing ordi-
nances to limit contagion. These extracts from the records of the Scottish town of Edinburgh
show the great lengths town leaders were prepared to go to protect the city's inhabitants.*

Source: modernized by M. Kowaleski, from *Extracts from the Records of the Burgh of Edinburgh A.D.
1403–1528*, ed. J.D. Marwick (Scottish Burgh Records Society, vol. 1, 1869), pp. 72, 74–76, selections.

28 March 1498. It is advised and thought expedient by the provost, bailiffs, and
council, because they are reliably informed that Swanston, the parishes of Currie,
Under Cramond, Groathill, Dreghorn, and the parish of Hailes [nearby villages]
are infected with this contagious infirmity of pestilence, wherefore we order immediately and command in our sovereign lord the king's name and ours, that no one
dwelling within the said bounds may proceed to come to this town [Edinburgh]
and enter it under pain of death. And that no inhabitants of this burgh and within
its bounds may house, harbor, or receive any of these persons or their goods, or any
others of suspect places, according to the first act, under pain of burning all of their
moveable goods and banishment from this town for all the days of their lives, unless
they first have been given license to do so by the provost and bailiffs.

17 November 1498. It is advised by statute and ordained by the provost, bailiffs,
and council, by the grace of almighty God, in as far as they may be diligent, to
eschew the danger of the perilous sickness of pestilence that has now risen to
the east and spread there, that from now on, by the charge and command in our
sovereign lord the king's name and ours, that any person dwelling within this
burgh and bounds cannot take in hand, in house, or harbor or receive anyone
who arrives on horseback or on foot to their house, place, or stables, whether rich
or poor, unless they come first to the bailiffs of this town and make themselves
known to them, and unless the bailiffs give them license to do so. Those that
break this ordinance are under pain of banishment from this town and confisca-
tion of all of their goods to the use of the common works of the town without
favor. And likewise, no one may go to Glasgow without license, under pain of
being thrown out of town for 40 days.

6 February 1499. It is advised by statute, in augmentation of the first statute [of 17
November], that no manner of persons may pass out of this town to buy or bring
to this town any type of merchandise, such as wool, skins, hides, or cloth, unless
they have license from the bailiffs and council, and with that they should bring
sufficient testimonials that they are coming from clean places, under pain of having their things burned and being thrown out of town if they break this statute.

27 April 1499. It is ordained by statute and forbidden for any person dwelling within this town to house, harbor, or receive any persons of Haddington [burgh to the east] or Kelso [to the south], considering the sickness that is largely spread there, under the pain of death, and also that none of those from these places may come within this town on pain of the burning of their cheeks with a hot iron and banishment.

Questions: What measures did the civic leaders of Edinburgh take to try and stop the spread of plague? Do you think the measures were effective?

131. THE URBAN MILITIA OF A SPANISH FRONTIER TOWN: CUENCA, 1190

Spanish border towns such as Cuenca faced constant threats of raids and violence because of their location on the frontier between the warring Christian kingdoms of Castile and Aragon, and the Muslim territories to the south. The fueros *or law code that governed Cuenca reflected these challenges, particularly in these clauses about guarding the town from the enemy, the citizens' military obligations (including the urban knights characteristic of Spanish towns: see doc. 36), and the division of spoils or booty.*

Source: trans. J. Powers, "Fuero de Cuenca (ca. 1190)," in *Medieval Iberia: Readings*, ed. O.R. Constable (Philadelphia: University of Pennsylvania Press, 1997), pp. 223–25.

XXX-Management of Military Expeditions
1. Military Regulations and Guarding of the Town
    When the council prepares an expedition [of the town's militia] against the enemy, prior to departure it should establish watchmen in each parish charged with the day and night surveillance of Cuenca. Also, two *alcaldes* [parish representatives] and an acting mayor should be appointed by the elected mayor. The appointed mayor and *alcaldes* are in overall charge of guarding the town. After the expeditionary militia has departed, all strangers should be expelled from the town. After sundown, should the night watch find anyone in the streets not carrying a light, the guards are to strip the offender and place him in confinement until morning. At that time, the offender should appear before the acting council; if the accused is a resident or the son of a resident, he should receive a beating. If the accused is a nonresident, he should be cast from the town cliff.
    The same guards will keep a fire-watch over the town, reminding householders to watch for fires in their vicinity; should a fire break out, residents should first hasten to the town gates to assure that these entries are well guarded, and only then extinguish the fire. This procedure is established

because in the past there have been occasions when traitors have set fires, and then while others were extinguishing them, the traitors opened the municipal gates and let enemies enter. If someone is suspected of potentially endangering the town in this way, the acting mayor and the *alcaldes* should expel him from the town, or hold him captive until the council returns. The same precautions should be taken to guard the town at harvest-time.

2. Concerning the Payments [Booty Shares] to the Town's Keepers
   Those compelled to remain in the town [during a military expedition] by the council should nonetheless have the same share of booty taken by the militia which is granted to any knight [who did serve]. This is done because those required to stay behind by council order had no opportunity to take any booty.

3. Concerning Those Who Remain [in the Town] Without Council Order
   All knights from the town or its territory who stayed home from the military expedition without council orders will pay a fine of two gold pieces. Foot soldiers in the same circumstance pay a fine of one gold piece, unless they were ill or out of the territory [thus receiving no call to arms].

4. The Master of the Household Sets Forth on Campaign
   Masters of each household are obliged to serve in campaigns of the militia, sending no substitutes. If the master is too old, he can send a son or nephew from his household, but no paid servant. Paid servants cannot excuse their masters from serving.

5. What Arms are Borne on Campaign, and Shares their Bearers Have
   Knights serving in militia expeditions who failed to bring a shield, lance, and sword will receive only one-half of their normal booty share. Foot soldiers who failed to bring a lance and a dagger or a club will receive no share. Foot archers bringing a bow with two bowstrings and one hundred arrows are due a half-share of booty for them; any substitution for this equipment denies them that half-share. Knightly archers trained in that skill who bring a bow with two bowstrings and two hundred arrows receive a full share of booty [for that equipment]; any substitution for this equipment denies them that share. A person wearing a long-sleeved mail jacket with a helmet should receive a full booty share for them, as does a person with a short-sleeved or sleeveless mail jacket with a helmet. Mail jackets worn alone receive a half-share of booty. Persons wearing only a helmet receive a quarter-share. Persons who bring chains with twelve collars [for holding prisoners] receive a full share. The share is reduced proportionately for a chain with fewer collars.

6.   That Children and Women are Prohibited from the Campaign
     Women and children do not go on campaign with the town's militia, nor
     receive any shares of booty.

*Questions: What dangers does the town anticipate when the civic militia is called away?
Who is required to serve in the civic militia? How are they equipped? What incentives does
the town offer its residents to serve its military interests?*

132. PARMA AT WAR

*Salimbene, a Franciscan friar from Parma, was an eye-witness to the constant warfare in
northern Italy during the thirteenth century as the German emperors tried to subdue the
Lombard communes (doc. 19) and wrest power and influence in the Italian peninsula away
from the pope in Rome. These struggles were also part of the ongoing disputes (docs. 30 and
38) between the Ghibellines (adherents of the emperor) and the Guelfs (who generally sided
with the pope). The shifting alliances stimulated by this warfare meant that communes could
be allies one year and enemies the next. In this part of his chronicle, Salimbene recounts his
experience of the siege of Parma.*

Source: trans. G.G. Coulton, *From St. Francis to Dante: Translations from the Chronicle of the Franciscan
Salimbene (1221–1288)*, 2nd ed. (New York: Russell & Russell, 1907), pp. 42, 116–22, abridged.

[1237: Parma is threatened by forces from the city of Bologna, which had destroyed a fortress of Modena] ... Then the advocate of the commune of Parma
(who was a man of Modena) rode on horseback, followed by a squire, through the
Borgo of St. Cristina, crying again and again with tears in his voice, "You lords of
Parma, go and help the men of Modena, your friends and brothers!" And hearing
his words my insides yearned for him with a compassion that moved me even to
tears. For I considered how Parma was stripped of men, nor were any left in the
city but boys and girls, youths and maidens, old men and women, since the men
of Parma, with the hosts of many other cities, had gone in the emperor's service
against Milan....

[1246. The Ghibellines of Parma expelled the principal Guelfs from the city and
burned their homes; the exiles regroup in Piacenza and return to Parma for revenge.] In the year of our Lord 1247 a few banished knights, dwelling at Piacenza,
who were valiant, vigorous, and strong, and most skilled in war—these men were in
bitterness of spirit, both because their houses in Parma had been torn to the ground,
and because it was an evil life to wander as guest from house to house—for they
were exiles and banished men, having great households and but little money, for

they had left Parma sudddenly lest the emperor should catch them in his toils. These men, I say, came from Piacenza and entered Parma, and expelled the emperor's party on the 15th day of June, slaying the podestà of Parma, who was my acquaintance and friend, and dearly beloved of the Franciscans.

Now there were many reasons why these banished men were easily able to take the city .... The third reason is that on that day the lord Bartolo Tavernario gave his daughter in marriage to a certain Lord of Bresci, who had come to Parma to fetch her. And those who met the exiles as they came to attack the city had eaten at that banquet, so that they were full of wine and over-much feasting; and they arose from table and fondly thought to overthrow all at the first onset. Seeing therefore that they were as men drunk with wine, their enemies slew and scattered them in flight. The fourth is that the city of Parma was wholly unfenced, and open in all directions. The fifth is that those who came to invade the city folded their hands on their breasts, thus making the sign of the Cross to all whom they met, saying, "For the love of God and the Blessed Virgin His Mother, who is our Lady in this city, may it please you that we return to our own city; whence we were expelled and banished without fault of our own; and we come back with peace to all, nor are we minded to do harm to any man." The men of Parma who had met them unarmed along the street, hearing this, were moved to pity by their humility, and said to them: "Enter the city in peace, in the name of the Lord, for our hand also shall be with you in all these things." The sixth is that they who dwelt in the city did not concern themselves with these matters, for they neither held with those who had come in, nor did they fight for the emperor; but bankers and money-changers sat at their tables, and men of other arts worked still at their posts as though nothing was wrong.

... When King Enzio heard that the Guelf exiles had entered Parma by force ... he came by a forced night march.... I lived in those days at Cremona, wherefore I knew all these things well. For at early dawn the men of Cremona were assembled forthwith with the king to a council, which lasted even [past 9 o'clock]; after which they ate hurriedly and went forth to the very last man, with the carroccio [war wagon] in their van. There remained not in Cremona one man who was able to march and fight in battle.... [King Enzio halts to wait for his father coming from Turin.] Meanwhile succour came daily from all parts to the men of Parma who had entered the city: and the citizens made themselves a ditch and a palisade, that their city might be shut in against the enemy. Then the emperor, all inflamed with wrath and fury at that which had befallen him, came to Parma [and gathers a large army] ... many nations came to [Emperor] Frederick's aid, such as the men of Reggio and Modena, who were for the emperor in their several cities, the men of Bergamo also, and other cities, as well of Tuscany and of Lombardy ... and they came from Burgundy and Calabria and Apulia and Sicily.... And Greeks, and Saracens from Nocera, and well-nigh from every nation under the sun....

Again, whereas the emperor thought in his heart utterly to destroy the city and transfer it to the city of Victoria which he had founded, and to sow salt in token of barrenness over the destroyed Parma; then the women of Parma, learning this (and especially the rich, the noble, and the powerful), betook themselves with one accord to pray for the aid of the Blessed Virgin Mary, that she might help to free their city, for her name and title was held in the greatest reverence by the Parmese in their cathedral church. And that they might the better gain her ear, they made a model of the city in solid silver, which I have seen, and which was offered as a gift to the Blessed Virgin....

[Salimbene returns to Parma, probably as a Guelf exile from Cremona.] Men went out daily from either side to fight: crossbowmen, archers, and slingers, as I saw with my own eyes; and ruffians also daily scoured the whole diocese of Parma, plundering and burning on all sides, and likewise did the men of Parma to those of Cremona and Reggio. The Mantuans also came in those days and burnt Casalmaggiore to the ground, as I saw with my own eyes. And every morning the emperor came with his men, and beheaded three or four, or as many more as seemed good to him, of the men of Parma and Modena and Reggio who were of the church party [the pope was associated with the Guelfs], and whom he kept in bonds; and all this he did by the riverside within sight of the men of Parma who were in the city, that he might vex their souls. The emperor put many innocent men to an evil death.... [Salimbene recounts several stories of torture, hanging, and drowning] ....

[The siege lasts from June 30, 1247, to February 18, 1248, when the emperor's new city of Victoria was taken.] For the men of Parma went forth from their city, knights and commons side by side, fully harnessed for war; and their very women and girls went out with them, youths and maidens, old men and young together. They drove the emperor by force from Victoria with all his horse and foot; and many were slain there, and many taken and led to Parma. And they freed their own captives, whom the emperor kept in bonds in Victoria. And the carroccio [a large war wagon used as a rallying point during battle] of Cremona, which was in Victoria, they brought to Parma, and placed it in triumph in the Baptistery ... Moreover the men of Parma spoiled the emperor of all his treasure—for he had a mighty treasure of gold and silver and precious stones, vessels and vestments....

Questions: What problems lay at the heart of this on-going conflict, and did it involve all or only some segments of the citizenry? How did different segments of the population view these conflicts? What can we learn about the Parmese fortifications and fighters, and the type of warfare they conducted?

Figure 11.2

The Civic Guard of Ghent

Communes were responsible for their own defense and so often needed to organize their own fighting forces, such as the civic guard of Ghent, a well-armored infantry unit depicted here. The most developed civic militias were in the Spanish towns (doc. 131). From a wall-painting in the chapel of St. John and St. Paul, Ghent, near the Gate of Bruges. Reproduced from Paul LaCroix, *Manners, Customs, and Dress During the Middle Ages and During the Renaissance Period* (London: Bickers and Son, 1870), fig. 36.

133. THE SIEGE OF CALAIS, 1346–47

The long siege of the northern French seaport of Calais by the English was one of the most important victories of the English during the Hundred Years War with France because it gave England a strategic landing place on the Continent that they held into the sixteenth century. This extract from Froissart, a Flemish chronicler who generally sided with the English, relates the story behind Rodin's famous sculpture of "The Burghers of Calais."

Source: trans. T. Johnes, *Chronicles of England, France, Spain and the Adjoining Countries*, by Sir John Froissart, 2 vols. (London: George Routledge and Sons, 1868), pp. v. 1, 169, 179, 185, 186–90, selections, revised.

On the king's [Edward III of England] arrival at Calais, he laid siege to it, and between the river and bridge built houses of wood, which were thatched in straw and brushwood and laid out in streets. And in this town built by the king, there was everything necessary for an army; besides a market-place, there were markets every Wednesday and Saturday for butcher's meat and all other sorts of merchandise. Cloth, bread, and everything else which came from England and Flanders could be had there, as well as all comforts, for money. The English made frequent excursions to Guines, and to the gates of St. Omer and Boulogne [towns in the region], bringing back great booty to the army. The king made no attacks upon the town, as he knew it would only be lost labor. He was sparing of his men and artillery, but said he would remain there as long as it took to starve the town into surrender, unless the king of France should come there to raise the siege.

When the governor of Calais [Sir John de Vienne] saw the preparations of the king of England, he collected together all the poor inhabitants, who had not laid in any store of provisions, and one Wednesday morning, sent upwards of 1,700 men, women, and children out of town. As they were passing through the English army, they asked them, why had they left the town? They replied, because they had nothing to eat. The king, on hearing this, allowed them to pass through in safety, and ordered them a hearty dinner, and gave to each 2 pence, as charity and alms, for which many of them prayed earnestly for the king....

The siege of Calais lasted a long time ... there were frequent skirmishes near the gates and ditches of the town, which never ended without several being killed and wounded.... The king of England and his council labored night and day to invent engines to annoy the town more effectively, but the inhabitants were equally alert to destroy their effect, and exerted themselves so much that they suffered nothing from them. However, no provisions could be brought into the place except by stealth, and with the help of two mariners.... By their means, the town of Calais was frequently victualled and by their boldness they were often in great danger, many times pursued and almost taken, but they escaped and slew and wounded many of the English. The siege lasted all winter.

The king had a great desire to be on good terms with the municipalities of Flanders, because he thought that through them he should more easily obtain his end. He made, therefore, frequent protestations of friendship to them to understand that, after he succeeded at Calais, he would reconquer for them Lisle, Douai, and all their dependencies. The Flemings, believing in such promises, put themselves in motion, about the time that the king was in Normandy, before he came to Crécy and Calais, and they laid siege to Bethune.... When the king of England came to Calais, he did not cease to send flattering messages and promises to the municipalities of Flanders, to preserve their friendship, and lessen their opinion of the king of France, who was taking great pains to acquire their affections....

[In the summer of 1347 King Philip of France gathered an army to relieve Calais, which was being steadily reduced by famine. The king of England set up a naval blockade to hinder French access to the town and sent a force to guard a bridge over the nearby river.] The French, therefore, were prevented from advancing further, unless they attempted crossing the marshes between Sangate and the sea, which were impassable. There was also, nearer to Calais, a high tower which was guarded by thirty archers from England. They had fortified it with double ditches, as a strong defense of the passage over the downs. When the French had taken up quarters on the hill of Sangate, those from [the town of] Tournai, about 1,500 men, advanced towards this tower. The garrison shot at them, and wonded some, but the men of Tournai crossed the ditches and reached the foot of the tower with pick-axes and mattocks. The engagement was then very sharp, and many of the men of Tournai were killed and wounded, but in the end, the tower was taken and thrown down, and all that were in it were put to the sword ...

[The French king is unable to relieve the siege, and negotiations go nowhere, so he gives up and the French army marches off.]

After the departure of the king of France with his army from the hill of Sangate, the people of Calais saw clearly that all hopes of succour were at an end, which caused them so much sorrow and distress that the hardiest could scarcely support it. They entreated, therefore, most earnestly, the lord John de Vienne, their governor, to mount the battlements and make a sign that he wished to hold a parley. The king of England, on hearing this, sent to him Sir Walter Manny and Lord Basset. When they had come near, the lord de Vienne said to them: "Dear gentlemen, you who are very valiant knights, know that the king of France, whose subjects we are, has sent us here to defend this town and castle from all harm and damage; this we have done to the best of our abilities. All hopes of help have now left us, so that we are most exceedingly straitened, and if the gallant king, your lord, have not pity upon us, we must perish with hunger. I therefore entreat that you would beg of him to have compassion on us, and to have the goodness to allow us to depart in the state we are in, and that he will be satisfied with having possession of the town and castle, with all that is in them, as he will find therein riches enough to content him."

To this Sir Walter Manny replied: "John, we are not ignorant of what the king our lord's intentions are, for he is resolved that you should surrender yourselves solely to his will, to allow those whom he pleases their ransom, or to put them to death. For the people of Calais have caused him so much trouble and have, by their obstinate defence, cost him so many lives and so much money, that he is mightily enraged."

[Sir Jean de Vienne asks for mercy, a message the two English knights bring back to their king, who refuses to agree, but the knights continue to plead the case of the Calais defenders.] Many barons who were then present supported this opinion. Upon which the king replied: "Gentlemen, I am not so obstinate as to hold my opinion alone against you all. Sir Walter, you will inform the governor of Calais, that the only grace he must expect from me is that six of the principal citizens of Calais should march out of the town, with bare heads and feet, with ropes around their necks, and the keys of the town and castle in their hands. These six persons should be at my absolute disposal, and the remainder of the inhabitants pardoned."

Sir Walter returned to the lord de Vienne, who was waiting for him on the battlements, and told him all that he had been able to gain from the king. "I beg of you," replied the governor, "that you would be so good as to remain here a little, while I go and relate all that has passed to the townsmen, for as they have desired me to undertake this, it is but proper that they should know the result of it." He went to the market-place, and caused the bell to be run, upon which all the inhabitants, men and women, assembled in the town-hall. He then related to them what he had said, and the answers he had received, and that he could not obtain any conditions more favorable, to which they must give a short and immediate answer. This information caused the greatest lamentation and despair, so that the hardest would have had compassion on them. Even the lord de Vienne wept bitterly.

After a short time, the most wealthy citizen of the town, by name Eustace de St. Pierre, rose up and said: "Gentlemen, both high and low, it would be a great pity to suffer so many people to die through famine, if any means could be found to prevent it, and it would be highly meritorious in the eyes of our Saviour, if such misery could be averted. I have such faith and trust in finding grace before God, if I die to save my townsmen, that I name myself as first of the six." When Eustace had done speaking, they all rose up and almost worshipped him; many cast themselves at his feet with tears and groans. Another citizen, rich and respected, rose up and said he would be the second to his companion, Eustace; his name was John Daire. After him, James Wisant, who was very rich in merchandise and lands, offered himself as companion to his two cousins, as did Peter Wissant, his brother. Two others then named themselves, which completed the number demanded by the king of England.

... There was the greatest sorrow and lamentation all over the town, and in such manner they were accompanied to the gate, which the governor ordered to be opened, and then shut upon him and the six citizens, whom he led to the barriers. He said to Sir Walter Manny who was waiting there for him: "I deliver up to you as governor of Calais, with the consent of the inhabitants, these six citizens. I swear to you that they were, and are at this day, the most wealthy and respectable inhabitants of Calais. I beg of you, gentle sir, that you would have the goodness to beseech the king, that they may not be put to death." "I cannot answer for what the king will do with them," replied Sir Walter, "but you may depend that I will do all in my power to save them." The barriers were opened, when these six citizens advanced towards the pavilion of the king, and the lord de Vienne reentered the town.

When Sir Walter Manny had presented these six citizens to the king, they fell upon their knees, and with uplifted hands, said: "Most gallant king, see before you six citizens of Calais, who have been capital merchants, and who bring you the keys of the castle and of the town. We surrender ourselves to your absolute will and pleasure in order to save the remainder of the inhabitants of Calais, who have suffered much distress and misery." ... All the barons, knights, and squires that were assembled there in great numbers wept at this sight. The king eyed them with angry looks (for he greatly hated the people of Calais for the great losses he had formerly suffered from them at sea) and ordered their heads to be stricken off. All present entreated the king to be more merciful to them, but he would not listen to them.

Then Sir Walter Manny said: "Ah, gentle king, let me beseech you to restrain your anger. You have the reputation of great nobleness of soul, do not therefore tarnish it by such an act as this, nor allow any one to speak in a disgraceful manner of you. In this instance, all the world will say you have acted cruelly if you put to death six such respectable persons who, of their own free will, have surrendered themselves to your mercy in order to save their fellow-citizens." Upon this, the king gave a wink, saying, "Be it so," and ordered the headsman to be sent for that, for the people of Calais had done him so much damage that it was proper that they should suffer for it.

The queen of England, who at that time was very big with child, fell on her knees and with tears said: "Ah, gentle sir, since I have crossed the sea with great danger to see you, I have never asked you one favor. Now, I most humbly ask as a gift, for the sake of the son of the Blessed Mary, and for your love to me, that you will be merciful to these six men." The king looked at her for some time in silence, and then said: "Ah, lady, I wish you had been anywhere else than here. You have entreated in such a manner that I cannot refuse you. I therefore give them to you, to do as you please with them." The queen conducted the six citizens to her apartments, and had the halters taken from around their necks, after which she newly clothed them, and served them with a plentiful dinner. She then presented each with six nobles [gold coins worth 6 shillings 8 pence each], and had them escorted out of the camp in safety....

The king, after he had presented these six citizens to the queen, called Sir Walter Manny and his two marshals, the earls of Warwick and Stafford, and said to them: "My lords, here are the keys of the town and castle of Calais. Go and take possession of them. You will put into prison the knights you find there, but you will send out of town all the other inhabitants, and all soldiers that may have come there to serve for pay, as I am resolved to re-people the town with English alone." ... They sent out of town all ranks of people, retaining only one priest, and two other old men, who were well acquainted with the customs and usages of Calais, in order to point out the different properties....

The king gave very handsome houses in Calais to Sir Walter Manny, Lord Stafford, Lord Warwick, Sir Bartholomew Burghersh, and other knights, that they might re-people it. His intentions were to send there, on his return to England, thirty-six substantial citizens, with all their wealth and to exert himself in such a manner that the inhabitants of the town should be wholly English, which he afterwards accomplished....

In my opinion, it was a melancholy thing for the inhabitants of Calais to be sent away from their inheritances with their children, leaving everything behind, for they were not allowed to carry off any of their furniture or their wealth.... They did, however, as well as they were able, and the greater part went to the town of St. Omer....

The king sent the thirty-six substantial citizens with their wives and families to Calais. Their numbers increased daily, for he multiplied and enlarged their privileges so much that many were eager to go there in order to gain fortunes.

Questions: What was life like in Calais during this long siege? How did its experience compare with the Parmese (doc. 132)? Why was the English king so angry at the people of Calais? Why did he demand that the six burghers of Calais appear before him as they did? What happened to the citizens of Calais and to the town of Calais after the siege?

134. CRIME PREVENTION IN LONDON

One of the chief means of crime prevention and detection in English towns was the city watch, to which all citizens were required to contribute in person. In some places the duty roster was set by the guilds, but in London it was set according to which city district or ward one lived in. The watch was the subject of many ordinances, including special instructions handed out for occasions when trouble might occur, such as major holidays (when celebratory bonfires could get out of hand), during political or wartime crises, or visits by royalty. The ordinances on the armor and weapons that members of the watch were required to have also make clear that the business of the watch could be dangerous.

Source: trans. H.T. Riley, *Memorials of London and London Life in the XIIIth, XIVth and XVth Centuries* (London: Longmans, Green, and Co., 1868), pp. 35, 80, 192–93, 272–73, 488.

(A) Watch and Ward at the City Gates, 1297

It was ordered that every beadle should make summons by day in his own ward, upon view of two good men, for setting watch at the gates. Those summoned should come to the gates in the daytime, and depart from there in the morning at daylight. These persons are to be properly armed with two pieces, namely a haketon [a quilted leather jacket used as body armor by foot soldiers] and gambeson [an inner jacket worn beneath a haketon or other armor], or else with a haketon and corset [a jacket of light armor], or with haketon and plates [metal armor]. If they neglect to come so armed, or make default in coming, the beadle should right away hire another person in his place, at the rate of 12 pence; this sum is then to be levied the next day on the person making the default.

In like manner, if any person summoned to watch within his ward makes his default, the beadle should substitute another in his place and on the next day take 3 pence from him for the use of the substitute.

(B) King's Concern with Crime Prevention, 1310

King Edward ... to the mayor and sheriffs of London, greetings. We have understood that many robberies, murders, and other trespasses are perpetrated, maintained, and iniquitously upheld by procurers and procuresses [and] common bawds in inns and other places in our city, the suburbs, and precincts. We are exceedingly surprised at this, seeing that you, who are most strictly bound to have decent as well as safe charge of the city and suburbs, not without negligence and default on your part, have hitherto allowed such crimes and misdeeds and other similar things to be perpetrated, maintained, and upheld there, to the disgrace of ourselves and the scandal of the city, and the grievous peril of very many persons coming to the city and its suburbs. We do therefore command you, on the fealty and love which you are bound to owe to us, strictly enjoining you to find a remedy to these matters and to cause these defaults to be corrected, so that honor may accrue from thence to ourselves, to you, and to the city, and due safety be ensured to the good men of our realm and all others who may have business to do in this city. Witness myself at Berwick upon Tweed, on 30 December, in the fourth year of our reign.

(C) Proclamation for the Safe-Keeping of the City, 1334

In the time of Reynald de Conduit, mayor of London. This proclamation was made on ... 13 December.... Because our lord king, whom may God save and preserve, is now engaged in his war against his enemies in Scotland, and every man ought to be most careful about keeping and and maintaining his peace, it is ordained and granted by the mayor, aldermen, and commonalty of the city of London, in order to maintain peace between all manner of people in the city, that no person, denizen or stranger, other than officers of the city and those who have to keep the peace, should go armed or carry arms by night or day within the franchise of the city, on pain of imprisonment and of losing the arms.

Also it is agreed that whoever should draw sword, or knife, or other arm, in affray of the people, should be attached straightaway and should be imprisoned without being able to find surety, according to the discretion of the mayor and of the aldermen of the city.

Also, we do forbid ... any people of the trades whose members may have committed an offence from making an alliance or understanding among themselves to support or to embolden the offenders or any man of these trades from seeking vengeance against another under color of such an offense. But let them make a good accord between the parties if they are able, and if not, let them bring the parties before the officers of the city and let them have redress before them, according to law and right demand.

Also, it is ordained and agreed that no person should be so daring, on pain of imprisonment, to go wandering about the city after the hour of curfew has rung out at St. Martin le Grand, unless it be some man of the city of good repute, or his servant, and then for reasonable cause and with light.

And because misdoers, going about at night, commonly gather in taverns more than elsewhere, and seek refuge there and watch their time for evil-doing, it is forbidden for any taverner or brewer to keep the door of his tavern open after the hour of the curfew, on pain of the same, that is: for the first time, on pain of being fined 40 pence; for the second time, ½ mark; the third time, 10 shillings; the fourth time, 20 shillings; and the fifth time, he is to forswear the trade.

Also, we forbid on the same pain of imprisonment any man at the feast of Christmas from going about with companions disguised with false faces [masks] or in any other manner, to play dice at the houses of the good people of the city, but let each one keep himself quiet and at his ease within his own house.

(D) Proclamation for Keeping the Peace within the City, 1353

It is ordered that every hosteler and innkeeper within the franchise of the city should warn his guests that they must leave their arms and armor in their hostels where they are lodging in the keeping of their hosts. And if the hosts do not give such a warning and any one is found bearing arms or in armor, for defaulting on this warning the host of these persons will be punished by imprisonment and other penalty at the discretion of the mayor and aldermen.

Also, that no alien should go in armor or should carry a sword, a pointed knife, or other arms in the city or in its suburbs, on pain of imprisonment and of losing such arms and armor.

Also, that every person of peace should come in aid of the officers of the city if need be to arrest felons and other misdoers and others contravening their [hue and] cry. And in the absence of the officers, every man of peace should have power to arrest such persons and to bring them to the houses of the sheriffs so that due punishment may be inflicted upon them.

Also, that no one should give maintenance, succor, prayer, or aid to any person who is of bad covin or alliance, or accused of evil, on pain of forfeiting as much as he may forfeit to our lord the king and to the city.

Also, that no one should hold an assembly within or outside of the city for making covin, confederacy, or alliance, nor make any collection of money in boxes or in any other manner, for the maintenance of his quarrels or for exciting evil riots, on pain of imprisonment and of forfeiture, as stated before.

Also, that no one should be so daring as to go wandering about the city or its suburbs after the hour of curfew is rung out at St. Martin's le Grand, unless he be a man of the city of good repute, or the servant of such a man, and he should do so for some real cause and with a light, under pain of imprisonment.

Also, that no taverner or brewer should keep the door of his tavern open after curfew is rung out at St. Martin's le Grand, under the same penalty ordained in the past.

(E) Setting the Watch During Summer Holidays, 1386

[Orders sent to aldermen] For the honor and safeguard of the city, we do command you to have good and sufficient watch of the people of your ward, well and befittingly armed and arrayed from that ward, on the eves of St. John [24 June] and of St. Peter and St. Paul [29 June] to come. And that you, arrayed in red, and your household and other good people who seem to you to desire the honor and profit of this city arrayed in white with a band of red, be in St. Paul's churchyard at 9 o'clock at the latest on these eves, with two cressets at least or more if you wish, to go with us through the city in the same manner as last year, or in better manner if you wish, to view and report on strangers. And do not omit doing this if you desire the honor and profit of the city.

Questions: Who served on the city watch and what were their duties? To what extent was the watch an unpaid police force? What law-and-order problems was the city of London most concerned to prevent in these ordinances?

135. CRIMINAL COURTS AND PUNISHMENT IN MARSEILLE, 1406–07

In late medieval Mediterranean cities like Marseille, a person found guilty by the criminal court was typically condemned to pay a fine to the clavaire, *the chief financial officer of the municipal government. Only in unusual circumstances (including insolvency) would someone suffer bodily mutilations or public humiliations (for punishments of more serious crimes, see docs. 72 and 73). Officials in charge of keeping track of municipal finances meticulously recorded the considerable income received from these fines. Several such registers have survived from medieval Marseille, containing thousands of entries. Each entry includes a brief description of the crime or violation and gives the name of the people involved. Below are some examples from the register covering the fiscal year 1406–07. Sixty royal shillings, a common fine, was roughly equivalent to two weeks' wages for an unskilled worker. There were 20 shillings per pound. A florin was roughly half again as much as a pound.*

Source: trans. D.L. Smail, from Archives Départementales des Bouches-du-Rhône B 1943, folios 2r and 46v–51v.

What follows are the monies received by the *clavaire* from the people listed below who were sentenced by the noble and distinguished lord Johan Dragoli, knight of the castrum of Pennes St. Julian, former royal vicar of the city of Marseille, in his first *parlement* [a public meeting held six times a year that dealt with important public business], held on Monday, the 14th of April, in the year of our Lord 1406.

And first of all, the *clavaire* received 60 royal shillings from Batrona Palhiere, who was condemned for this reason. Last year, on the authority of Johan de Ysia, a jurist and former associate judge of the courts of the city, and at the request of master Mosse Cohen, a Jew and physician, a certain ass was taken from her as security for a certain dry good [that she had not paid for]. Notwithstanding this, she stole back the ass.

[The following condemnation notices come from the last *parlement* of the year.]

The *clavaire* received 60 shillings. from Dominic de Scalis, a fisherman, who was condemned to pay 6 pounds for two crimes. First, he cast his net in front of the net of Jacme Turel, another fisherman. Second, he pursued Jacme over the sea by boat, throwing rocks at him. His fine was reduced to 60 shillings because he is a cleric.

Also 25 shillings from Franqueta, a Jewess…. She had spoken against Silona Gautelme, saying that Silona had stolen five sheets from her.

Also 60 shillings from Gabriela Borgone…. To the defamation of the good name and reputation of Ugueta, the wife of Guilhem Velans, a gardener, Gabriela said that she had seen Soldan the shoemaker lying in bed with Ugueta. She said that "she believed him to be a decent man."

Also 100 shillings from Jacme Albin, a smith…. He struck Ugona, the wife of Rostahn Cavalhon, two blows with a staff.

Also 50 shillings from Peire Toesco…. Against the tenor of a municipal proclamation, he was carrying a knife whose blade was too long.

Also 5 shillings from Ugona, the wife of Rostahn Cavalhon…. She called Jacme Albin, a smith, a "horrible dirty highland peasant."

Also 10 pounds from Peire Bacon…. With his dagger or knife, he wounded Johan Guerre, a goldsmith.

Also 100 shillings from Gabriela, the wife of Gabriel Borgon…. With her hand, she maliciously struck Ugona, the wife of Antoni Somorie, who was pregnant.

Also 40 shillings from Peire Johanin…. He thrashed a certain stranger with his fists.

Also 100 shillings from Honorat de Cavalhon…. He sold fish outside the fish market against the tenor of a municipal proclamation.

Also 10 pounds from Johan Ricau…. While quarreling with the wife of Johan Rohier over the rent of a certain house, she said to him: "If it seems to you that I have done you wrong, go complain to the Lord," and Johan shamefully responded: "there is neither lord nor lady."

Also 32 shillings from Ricavet Ricau.... He grabbed Guillemet de Montels by the arm so as to attack him. He had been condemned to pay 60 shillings but composed in the amount of 32 shillings because he is a cleric.

Also 100 shillings from Johan Mesquin and 100 shillings from the late Rostahn Chabert.... They bribed lord Johan Mounier [a municipal judge] with 75 florins to absolve Guilhem Terrussi and the late Isnard Brachet from a sentence of hanging.

Also 40 shillings from Ricart de Porto.... He gave a slap to Abrahamet de Bederida, a Jew.

Questions: What do these sources tell us about the criminal activities of women, men, Jews, Christians, and others? What sorts of conflict or dispute might have prompted some of these condemnations? Given the stereotype of the Middle Ages as a period of cruel and unusual punishments, how would you characterize Marseille's attitudes toward violent crimes? How did some of these disputes come to the attention of the court? What kinds of crimes merited heavy fines? Which were considered less serious?

136. THE ROAD TO RUIN IN DIJON, 1492

This deposition of a poor country girl whose father found her a low-paying job in the big city of Dijon shows the circumstances that led to her ending up in a private brothel. Doc. 92 tells a similar tale of a young migrant girl victimized by the difficulties of making a living in the big city. This inquest shows the path taken by one girl as she slid from poorly paid work to occasional and then regular prostitution to make a living.

Source: trans. L.G. Cochrane, *Medieval Prostitution*, by J. Rossiaud (Oxford: Basil Blackwell, 1988), pp. 179–81, revised.

Jehanne, daughter of Claude Joly of Charentenay, near Roy in the county of Burgundy, aged about fifteen years, as she says. Witness sworn on the Holy Gospels of God our Lord, says and deposes by her oath that it is true that about one year ago today her father, Claude, because the mother of the deposant went from life to death and because he had charge of other children, brought the deposant to this city of Dijon to serve a master. And put her [to work] in the *rôtisserie* [shop selling roasted meat] in this city of Dijon in the service of one named La Pucelle, where she lived during about ten months and even on a certain evening of this past winter [when], as she was going by candlelight up to the town to get some wine on the order of her mistress, a companion whom she did not know and knows not who he might be came to her and extinguished her candle and dragged her and lay her down under a sign for selling meat in the butcher shop and because she attempted to start to scream, covered her mouth with his apron, tumbled her on her back and knew her carnally. And from that day [she] has done no evil with her body.

When the fields were being weeded the deposant went [to work] by the day in a certain field outside the new gate with other girls and women, among whom there was one who was named Claude, whom she did not know otherwise, who interrogated her on her lodging and the earnings she made from her service, the deposant answering that she earned 2 francs, and this Claude said to her that this was not much, and that it would be better to go weeding at the harvests and the grape harvests by the day than to serve a year for 2 francs, and if she wanted to leave her service she could be well lodged with others in the house of an old woman named Jambe de Fer living near the Guillaume gate of Dijon. And by this means she was so induced that she left her service and went to the lodging of Jambe de Fer [Iron Leg], where she requested to be lodged to go to work daily like the others, paying for her lodging for every night one *niquet*, and on [this agreement] she was received. And from that time on [she] went on some days to hoe the fields, and other days stayed home and went down from the city and over the moat, and since it was known that she came and went and was idle, she was immediately hunted by the young men of the city, who pursued her so that she began to give them the pleasure of her body. And she could not name them except for a carpenter who she said was the son of Mongin the Carpenter, who brought with him other companions by night to the house of Jambe de Fer who, some fifteen days later remarked on the behavior of the deposant, who had known [a certain] Pierre Bouju when he was plastering the house of Philibert Truchot in the said butcher shop near the house of the said Pucelle, and whom she had served by carrying the mortar, and from then had known that he lived in the faubourg of St. Nicholas. She met Pierre on a certain day and asked him if he could lodge her in his house, who answered her. And in fact the deposant went into that house where she was in the daytime and until this present day has only slept two nights.

Questions: What factors hastened Jehanne's descent into prostitution? What was the role of reputation in Jehanne's plight? How did the places she lived mirror the life she led? How does her fall into prostitution compare with the tale in doc. 92?

CHAPTER TWELVE

THE URBAN ENVIRONMENT

Figure 12.1

Three-Storey House with Shop on First Floor

This drawing depicts a fifteenth-century house in Double Butcher Row, in the English town of Shrewsbury. The shop was on the ground floor, living quarters on the second floor, and bedrooms on the top floor. For a group of such shop/houses depicted in a French manuscript, see fig. 4.1. Reproduced by G.G. Coulton, *Social Life in Britain From the Conquest to the Reformation* (Cambridge: Cambridge University Press, 1919), fig. 20, facing p. 287.

137. AIR POLLUTION IN SOUTHWARK, 1307

Air pollution became a problem in the bigger cities, particularly in industrial suburbs such as Southwark, which lay on the south bank of the Thames across from the city of London. Sea-coal is mineral coal dug from the earth, as opposed to charcoal, which is made from wood. Both sources of fuel emit strong odors and smoke when burned.

Source: from *Calendar of the Close Rolls preserved in the Public Record Office. Edward I. vol. V. 1302–1307* (London: H.M.S.O., 1908), p. 537.

[To the sheriff] of Surrey. Order to cause proclamation to be made in the town of Southwark that all who wish to use kilns in that town or its confines, shall make their kilns of brushwood or charcoal in the usual way, and shall not use from now on in any way sea-coal, under pain of heavy forfeiture, and the sheriff shall cause this order to be observed inviolably. The king has learned from the complaint of prelates and magnates of his realm, who frequently come to London for the benefit of the commonwealth by his order, and from the complaint of his citizens and all his people dwelling there and in Southwark that the workmen in that city and town now burn [fires] and construct them of sea-coal instead of brushwood or charcoal, from the use of which sea-coal an intolerable smell diffuses itself throughout the neighboring places and the air is greatly infected, to the annoyance of the magnates, citizens and others there dwelling and to the injury of their bodily health.

The like [is issued] to the mayor and sheriffs of London.

Questions: Whom did the proclamation target as responsible for the air pollution? Who appeared to have initiated the complaints?

138. REGULATIONS FOR LONDON'S STREETS, 1297

Large cities such as London passed numerous ordinances to regulate the use and appearance of city streets. The abuses targeted by such proclamations give us a good idea of the everyday activities occurring in the streets of medieval towns.

Source: trans. H.T. Riley, *Memorials of London and London Life in the XIIIth, XIVth and XVth Centuries* (London: Longmans, Green, and Co., 1868), pp. 34–35, revised.

On ... [14 September] in the 25th year of the reign of King Edward, the following proclamation was ordered by Sir John Bretun, warden, and the aldermen, for maintaining the peace of our lord the king.

On behalf of the king and his son and their council, the warden and the alder-men ordain that no person should dare to be found walking through the streets after curfew rung at St. Martin's le Grand, and that every one, under the penalty that is usually awarded, should come when he is summoned to the watch, as well at the city gates as in the streets, armed and arrayed as he ought to be.

And that every one shall keep clean the front of his tenement, so that the streets are delivered from all incumbrances before Friday next at Vespers [in the evening], and where incumbrances are found after this time, let the owner be amerced [fined] ½ mark.

And that the stands placed in the streets for the sale of wares should be removed immediately, before Vespers.

And that on Sunday every alderman in his own ward should take such stands as can be found in the streets, and do what he wants with them. And if after that time any stand is found in the streets, the warden should do what he wants with them.

And that no taverner or brewster should keep the door open after curfew rung as mentioned above, and that whoever is convicted of this should be amerced ½ mark, which should be spent on repairing the walls and the gates of the city.

And that fullers' implements shall be immediately removed [from the streets] before Vespers.

And that pentices [a sloping roof or ledge that projects outwards over the edge of the building wall] which are too low shall be immediately pulled down, so that persons may ride on chargers [large war horses] beneath them.

And also that pig-sties that are in the streets should be speedily removed, and that no swine should be found in the streets, on pain of forfeiting them, in aid of making the walls and gates.

Questions: What problems is the proclamation trying to address? What do the regulations tell us about what citizens encountered as they walked the streets of London?

139. GARBAGE REMOVAL IN ENGLISH TOWNS, 1385

This national statute attempts to solve the age-old problem of how to dispose of town garbage.

Source: trans. G.G. Coulton, *Social Life in Britain from the Conquest to the Reformation* (Cambridge: Cambridge University Press, 1918), pp. 330–31, revised.

So much dung and filth of garbage, as well as entrails of slaughtered beasts, and other corruptions are cast and put into ditches, rivers and other waters and also in many other places within and around cities, boroughs, and towns of the realm and their suburbs, that the air there is greatly corrupt and infected, and many maladies and other intolerable diseases do daily happen to the inhabitants as well as to those dwelling, visiting and traveling to the cities ... to the great annoyance, damage and peril of the inhabitants, dwellers, visitors, and travelers. It is thus agreed and assented that proclamation be made in the city of London as well as in other cities, boroughs, and towns through the realm of England, where it shall be needed, within as well as without franchises, that all who cast and lay all such annoyances, dung, garbage, entrails, and other ordure in ditches, rivers, waters, and other places, should make sure they are completely removed, avoided, and carried away between this and the next feast of St. Michael [29 September] after this Parliament, upon pain of losing and forfeiting £20 to the lord king.

Questions: Where did the garbage come from, where did people dump it, and how did the authorities propose to remove it?

140. THE WATER SUPPLY OF DUBLIN

Access to clean water for drinking and cleaning was a high priority in medieval towns, which depended on wells and fresh-water streams and springs for drinking water. As towns became larger and more spread out, however, a patchwork of pipes and underground conduits connecting individual houses and whole neighborhoods to the main sources of water became more common. These extracts for Dublin show how these underground water systems were built up over time, as well as the combination of private and public funding used to construct them.

Source: trans. J.T. Gilbert, *Calendar of Ancient Records of Dublin in the Possession of the Municipal Corporation of that City* (Dublin: Joseph Dollard, Wellington-Quay; London: Bernard Quaritch, 1889), pp. 109, 114, 119, revised.

Transfer of a grant of access to the water supply, 1288
The mayor and commonalty granted recently to Sir Richard of Exeter, knight, a small supply of the city water through a pipe of the diameter of a goose-quill. His son and heir, Richard, transferred that grant to Henry le Mareschal, their well-beloved fellow-citizen. The mayor and commonalty confirm this transfer to Henry, on his petition, and especially on account of its usefulness to the neighborhood. The water is to be taken from the city pipe towards the corner which extends to Kilholmok Street, and to be brought at Henry's own cost to his house near the church of the Holy Trinity. It is agreed that one portion of that water may be taken from the pitcher of Henry for the use of the neighbors and others, reserving to him the pipe of the above-named diameter. For the grant of the water

to him and his heirs, he and they are to present annually to the mayor a chaplet of roses on the festival of St. John the Baptist [24 June].

Grant of overflow water in exchange for maintaining a part of the water conduit, 1329
The mayor and commonalty grant to William le Mareschal, their fellow-citizen, a plot of ground, and appurtenances, between the wall of the abbey of St. Thomas the Martyr and the curtilages [large yards] of divers citizens in the street of St. Thomas. The ground extends in length from the Abbey gate so far as the city cistern of the water-course, towards the west, and from there to the place where the water-course crosses, and, in breadth, between the ground of Robert Rowe, from the north, and the grounds of the canons of the same abbey, from the south, and, in length, so far as the small cross which stands in the raised way towards Kylmaynan, together with the fosse [ditch] towards the north near the gate at the Barrs. Permission is given to Le Mareschal to conduct and discharge at his will the overflow water through the fosse. He is to hold the ground by service of well and efficiently conducting and sustaining at his cost and labor the common city water-course from the last place at which water is brought towards the city so far as the city cistern, which is near the above-named abbey. The mayor and commonalty reserve the right of distraint [confiscation] and re-occupation, in event of temporary or continuous non-performance of the stipulated service.

Grant to access a cistern, 1329
The mayor, bailiffs and commonalty grant to Nicholas Fastolf and Cecilia, his wife, a reasonable supply of water from the cistern of Master Walter de Istelep, in the parish of St. Nicholas, so far as the tenement of Fastolf, in the same parish, through the middle of Rochelistrete. The pipe, in the narrowest part of its head, is to be of the width of a goose-quill. The annual rent is 1 penny. Nicholas and Cecilia are permitted to have water from the cistern in all their tenements in the parish through the pipe, with liberty to open the street for laying it there, and to repair and improve the conduit as often as necessary, provided that it be speedily done, and that they repair the street and sufficiently pave it at their own cost.

Questions: What were the main physical components of the Dublin water system? What type of responsibility for building, maintenance, and access did private citizens have as opposed to the town corporation or other institutions?

141. THE SOUNDS OF THE CITY: BELLS, HORNS, AND TOWN CRIERS

Every town had bells to signal such daily events as the dispersal of the watch at daybreak or the closing of the gates at curfew. They were also used to spread the alarm about a fire or the approach of the enemy. These bells were atop parish churches (where they were used to remind people when to pray or when services began), as well as a host of other ecclesiastical and civic buildings. Indeed, the cacophony of bell-ringing that must have taken place at some times of the day meant that towns often went out of their way to designate one particular bell as the most important. Horns were also used for a variety of purposes such as summoning people to court, while town criers made public announcements about, for example, new town ordinances, the latest news from the war front, or the capital punishments of felons. The following extracts show the ways that bells, horns, and town criers were employed in several English towns. For other references to the role of bells in medieval towns, see doc 138.

Source: (A) trans. W.H. Black and G.M. Hills, "The Hereford Municipal Records and Customs of Hereford," *Journal of the British Archaeological Association* 27 (1871): 466, revised; (B) trans. H.T. Riley, *Memorials of London and London Life in the XIIIth, XIVth and XVth Centuries* (London: Longmans, Green, and Co., 1868), p. 21; (C) trans. M. Bateson, *Borough Customs*, vol. II (Selden Society, vol. 21, 1906), p. 41, revised (New Romney and Sandwich); (D) trans. T. Smith and L. Toulmin Smith, *English Gilds* (Early English Text Society, original series, vol. 40, 1870), pp. 288–91, abridged.

(A) Hereford, c. 1154

… Concerning our bell, we use it in a public place where our chief bailiff may come by day or by night to give warning to all men living within the city and suburbs. And we do not say that it ought to ring unless it be for some terrible fire burning any row of houses within the city, or for any common contention whereby the city might be terribly moved, or for any enemies drawing near to the city, or if the city is besieged, or if there is any sedition between any people, and notice should be given of [these problems] to the chief bailiff [before the bell is rung]. And in these and all cases, everyone abiding within the city and suburbs and liberties of the city, of whatever degree they may be, ought to come at any such ringing, or motion of ringing, with such weapons as fit their degree, etc.…

(B) London, 1282

… At every parish church, curfew is to be rung at the same hour as at St. Martin's le Grand, so that they begin together and end together. And then all the gates are to be shut, as well as all taverns for wine or for ale, and no one is then to go about the streets or ways.…

(C) New Romney and Sandwich

New Romney, Early Fourteenth Century
... The horn should be sounded for the court. It is customary that at the hour when the bailiff is to hold the town court, he should have the common horn sounded at least twice in two parts of the town—in the market and at the cross—to warn the parties of the plaintiff and defendant, and the good folks and people of the town, who have business in the court or choose to come to the court.

Sandwich, Fifteenth Century
... When the Monday comes on which the hundred is to be held, the mayor's sergeant should go forth with the horn around 6 a.m. to certain places to sound his horn. And having sounded it, he should say these words: "Every man of twelve years or more, go to St. Clement's church to the hundred court, haste, haste!" And when the mayor, with the bailiff and jurats and all the community are assembled there, and the sergeant has come with the horn, the mayor's sergeant should stand outside the bar to proclaim the peace, and the bailiff's sergeant should stand to call the parties who are to plead there....

(D) Bristol, Ordinances of the Guild of the Ringers, Fifteenth Century

It is agreed and determined that every one that is or will be of the company or society of St. Stephen's Ringers should keep all articles and decrees that are or will be specified in this ordinance concerning the good government and peaceable society of the company. And no one should belong to the society except those who are of honest, peaceable and good conversation, and they should be ready at all times to defend whatsoever should be alleged against the company ... so that we ... may gain credit and reputation by our musical exercise. When others of our rich neighbors, hearing these loud cymbals with their ears may, by their sweet harmony, be enlarged in their hearts to pull one string to make it more sweet.... [There follows the usual guild ordinances on choosing officers, attending meetings, paying dues, and selecting new members.]

10. If the master [chief officer of the guild] ... should send to the Sexton concerning a peale that should be rung, either at night or in the morning, or at any other time that the master should want to ring, if he [the Sexton] refuses or neglects to come at the very hour that the master wants him to come, he should pay 2 pence for his offence, to be divided among the company.

12. If any one of the company, after the time when he comes into the church to ring, should curse or swear, or make any noise or disturbance, either in scoffing or unseemly jesting, the offender should pay 3 pence for his offense, to be divided as noted above.

14. If any one of the company should miss to strike his bell at the second sway, in the rising of the peale, he should, for his offense, pay 1 penny to the company.

16. If any one of the company should take a rope out of his fellow's hand when the bells [are] doing well, and make a fault, or fly off or come too near, he should pay 1 penny to the company for his offense.

Questions: When urban residents heard bells ringing or horns sounding, what did it mean to them? What problems did the Bristol guild of bell-ringers think might arise among their members?

142. LONDON BRIDGE, 1404

The original London Bridge was built of wood, but by the late twelfth century it had been reconstructed on stone piers separated by nineteen arches over the water to allow boat traffic to pass under the bridge. This extract from a rental of property whose revenues helped to maintain the bridge shows the variety of shops and houses on the bridge itself, where a chapel dedicated to St. Thomas Beckett (an archbishop of Canterbury murdered for political reasons) was also located. The bridge must have been very crowded since the rental records some 138 different tenements on it. This extract also shows the updating of the rental as old tenants (the first names which are crossed out) were replaced by other tenants, whose names (in curly brackets) were then crossed out as newer tenants (in pointed brackets) took their place in the next few years. The rents could be quite substantial when we keep in mind that the weekly wage of a skilled laborer at this time was about 2 shillings (which equaled 24 pence).

Source: trans. V. Harding and L. Wright, *London Bridge: Selected Accounts and Rentals, 1381–1538* (London Record Society, vol. 31, 1995), pp. 38–40, abridged.

On the Bridge.
On the east of the bridge beginning at the Staples [the bollards protecting the entry to the bridge] towards London there are divers shops which are worth yearly as appears.

Of ~~the wife of Abraham Seyntfeyth~~ {~~Thomas Paxon grocer~~} <Robert Oteleye> 53 shillings 4 pence.
Of ~~Thomas King~~ <Robert Oteley> 53 shillings 4 pence.

Of ~~Thomas Naunby~~ {~~Richard Burgeys~~} <Thomas Kyng> 53 shillings 4 pence.

Of ~~Simon Warle~~ <Thomas Kyng> 40 shillings.

Of ~~Peter Blak~~ <James Grene> 36 shillings 8 pence.

Sum total of the page ...

Of John ~~Hyde~~ <Westowe> £3 6 shillings [in margin:] <2 tenements>

Of Roger Gylot and Avice his wife 36 shillings.

Of ~~Michael Mordon~~ <John Soler> and Agnes his wife 30 shillings.

Of ~~Gilbert Peryman~~ <Richard Osgood> 32 shillings.

Of ~~John Goldesburgh~~ {~~Walter Laurence~~} <William Waryn> 26 shillings 8 pence.

Of Thomas Foule spurrier <and others licensed there by t'> 26 shillings 8 pence.

Of ~~John Chymbeham~~ {~~Richard Clyf~~} <John Welys cutler> and Johan his wife 32 shillings.

[in margin:] <Entered about 30 September 1410 ... Memorandum of glazed windows bought {~~lost~~} and benches in the hall, wooden wall {~~lost~~} <and 1 lattice>, shelves, partitions, chests {~~lost~~} hall and glazed windows in the shop>.

Of John ~~Vylere~~ <Gilot> 26 shillings 8 pence.

Of ~~Thomas Bromley~~ {~~William Kynton~~} <Thomas Robelard> 26 shillings 8 pence.

Of Walter Peryman 32 shillings.

Of ~~Margery Lynne~~ {~~Walter Weddesbury~~} <Thomas Hamond cutler> 23 shillings 4 pence.

Of ~~Peter Frenssh~~ <Walter Home and Isabella his wife> 33 shillings 4 pence.

Of ~~William Fouche~~ <John Chapman haberdasher and Agnes his wife> 31 shillings 8 pence.

Of ~~Richard Burgeys~~ {~~Thomas Jolyf~~} <Robert Darcok armourer and Geliana his wife> 21 shillings.

Of ~~Thomas Jolyf~~ <the same Robert and Geliana> 43 shillings [in margin:] 2 tenements.

Of ~~Richard Tabelmaker~~ {~~Alice Blak, late his wife~~} {~~John Trot~~} <William Rotour and Cristiana his wife> 21 shillings.

Of ~~Matilda Gerars~~ <Richard Brydbrook> 21 shillings.

[in margin:] <Memorandum of the necessities bought for the said house, as appears in the purchases in the 52 pence week of [the account for the year] ... 1406–7> ...

Of ~~Matilda Foulhardy~~ <Walter Takeneswell> 16 shillings.

Of ~~William Moger~~ {~~for 2 Katherine Moger~~} ~~36 shillings~~ <46 shillings 8 pence> [in margin:] <Increase 10 shillings 8 pence beginning from Midsummer 1408>.

Of ~~John Hert~~ {~~Richard Whityngton~~} {~~Andrew Rede~~} {John {~~Grene~~} ~~Yerde~~} <John Spen e *brochemaker*> 40 shillings.

Of John Verne <William Dyngewyk> 16 shillings.

Of Robert Whyte <Bartholomew Bownde purser> <and Margaret his wife> 16 shillings.

Of <the wife of> John Page <now {Thomas Waleys} his wife> 20 shillings.

Of <the wife of> John Page <now {Thomas Waleys} his wife> 16 shillings.

Of <the wife of> Walter Eggelof 20 shillings.

Of John Bury {Drury} <Robert Breton bowyer> and <Felice his wife> 13 shillings 4 pence.

Of John Charryng {Agnes Babyngton, art of linendraper} <Robert Breton boywer {and Felice his wife}> 13 shillings 4 pence....

On the west part of the Bridge.
On the west part of the Bridge beginning at the Staples towards Southwark [the suburb on the south bank of the Thames] are divers shops which are worth as appears.

Of Thomas Lydeyard cook for the first shop {Richard Abraham} {John Doke} <John Esgaston for both houses> 53 shillings4d <£4 13 shillings 4 pence[for both this and next entry]> <Memorandum of necessaries bought on 29 [rest of date lost]>

Of the same Thomas for the second shop {Richard} <John> 53 shillings 4 pence.

Of John Foster <Richard Peryman> 40 shillings <33 shillings 4 pence>
[in margin:] <Vacated at Christmas 1406. Entered at Michaelmas [29 September] 1407. Decreased from Midsummer 1408 6 shillings 8 pence a year> ...

Of John Marchall 40 shillings33 shillings 4 pence [in margin:] <Decrease beginning Midsummer 1408 6 shillings 8 pence a year>

Of William Banastre {John Sherman} {Edward Uphewe} {John Tornour} <John Ruston> 40 shillings <33 shillings4d> [in margin:] <Banastre vacated at Easter 1406 and the said Sherman entered at Midsummer 1405 [sic] with decrease 6 shillings 8 pence yearly beginning at Misdummer 1408>

Of Joan Blount {John Esgaston} <Robert Fairford> 60 shillings <53 shillings 4 pence> [in margin:] <decrease of 6 shillings 8 pence yearly beginning at Christmas 1404>

Of John atte Wode <the same Robert> 40 shillings 33 shillings 4 pence [in margin:] <Decrease 6 shillings 8 pence beginning at Midsummer 1408> ...

Of John Byle <John Goldisburgh and Joan his wife> 46 shillings 8 pence <21 shillings> [in margin:] <This John Byle twice paid a fine for his tenement in the time of William Chicheley, then warden of the Bridge, for putting in a tenant without licence.> ...

Of ~~Walter Crane~~ {~~Thomas Sawyer~~} <Alan Brymmmesgrove> <and Alice his wife> 26 shillings [in margin:] 2 October 1406 it was granted to the same T. that he might have his kitchen in the said house by licence of the masters [of the Bridge]....

Of ~~William Ayston~~ <John Hale fletcher> <and Anne his wife> for 1 <new> house with a stone pit over the cellar of Andrew Hunte there 46 ~~shillings~~ 8 ~~pence~~ <£3>
Of John Chyld <junior and Alice his wife and John Child senior and Matilda his wife> 36 ~~shillings~~ <£3> [in margin:] <2 tenements>

Questions: What types of shops or businesses were on the Bridge? What does this extract tell us about the rental market for property on the Bridge in terms of types of tenants, turnover, and rent fluctuations? Why were London residents willing to pay these relatively high rents for properties on the Bridge?

143. THE TOWN RENTS OF EDINBURGH, 1457

We can get an idea of the value of the properties owned by towns as a corporate body from the rentals they kept to keep track of their tenants and income they received, which represented an important source of urban revenue (see doc. 65); other urban institutions, such as the London Bridge (doc. 142) kept similar rentals, which also allow us to see the distribution of different types of properties in the town. The Edinburgh Tollbooth was a type of town hall where courts and town meetings were held, tolls and rents collected, and prisoners incarcerated. The "booths" rented out were market stalls. The "surety" was someone willing to pledge or guarantee that the tenant would pay the rent.

Source: trans. J.D. Marwick, *Extracts from the Records of the Burgh of Edinburgh* (Scottish Burgh Records Society, vol. 1, 1869), pp. 15–18, revised.

The setting of leases of the lands and annual rents of the burgh made in the Tollbooth, 10 November 1457, from the feast of St. Martin [11 November] of the present year to the feast of St. Martin 1458, and the following leases were made in the presence of the provost, bailiffs, and community of the burgh....

The first booth of the chamber of the Tollbooth is let to Allan Broun for 40 shillings. Surety Adam Cant.
The second booth is let to John de Dalrimpill for 40 shillings.
The third booth is in the hands of Malcolm Baird for 40 shillings.
The fourth booth is let to Henry Fowler for 45 shillings, on his own security.

The fifth booth is let to Jonete, spouse to the late William Scott, for 45 shillings. Surety James Dodd.

The sixth booth is let to Thomas Williamson for 45 shillings. Surety Walter Young.

The seventh booth is in the hands of Nicholas Spathy for 15 shillings.

The next booth is in the hands of George Fawlau for 45 shillings.

The two booths on the west side of the Tollbooth are let to Robert Murray for 43 shillings. Surety Walter Young.

The east booth on the south side of the Tollbooth is let to John Law for 20 shillings. Surety William Lawder.

The second booth is let to John best and is given to him gratis for his fee.

The third booth is in the hands of the town.

The fourth booth is let to John Gullane for 20 shillings. Surety James Schele.

The fifth and sixth booths [are] in the hands of the town.

In the bell-house, the house above the stair is let to James Taylor for 50 shillings. Surety Alexander Schele.

The second house is let to William Balfour for 45 shillings, on his own security.

The third house is let to Thomas Nort for 18 shillings.

The fourth house is let to Walter Carnis for 20 shillings.

The penthouse [a lean-to] under the stair is let to Adam Cant for 19 shillings 6 pence, on his own security.

The uppermost chamber is let to Malcolm Boyd for 30 shillings, on his own security.

The booth next to the penthouse is let to Thomas Whitelock for 40 shillings, on his own security.

The next booth is let to William Turner for 40 shillings, on his own security.

The next booth is let to William Hall for 44 shillings 5 pence. Surety William Turner.

The next booth is let to Harman Beltmaker, for 44 shillings 6 pence. Surety James Schele.

The next booth is let to Adam Spens for 44 shillings 6 pence. Surety Walter Young, deacon.

The fleshhouse [butcher's market] is let to the fleshers [butchers] for 10 marks, each being cautioner [pledge] for the other.

The butter trone [weighing machine] is let to Margaret Bertrem for £4 6 shillings. Surety Adam de Cranstoun.

The mills remain in the hands of the town.

Questions: What types of property did the town of Edinburgh own? Which were most profitable? Why were some tenants required to find sureties (pledges that they would pay their rent on time)? Do we have any idea who the tenants and sureties were?

144. BUILDING REGULATIONS IN LONDON, 1189

One of the earliest surviving ordinances about buildings in London was the "assize" of Henry Fitz-Elwyne, the first mayor of the city. The ordinances covered such matters as judicial procedures for settling property disputes, the responsibilities of neighbors who wish to build a wall between their properties, how to deal with the run-off of rain water from one property to another, building latrines, and obstructing the view.

Source: trans. H.T. Riley, *Liber Albus the White Book of the City of London compiled in 1419 by John Carpenter and Richard Whittington* (London: Richard Griffin and Co., 1861), pp. 279–81, 284–85, abridged and revised.

On Stone-Walls and Rain Gutters

If any person has his own stone-wall upon his own land of the height of 16 feet, his neighbor should make a gutter under the eaves of the house that is situated upon the wall, and to receive in it the water falling from the house and lead it to his own land, unless he can siphon it off into the street. And he should, notwithstanding, have no interest in this wall if he builds beside it....

Also, no one of those who have a common stone-wall built between them may, or ought to, pull down any portion of his part of the wall, or lessen its thickness, without the assent and will of the other.

On Building Latrines

Also, concerning necessary-chambers [latrines] in the houses of citizens, it is enacted and ordained, that if the pit made in a chamber be lined with stone, the mouth of the pit should be 2½ feet distant from the neighbor's land, even though they have a common stone-wall between them. But if it is not lined with stone, it should be 3½ feet from the neighbor's land. And the assize affords and grants to every one [this same right] in reference to those of former construction as well as to new ones, unless [the latrine] was made before the provision and ordinance which was enacted in [1189]. Provided always, that it should be discussed by view of twelve men or the greater part of them whether such pits have been reasonably made or not.

In the same manner, proceedings must be taken where disputes arise as to any kind of pits made for receiving water, whether clean or foul.

On Obstructing the View from Windows

Also, if any person has windows looking upon his neighbor's land, although he may have been for a long time in possession of the view from these windows, and even though his predecessors may have possessed the windows, nevertheless, his neighbor may lawfully obstruct the view from these windows by building opposite to them, or by placing [anything] there upon his own land, unless the person who has the windows can show any writing or reasons for why his neighbor may not obstruct the view from those windows....

On Impeding the Construction of Buildings

Be it known, that if a person builds near the tenement of his neighbor, and it appears to the neighbor that the building is unjust and to the injury of his own tenement, it is fully lawful for the neighbor to impede the erection of the building [by] giving pledge and surety to the sheriff of the city that he will prosecute. And thereupon the building should cease until a [jury of] twelve men or the greater part of them have discussed whether the building is unjust or not. And then it is necessary that he whose building is impeded should demand the Assize [that is, he could go to court to plead his case]....

The Advantages of Stone Houses

It should be remarked, that in ancient times the greater part of the city was built of wood, and the houses were covered with straw, stubble, and the like.

Hence it happened, that when a single house had caught fire, the greater part of the city was destroyed through such conflagration, which occurred in the first year of the reign of King Stephen [1135] when, by reason of a fire that broke out at London Bridge, the church of St. Paul was burnt. From this spot the conflagration extended, destroying houses and buildings as far as the church of St. Clement Danes.

After this, many of the citizens, to the best of their ability, to avoid such a peril, built stone houses upon their foundations, covered with thick tiles, and so protected against the fury of the flames. Thus it has often been the case that, when a fire has broken out in the City, and has destroyed many buildings, upon reaching such houses, it has been unable to do further mischief, and has been extinguished there so that the houses of the neighbors have been saved from being burnt.

Hence ... this ordinance, called the "assize," provided and ordained, in order that the citizens might be encouraged to build with stone, that every one who should have a stone-wall upon his own land sixteen feet in height, might possess the same freely and meritoriously ... it always being the duty of his neighbor to receive upon his own land the water falling from the house built upon such a wall, and at his own cost to carry off the same. And if he shall wish to build near the wall, he is bound to make his own gutter under the eaves of the house for receiving the water from it in order that the house may remain secure and protected against the violence of fire when it comes, and so, through it, many a house may be saved and preserved unharmed by the violence of the flames.

Questions: What do these regulations tell us about neighborly relations in large medieval cities? How were disputes about buildings between neighbors solved? What was the city's interest in making these building regulations—what problems were they trying to head off?

145. THE RISE AND FALL OF URBAN TOWERS IN ITALIAN TOWNS

By the twelfth and thirteenth centuries, noble families in the Italian city-states were constructing tall, thin towers meant to serve as strongholds and places of refuge when violent feuds broke out with other families. The Italian urban landscape was full of these towers; in Rome alone, there were over 300. Although the towers' military functions declined over time, they remained a potent symbol of the family's prestige and wealth. Tower building began to falter in many towns, however, as guilds or Signori (city officials drawn from the wealthy merchant class) challenged the noble elite's political power, and as vendetta was increasingly discouraged. These selections from communal statutes and a memoir also show the different attitudes taken toward the towers by the authorities and by the owners of towers.

Source: trans. T. Dean, *The Towns of Italy in the Later Middle Ages* (Manchester: Manchester University Press; New York: St Martin's Press, 2000), pp. 40–41.

(A) From the Statutes of the Commune of Parma, 1266

So that the men of Porta Nova wishing to come to the communal piazza to assist the commune and to maintain the podestà and the honor of the city, may come safely and without any impediment, and lest anyone might obstruct them, as has often been done by enemies of the commune and of the Guelf party ... the podestà is to have the whole tower and arch of the Ildizoni [family] destroyed to its foundations, and is to have the road opened up in a straight line going from the Porta Nova along the communal canal to the communal piazza ... and this at the expense of the men of Porta Nova, whether of the city or territory....

(B) From the Statutes of the Commune of Lucca, 1308

If during my term of office any person of the city or suburbs of Lucca builds or causes to be built a tower, whose height exceeds the tower of the sons of Paganello, Baratella and Boccella ... or that of the sons and grandsons of Bongioro as it now is, I [the podestà], having measured them, shall absolutely prohibit it from exceeding that measure. And I shall not permit towers already made and begun ... to be raised or built above the measure of those towers. And within one month ... I shall have all the towers in the city inspected by good and worthy masters, and those that I find taller than the said towers I shall have destroyed within two months at the expense of their owners....

(C) From the Statutes of Perugia, 1342

As cities, castles, and fortresses acquire great beauty and sometimes benefit from towers, and to knock them down in any way seems a disfigurement of the city, we decree and ordain in perpetuity that no one in the city and *contado* of Perugia ... may sell, donate, bequeath or give in any other way any tower in the city and suburbs to be demolished or destroyed ... and if he contravenes, he is to be punished with a fine of 200 lire. And from henceforth, no one is to dare or presume to demolish or destroy any tower in the city or suburbs, on pain of 1,000 lire for each tower.... And from henceforth no one is to dare or presume to undermine ... insert windows in or do any alteration to any tower as a result of which it might fall down or be in danger of collapse.

(D) From the Statutes of the City of Rome, 1360s

If from any tower or house taller than five *palariae* are thrown stones in any battle, fight or affray, the tower or house is to be confiscated to the city fisc, except that, if the owner wishes, he may redeem the tower or house for 50 lire ... but if stones are thrown from a house jointly owned among several kinsmen in a battle or affray of one more of the kinsmen, he in whose cause the stones were thrown is required to redeem and to pay the said penalties....

(E) From Matthew de Griffonibus, *Memoriale historicum de rebus bononiensium*, 1389

The tower of the Rodaldi family, which was opposite the houses of the Bianchi family, fell to the ground and destroyed four houses, two belonging to the sons of fra Bagarotto de' Bianchi, one to a merchant, Giorgino Cospi, and one to Enrico da Ferro. Giorgino later bought the site and built on it a most beautiful residence.

Questions: Why were the Italian communes anxious to control the building and height of towers? What do these readings suggest were some of the reasons why towers eventually became less common in the Italian cities?

146. BUILDING CONTRACTS FOR A TAVERN AND HOUSE, 1342

Few building contracts survive, but many must have been made to ensure that carpenters finished on time, charged the agreed-upon costs, and worked to the specifications desired by the client. In the first contract, a mason agrees to construct an underground vaulted cellar for a tavern, with a latrine at one end, stairs connecting the cellar to the ground floor, and a fireplace at either end of the cellar. The second agreement concerns the construction of a new house above the tavern. It was to have two upper storeys that jutted out and were topped by gabled roofs. One gabled section was to have a garret, and the other a hall with a larder (food storage area) and kitchen. Part of the ground floor and first floor were to be partitioned off to serve as a tavern. Further specifications are made regarding construction materials, the size of rooms, windows, and other parts of the buildings.

Source: trans. M. Kowaleski, from *Building in England down to 1540: A Documentary Study*, by L.F. Salzman (Oxford: Oxford University Press, 1951), pp. 433–34.

This is the agreement made between William Marbrer, citizen and vintner of London on one part, and Philip de Cherche, mason, on the other part. Philip is to dig to the depth of 17 feet beneath William's place on Paternoster Row in the parish of St. Michael at Corn where there are five shops ... and build there a vault with one garderobe [for a latrine] 7 feet in length and 7 feet in width and as deep as the water allows. And the vault of the garderobe should be of chalk [stone], and he will build the pipe of the garderobe of stone along the stone wall to the height of the first jetty [the projecting upper storey].... And the walls of the cellar's vault are to be of good ragstone [irregularly-shaped stone] as high as the first jetty towards the place and tenements of Thomas Leg, citizen of London.... And the vault and its arches are to be of freestone and the filling of the vault of chalk.... And the wall of the vault on the side of the street should all be of ragstone to the height of 2 feet above the pavement with 4 windows overlooking the street. And all the steps of the stairs of the cellar should be of good ragstone and cleanly made and the jambs of the door of the cellar should be of good ragstone. And he will build another stair of chalk with steps of ragstone ... between the first floor ... and the cellar. And he will build the steps of the door of the room of ragstone. And he will build good stone fireplaces on both ends of the cellar up to the height of the jetty. And all the walls of the vault facing the street should be 3 feet thick. Philip is to have for his work £26 and 1 mark sterling [13 shillings 4 pence] for a robe and he will supply all the masonry work, stone, chalk, lime and sand.... And underneath the steps he will build a vaulted stone "cave" [recess] with a door to the cellar....

This is the agreement made between William Marberer, citizen and taverner of London on one part, and Richard of Felstede, citizen and carpenter of the same city on the other part. Richard will build upon the plot of William in Paternoster Row in London, where there were five shops, a new house with two gabled roofs toward the street, each with two jetties. [It will be] between the room beneath the gate of the tavern of Thomas Legge, citizen of London, on the east (which is held by Sir John of Oakbrook, chaplain, for the term of his life) and the tenement of Thomas on the west and the south ... and along the street on the north.... And [there should be] two storeys above, beneath the one roof, a garret with support-ing posts six feet high, and beneath the other roof, towards Paternoster Row, he will build a room on the highest storey, and at one end of it, towards the north, a larder and a kitchen. And he will build all the partitions throughout the whole new house, and upon the lowest floor above the vault a closed room, and on the rest of the same floor he will build thirty seats for the tavern, and a partition ex-tending along the whole length of the lowest floor. And on the second floor above, he will build thirty seats for the tavern, and in the room a bay window towards the street and on either side of it a linteled window, and in the bedroom another bay window, with other such linteled windows on either side. And everywhere he will build windows ... [and] steps as they are required, and in the bedroom the canopy over the bed ... and William will supply all the timber and sawing of timber and will assume responsibility for the cost of all other things. And Rich-ard will receive for his carpenter's work £24 and a gown worth 20 shillings or its value in money ... Done at London on the day of St. Thomas in Christmas week in [1342]. And all the work should be done by the next feast of St. Michael [29 September 1343] and he will pay £10 in advance and the remainder as each stage is completed.

Questions: Do the contracts offer enough information to make a rough sketch of what the tavern and house would have looked like? What purpose did the various parts of the tavern serve? How many rooms were in the house, and what were they to be used for? Why does the contract specify specific building materials for some parts of the tavern and house?

147. A MERCHANT'S HOUSE IN KING'S LYNN

Extensive archaeological excavations and a good cache of surviving documentation have made it possible to sketch what one wealthy merchant's house and warehouse looked like in the eastern English port of King's Lynn at the end of the fifteenth century. Built around a courtyard, this house provided domestic accommodation in one wing as well as space for the merchant's business dealings, including storage of bulk goods shipped by sea.

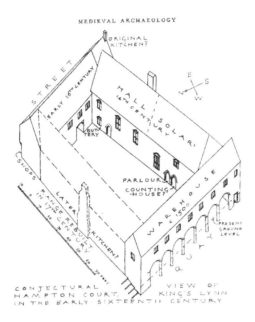

Figure 12.2

A Late Medieval Merchant's House at King's Lynn

This drawing, made after an extensive archaeological investigation, shows how wealthy merchants combined their work and domestic spaces. This complex, situated on the river Ouse in the English port of King's Lynn, is called Hampton's Court and is built around a courtyard. The south range was constructed in the fourteenth century and contains living space—the parlor and buttery on the ground floor, hall on the first floor, and solars (usually bedrooms) upstairs—and the merchant's office, called the counting house. The west range was built c. 1500 and contained an arcaded warehouse opened to the river quay. In the east range, built early in the sixteenth century, were located shops opening up to the street; the west range was not built until the seventeenth century. From W.A. Pantin, "The Merchants' Houses and Warehouses of King's Lynn," *Medieval Archaeology* 6–7 (1962–63): 180.

Questions: Were there obvious divisions and differences between the "private" space employed for domestic life, and the "public" spaces used for business in this housing complex? What helped to determine where certain rooms or sections of the house were located? Are there any features of this house that were similar to those sketched out in doc. 146?

148. CLOTHING AND HEAD-GEAR

Historians of dress have drawn heavily on manuscript illustrations of medieval people to analyze what medieval urban dwellers wore, how their dress may have changed over time, and how clothing (including fabrics, color, and design) varied according to gender, occupation, wealth, and region. The illustrations here depict the different types of clothing and head-gear worn by medieval people during the late Middle Ages, when the pursuit of "fashion" had become more important among the well-off. For documentary evidence of the clothing and household goods owned by medieval townspeople, see the inventory in doc. 45. For attitudes toward "fashion," see doc. 87.

Figure 12.3
Female Dress in Early Fourteenth-Century England
Two well-off urban ladies flank what appears to be a maid servant wearing an apron. Compare the head-gear worn by these women with the depictions in fig 12.7. Married women usually signaled their marital status by wearing their hair up and bound by a veil or other type of hat. Copied from medieval manuscript images, reproduced from Charles Knight, *Old England: A Pictorial Museum of Regal, Ecclesiastical, Municipal, Baronial, and Popular Antiquities*, 2 vols. (London: James Sangster and Co., 1850), fig. 1137.

Figure 12.4
A Rich Burgher of Ghent and His Wife
The long *houppelandes* worn by this man and his wife fall open to reveal tighter-fitting garments beneath. The quantity of fabric and the fur lining are indicative of their wealth. From a fifteenth-century painted window in a chapel in Ghent. Reproduced from Paul LaCroix, *Manners, Customs, and Dress During the Middle Ages and During the Renaissance Period* (London: Bickers and Son, 1870), fig. 58.

Figure 12.5
Male Dress in Early Fourteenth-Century England
The man on the left is dressed more richly than his companions, whose less elaborate dress signals their lower station in life. Compare the plainer head-gear favored by these men to the more lavish styles in fig. 12.6. Copied from medieval manuscript images, reproduced from Charles Knight, *Old England: A Pictorial Museum of Regal, Ecclesiastical, Municipal, Baronial, and Popular Antiquities*, 2 vols. (London: James Sangster and Co., 1850), fig. 1122.

Figure 12.6

Male Hats and Head-gear

These elaborate hats and head-gear were worn by wealthier men who could afford the fabric, linings, and decorations. Drawn from a variety of medieval manuscript illustrations, reproduced by Joseph Strutt, *A Complete View of the Dress and Habits of the People of England* (London: Henry G. Bohn, 1842), plate LXXXVII.

Figure 12.7

Female Veils and Head-gear

These drawings from a variety of medieval manuscript illuminations depict the different hairstyles and head-gear favored by medieval women. Reproduced by Joseph Strutt, *A Complete View of the Dress and Habits of the People of England* (London: Henry G. Bohn, 1842), plate XCVIII.

Questions: Why do you think medieval people favored such elaborate head-gear? What differences can you discern between the head-gear and other clothing worn by men and by women? How could the wealthy use clothing to distinguish themselves from those lower down the social ladder (see also figs. 2.1, 3.2, and 5.1 for depictions of the dress of the wealthy merchant class, and figs. 3.3, 3.4, 4.2, and 7.1 for depictions of the clothing of artisans and laborers)? Note also the differences between the appearance of the laity and the clergy, who are pictured in figs. 8.1 (a friar), 8.2, 8.3, and 9.2.

149. MEDIEVAL FAST FOOD

The cooks and pasty-makers operated the medieval equivalent of fast-food outlets since they sold ready-made "take-away" food. The ordinances governing this guild in London show the variety of roasted and baked meats and other items available to medieval townspeople. A "pasty" was a pie with a sturdy crust in which meat or another filling was cooked. To get some idea of the prices, keep in mind that an unskilled laborer in London could make about 4 to 5 pence a day in this period.

Source: trans. H.T. Riley, *Memorials of London and London Life in the XIIIth, XIVth and XVth Centuries* (London: Longmans, Green, and Co., 1868), (A) pp. 426, (B) 438.

(A) Ordinance of the Cooks and Pastelers, or Piebakers, 1378

The ordinances of the Cooks, ordered by the mayor and aldermen, as to divers flesh-meat and poultry, roasted as well as baked in pasties.

The best roast pig for 8 pence.

Best roast goose, 7 pence.

Best roast capon, 6 pence.

Best roast hen, 4 pence.

Best roast pullet, 2½ pence.

Best roast rabbit, 4 pence.

Best roast river mallard [wild duck], 4½ pence.

Best roast dunghill mallard [domesticated duck], 3½ pence.

Best roast teal [duck], 2½ pence.

Best roast snipe [game birds], 1½ pence.

Five roast larks, 1½ pence.

Best roast woodcock, 2½ pence.

Best roast partridge, 3½ pence.

Best roast plover [shore birds], 2½ pence.

Best roast pheasant, 13 pence.

Best roast curlew [long-legged birds], 6½ pence.

Three roast thrushes, 2 pence.

Ten roast finches, 1 pence.

Best roast heron, 18 pence.

Best roast bittern [small nocturnal herons], 20 pence.

Three roast pigeons, 2½ pence.

Ten eggs, 1 penny....

The best capon cooked in pasty, 8 pence.

The best hen baked in a pasty, 5 pence.

The best lamb, roasted, 7 pence.

(B) Ordinances of the Pastelers, or Piebakers as to Pasties, 1379

Because the pastelers of the city of London have heretofore baked in pasties rabbits, goose and entrails not befitting and sometimes stinking, in deceit of the people, and also have baked beef in pasties and sold the same for venison in deceit of the people; therefore, by assent of the four master pastelers, and at their prayer, it is ordered and assented to:

In the first place, that no one of this trade shall bake rabbits in pasties for sale, on pain of paying, the first time if found guilty, 6 shillings 8 pence, to the use of the chamber [city council], and of going bodily to prison, at the will of the mayor; the second time, 13 shillings 4 pence to the use of the chamber, and of going etc.; and of the third time, 20 shillings to the use of the chamber, and of going etc.

Also, that no one of the trade should buy of any cook of Bredestreet, or, at the houses of the great lords, of the cooks of such lords, any entrails from capons, hens, or geese, to bake in a pasty and sell it, under the same penalty.

Also, that no one should bake beef in a pasty for sale, and sell it as venison, under the same penalty.

Also, that no one of the trade should bake either whole geese in a pasty, halves of geese, or quarters of geese, for sale, under pain of the same penalty.

Questions: How did the fast food of medieval London compare with fast food today in terms of types and prices? Based on price, what were the most prized delicacies? Can these ordinances tell us anything about the diet of city dwellers? What problems were the ordinances trying to stamp out in the sale of fast food?

150. MEAT CONSUMPTION

We can find out a good deal about the diet of medieval townspeople from archaeological ex-cavations. The animal bones found in back-yard pits, for example, can tell us about the type of meat consumed, whether it was from a young or old animal (or male or female), how it was butchered, and what cuts of meat were most popular. Even more interpretation is possible when the pits can be associated with a particular time period, or the property of an individual of a particular social group. There are two major ways to analyze the bone data, illustrated here with data from excavations in the small English town of Exeter. One (Table 12.1) counts the number of bone fragments found for each species; the second method calculates the actual amount of meat that would have been available for the number of bones found (obvi-ously, a cow provided more meat than a pig). The second table (Table 12.2), which draws on documentary evidence, is compiled from information in the household accounts of the bishop of Arles, a medium-sized town in southern France. The accounts record what the bishop's household—including his officials, visitors, staff, and servants—ate each day, allowing us to see the frequency with which certain types of meats were consumed.

Source: (A) data from M. Maltby, *Faunal Studies on Urban Sites: The Animal Bones from Exeter 1971–1978* (Exeter Archaeological Reports, vol. 2, 1979), pp.137, 140; (B) trans. M. Kowaleski, from *Ravitaillement et alimentation en Provence aux XIV* et XV* siècles*, by L. Stouff (Paris-La Haye: Mouton, 1970), p. 244.

(A) Table 12.1: Analysis of Animal Bones from Principal Livestock in Medieval Exeter

Species	Years			
	1100–1200	1250–1300	1300–1350	1350–1500
I: Bone Fragments Found				
Cattle	43.1%	40.5%	43.1%	44.1%
Sheep/Goat	42.6%	45.5%	45.9%	46.1%
Pig	14.3%	14.0%	11.0%	9.8%
II: Meat Weight Supported by Bone Fragments				
Cattle	76.7%	75.7%	73.6%	n/a
Sheep/Goat	12.7%	14.0%	18.2%	n/a
Pig	10.6%	10.3%	8.2%	n/a

(B) Table 12.2: Meat Consumption in the Household of the Bishop of Arles

Type of Meat	No. of Days Eaten (by Year)		
	1424	1429	1430
Meat, unspecified type	15	–	–
Mutton (sheep)	179	191	178
Lamb	34	34	3
Ewe (female sheep)	–	2	4
Goat	31	7	15
Beef	65	68	74
Veal	8	–	14
Fresh pork	22	7	16
Young chicken	11	6	8
Chicken	2	1	1
Pigeon	5	1	–
Goose	–	–	1
Partridge	1	1	1
Capons	1	–	–
Boar	1	–	–
Tripe	–	–	7
Rabbit	3	10	7
Hare	–	–	1

Questions: What meat did Exeter residents consume in the largest quantitites? What could account for the slight rise in meat from sheep and goat by the early fourteenth century, a period when the countryside was overpopulated? How often did the bishop's household at Arles consume the categories of meat counted in the Exeter archaeological exercise (beef, mutton/goat, and pork)?

CHAPTER THIRTEEN

THE IDEALIZED CITY

Figure 13.1

A Cityscape

Although the top of this engraving of late medieval city streets shows rather fanciful spirelets and vanes on top of the towers and turrets, the lower part accurately represents a medieval street. On the right, timber houses with the narrow gable ends turned toward the street (in order to maximize valuable street frontage) contain shops on the ground level (see also figs. 4.1, 12.1, 12.2) protected by a projecting half roof or "penthouse" (doc. 68). Note the patterns produced by the timbers showing through the stucco walls of the houses, as well as what may be raised plaster ornamentation. To the left is a grander civic building, perhaps the town hall or a guild hall since it too has shops on the ground floor. The elaborate windows and exterior wall paintings proclaim the wealthy status of the building. On the far left is a pulley being used to haul a bucket of mortar up to a mason who is constructing the wall of another building (the perspective of the scene, as in many medieval drawings, does not necessarily conform to modern rules of perspective). The size and elaborate decoration of the buildings, as well as the activities of the workmen, craft assistants, shoppers, shopkeepers, and simple passers-by give us a good idea of the busy ambience of a medieval town. Based on a fifteenth-century French engraving, reproduced from E.L. Cutts, *Scenes and Characters of the Middle Ages* (London: H. Virtue and Co., 1902), p. 536.

151. A DESCRIPTION OF LONDON, C. 1173

This description of London was written by William Fitzstephen, who placed it at the begin-ning of his biography of his employer, Thomas Beckett, an archbishop of Canterbury whose murder in the cathedral (by henchmen of King Henry II of England) encouraged William and others to propose him for sainthood. In writing this laudatory description of the city where both he and Thomas were born, Fitzstephen makes many classical allusions that were meant to elevate the tone of the description and thus Thomas's importance.

Source: trans. H. Morley, *A Survay of London*, by John Stow (London: George Routledge and Sons, 1890), pp. 22–29, revised.

Of Its Site

Among the noble cities of the world that fame celebrates, the city of London of the kingdom of the English is the one seat that pours out its fame more widely, sends to farther lands its wealth and trade, and lifts its head higher than the rest. It is happy in the healthiness of its air, in the Christian religion, in the strength of its defenses, the nature of its site, the honor of its citizens, the modesty of its matrons; pleasant in sports, fruitful of noble men. Let us look into these things separately.

Of the Mildness of Air

If the clemency of the skies there softens minds, it is not so that they corrupt in Venus [the Roman goddess of love and beauty], but that they be not fierce and bestial, but rather benign and liberal.

Of Religion

There is in the church there the episcopal seat of St. Paul; once it was a metropoli-tan [where one of the highest church leaders resided], and it is thought will again become so if the citizens return into the island, unless perhaps the archiepiscopal title of Saint Thomas the Martyr, and his bodily presence, preserve to Canterbury, where it is now, a perpetual dignity. But as Saint Thomas made both cities illus-trious, London by his rising, Canterbury by his setting [as archbishop there], in regard of that saint, with admitted justice, each can claim advantage of the other. There are also, as regards the cultivation of the Christian faith, in London and the suburbs, thirteen larger conventual [attached to a religious insitution], besides 120 lesser parish churches.

Of the Strength of the City

It has on the east the Palatine Castle [the Tower of London], very great and strong, of which the ground plan and the walls rise from a very deep foundation, fixed with a mortar tempered by the blood of animals. On the west are two towers very strongly fortified, with the high and great wall of the city having seven double gates, and towered to the north at intervals. London was walled and towered in like manner on the south, but the great fish-bearing Thames river which glides there, with ebb and flow from the sea, by course of time has washed against, loosened, and thrown down those walls. Also upwards to the west the royal palace [at Westminster] is conspicuous above the river, an incomparable building with ramparts and bulwarks, two miles from the city, joined to it by a populous suburb.

Of Gardens

Everywhere outside the houses of those living in the suburbs are joined to them, planted with trees, the spacious and beautiful gardens of the citizens.

Of Pasture and Tilled Lands

Also there are, on the north side, pastures and a pleasant meadow land, through which flow river streams, where the turning wheels of mills are put in motion with a cheerful sound. Very near lies a great forest, with woodland pastures, coverts [lairs] of wild animals: stags, fallow deer, boars and wild bulls. The tilled lands of the city are not of barren grave, but fat plains of Asia that yield luxuriant crops, and fill their tillers' barns with Ceres's [the Roman goddess of agriculture] sheaves.

Of Springs

Three are also around London, on the north side, excellent suburban springs, with sweet, wholesome, and clear water that flows rippling over the bright stones; among which Holy Well, Clerken Well, and St. Clement's are held to be of most note. These are frequented by great numbers of people, and visited more by scholars and youth of the city when they go out for fresh air on summer evenings. It is a good city indeed when it has a good master.

Of Honor of the Citizens

That city is honored by her men, adorned by her arms, populous with many inhabitants, so that in the time of slaughter of war under King Stephen [a civil war in the mid-twelfth century], of those going out to a muster 20,000 horsemen and 60,000 men on foot were estimated to be fit for war. Above all other citizens, everywhere, the citizens of London are regarded as conspicuous and noteworthy for handsomeness of manners and of dress, at table, and in way of speaking.

Of Matrons

The city matrons [wives] are true Sabine women [noteworthy for their bravery and loyalty].

Of Schools

In London the three principal churches have, by privilege and ancient dignity, famous schools; yet very often by support of some personage, or of some teachers who are considered notable and famous in philosophy, there are also other schools by favor and permission. On feast days the masters have festival meetings [for their pupils] in these churches. Their scholars dispute, some by demonstration, others by dialectics; some recite enthymemes [syllogisms in which one of the premises is implicit], others do better in using perfect syllogisms. Some are exercised in disputation for display, as wrestling with opponents; others for truth, which is the grace of perfectness. Sophists who feign are judged happy in their heap and flood of words. Others parlogize [make an illogical argument]. Some orators, now and then, say in their rhetorical speeches something apt for persuasion, careful to observe rules of their art, and to omit none of the contingents. Boys of different schools strive against one another in verses, and contend about the principles of grammar and rules of the past rhymes, and verses the old trifling banter, and with Fescinnine [ribald] license freely pull their comrades to pieces, without giving their names, fling at them scoffs and sarcasms, touch the faults of schoolfellows or perhaps of greater people with Socratic salt, or bite harder with Theonine tooth....

Of the Ordering of the City

Those engaging in the several kinds of business, sellers of several things, contractors for several kinds of work, are distributed every morning into their several localities and shops. Besides, there is in London on the river bank, among the wines in ships and cellars sold by the vintners, a public cook shop. There, eatables are to be found every day, according to the season, dishes of meat, roast, fried and boiled, great and small fish, coarser meats for the poor, more delicate for the rich, of game, fowls and small birds. If there should come suddenly to any of the citizens friends, weary from a journey and too hungry to like waiting till fresh food is bought and cooked, with water to their hands comes bread ... while one runs to river bank, and there is all that can be wanted. However great the multitude of soldiers or travellers entering the city, or preparing to go out of it, at any hour of the day or night—that these may not fast too long and those may not go out supperless—they turn hither, if they please, where every man can refresh himself in his own way. Those who would care for themselves luxuriously, when set before the delicacies there to be found, would not desire sturgeon nor the bird of Africa not the Ionian godwit. For this is the public kitchen, very convenient to the city, and part of its civilisation.... Ouside one of the gates there, immediately in the suburb, is a certain smooth field [Smithfield], field in fact and name. Every Friday, unless it be a higher day of appointed solemnity, there is in it a famous show of nobles horses for sale. Earls, barons, knights, and many citizens who are in town, come to see or buy. It is pleasant to see the steppers in quick trot going gently up and down, their feet on each side alternately rising and falling ... [he then offers an extended description of the different kinds of horses available for every age, social status, and occupation.] To this city from every nation under heaven merchants delight to bring their trade by sea....

London is, on the faith of the chroniclers, a much older city than Rome, for by the same Trojan forefathers it was founded by Brutus before [Rome was founded] by Romulus and Remus. Whence it is that they still have the same laws established in common. This city, like that, is divided into wards, has annual sheriffs for its consuls, has senatorial and lower magistrates, sewers and aqueducts in its streets, its proper places and courts for cases of each kind—deliberative, demonstrative, and judicial. It has assemblies on appointed days. I do not think there is a city with more commendable customs of church attendance, honor to God's ordinances, keeping sacred festivals, contracting marriages, celebration of nuptials, preparing feasts, cheering the guests, and also in care for funerals and the interment of the dead. The only pests of London are the immoderate drinking of fools and the frequency of fires. To this may be added that nearly all the bishops, abbots, and magnates of England are, as it were, citizens and freemen of London; having there their own splendid houses, to which they resort, where they spend largely when summoned to great councils by the king or by their metropolitans [ecclesiastical leaders], or drawn by their own private affairs.

Of Sports
[Here Fitzstephen enumerates the different games and past-times of Londoners; see doc. 117.]

The city of London has brought forth some men who made many kingdoms and the Roman empire subject to themselves; and many others, lords over the world, whom virtue lifted to the skies, as was promised in Apollo's [god of sunlight, prophecy, music, and poetry] oracle to Brutus....

In Christian times London brought forth that noble emperor Constantine, who gave the city of Rome and all the insignia of the empire of God and Saint Peter, and to Pope Silvester, whom he served in office of a stirrup-holder, rejoicing not to be called Emperor, so much as defender of the holy Roman church; and lest his presence should cause noise of secular affairs to break the peace of our lord the pope, he departed from the city given by him to our lord the pope and built for himself the city of Byzantium [Constantinople]. London also in modern times has produced illustrious and magnificent rulers: the empress Matilda, King Henry III [a son of Henry II], and Saint Thomas, the archbishop, glorious martyr of Christ, than whom it bore none purer, and there was none more bound to whatever is good in the Roman world.

Questions: Why did Fitzstephen go out of his way to compare London to Rome? What physical attributes of the city of London did Fitzstephen think are most noteworthy? What aspects of the personalities of Londoners does he single out? Which attributes or characteristics of London do you think he believed most admirable—features of London's topography, its economy, its intellectual or ecclesiastical life, its politics, or its sociability? What parts of Fitzstephen's description might accurately reflect the real London of the late eleventh century? What aspects of London in this period can also be found in large cities today?

152. IN PRAISE OF MILAN'S TOWNSCAPE, 1288

These extracts are from "On the Marvels of the City of Milan," by Bonvesin dell Riva, a thirteenth-century friar writing enthusiastically about his home town. Although we cannot take his figures as accurate, they are not as exaggerated as some medieval statistics are. Milan at this time probably had a population close to 200,000, while the surrounding countryside under its jurisdiction (the contado, *here called its "county"), was much larger. A cubit is a little less than one-half of a meter.*

Source: trans. R.S. Lopez and I.W. Raymond, *Medieval Trade in the Mediterranean World* (New York: Columbia University Press, 1955), pp. 61–65, abridged.

In Praise of Milan's Housing

In regard to housing ... the truth is there before the eyes of those who see. The streets in this city are quite wide, the palaces quite beautiful, the houses packed in, not scattered but continuous, stately, adorned in a stately manner.

1. Dwellings with doors giving access to the public streets have been found to number about 12,500, and in their number are very many in which many families live together with crowds of dependents. And this indicates the astonishing density of population of citizens.

2. The roofed commons [opens to all] neighbors in those squares which are popularly called *coperti* [a roofed arcade] almost reach the record number of 60.

3. The court of the commune, befitting such a great city, spreads over an area of ten *pertiche* [roughly equal to 66 acres] or thereabouts. And in order to make this more easily understandable perchance to some people, [I shall specify that it] measures 130 cubits from east to west and 136 from north to south. In the midst of it stands a wonderful palace, and in the court itself there is a town, in which are the four bells of the commune. On the eastern side is a palace in which are the rooms of the podestà and of the judges, and at its end on

the northern side is the chapel of the podestà, built in honor of our patron, Blessed Ambrose [an early bishop of Milan]. And another palace prolongs the court on the north; so, similarly, on the west. To the south there is also a hall where the sentences of condemnation are publicly proclaimed.

4. The city itself is ringed as a circle, and its wonderful rounded shape is a mark of its perfection ... [a description of the walls and moats follows.]

5. Outside the wall of the moat there are so many suburban houses that they alone would be enough to constitute a city....

6. The main gates of the city are also very strong, and they reach the number of six. The secondary gates, named *pusterle*, are ten....

7. The sanctuaries of the saints ... are about 200 in the city alone, having 480 altars....

8. [In honor of the Virgin Mary] 36 churches have been built in the city, and undoubtedly there are more in the surrounding county....

9. The steeples, built in the manner of towers, are about 120 in the city....

10. In the county there are pleasant and delightful localities, even stately towns, 50 in number; and among them is Monza, ten miles distant from the city, worthier to be named a city than a town. Indeed, 150 villages with castles are subject to the jurisdiction of our commune, and among them there are a great many, each of which has more than 500 inhabitants able to bear arms. And in these very towns as well as in the villages not only farmers and craftsmen live but also very many magnates of high nobility. And there are also other isolated buildings, some of which are called mills and others, popularly, *cassine* [farm houses]—the infinite number of which I can hardly estimate....

In Praise of Milan's Population

4. Then there are in the city 94 chapels....

5. In the city there are six convents of monks, and the nunneries are eight....

6. Again, in the city, including the suburbs, which are always to be regarded as included whenever the city is mentioned, there are ten hospitals for the sick, all properly endowed with sufficient temporal resources. The principal one of these

is the Hospital of the Brolo, very rich in precious possessions; it was founded in 1145 by Goffredo de Bussero. In it, as its friars and deacons testify, at times and particularly in the days of dearth [during Lent?], when count is made, there are found more than 500 poor bed patients and just as many more not lying down. All of these receive food at the expense of the hospital itself. Besides them, also, no less than 350 babies and more, placed with individual nurses after their birth, are under the hospital's care. Every sort of the poor people ... except the lepers, for whom another hospital is reserved....

7. There are also houses of the second order of the Humiliati of each sex which in the city and the county reach the number of 220; inside them are copious number of persons leading the religious life while working with their own hands....

8. The houses of the order of St. Augustine of each sex undoubtedly are 60 [a long list of the convents of other religious orders follows....]

11. This, however, I affirm with certainty, that inside as well as outside the city, counting priests and other clerics of all orders ... [there are] more than 10,000 religious....

12. What else can be said of the huge number of the multitude living in Milan and in the county? ... For as I roughly estimate—and many definitely assert the same—more than 700,000 mouths of the two sexes, including all infants as well as adults, obtain their sustenance [here]....

14. Let therefore anyone who can count how many persons live in such a city. And if he is able to do it accurately, he will count up to the number of about 200,000, as I firmly believe....

[The author goes on to say that in Milan there are also 120 doctors of canon and civil law, 1,500 notaries, 600 messengers of the commune, 28 physicians, 150 surgeons, 8 professors of grammar, more than 70 elementary teachers, 300 bakeries, more than 1,000 shopkeepers, more than 440 butchers, and about 150 inns.]

Questions: What types of buildings were in the physical townscape of Milan, and what do they tell us about the services available to the Milanese? What do we learn about the layout of the town? What does this passage tell us about how the Milanese envisioned and idealized their city?

153. THE EVILS OF THE BIG CITY

Not all writers idealized the city in the same way as in the previous selections. Another school of thinking—which we are also familiar with today—focused on the evils and temptations of big city life, as the chronicler Richard of Devizes did in relating a warning given to a young man about to go to London, c. 1192.

Source: trans. J.A. Giles, *Chronicles of the Crusades*, by Richard Devizes (London: H.G. Bohn, 1848), pp. 49–50, revised.

When you have entered England, if you should come to London, you should pass through it quickly since that city greatly displeases me. Every race of men, out of every nation which is under heaven, resorts there in great numbers; every nation has introduced into that city its vices and bad manners. No one lives in it without offence; there is not a single street in it that does not abound in miserable, obscene wretches; there, in proportion as any man has exceeded in wickedness, so much is he the better. I am not ignorant of the disposition I am exhorting; you have, in addition to your youth, an ardent disposition, a slowness of memory and a soberness of reason between extremes. I feel in myself no uneasiness about you, unless you should abide with men of corrupt lives; for from our associations our manners are formed. But let that be as it may. You will come to London. Behold! I warn you, whatever of evil or perversity there is in any, whatever in all parts of the world, you will find in that city alone. Go not to the dances of panders, nor mix yourself up with the herds of the houses of ill fame; avoid the talus [oblong-shaped dice] and the dice, the theater and the tavern. You will find more braggadacios there than in all France, while the number of flatterers is infinite. Stage-players, buffoons, those that have no hair on their bodies, *Garamantes* [gossips?], pickthanks [flatterer or tattle-tale], catamites [boys kept for unnatural purposes], effeminate evildoers, lewd musical girls, drug dealers, lustful persons, fortune-tellers, extortioners, nightly strollers, magicians, mimics, common beggars, tatterdemalions [those wearing tattered clothes]—this whole crew has filled every house. So if you do not wish to live with the shameful, you will not dwell in London.

Questions: What were the dangers of the city according to this author? How similar are these ideas to those current today about the evils of the "big city"? How does this view of urban life compare to that expressed in docs. 151 and 152?

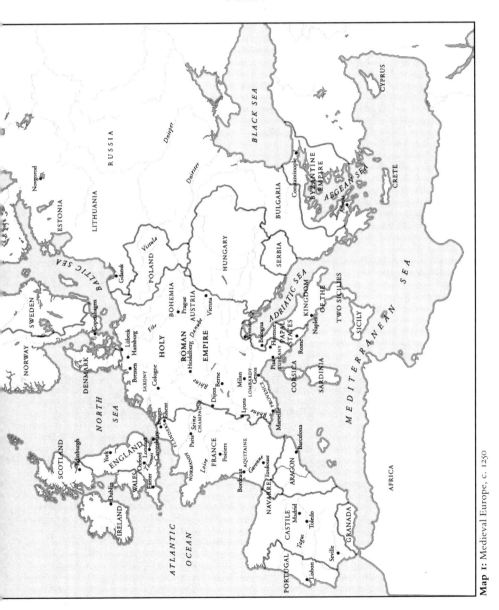

Map 1: Medieval Europe, c. 1250

Map 2: Towns in Britain and North-Western Europe, c. 1250

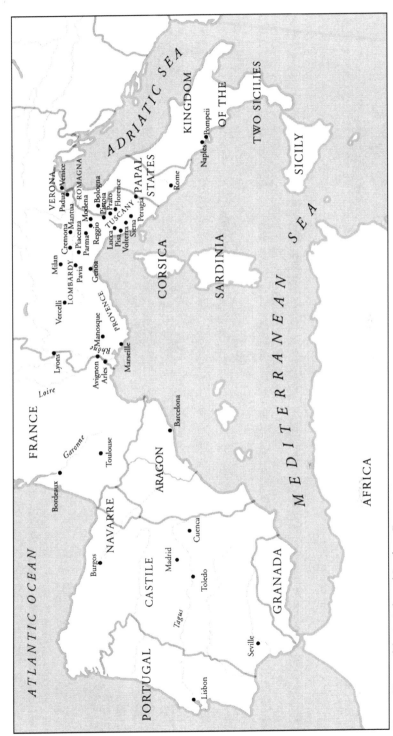

Map 3: Towns of Iberia, Italy, and Southern France, c. 1250

INDEX OF TOPICS

Topics are listed by document number.

INDEX OF TOWNS

References are to document numbers. The modern country where the town is located is noted in parentheses.

INDEX OF TOWN OFFICIALS

References are to document numbers.

SOURCES

The Author of the book and the Publisher have made every attempt to locate the authors of the copyrighted material or their heirs or assigns, and would be grateful for any information that would allow them to correct any errors or omissions in a subsequent edition of the book.

Allmand, C.T., ed. *Society at War: The Experience of England and France During the Hundred Years War.* New York: Harper & Row Publishers, Inc, 1973, pp. 182–83 [doc. 56]. Reprinted by permission of Chirstopher T. Allmand (translator).

Amt, E.A., ed. *Women's Lives in Medieval Europe: A Sourcebook.* New York: Routledge, 1993, pp. 263–67 [doc. 97].

Baca, M, ed. *Merchant Writers of the Italian Renaissance from Boccaccio to Machiavelli.* Ed. Vittore Branca. New York: Marsilio Publishers, 1999, pp. 37–41 [doc. 128]; 115–16 [doc. 82]; 149–52 [doc. 109]. Reprinted by permission of Murtha Baca.

Baxendale, S.F., trans. "Florence: Catasto of 1427," *Readings in Medieval History.* Ed. P.J. Geary. Peterborough, ON: Broadview Press, 1989, pp. 812–14, 815–16, abridged [doc. 66]. Reprinted with permission.

Benton, John F., ed. *Self and Society in Medieval France.: The Memoirs of Abbot Guibert of Nogent,* copyright © 1984, the Medieval Academy of America, pp.165–68 and 171–76 [doc. 17]. Reprinted by permission of the estate of John F. Benton.

Brucker, G., ed. *The Society of Renaissance Florence: A Documentary Study.* New York: Harper and Row Torchbooks, 1971, pp. 32–37 [doc. 74]; 93–94 [doc. 63]; 231–33 [doc. 106]; 236–39 [doc. 49]. Reprinted with the permission of the Renaissance Society of America.

Cave, R.C. and H.H. Coulson, eds. *A Source Book for Medieval Economic History.* Milwaukee: The Bruce Publishing Co., 1936; reprint New York: Biblio and Tannen, 1965, pp. 250–52 [doc. 58]; p. 145 [doc. 60].

Cochrane, Lydia G., trans. *Medieval Prostitution.* Ed. Jacques Rossiaud. Copyright © 1988, Basil Blackwell Ltd., Oxford. First published in Italian as *La Prostituzione nel Medioevo* © Editori Laterza, Poma-Bari, 1984. pp. 179–81, revised [doc. 136]. Reprinted by permission of Blackwell Publishing Ltd.

de Rosen Jervis, A., ed. *A Florentine Diary from 1450 to 1516.* By Luca Landucci. New York: E. P. Dutton & Co., Inc., 1927, pp. 74–75, 76, 79, 80, 85, 101–02 [doc. 104]. Reprinted with the acknowledgement of JM Dent (a division of the Orion Publishing Group).

Dean T., ed. *The Towns of Italy in the Later Middle Ages.* Manchester: Manchester University Press; New York: St Martin's Press, 2000, pp. 40-41 [doc. 145]; 72–75 [doc. 122]; 185-87 [doc. 71]; 222–24 [doc. 24B]. Reprinted by permission of the publisher.

Dutton, P., ed. "Abbo's Account of the Siege of Paris by the Northmen," *Carolingian Civilization: A Reader.* Peterborough, ON: Broadview Press, 1993, pp. 483–85. [doc. 7]. Reprinted by permission of the editor, Paul Dutton.

Fanning, S. and B.S. Bachrach, ed. *The Annals of Flodoard of Reims 919–966.* Peterborough, ON: Broadview Press, 2004, pp. 12, 15, 23, 26, 29, 56, 61 [doc. 8]. Reprinted by permission of the editors, Steven Fanning and Bernard S. Bachrach.

Goldberg, P.J.P., ed. and trans. *Women in England c. 1275–1525: Documentary Sources.* Copyright © 1995, Manchester University Press, Manchester, (Manchester Medieval Sources Series), pp. 230–31 [doc. 86B]. Reprinted by permission of P.J.P. Goldberg and Manchester University Press.

Gragg, Florence Alden, ed. Gabel, Leona C. ed. and annotator. *Pius II: Memoirs of a Renaissance Pope.* Northhampton, MA, Smith College, Department of History, 1940, pp. 135–37 and 153 [doc. 35]. Reprinted by permission of the publisher.

Hall, Richard. *The Viking Dig: The Excavations at York.* London: The Bodley Head, 1984. Summary of pp. 67–116 and Figures 65, 93, 108, 137, 138 [doc. 15]. Reprinted by permission of the publisher.

Harding, V. and L. Wright, eds. *London Bridge: Selected Accounts and Rentals, 1381–1538.* London Record Society, vol. 31, 1995, pp. 38-40, abridged [doc. 142]. Reprinted by permission of Vanessa Harding on behalf of the London Record Society.

Johnson, H., ed. *Annals of Ghent.* New York: Oxford University Press, 1951, pp. 12–19, abridged [doc. 48]. Reprinted by permission of the family of Hilda Johnson.

Kowaleski, M. *Local Markets and Regional Trade in Medieval Exeter.* Cambridge: Cambridge University Press, 1995, p. 102 [doc. 39D]. Reprinted with permission.

Lewis, Bernard, ed. and trans. *Islam: From the Prophet Muhammad to the Capture of Constantinople, Volume 2 Religion and Society.* New York: Oxford University Press, 1987, pp. 157–61 [doc. 50]. Copyright © Bernard Lewis. Used by permission of Oxford University Press.

Lewis, N. and M. Reinhold, eds. *Roman Civilisation Sourcebook II: The Empire.* New York: Columbia University Press, 1955, pp. 488–89 [doc. 1B]; pp. 326–27, 358–60, selections [doc. 3]. Reprinted by permission of Columbia University Press.

Lopez, R.S. and I. W. Raymond, eds. *Medieval Trade in the Mediterranean World.* New York: Columbia University Press, 1955 (reprinted 2001), pp. 61–65, abridged [doc. 152]; 400–03 [doc. 55]. Reprinted by permission of Columbia University Press.

Marcus, Jacob R., trans. *The Jew in the Medieval World: A Source Book, 315-1791*. Copyright © 1938 by Union of American Hebrew Congregations, Reprinted in 1960 by the Jewish Publication Society, Philadelphia and Meridian Press, New York. pp. 45-47 [doc. 95]. Reprinted with the permission of the Hebrew Union College Press and the Jacob Rader Center of the American Jewish Archives.

Martines, Julia, trans. *Two Memoirs of Renaissance Florence: The Diaries of Buonaccorso Pitti and Gregorio Dati*. Ed. Gene Brucker. Long Grove, IL: Waveland Press, 1967 [reissued 1991]), pp. 139–40 [doc. 40]. Reprinted by permission of Waveland Press, Inc. All rights reserved.

Pantin, W.A. "Some Medieval English Town Houses: a Study in Adaptation," *Culture and Environment—Essays in Honour of Sir Cyril Fox*. Ed. I.LL. Foster and L. Alcock. London: Routledge and Kegan Paul, 1963, p. 454, fig. 104: "Hampton Court, King's Lynn: conjectural view in the early sixteenth century," (illustration only) [doc. 147]. Reprinted by permission of the publisher.

Power, E., ed. *The Goodman of Paris*. London: George Routledge & Sons, Ltd., 1928, pp. 208–11, 213–14, 218–19, abridged, revised [doc. 91]. Reprinted by permission of Routledge Publishing.

Powers, J., trans. "Fuero de Cuenca (ca. 1190)." *Medieval Iberia: Readings*. Ed. O.R. Constable. Philadelphia: University of Pennsylvania Press, 1997, pp. 223–25 [doc. 131]. Reprinted by permission of the University of Pennsylvania Press.

Riesenberg, P., ed. "The Statutes of Volterra, 1224." *The Medieval Town*. Ed. J.H. Mundy and P. Riesenberg. New York: Van Nostrand Co., Inc., 1958; reprint Huntington, NY: Robert E. Krieger, 1979, pp. 154–57 [doc. 23]. Reprinted by permission of Peter Riesenberg and the estate of John H. Mundy.

Rowe, M.M. and A.M. Jackson, eds. *Exeter Freemen 1266–1967*. Devon and Cornwall Record Society, extra series 1, 1973, pp. 32–33 [doc. 39A]. Reprinted with permission.

Ruiz, T., trans. "Charter to the Non-Noble Knights of Burgos (1256)." *Medieval Iberia: Readings*. Ed. O.R. Constable. Philadelphia: University of Pennsylvania Press, 1997, pp. 225–27 [doc. 36]. Reprinted by permission of the University of Pennsylvania Press.

Shirley, J., ed. *A Parisian Journal 1405–1449*. Oxford: Clarendon Press, 1968, pp. 62–65 [doc. 124]; 230–35 [doc. 99]. Reprinted by permission of Oxford University Press.

Smail, Daniel Lord. *The Consumption of Justice: Emotions, Publicity, and Legal Culture in Marseille, 1264–1423*. Copyright © 2003 by Cornell University, pp. 67–68 [doc. 70]. Used by permission of the publisher, Cornell University Press.

Thorndike, L., ed. *University Records and Life in the Middle Ages*. New York: Columbia University Press, 1944; rpt. New York: Octagon Books, 1971, pp. 32–35 [doc. 113]. Reprinted by permission of Columbia University Press.

Tschan, F.J., ed. *The Chronicle of the Slavs, by Helmold, priest of Bosau*. New York: Columbia University Press, 1935, pp. 168–69, abridged [doc. 14]. Reprinted by permission of Columbia University Press.

New Translations

This volume contains several new translations from a variety of languages, as indicated below. For full references to the sources used, see the passages in the text. Those translated from manuscript sources are marked with a star (*).

Doc. 6. "Toll Exemptions in French Towns," trans. Maryanne Kowaleski, from Latin.

Doc. 9. "The Creation of Bruges," trans. Maryanne Kowaleski, from Latin.

Doc. 13. "Grant of Privileges to the Castilians, Mozarabs, and Franks of Toledo, 1086," trans. Maryanne Kowaleski, from Latin.

Doc. 21. "Lübeck Is Made an Imperial City, 1226," trans. Maryanne Kowaleski, from Latin.

Doc. 38. "Factionalism and the Concerns of an Exile, 1312," trans. Laura Morreale, from Italian.

Doc. 39B. "The Murage Tax Roll of Exeter, 1377," trans. Maryanne Kowaleski, from Latin.*

Doc. 39C. "Election Returns for the City of Exeter, 1377," trans. Maryanne Kowaleski, from Latin.*

Doc. 44. "A Day in the Life of a Carpenter," trans. Thelma Fenster and Maryanne Kowaleski, from French.

Doc. 46A: "Searching for a Runaway Slave in Florence, 1388," trans. Maryanne Kowaleski, from French.

Doc. 46B. "Contract for the Purchase of a Slave in Ferrara," trans. Maryanne Kowaleski, from Latin.

Doc. 51A. "Fair Profits in the Extent of the Lands of the Count of Champagne and Brie, 1276–1278," trans. Anne Lester, from Latin.

Doc. 51B. "Rental contract for a House during the Fair in Bar-sur-Aube, 1275," trans. Anne Lester, from Latin.

Doc. 59. "Regulations of the Guild of Skinners in Copenhagen,"trans. Martin Chase, S.J., from Old Danish.

Doc. 60B. "Apprenticeship to a Weaver in Arras," trans. Maryanne Kowaleski, from Old French.

Doc. 64. "Accounts of the City of Siena," trans. Maryanne Kowaleski, from Latin.

Doc. 76A. "Marriage in York, 1417." trans. Caroline Dunn, from Latin.

Doc. 76B. "Marriage in Paris, 1488," trans. Caroline Dunn, from Latin.

Doc. 77. "Women, Family Relations, and Inheritance in Aragon," trans. Jennifer Speed, from Latin.

Doc. 81. "Family and Household in Manosque, 1418-26," trans. Maryanne Kowaleski, from French.

Doc. 83A. "Retirement at Home," trans. Maryanne Kowaleski, from Latin.★

Doc. 83B. "Retirement to a Religious House." trans. Maryanne Kowaleski, from Latin.★

Doc. 86A. "Women and Gossip in the Exeter Borough Courts," trans. Maryanne Kowaleski, from Latin.★

Doc. 89. "Women in the Parisian Craft Guilds, c. 1270," trans. Maryanne Kowaleski, from Old French.

Doc. 103. "The Accounts of the Churchwardens in Canterbury, 1485–86," trans. Maryanne Kowaleski, from Latin.

Doc. 107. "Charitable Bequests in Siena, 1300–25," trans. Allison Clark, from Latin.★

Doc. 108. "The Cost of Schooling, 1394–95," trans. Maryanne Kowaleski, from Anglo-Norman.

Doc. 121. "Feast and Festival in Venice," trans. Laura Morreale, from Franco-Venetian.

Doc. 127A. "Account of the City of Ypres, 1316," trans. Maryanne Kowaleski, from French.

Doc. 127B. "Corpses Collected at the Expense of the Towns of Bruges and Ypres in 1316," trans. Maryanne Kowaleski, from French.

Doc. 135. "Criminal Courts and Punishment in Marseille, 1406–07," trans. Daniel Lord Smail, from Latin.★

Doc. 146. "Building Contracts for a House and Tavern, 1342," trans. Maryanne Kowaleski, from Anglo-Norman.

Doc. 150. "Meat Consumption in the Household of the Bishop of Arles," trans. Maryanne Kowaleski, from French.

READINGS IN MEDIEVAL CIVILIZATIONS AND CULTURES
Series Editor: Paul Edward Dutton

"Readings in Medieval Civilizations and Cultures is in my opinion the most useful series being published today."
— William C. Jordan, Princeton University